SPORTS LAW
IN A NUTSHELL
FOURTH EDITION

By

WALTER T. CHAMPION
George Foreman Professor of
Sports and Entertainment Law,
Texas Southern University
School of Law

WEST®

A Thomson Reuters business

Mat #40806687

Nutshell Series, In a Nutshell and the Nutshell Logo are trademarks registered in the U.S. Patent and Trademark Office.

© 1993 WEST PUBLISHING CO.
© WEST, a Thomson business, 2000, 2005
© 2009 Thomson Reuters

    610 Opperman Drive
    St. Paul, MN 55123
    1–800–313–9378

Printed in the United States of America

ISBN: 978–0–314–20446–2

*To George Foreman,
boxer, preacher, entrepreneur, and
philanthropist*

*

PREFACE

This Nutshell will explain all elements of Sports Law in an organized, reasonably coherent manner. Sports Law flows through our lives in many different formats and impacts on many different people: from agents to lawyers to athletic directors to fans. This book is a review of sports law; it can also be used as a course book, a student outline, a primer for would be professionals (whether agent, athletic director, athlete, or coach), or just a nice way to mull away an afternoon.

This is my fourth edition, and the first one after I was selected as the ''George Foreman Professor of Sports and Entertainment Law'' at Texas Southern University's Thurgood Marshall School of Law. In some ways, I find myself in the position of ombudsman to the genre. The field has changed dramatically in the last four years including moral dilemmas in drug testing, athletic discipline, referee gambling, and, of course, the Mitchell Report! Hopefully, this edition will help resolve some of the conundrums. Now, more than ever, the maxim of

French philosopher/historian Jacques Barzun remains true: "Whoever wants to know the hearts and minds of America had better learn baseball."

WALTER CHAMPION

Houston, Texas
May 2009

ACKNOWLEDGMENTS

A good book needs good contributors. To begin with, I was lucky enough to have coerced three exemplary sports professionals to write introductions for the first three editions, namely, Steve Patterson, former President of the Portland Trailblazers; Nick Nichols, the "father" of participant litigation; and Oliver Luck, former C.E.O., Harris County- Houston Sports Authority.

I was also lucky to secure contributions, advice, revisions, and consultations from several outstanding legal scholars, namely: Patrick Thornton (intellectual property) and McKen Carrington (financial considerations).

A good book needs good people behind it, and that we have in abundance. Special thanks goes to my students: Sharita Thomas, the Samavarti sisters, Michael Campbell, Nelson Ocampo, and Bianca Castillo; to Steve Kauffman, sports agent extraordinaire; to Ricky Anderson, entertainment lawyer extraordinaire; to Steve Underwood, President of the Tennessee Titans; and to my crackerjack Bomber Squadron of Sports Law afficianados who have assisted me in bringing the Good News of Sports Law through continuing education seminars (they are, in no particular order), Ricky Anderson, Pat Thornton, Carl Poston, Oliver Luck, Steve Underwood,

ACKNOWLEDGMENTS

Bill Frizzell from Tyler, Texas, Kary Wilson, from Sweetwater, Texas, Steve Patterson, Nick Nichols, the Hon. Harold Dutton, Randy Hendricks, and Judge Gregory "Scrap" Simmons.

I especially want to thank my two reference librarians, Soto Babatunda, LL.M., Dany Norris, Esq., and Prof. Patrick Thornton, to whom I offered about 35 questions about statistics and/or legal nuances for them to decipher. The winner gets an autographed copy of this book.

Another sincere acknowledgement to George Foreman, who has the foresight to use his position to improve the field of Sports Law. In the last three years, we have posed and in some ways tried to add insight to the perceived problem of "Sports Ethics."

WALTER CHAMPION

Houston, Texas
May 2009

INTRODUCTION TO FOURTH EDITION
BY: GEORGE FOREMAN

The following is a letter from George Foreman to the sentencing judge for Michael Vick, asking for leniency. I think it serves as a poignant introduction to this edition of the Nutshell, which covered some particularly turbulent years in the field. The question that George Foreman poses is an important one—namely, is the public better served by the education and rehabilitation of Michael Vick, and others, as opposed to mindless punishment and humiliation? W.T.C.

INTRODUCTION TO FOURTH EDITION

GEORGE FOREMAN

Honorable Henry E. Hudson
United States District Court for Eastern District of Virginia
Lewis F. Powell, Jr., U.S. Courthouse
1000 East Main Street, Suite 305
Richmond, Virginia 23219

Dear Judge Hudson:

I'm a fulltime minister at the Church of the Lord Jesus Christ in Houston, Texas, former two-time Heavyweight Champion of the world, and known all over the world as the king of the grills because of the George Foreman Lean Mean Fat Reducing Grilling Machine.

But the real story is that as a young boy I prowled the streets of Houston, TX as a thief, and a teenage mugger until one night while trying to escape the police, I laid in a hole and covered myself with mud from a busted sewage pipe under a house so the police dogs couldn't sniff me out. For the first time I realized that my life was in shambles, and that I had disappointed my mother, father, and all of my family. I was no more than a criminal, but that night I said to myself, "I'm going to change my life. I'm going to be a different person, if I can just get from underneath this house and not be caught by the police."

I made it home that night all stinky and filthy from the sewage and I promised myself that I was going to be a better person and that I would never steal from, nor harm another human being as long as I live. I didn't believe in religion, and I laughed at songs such as Amazing Grace, with words like, "I once was lost but now I'm found, was blind but now I see."

Judge, my friend Michael Vick is a bit older in "years", but I still feel that this man has come to that same crossroads in his life where he can see his errors, and like me under the house that night, he recognizes that he cannot blame anyone but himself for his mistakes. But God in heaven gave me another chance. On behalf of Michael Vick, I'd like to say that it's not too late for Michael. I have seen him grow personally, and have sensed his genuine remorse over his misdeeds of the pass. With assistance from myself, and all the wonderful people he has now surrounded himself with who want to see him do well, I believe he can still be a productive member of our society. At the very least Michael Vick can serve as an example to all American youth on how abhorred behavior can ruin your life and the lives of people around you.

INTRODUCTION TO FOURTH EDITION

GEORGE FOREMAN

I therefore ask you to consider leniency in the sentencing of Michael Vick. This is a good tree, and with a little turning of the earth, and fertilizer he can bring forth a lot of good fruit.

St Luke 12:9

Sincerely,

George Foreman
1968 Olympic Gold Medalist
Two-time World Boxing Champion
Pastor of the Church of the Lord
Jesus Christ, Houston, TX

*

OUTLINE

OUTLINE

XVII

OUTLINE

Page

*

TABLE OF CASES

References are to Pages

A

C

D

H

L

M

O

P

T

U

V

TABLE OF CASES

Z

*

SPORTS LAW

IN A NUTSHELL

FOURTH EDITION

*

CHAPTER 1

CONTRACTS

A. FORMATION

A valid contract is formed only if both parties intend the act of signing to be the last act in the formation of a binding contract. In evaluating contract validity, first identify the offeror and the offeree and then ascertain whether there was a proper acceptance. If the player's response includes a variance, it is a counter-offer.

In earlier versions of the contract between players and management, the wording of the contract was such that the commissioner's signature in approving the agreement was a condition precedent to the formation of a binding contract. Without that approval the player's signature was merely a counter-offer. The failure to obtain the commissioner's signature was deemed a material breach of the agreement pursuant to the contractual language of the contract. *Los Angeles Rams v. Cannon*, 185 F.Supp. 717 (S.D.Cal.1960). Without the commissioner's signature, the player's signing was a revocable offer. *Detroit Football Co. v. Robinson*, 186 F.Supp. 933 (E.D.La.1960).

1

1. Offer

A player's contract is drafted by the team, and it is the team that seeks out the services of the player. The team makes the offer and the player expresses his acceptance by signing the contract. However, if the signing is not accompanied by consideration and a withdrawal is advanced to the team before an acceptance, then the signing is an authentication of a revocable offer as opposed to the formation of a binding contract. It is the intent of the parties that will determine this conflict.

2. Acceptance

The problem that arises with an acceptance is the timeliness of the alleged acceptance. Acceptance is indicated by any showing that expresses the player's willingness to be bound by the offer's exact terms.

3. Interpretation

In determining the meaning of an indefinite or ambiguous term in a contract, the language should be read in light of all the surrounding circumstances. The interpretation that is placed on a contract by the parties prior to the time that it becomes a matter of controversy is entitled to great, if not controlling influence in ascertaining the intent and understanding of the parties.

In *Pasquel v. Owen*, 186 F.2d 263 (8th Cir.1950), the ambiguous term in question was "player-manager." The defendant, Mickey Owen, a major league baseball player, abandoned his contract to play baseball in the Mexican League when he was relieved of his duties as manager but still continued as a player. The question is whether the removal of Owen as either a player or a manager constituted a breach of contract by one party that was of such a character as to warrant abandonment of the contract by the other party. But to permit abandonment, the failure to perform by the defaulting party must go to the substance of the contract. In this case, although the contract referred to defendant as a "player-manager," it did not indicate at what time he was to function as either a player or a manager or both. Therefore, the act of relieving Owen as a manager but continuing to pay his whole salary resulted in no financial loss to the player and thus did not constitute a breach of contract sufficient to warrant the player's abandonment of the contract.

In *Ford Motor Co. v. Kahne,* 379 F.Supp.2d 857 (E.D.Mich.2005), Ford sued Kasey Kahne, a famous NASCAR driver, alleging breach of personal services contract. In 2000, Kahne entered into his first contract with Ford, which was to be effective until August 2002. Kahne's contract with Ford provided Ford the opportunity to match any racing-related or driving-related employment offer. On February 4, 2002, Kahne executed a "Contract for Services" with Robert Yates Racing, which provided that Kahne would drive exclusively for them in NASCAR sanctioned racing series. The court found that Ford and Kahne did not reach an agreement on all essential terms of the personal services contract under which the driver would have "opportunities to participate in one or more mutually acceptable racing series with a reasonably competitive team," and thus the agreement was unenforceable because the contract's clear and unambiguous language indicated that the parties intentionally left the meanings of "series" and "team" unexpressed.

B. STANDARD PLAYER'S CONTRACT

Contracts in sports define the rights and responsibilities of the various participants in the business of professional sports. The so-called Standard Player's Contract (SPK) (see Appendix), is an employment contract which specifies the player's rights. The SPK will state that the player has unique skills and that the team will control the activities of the player.

The average player has little job security. For him the SPK is a contract of adhesion. However, the SPK can be modified if that particular player has "juice". "Juice" is the ability to write your own ticket based on unique skills or rampant popularity (e.g., Michael Jordan). Alex Rodriguez or Manny Ramirez has juice; Bobby Nobody, a free agent from Slippery Rock, does not. The more juice a player possesses, the greater his ability to modify his SPK by attaching standard modifications such as no-cut, no-trade or attendance clauses. Management will usually not give their players anything.

The SPK can be modified through collateral agreements, e.g., the incorporation of the collective bargaining agreement (c.b.a.) and the League's By–Laws and Constitution into the contract.

The parol evidence rule is incorporated into the SPK. If the agreement is written and it is their final expression then the contract as it stands cannot be modified by other agreements or promises. In the interpretation of ambiguous terms, the contract will be interpreted against the writer of the contract. Handwritten provisions will prevail over printed provisions. *Johnson v. Green Bay Packers, Inc.*, 272 Wis. 149, 74 N.W.2d 784 (1956).

The club's responsibility for liability for injuries is limited by the terms of the SPK.

There is no right by the team to demand performance of a player for a player's non-performance as exhibited by his jumping to another team, however, they can obtain equitable performance by way of injunctive relief through a contractual clause. *Philadelphia Ball Club v. Lajoie*, 202 Pa. 210, 51 A. 973 (1902).

The SPK calls for annual physical examinations. In these examinations, the club can ascertain if the player suffered an off-season injury. If a player passes this examination, then the club cannot later claim that a current (under contract) injury is a result of a previous (non-contract) injury. *Tillman v. New Orleans Saints*, 265 So.2d 284 (La.App. 4 Cir.1972). The player further promises to be in "good physical condition" and to swear "loyalty" to the club.

The SPK includes a termination clause which gives the team the right to terminate the athlete's contract. The termination must be "for cause," but "for cause" could be simply that the employee no longer fits the team's needs. There is also a no-tampering clause which avers that one player cannot attempt to entice another employee to enter negotiations with another club while under contract to a different team. The SPK demands that a copy of the contract must be filed by the team with the office of the league's commissioner within 48 hours of the execution of the contract. The wording of current SPKs contain language such that the filing of a copy is merely a condition precedent to the execution of the contract.

The SPK further provides that the Commissioner possesses the ability to fine players for infractions of league rules. The Commissioner, in his sole discretion, can expel a player for gambling on a game's outcome if the player is a participant in that game. *Molinas v. National Basketball Association*, 190 F.Supp. 241 (S.D.N.Y.1961) and *Molinas v. Podoloff*, 133 N.Y.S.2d 743 (N.Y.Sup.1954).

The SPK merges all the peculiarities of contract formation into one document that must be signed before an athlete can participate. The SPK, since it is drawn by the team, is drawn in their favor and, therefore, if ambiguities arise, they are interpreted against the team. However, since the particular wording of each SPK is essential, it must be carefully read and completely understood.

C. SPECIALTY CLAUSES

The more juice a player possesses, the more specialty clauses he can add to his SPK so as to enhance it. This is where negotiation skills come in handy; negotiation-wise, the SPK is a dead issue.

The preeminent specialty clause is the signing bonus. To secure this bonus, a player at a minimum, must appear in training camp in good shape and ready to play. It is not considered salary. The employee may receive it for merely signing and not actually playing. If he is "cut" later on, he will still keep the signing bonus. To secure the bonus, the player must at least try to perform. Or, in the case of a team folding before camp, the signed player must show his willingness to perform by allowing the team to use his good name for public relations purposes. *Alabama Football, Inc. v. Stabler*, 294 Ala. 551, 319 So.2d 678 (1975) and *Alabama Football, Inc. v. Greenwood*, 452 F.Supp. 1191 (W.D.Pa. 1978).

On March 20, 2006, a special master ruled that the Seattle Seahawks would have to match all of the terms in the seven-year $49 million offer that the Minnesota Vikings made to Seahawks All–Pro left guard Steve Hutchinson, including the term providing that the entire contract amount would become fully guaranteed if Hutchinson were not the highest paid offensive lineman of the team. He became their transition player, meaning that the Seahawks retained the right to match any offer. Sixteen million of the 49 million was guaranteed, but it still contained the "poison pill" "escalating clause". In order for the Seahawks to match the Vikings offer they would have to include the clause guaranteeing the full $49 million since Seahawks tackle Walter Jones now made more money. The Seahawks claimed that the right to match only required to match the financial terms, not an ancillary term like the guarantee provision. The Special Master rejected this argument. The Seahawks declined to match (and guarantee) the Vikings offer. Hutchinson signed with the Vikings on March 20, 2006. Just prior to the hearing, the Seahawks restructured Jones' contract so that the annual average was reduced to $6.68 million. However, the maneuver failed, since at the time of the offer, Jones still averaged $7.5 million.

On April 26, 2007, an arbitrator concluded that San Francisco 49ers wide receiver Ashley Lelie must repay the Denver Broncos nearly $600,000 of his rookie signing bonus. In 2002, Lelie was drafted by the Broncos and signed a contract including a $3.3 million signing bonus. Prior to the 2006–07 season, Lelie refused to attend off-season workouts or training camp after the Broncos acquired a new wide receiver. The Broncos fined him $14,000 for each day missed, eventually totaling over $300,000. The Broncos traded Lelie to the Atlanta Falcons, but sought to recover a portion of his signing bonus and the fines. The arbitrator ruled that Lelie had to pay back a prorated amount of his signing bonus for holding out and forcing the trade to Atlanta. However, the arbitrator determined that Lelie did not have to pay the Broncos the $300,000 in fines because franchises could not collect fine money from players that have been traded. In a related grievance, the Special Master ruled that the Broncos were not entitled to a portion of Lelie's $1.1 million option bonus because that was barred by an express clause in an extension of the c.b.a., a decision that was appealed and then upheld by U.S. District Judge David Doty in Minneapolis, who continues to oversee "system" matters controlled by the 1994 *White* litigation settlement. See *White v. NFL (App. of Ashley Lelie)*, 2007 WL 939560 (D. Minn.)

1. Option

Another part of the SPK is the so-called option clause which allows the team to unilaterally bind the player for another year at a stated per cent (usually ten per cent less) of the prior year's salary. Since this clause restrains trade, it often exhibits antitrust implications. However, the option year is usually softened through collective bargaining. As an agent, when an option clause is sent to a player, advise him not to sign it, since it may be interpreted as yet another signed contract and if so, will include another mandatory option year. Also, make sure that all the benefits of the original contract are carried over to the option year. See *Hennigan v. Chargers Football Co.*, 431 F.2d 308 (5th Cir.1970).

2. Reserve

Baseball's former infamous reserve clause was truly unconscionable since it gave management a perpetual option year. Under baseball's old reserve system a player belonged to a team for life. The only alternatives left to a player was to either request a trade or retire from the sport. However, the team could at their whim, release a player or trade him without consent to another team. This hated version of the option clause was eradicated from baseball's lexicon in 1975 as a result of a bargained-for grievance procedure.

3. No–Cut

This type of clause assures the player that he will not be "cut" during the life of the contract. There are many ways and reasons that a player can be terminated: skill, physical condition, off-season injuries, suspension, death, etc. Because of this, a standard no-cut clause does not exist since each clause only protects the player from a certain type of termination.

The basic types of no-cut clauses are the *Cunningham* model, the standard NFL clause and the *Hudson* model. In *Munchak Corp. v. Cunningham*, 457 F.2d 721 (4th Cir.1972), the parties agreed to a "no-cut contract" using that term and anticipating that this clause would protect the player from a cut based on a lack of skill. This clause would still not protect the player from "cuts" due to bad physical or mental condition, inability to perform as a result of off-field injuries and suspension without pay for disciplinary reasons. The standard NFL "no-cut" clause is comparable to the *Cunningham* model except that it is more specific concerning the necessity of the player to maintain a superior physical condition. The best for the player, is the *Hudson* model (*Minnesota Muskies, Inc. v. Hudson*, 294 F.Supp. 979 (M.D.N.C.1969)), which employs the following language: "salary payable in any event." Even with this language, the club will still not waive its right to suspend a player; nor will it protect a player who fails to exhibit a good faith effort. Any no-cut clause, however, only guarantees that the player will continue to be paid; it does not correspondingly guarantee a player an automatic spot on the roster.

D. COLLATERAL AGREEMENTS

A sports contract can also be modified through inclusion of collateral agreements by way of an incorporation clause. The standard collateral agreements are collective bargaining agreements and the league's constitution and by-laws; these additional documents will then be incorporated into the SPK as if they were a part of the contract. Less standard agreements can also be incorporated into the contract, for example, drug usage guidelines, player-agent standards, etc. When a player signs an SPK he not only agrees to abide by the ten pages in that contract but he also impliedly agrees to abide by the some 300 pages of responsibilities and obligations contained within the collateral documents.

E. TERMINATIONS

The termination of an athlete will be construed as a breach of contract if the termination is not justified. An employer can terminate an athlete if he is physically unable to perform. If a team terminates an employee on the basis of an injury there is usually a procedure that will cover this situation in the collective bargaining agreement.

A club must act within its rights when it terminates a contract. A player can be rightfully terminated for being out of shape, a lack of skill, defying club and league rules or a material breach of the SPK. In reality, a player with unique and proven skills will not be released, whereas, a marginal player will be released due to a lack of skills judged solely by the club.

F. ASSIGNMENTS

A necessary evil of a professional sports environment is the assignment of contracts, that is, trading players. SPK's contain a clause that allows the team to trade players at will. Players can, of course, negotiate "no trade" contracts; another alternative is that c.b.a.'s can also provide certain agreed-upon no-trade provisions.

G. REMEDIES

A breach of contract can usually be remedied by either money damages, restitution or specific performance. In the typical scenario, a party will seek the benefit of that bargain, that is, that which was promised in relation to what was received. If the legal remedy is inadequate then the aggrieved party may seek specific performance if the services are unique.

As regards specific performance, a court will not force an athlete to play against his will. But because an athlete's particular skills are unique and the addition of his participation to the chemistry of a team can never be successfully delineated, divided or understood, a court will allow the prevailing team to enjoin the athlete from playing for another team.

The use of injunctions as a remedy in professional sports was established in *Philadelphia Ball Club v. Lajoie*, 202 Pa. 210, 51 A. 973 (1902) which allowed a ball club to enjoin a professional baseball player, a future Hall of Fame member, one Napoleon Lajoie, when he attempted to play for another team. The injunction was authorized to restrain Lajoie from rendering services to another team since his services were of a unique character which would render them of peculiar value to the baseball club. In short, it would be difficult to find a substitute for the services of Napoleon Lajoie.

Because of this uniqueness, the first team can enjoin the player from playing for another team during the continuation of the contract. The provisions in the contract which prohibited the athlete from jumping to another team were a part of the consideration for the employer's agreement to pay the athlete his salary. These promises were not lacking mutuality of remedy or were they so unreasonable as to prevent the issuance of an injunction. Another rationale was that the contract was already partially performed and the employer was desirous of its continuance.

In *Lincoln Hockey, LLC v. Semin*, 2005 WL 3294008 (D.D.C.2005), a professional hockey player, signed a three-year contract to play hockey for the Washington Capitals. The contract stated a specific time and place to which he must report to play hockey, unless he was released from the terms of the deal. Plaintiff's skills were exceptional and thus his loss could not have been justly compensated by damages. The plaintiff agreed to a term in the contract that an injunction was the proper remedy to prevent him from playing for another team. The NHL's season was cancelled for the 2004–05 season due to a labor dispute. He left the country and played in Russia and the Capitals fined him $1,000 per day. Plaintiff claims that he was required to serve in the Russian military and could not perform under the terms of his original contract with the Capitals. He made arrangements with the Russian military that allowed him to play hockey in lieu of formal military service. When the lockout ended, the team asked that the plaintiff report to training camp.

Plaintiff claimed that he had worked out another arrangement with the military and he would be allowed to return to the country to play hockey. After hiring new agents, Semin was suddenly no longer allowed relief from his military obligations.

The Capitals initiated this lawsuit and asked the court for injunctive relief. The club also filed a suit for tortious interference with a contractual obligation against Semin's new agents. The court granted a temporary restraining order and held a hearing discussing the injunction on December 1, 2005. The court found that arbitration was the potential forum for such a dispute, reducing further the Capitals chances of success.

H. DEFENSES

When there is an alleged breach of contract, there are several defenses that can be posited. Of course, when an employer terminates the contract due to an injury, the c.b.a. will spell out the appropriate procedures. Usually, the team doctor's diagnosis will be submitted to arbitration after a review by a neutral physician. Club's defenses that can be raised in arbitration are: failure to pass the preseason physical exam, failure to make complete disclosure of a physical or mental condition, injury occurring prior to exam, a non-sport injury, no new sports-related injury after exam and no aggravation of prior injury after exam.

1. Unclean Hands

It is axiomatic that one cannot request a remedy in equity if he comes to court with unclean hands. Players have successfully used the doctrine of unclean hands in defending against suits by management for negative injunctions. A court of equity will not grant injunctive relief to a plaintiff who has acted in bad faith as regards the problem to be litigated. See *New York Football Giants, Inc. v. Los Angeles Chargers Football Club, Inc.*, 291 F.2d 471 (5th Cir.1961).

In *Minnesota Muskies, Inc. v. Hudson*, 294 F.Supp. 979 (M.D.N.C.1969), plaintiff was not entitled to enjoin defendant basketball player from joining another team during the life of his contract since plaintiff professional basketball team had already soiled its hands in negotiating a contract with the player while the player was still bound by contract to another professional basketball club in a different basketball association. Therefore, plaintiff club was not entitled to enjoin breach of that contract by the player, who after signing with plaintiff then signed a new contract with the original club and honored that contract by performing under it.

2. Unconscionability

Another defense could be that the contract was illegal or unfair. A court, for example, will not permit equitable enforcement if the terms of the contract are too harsh and one-sided. *Connecticut*

Professional Sports Corp. v. Heyman, 276 F.Supp. 618 (S.D.N.Y.1967). Historically some form of the reserve clause might well have been unconscionable and thus unenforceable. At present, the once overly harsh player retention systems have all been, to a certain extent, ameliorated by collective bargaining; as a result, they are now more narrowly drawn and less likely to be viewed as unfair, illegal or unconscionable.

3. Mutuality

Another defense to a club's suit for a negative injunction is the lack of mutuality. That is, either inequality between the player's obligation of many years and the team's obligation for a minimal amount of time or the fact that the club can avail itself of an opportunity to obtain the specific performance of an athlete's negative promise, whereas, specific performance is unavailable to a player.

I. INSURANCE AND PENSIONS

Insurance and pensions are types of contracts that have a great influence on the relative success and well being of athletes. Many athletes, both professional and amateur, take out insurance policies against the possibility of injury. In addition, many teams, arenas, leagues, universities, school districts, etc., take out liability insurance so they can be paid by the insurer for loss that results from legal liability to a third person. It protects the insured against the financial loss brought upon by lawsuits based on negligence. "Common subjects for liability insurance are risks from use of the premises, from faulty products, from use of vehicles, and from the practice of professions." NCAA, 2002–2003 NCAA Division I Manual 31.7.4.1. Host institutions and sponsoring agencies of NCAA championships are similarly obligated to provide "primary comprehensive general public liability insurance coverage" of "at least $1 million per occurrence for bodily injury and property damage." NCAA, 2002–2003 NCAA Division I Manual 31.7.4.1

Another form of contract that is extremely important to sports participation due to the nature of its inherent physical abuse are the pension systems that are usually made part of the employment contract within the plan itself and in the collective bargaining agreement and incorporated into the contract by way of the incorporation clause. For example, the NFL retirement and disability benefits, as worked out through the collective bargaining process, are now covered by the Bert Bell/Pete Rozelle NFL player retirement plan.

The Houston Astros Baseball Club purchased a total disability insurance policy from Defendant Connecticut General Life Insurance Company that covered Astros first baseman Jeff Bagwell. The policy provided that if Mr. Bagwell became totally disabled before the policy terminated on January 31, 2006, the Astros would recover. See *Houston McLane Co. v. Connecticut General Life Ins. Co.*, 2006 WL 3050812 (S.D.Tex.).

Mr. Bagwell suffers from a degenerative arthritic condition in his right shoulder. He was placed on the disabled list in May 2005, and he underwent surgery on his shoulder in June 2005. After a period of physical therapy and rehabilitation, Mr. Bagwell was activated and returned to the Astros' roster in September 2005 for the end of the regular season, as well as the playoffs and World Series. After the conclusion of the 2005 season, the Astros directed Mr. Bagwell to be examined by a sports medicine physician. The physician concluded that Mr. Bagwell was disabled completely from playing professional baseball and based on that evaluation, the Astros filed a claim for total disability on January 24, 2006. In February 2006, Mr. Bagwell reported to Astros spring training, and Connecticut General subsequently denied the Astros' disability claim on March 13, 2006. On March 25, 2006, the Astros placed Bagwell on the team's disabled list. He was subsequently retired. The Astros filed suit against Connecticut General, alleging breach of contract, violations of the Texas Insurance Code, and breach of common law duty of good faith and fair dealing. The court denied Connecticut General's motion for separate trials to bifurcate the causes of action.

On December 15, 2006, Connecticut General Life Insurance Company settled a lawsuit with the Houston Astros over the team's entitlement to recoup $15.6 million of the $17 million veteran first baseman Jeff Bagwell was paid for the 2006 season in which he was unable to play because of injuries. Bagwell, Houston's first baseman for nearly 15 years, formally announced his retirement on December 16, 2006.

On December 13, 2006, the U.S. Court of Appeals for the Fourth Circuit affirmed a ruling that the NFL players pension fund must pay the estate of NFL Hall of Fame center Mike Webster close to $2 million in back disability benefits for the brain damage he suffered during his playing days that left him unable to work after retirement. The amount is the difference between the disability benefits he received and the amount he should have received, plus interest, and legal fees.

Webster played 16 seasons in the NFL, 14 of which were spent with the Pittsburgh Steelers, including their glory years in which they won several Super Bowls. After his retirement in 1991, Webster was homeless at times, sleeping in his car, or on the floor of the Kansas City Chief's equipment room, when the team briefly employed him. Webster often needed to be reminded to do rudimentary tasks such as changing his clothes, going to bathroom, and eating meals.

In 1999, Webster applied for disability benefits under the NFL's pension plan. If his disability was caused by playing football, he would be entitled to higher level payments. The NFL players' retirement and disability board voted that the condition was not caused by playing football, despite medical testimony to the contrary. The court states that the board "completely ignored overwhelming evidence" that Webster was totally and permanently disabled as a result of brain injuries incurred while playing professional football. The court said that the board could not simply ignore the opinion of its own expert and others who found that Webster was disabled after retirement. The financial recovery will benefit Webster's widow and four children. This decision is the first time the NFL and NFLPA ever lost a disability status challenge case.

See *Jani v. Bert Bell/Peter Rozelle NFL Player Retirement Plan*, 209 Fed.Appx. 305 (4th Cir.2006).

J.　COACHING CONTRACTS

Professional coaches received salaries nearly as staggering as some of their players contracts. The salaries that collegiate basketball and football coaches can receive in some premier sports programs have also exceeded the multi-million-dollar barrier. However, coaches absolutely lack job security. Coaches have no real union or standardized contract.

The modern coach must perform many diverse duties: each duty, if not performed to the desires and satisfaction of the university's administration, can result in immediate termination.

Another part of a college coach's responsibility is to assist in achieving high graduation rates. This responsibility includes monitoring their athlete's grade point average so as to continue NCAA eligibility.

Many of these university athletic programs have the capacity to generate great sums of money.

These generated funds are needed to pay for other athletic programs in that university and to provide money that is used for that school's general fund. Lastly, a winning athletic program affords the university with heightened prestige and boosts their status vis-à-vis attracting better and more affluent students.

A collegiate coach's contract will offer not only a salary with institutional fringe benefits, but also additional compensation packages, which might include shoe, apparel, and equipment endorsements, television and radio shows, speaking engagements, personal appearances, and summer camps. Additionally, the job may also provide for housing, insurance premiums, country club memberships, business opportunities, and the use of university automobiles.

Most coaches, because of the variety of their tasks, have historically been able to leave their position virtually at will despite their prior contractual commitments. However, as in standard player's contracts, a university can include a clause within the coach's contract that allows an injunction to prohibit a coach from "jumping" his contract and working for another school. Upon termination prior to contract expiration, the courts will usually allow the coach to recover monetary damages. The coach's right to be compensated, however, may be reduced if there is a mitigation of damages clauses, which will offset the relief if he or she obtains other employment. The question of severance pay will usually involve the amount of money earned in related contracts (perquisites), such as shoe endorsements.

There is no standard coach's employment contract. There is no formal union that represents coaches. The crux of the contract is whether the coach agrees to perform all duties and responsibilities that accompany the position. The coach must also agree to comply with all pertinent NCAA regulations. Collegiate coaching contracts are usually three to five years in length. Many contracts contain a "rollover" provision, which extends the contract for an additional year. That is, if a coach had a five-year contract with a rollover, the university, at the end of each season, with the coach's consent, has the right to extend it for an additional year.

A coach's contract may also contain a reassignment clause which will allow the university to remove a person as a head coach, without per se ending his contract, by assigning him to a new title or new responsibilities. This clause may contain a caveat that will stipulate that this job reassignment will not be inconsistent with the coach's education and experience. If the coach refuses to accept this reassignment then the school may dissolve the employment contract pursuant to the contract's termination provisions.

In regards to compensation, every coaching contract will contain a guaranteed base salary. For example:

The guaranteed based salary paid by the University to the coach for services and satisfactory performance under the terms and conditions of this Employment Agreement shall be at rate of $_____ per year, payable in _____ installments by the University to the Coach on the _____ day of each calendar month during the term of this Agreement.

The contract will usually stipulate periodic increases to the guaranteed base salary during the length of the contract.

The contract will also contain a provision for fringe benefits, which may include: life and health insurance, vacation with pay, retirement, travel, out-of-pocket expenses, use of an automobile, auto insurance, gas credit card, car maintenance, tuition waiver, for family members, complimentary tickets, country club and health club memberships, and possibly living accommodations, etc. See *Rodgers v. Georgia Tech Athletic Ass'n*, 166 Ga.App. 156, 303 S.E.2d 467 (1983). There will also be bonus clauses. They may be in the form of a set amount or a percentage of either base salary or net revenues. The bonus mat be in the form of a signing bonus or based on post-season tournament participation or win/loss record, home attendance, graduation rate, or length of service. All contracts will also provide the coach with outside or supplemental income sources common to many major sport-coaching contracts, e.g., added benefit of payment for radio and TV talk show programs. Perhaps the most consistent moneymaker in coaching contracts is the caveat that the coach supervises summer athletic camps and clinics.

Coaching often attracts endorsement offers. The types of product endorsements run the gambit from car dealerships to sporting goods to restaurants to health clubs, etc. Apparel and equipment contracts are usually negotiated between the coach and the merchandise company. This company will pay the coach to act as a consultant and provide shoes, etc., in exchange for the players wearing their products.

In *McBryde v. Ritenour Sch. Dist.*, 207 S.W.3d 162 (Mo.App.2006), plaintiff was an assistant high school basketball coach. When the plaintiff was hired, he was told by the head basketball coach that he needed an African American coach that could relate to his players. Plaintiff was the only African American on the basketball coaching staff. All other assistant coaches received full time teaching positions at the school, received contracts before the start of the basketball season, and received only verbal warnings as a result of misconduct. Plaintiff was offered a position as a teaching assistant only during the basketball season, always received his contracts after the start of the basketball season, and was suspended as a result of misconduct without first receiving a verbal warning. In his suit claiming racial discrimination, the trial court awarded damages and attorney's fees for plaintiff. The high school appealed claiming the instructions were incorrect. The court affirmed the circuit court's decisions because the court had used Missouri Model Instructions, and a Missouri court is not bound to follow Eighth Circuit case law.

K. NEGOTIATING THE CONTRACT

The art of negotiating a contract in sports is very similar to the art of negotiating in other more standard venues. Although the SPK is in many ways a contract of adhesion, there are ways to flesh out the contract in an attempt to get the best deal for your client. As an overview, the more money up front the better; the more money in the signing bonus the better. Also, management will usually not object to the addition of incentive clauses (e.g., bonus money for achieving "all-rookie" status, attendance clauses, etc.).

The unions have greatly improved an agent's ability to successfully negotiate by providing players and agents with a complete statistical file of the relative worth of each potential professional athlete. This way, the athlete and his agent will have a clear idea of the contracts that similarly-positioned athletes were able to obtain. This takes the guess work out of ascertaining the "bottom line" and shows the athlete his market place comparative worth figure.

As an aside, much of the athlete's would be negotiation strengths are defined and refined through collective bargaining. Therefore, it would behoove the good agent to immerse himself into the c.b.a. before attempting contract negotiation. Although the SPK and c.b.a. include rules and benefits that automatically accrue to a player there are still certain concerns that reside completely in the domain of the individual contract negotiator. For example, signing bonus amount, time of payment of the bonus, desirability of a loan, insurance, contract length, injury or skill guarantees, ascertaining the appropriate mix of initial year salary and annual installments, option clauses, salary adjustments, roster bonuses, individual and team incentives, etc.

Suppose an athlete chooses you as his agent. What does your job description include? Although agents aren't required to be attorneys, the first document that you must be familiar with is the collective bargaining agreement (c.b.a.), a legal document (written by lawyers). The document that the agent must negotiate is the standard player's contract (SPK). This agreement is part of the c.b.a. which controls the union-management relationship in that sport. Most team sports have some form of a salary cap (or, at least, a luxury cap). The salary cap information is found in the c.b.a. It is imperative that you must know the "cap status" of the team that you are negotiating with.

CHAPTER 2

AGENTS

A. BACKGROUND

With the great increases in salaries and benefits in professional sports, a need developed for athletes to have personal representatives, or agents, to manage their affairs. This representation includes the negotiation of a personal services contract with a professional sports team. There is a fiduciary relationship between agents and athletes; therefore, agents are under an obligation to exercise the utmost care and good faith in their dealings with athletes.

B. STANDARD REPRESENTATION AGREEMENTS

The main connection between player and agent is the standard representation contract (SRK). This contract establishes the rights and responsibilities between the parties. It only calls for a good faith effort. The actions of the agent do not necessarily have to prove successful. *Zinn v. Parrish*, 461 F.Supp. 11 (N.D.Ill.1977).

However, the agent does have the obligation to make a full and complete disclosure of all areas of potential conflicts of interest and must receive prior consent from the athlete if representation is continued after this disclosure. *Detroit Lions, Inc. v. Argovitz*, 580 F.Supp. 542 (E.D.Mich.1984). Like any other contract, the key to an SRK is its particular wording. There are at least four essential clauses within an SRK: notice in writing of potential conflicts, a negotiation in good faith clause, an arbitration provision, and a clause that stipulates which state's law will govern if interpretation of the contract is necessary.

The basic responsibility of an agent is to exercise good faith effort overall and to act as a trustee for his client's money when investing it. Investments must be similar to those that a prudent investor would engage in for his own account, keeping in mind both safety and income.

C. DUTIES

The most essential part of the SRK is the agent's obligation to negotiate a contract. Implied in this obligation is the understanding that the agent possesses the necessary background, skills, experiences, and expertise to perform this task to a degree that corresponds with the skills and knowledge that are standard to the profession. An agent does not have to secure the best contract; the agent must only negotiate the contract in good faith using his or her best abilities.

The responsibilities of the agent will usually include contract negotiation, investments, taxes and public relations. The number of functions that an agent can perform is limited only by the agent's imagination. The list of functions that might be covered include: 1) contracts, 2) taxes, 3) financial planning, 4) money management, 5) investments, 6) income tax preparation, 7) incorporation, 8) estate planning, 9) endorsements, 10) sports medicine consultations, 11) health and physical training consultations, 12) career and personal development counseling, 13) post-career development, 14) insurance and 15) legal consultations.

Zinn v. Parrish, 461 F.Supp. 11 (N.D.Ill.1977), established the obligations that an agent must meet in his effort to satisfy his client. Plaintiff, an agent, brought an action to recover commissions that were allegedly due under an SRK. The agent secured three professional football team contracts for his client and pursuant to the SRK was entitled to a 10% agency fee. The agent was to negotiate contracts, furnish advice on business and tax matters, seek endorsements and assist with off-season employment. The plaintiff performed some of these obligations; he solicited some investment advice and assisted defendant in investing a small amount of his money in buying a house. No jobs, though; no endorsements; no off-season employment and, for tax advice, plaintiff sent his client to H & R Block.

Defendant alleged that his agent acted as an investment advisor under 15 U.S.C.A. § 80(b)–2(a)(11) and since he was not registered, the contract was void. However, the court held that the investment advice was merely an incident to the primary purpose of the management contract which was to negotiate a professional contract. In short, defendant alleged that plaintiff failed to perform his duties competently. However, plaintiff satisfied his obligations by performing these duties in good faith.

D. CONFLICTS OF INTEREST

The agent must not have any conflicts of interest that might influence or affect his ability to do the best job for his or her client. The agent must inform the principal of all facts that come to his knowledge which may be material or might affect his principal's rights or interests or influence the actions that the athlete may or may not take. *Detroit Lions, Inc. v. Argovitz*, 580 F.Supp. 542 (E.D.Mich.1984).

An agent should err on the side of a complete and detailed disclosure of any possible or potential conflicts of interest that might occur between the agent and the athlete.

Avoidance of conflicts of interest is even more important if the agent is also an attorney. Under the rules of professional conduct, an attorney must decline representation if it will be directly adverse to the interests of another client or if the attorney's personal interests materially limit his responsibilities to his client.

An attorney must perform his legal duties with unabated loyalty. This loyalty is necessarily questioned if the agent has conflicting interests that appear to be adverse to the interests of the athlete, e.g., representation of a competing athlete or ties with management. The attorney-agent is under the restriction of the attorney-client privilege of confidentiality. The agent cannot use confidential information to the athlete's disadvantage.

E. REGISTRATION OF AGENTS

Although their relationship is fiduciary in nature, sports agents were unregulated for many years. As a result of this, there were many infamous cases of abuse on the part of the agents. The perceived need for reform created a public outcry that resulted in attempts to regulate agents by both the states and the professional sports unions.

1. State Legislation

Many state legislatures entered into the controversy by enacting legislation that requires that agents register with that state if they are from that state or if they sign an athlete from that state. Registration must occur before they proceed with contract negotiations for an athlete.

The earliest registration model came from California. It requires that any agent who represents an athlete in an attempt to gain an employment contract with a professional sports team must register with the state labor commission. The act does not include "advisors" who do not negotiate contracts nor does it include California attorneys that act as legal counsel. Non–California attorneys are not exempted, they're treated as non-attorney agents. The act requires that agents must register and post a $10,000.00 surety bond to satisfy any damages for misrepresentation or fraud. The labor commissioner acts as an arbitrator for agent-athlete disputes. Any violation of the statute is a criminal misdemeanor. West's Ann. Cal. Labor Code § 1546.

A newer, "tougher" approach is represented by a Florida statute which targets both the agent and the athlete for criminal and civil penalties for violations. This act requires registration of all agents who do business in Florida. However, the registration itself is routine and is accompanied by only a minimal fee. The act applies to all agents who communicate with any Florida athlete regardless of whether the athlete is or is not ultimately signed. Failure to register is a third-degree felony with penalties of up to five years incarceration and a $5,000.00 fine. The athlete and the agent must notify the college's athletic director within 72 hours of the signing of an SRK. There are sanctions involved which include voiding the SRK as unenforceable, subjecting both the athlete and the agent to criminal penalties and allowing the school an opportunity to bring a civil suit against the athlete and the agent. West's Fla.St.Ann. § 468.451, *et seq.*

2. Union Regulations

Another way to curb abuses is through mechanisms provided by the sports unions. Basically, the unions created their own plan so that any agent who wanted to represent a union member must first register with, or be certified by, the union. This gives the union a certain amount of control. They can keep out unsavory would be agents while also mandating continuing education to improve the overall caliber of representation. All major sports unions currently maintain some form of agent registration.

However, the seminal model is from the National Football League Players' Association (NFLPA), which in 1983 established guidelines requiring agents to become certified as contract advisors. To gain certification, an agent must apply; pay a fee; submit an application providing information about education, employment, membership in business and professional associations, and criminal history; and pass a test. Two major aspects of the qualification process are 1) full disclosure and 2) an absence of a prior history that reveals incidents of serious misconduct. A procedure such as this, however, only excludes those whose conduct is egregious.

After they become contract advisors, the newly certified agents must use an NFLPA SRK, agree to abide by NFLPA limits to the percentage of the athlete's compensation that the agent can receive for representation, attend annual NFLPA continuing education seminars, agree not to give a player anything of value in exchange for the opportunity to secure representation, fully comply with applicable state and federal rules and regulations, and agree to avoid potential conflicts of interests by not having any financial interest in a professional sports teams. A violation of these rules will subject the agent to fines and penalties along with the possibility of a revocation of his contract advisor status.

The purpose of this type of regulation is to provide quality control in representation and to limit the fees that agents can charge NFLPA members for contract negotiation. However, its protective umbrella will not cover charlatans that might masquerade as publicity consultants or marketing experts. All other union-orchestrated, agent-certification schemes copy to a large extent the NFLPA model. In 2003, the NFLPA established a similar certification program for financial advisors.

In *Smith v. IMG Worldwide, Inc.,* 360 F.Supp.2d 681 (E.D.Pa.2005), the defendant, an NFL agent, and his company attempted to compel arbitration under the NFLPA Bylaws. The plaintiff argued that the defendant made defamatory statements about him and intentionally interfered with a prospective contract. Both the plaintiff and defendant are certified NFL agents. The defendant did not file a motion to compel arbitration until after the discovery period was ending. The court concluded that arbitration was appropriate because the claims fell within the scope of the arbitration clause. However, defendant waived his right to arbitrate by not timely requesting arbitration and actively litigating the case for 16 months, resulting in prejudice to plaintiff.

On June 23, 2006, seven current and former players sued the NFL and NFL Player's Association in U.S. District Court for the Northern District of Georgia for negligence in not investigating and warning the players about a financial advisor with whom they entrusted money and who subsequently lost it. The NFL and NFLPA listed Kirk Wright as an acceptable financial adviser. The players claim that the NFL and NFLPA are responsible for their losses because an investigation of Wright, should have shown that there were several outstanding tax liens and judgments against him and that he was uninsured.

Wright was also indicted on May 25, 2006 on 48 counts of mail and securities fraud. Wright and his company were sued in February 2005 by the SEC for numerous violations. Wright's company filed for bankruptcy later in 2005. More than 500 investors lost over $110 million entrusted to Wright. He used false statements and documents to mislead some investors into believing that the value of their investments was increasing when in fact, they were significantly decreasing. The players seek compensatory and punitive damages as well as an injunction to ensure that the NFL and NFLPA provide background checks of listed financial advisors to protect players from fraud in the future. In *Atwater v. NFLPA,* all of the NFL's and NFLPA's pretrial motions to dismiss were denied and he was convicted of 47 counts of fraud and money laundering on May 21, 2008. He killed himself in his jail cell on May 31, 2008. See *Atwater v. NFLPA,* 2007 WL 1020848 (N.D.Ga.) and *S.E.C. v. Wright,* 261 Fed. Appx. 259 (11th Cir.2008).

3. NCAA–Based

The National Collegiate Athletic Association (NCAA), an unincorporated association of individual schools, is the primary regulator of intercollegiate athletics. It also promulgates regulations that attempt to police agents. Athletes will lose their remaining collegiate eligibility if they accept gifts or enter into contracts with agents. In 1984, the NCAA established a voluntary "Player Agent Registration Plan" which urges agents to register with the NCAA. Once the agent chooses to register with the NCAA, the agent must provide information on employment and education background. In addition, he or she must notify the athlete's coach or athletic director before contacting an athlete who still possesses NCAA eligibility. Through this process, the agent's name is placed on a list of registered agents that is then provided to NCAA schools. An agent is removed from this list if he or she provides gifts to a still eligible athlete or if the agent fails to contact the school's athletic director before contacting either the athlete or the athlete's coach.

Many states have designed their regulatory legislation so that it facilitates and corresponds to the NCAA rules. These statutes are considered NCAA-based in that they put teeth into the NCAA eligibility rules. Although these statutes vary greatly, many are similar in that they provide for 1) a written notice regarding the possibility of losing eligibility upon the signing of an SRK and 2) a cooling off period which allows the athlete an opportunity to rescind the contract. Usually an SRK which violates the statute is void. Also, an agent must notify the school of a potential contract. Some statutes require that notice be given to the university prior to the proposed signing. Other statutes simply prohibit the signing of an athlete before the expiration of his NCAA eligibility.

F. CRIMINAL LIABILITY

Some state statutes regulate the conduct of professional sports agents by the imposition of criminal sanctions. For example, in Alabama, an agent can be prosecuted under a statute that prohibits tampering with a sporting event. Ala.Code § 13A–11–143 (1982). Criminal sanctions are applicable. Ala.Code § 8–26–1 to 8–26–41 (Supp.1989). The penalty provisions of the Alabama act establish that all offenses under the act are felony violations. These offenses range from failure to properly register to failure to provide a ten-point type on the face of the SRK warning that the athlete's amateur standing might be jeopardized by entering into the contract.

G. REPRESENTING THE ATHLETE

The agent-athlete agreement typically demands that the agent will be the exclusive representative for the athlete. The fee for these services can range from 3% to 50% of the athlete's contract; the specific share will depend on the agent's responsibilities, the sport, etc. The athlete should expect that the agent's results will be comparable to the results of other agents. The agent has an affirmative duty to be aware of the customs and practices that are relevant to that particular professional sport. Also, as regards publicity, the agent must use his best efforts in a good faith attempt to find employment opportunities outside of the sporting arena.

As regards negotiating a contract, it is essential to acquire the necessary background and then map the most appropriate strategies. One must also possess the flexibility to counter management's negotiation thrusts.

Other aspects of representation may include counseling, managing the athlete's assets, marketing his image through personal appearances and commercial endorsements, assisting the athlete to resolve his disciplinary or salary disputes through mediation or arbitration, and planning life-time strategies that will guarantee the athlete financial, mental and emotional security at the time of the athlete's retirement from the work force.

The goal is to spread income from a short period of time so that it extends through a long period of time, and/or to create employment and business opportunities after retirement from the playing field in order to continue the athlete's standard of living past his days as an athlete.

H. TORTIOUS INTERFERENCE WITH CONTRACTUAL RELATIONS

Many times in the field of sports agency, one associate leaves the firm and takes clients when he departs. Alternatively, one agent sues another for tortious interference with contractual relations when the second agent woos away a signed athlete.

The U.S. Court of Appeals for the Ninth Circuit in San Francisco reversed a jury award of $44.6 million and ordered a new trial in the dispute between NFL agent Leigh Steinberg's former athlete representation firm and his ex-partner David Dunn. After Dunn left Steinberg, Moorad & Dunn, which had been acquired and was then part of the mega-agency firm Assante, to set up a rival agency, Athletes First, Steinberg accused Dunn of violating a noncompete clause in his employment contract and of breaching his fiduciary duty to Steinberg, Moorad & Dunn by stealing a number of its clients. In 2002, a jury ordered Dunn to pay $22 million in compensatory damages and $22.6 million in punitive damages.

However, a unanimous three judge panel of the Ninth Circuit found that U.S. District Judge Ronald S.W. Lew erred by: (1) allowing a statutory unfair competition claim to be submitted to the jury in contravention of the pre-trial conference order; (2) rendering evidentiary rulings related to Dunn's employment contract that prejudiced the jury; (3) failing to instruct the jury that the employment contract's noncompete clause was invalid under California law; and (4) failing to instruct the jury that Dunn's assignment agreement was invalid.

While the Ninth Circuit observed that Judge Lew recognized and tried to rectify his mistake, it concluded that his jury instruction that liability for common law unfair competition could be found on the basis of conduct intended to comprise statutory unfair competition was reversible error. In addition, the Ninth Circuit, ruled that Judge Lew abused his discretion by sustaining multiple hearsay objections when Dunn attempted to testify about what he was told during his contract negotiations. Further, the appellate court found the noncompete clause to be invalid under California state law, which establishes that such clauses are unenforceable whether or not the term of employment has ended. See Cal. Bus. & Prof. Code 16600 (2005). Finally, the panel similarly ruled that the assignment agreement was unenforceable to the extent that it required Dunn to assign all proceeds earned from representing Steinberg, Moorad, & Dunn clients in perpetuity. The Ninth Circuit felt that the entire judgment against Dunn was tainted by the submission of the statutory unfair competition claim because, under California state law, it is an equitable claim and does not provide for either damages or a jury trial. See

Steinberg Moorad & Dunn Inc., a California Corporation v. Dunn, 136 Fed.Appx. 6 (9th Cir.2005).

CHAPTER 3

FINANCIAL CONSIDERATIONS

The astute agent of a professional athlete, through tax and financial planning, should maximize the athlete's income and minimize the tax bite on his earnings. Success is measured by the athlete's financial security at the time of his retirement from the work force rather than at the end of his playing career. One must strive to preserve capital and lessen any adverse tax consequences during the peak income period.

A. TAXATION

Taxation is the application of tax rates to taxable income during a given tax year. To determine an athlete's tax liability one must calculate the gross amount of all income attributed to the athlete-taxpayer during the taxable year. After that, subtract from this gross amount, all deductions; that amount is the taxable income figure which will be used to determine the athlete's tax liability by the application of rates.

Income is a gain derived from any source whatsoever. It includes not only salary, but also bonuses, prize money, the value placed on interest-free loans, endorsement revenues, sportswear companies' gift products, gifts for radio or TV appearances, employer-provided insurance benefits in excess of $50,000.00, "free use of an automobile," etc.

1. Gross Income

An athlete's gross income is where many of the athlete's expenses can be deducted. Gross income can be reduced by deductions for business-related expenses. Business-related expenses are all the ordinary and necessary expenses that are incurred by reason of an athlete's performance in an athletic event including the cost of tools of his trade, expenses related to maintaining a good physical condition, travel, professional services, business entertainment and necessary gratuities. In order to prove the deductibility of an expense, the athlete must maintain a system of record-keeping of expenditures so that the business expense deduction can be maximized and all expenses can be monitored to determine if they are excessive.

2. Planning

The crux of the "problem" is that, typically, athletes receive a large amount of income in a very short amount of time. Therefore, tax planning is imperative. The purpose of this planning is to maximize the benefit from those years in which a high income is recognized by spreading the tax liability to those years of lower income. There are many different ways that one can arrange a tax plan. These arrangements can include deferred compensation plans, tax sheltered investments, and other contractual arrangements that spread out the receipt of income over a period longer than the playing period of the athlete.

B.   ASSIGNMENT OF INCOME

The idea behind income assignment is to avoid realization of income from professional services as an athlete by assigning a portion of that income to a third person. This assignment would reduce overall tax liability by spreading the income to another person who is in a lower marginal tax bracket than the athlete.

It is a good strategy, however, an attempted assignment will be nullified unless it avoids the assignment of income doctrine which stipulates that he who is entitled to income cannot circumvent tax liability by causing it to be paid to another through an anticipatory assignment. There must be a legitimate basis for the other person to receive the assigned income from the athlete. The way to establish this basis is to show that the recipient performed valuable services which aided in the production of the income so as to be entitled to the assignment. Because the highest tax rate in 2009 is 35 percent, any technique that required the assignment of $1.00 to save 35 cents will be of dubious value. This technique is advisable only if tax rates increase.

C. DEFERRALS

The principle behind deferring income is to lessen tax liability by prolonging the incident of taxation from the years in which the athlete earns income to a time in the future. An employee can arrange income deferral through his employer by way of the contract or it can be arranged separately by either the athlete or the athlete's agent. Income can be deferred through pension plans, by contract or by the receipt of restricted property. The latter technique can be accomplished through "substantially nonvested property." That is, property that is not required to be included as income until the first time that the beneficial percentage in the property becomes substantially vested.

1. By Contract

Deferral of the receipt of income can be arranged by way of contract through the SPK. The contract can stipulate that the payment of income will be extended over a period of years and paid in equal sums during each year of that period.

2. By Pension Plans

An extremely popular deferral plan is one arranged by a pension plan that can be created by or for the benefit of a professional athlete. These plans can be individually negotiated or they can be the result of a collective bargaining agreement. A qualified pension plan will provide several benefits including deferring the income to later years to the extent of the employer's contributions; making the employer's contribution deductible, and tax-deferring the pension income.

For relatively high-paid athletes, the most important fact of a qualified pension plan is the extent of the tax reduction on current income. Usually, the athlete will receive monthly payments on retirement or disability. These payments are a part of the athlete's income. The athlete, however, can exclude an amount equal to a portion of the higher payment into the plan. This portion is determined by the exclusion ratio which is determined by dividing the athlete's investment by its expected return. The amount to be excluded will equal the figure that is produced by multiplying payment by the percentage. Since most athletes do not personally contribute to the pension plan, then all of the payments will be included as income.

One other option is a pension plan that is available to the athlete who does not participate in team or league plans. These plans usually cover non-team sports, such as tennis or golf, and allows the athlete as a self-employed person to be treated as both employer and employee for pension plan purposes.

The final option concerns individual retirement accounts. These accounts are for those people who are not active in a qualified plan and could be established by the athlete for a non-working spouse. The athlete then can contribute and deduct a maximum of $5,000 of the compensation included in the gross income for the taxable year. The nondeductible contribution is advisable because the income earned on the contribution is tax-deferred until final withdrawal. Penalty-less withdrawals are not permitted prior to age 59 ½ and do not qualify for the five year forward averaging rule for lump sums under qualified plans. Currently, the most attractive option appears to be the Roth IRA; this is yet another retirement vehicle that affluent athletes can utilize. A tax advisor should suggest the appropriate retirement option.

3. Substantially Non–Vested Property

Another deferral technique concerns substantially non-vested property which is property that is transferred in connection with the performance of services. The value of this property does not have to be included in the athlete's income until the first time its beneficial interest becomes substantially vested; that is, until it is transferable or no longer possesses a substantial risk of forfeiture. This mechanism can provide the athlete with a means of deferring income recognition while providing some security.

The athlete can acquire possession of property at the time services are rendered while allowing taxation deferral until the time when there is a lapsing of a substantial risk of forfeiture. For this to work, the athlete must have the party to whom the services are to be rendered take the deferred amount and purchase the type of property that is preferred by the athlete, e.g., corporate stock or real property. This property then must be transferred to the athlete with a restriction that would qualify as a substantial forfeiture risk such as a provision that would require the athlete to transfer the property to the other party in the event that the athlete ends his athletic services during a particular period of time.

D. TAX–SHELTERED INVESTMENTS

Another method to lessen taxes is through tax-sheltered investments. These investments are those that through appropriate deductions shelter the athlete's income from tax liability. Although such investments vary in kind and activity, they often possess the following tax-minimizing characteristics: leveraging, tax-deferral and tax-free cash flow.

Leveraging: Some tax-shelters offer the investor the use of someone else's money to finance an investment. This is called leveraging.

Tax-deferral: When an investment permits deductions to be accelerated in the early years of the investment and applied to the investor's other income, such an investment offers tax-deferral.

Positive cash flow: When a tax-sheltered investment combines deductions with investment income and generates both simultaneously; the investor receives all the cash that exceeds actual expenses.

Two programs that remain viable are real estate investments especially in low income housing, and oil and gas. However, as with any investment, these programs involve a degree of risk. Thus, a professional athlete must carefully evaluate each program prior to making the investment.

E.   INCORPORATION

Another form of temporary tax planning is to create a personal services corporation based on the athlete's athletic participation, commercial endorsements, etc. This type of corporation is organized for the purpose of using the athlete's abilities. The athlete will form the corporation and then become its major shareholder. He is obliged to perform specialized services with the corporation which would then contract with the sports team. This type of corporate structure allows a deferral of income by the adoption of a corporate pension and profit sharing plan along with a corporate fiscal year.

The corporation can adopt corporate fringe benefits programs and can also allow the creation of various estate planning advantages that are offered by the corporate form of organization. The corporation, though, must have some other purpose than merely avoiding taxes. See *Leavell v. C.I.R.*, 104 T.C. 140 (1995).

F.   FINANCIAL PLANNING

The aims of planning should be capital preservation, tax minimization, protection against risk and an orderly estate plan. The primary objective of financial planning is to increase long-term capital at the expense of current income.

The four basic ways of managing an athlete's assets are to let him decide his own choices, invest in mutual funds, turn the account over to a broker or retain an investment manager. The latter is the most preferred since the investment manager acts as a personal agent and is not a broker.

An investment manager makes decisions on an investor's behalf based upon research of the investment's potential. Rather than receiving payment for each stock transaction, the manager is paid an annual fee for structuring an investment portfolio. As part of this structure, the manager will invariably attempt to achieve financial security for the athlete's investments.

1. Preservation of Capital

The number of years the average professional athlete can compete is extremely short: for example, approximately two years in football and four and a half in baseball. Since the athlete will probably have 40 or so years until retirement age it is imperative that a strategy be adopted to maximize his investment portfolio. There are many products that can assist in achieving the goal of capital preservation such as certificates of deposit, common stock and annuities. An annuity is a contract between the athlete and an insurance company for fixed payments at regular intervals over some period of time. An example would be a 30–year–old athlete who purchases an annuity for $100,000 with payments of money per month beginning at age 45.

2.   Tax Minimization

The planner also should consider the following tax measures to minimize the income tax burden of the athlete:

1.   Making a contribution to an IRA for a non-working spouse. All income earned on the IRA is tax-deferred until final distribution.

2.   Making Keogh contributions: for athletes with substantial endorsement income, contributions of up to the lesser of $49,000 or 25% of this self-employment income are allowable. Endorsement income is normally self-employment income. This presents an opportunity for savings.

3.   Converting taxable income into tax-exempt income.

4.   Making family gifts so that earnings can be removed from income.

5.   Making contributions to a college fund for the athlete's children.

6.   Converting personal non-deductible interest into qualified residence income.

3.   Protection Against Risk

There is an ongoing struggle between investing in assets that appreciate rapidly and investing in assets that protect against risk. Since the money that the athlete can earn from his skills is finite, it is imperative that he does not lose money. Therefore, investment plans should be balanced against his risk. Conservative instruments such as certificates of deposit and money market funds are available but the skilled investment professional should be capable of structuring a more profitable conservative plan while retaining emphasis on preservation of capital. This approach can achieve a higher return at little risk to the athlete/investor.

4. Estate Planning

Estate planning is important for athletes since they risk accidental death with every tackle or misplaced fast ball. An athlete should have a will to pass title to property on death. A will can be used to place funds in a trust for the benefit of others unable to manage property. For example, a trust can be used to educate and care for the deceased athlete's children; and when they reach maturity, provide for the principal to be paid out as specified in the will.

Another aspect of estate planning is the creation of a revocable trust. A trust takes effect at the time of its creation and operates as a will substitute. A trust is an agreement between grantor and trustee which contains instructions to the trustees so as to assist in the disposition of the property that is transferred to the trustee. Revocable trusts seldom establish a workable asset management arrangement during the athlete's life; a durable power of attorney provides for continued action on behalf of the athlete upon disability that renders him incompetent. An added advantage of a trust is that trust property is not subject to probate upon the owner's death. The trust can be freely revoked or amended during the owner's life and the cost and delays are less than those in an administration of a will.

Estate tax is the government's tax on the value of property that passes from a person who has died to his beneficiaries. The tax is assessed against the fair market value of all property that was owned by the decedent upon death. Estate tax is calculated on the taxable estate which is the gross estate less deductions and credits. There is a marital deduction which allows an unlimited deduction for property passing from the decedent to the surviving spouse. There is also a charitable deduction which can benefit the athlete in his estate plan by providing a deduction from estate taxes. Like property that passes to a spouse, property that passes to a qualified charity is also deductible from the gross estate. While spousal and charitable deductions are deducted from the athlete's gross estate, the "unified credit" is applied to reduce the tax itself. This credit can currently eliminate estate taxes on $3,500,000 worth of property.

There is also a generation skipping tax which is a separate tax designed to prevent avoiding estate or gift taxes which would have been applicable if the property in question had first been given to the intervening generation and then transferred to the grandchildren. However, there's a significant exemption from generation-skipping taxes which allows each individual today to transfer up to $3,500,000 of property, free from this tax.

Life insurance is yet another aspect of many financial plans. Because of their age and robust physical condition life insurance is readily obtainable at a reasonable price by professional athletes. Insurance proceeds can be important to his family if the athlete does die young. These proceeds can be used to pay debts, taxes, bequests, and/or provide funds for trusts for family members of the athlete.

CHAPTER 4

LABOR LAW

A. NATIONAL LABOR RELATIONS ACT

Union-management relations in professional sports are controlled under the auspices of the National Labor Relations Act (NLRA), 29 U.S.C.A. §§ 151–166. However, sports for many years was viewed as an anomaly that was not a business, and it thus escaped the protection of the NLRA during those years. Baseball, for example, in the early days was a classic case of management abuse. Yet, in *Federal Baseball Club, Inc. v. National League of Professional Baseball Clubs*, 259 U.S. 200 (1922), the Supreme Court excepted baseball and the reserve clause from antitrust regulations, thus stagnating any attempts by the players to organize as a union.

But, professional sports include other employees than just athletes. There are also the relatively low-paid club house attendants, bat boys, traveling secretaries, physical therapists, ushers, ticket sellers, etc. Collective bargaining and the umbrella protection of the NLRA finally came to baseball in 1969.

In *American League of Professional Baseball Clubs*, 180 N.L.R.B. 190 (1969), the National Labor

Relations Board (NLRB) moved to take jurisdiction over professional baseball. The NLRB can decline jurisdiction when a particular industry's impact on interstate commerce is deemed to be insubstantial. The NLRB has accordingly declined jurisdiction over some forms of recreational activity, for example, harness racing. *Yonkers Raceway, Inc.*, 196 N.L.R.B. 373 (1972); see also *Centennial Turf Club, Inc.*, 192 N.L.R.B. 698 (1971). However, the NLRB will generally take jurisdiction of all organized team sports.

American League of Professional Baseball Clubs involved baseball umpires. The NLRB held that since baseball is an industry that affects commerce it is subject to the coverage and the jurisdiction of the NLRB. The policy of the NLRB is to encourage collective bargaining through the protection of the rights of employees to self-organize and choose the representation of their choice. These goals were felt to be best served by asserting jurisdiction over professional baseball and thus subjecting all labor disputes to determination under the NLRA. The NLRB also specifically took jurisdiction over professional football in *National Football League Management Council*, 203 N.L.R.B. 958 (1973).

The NLRB's § 7 demands that "employees should have the right to self-organization, to bargain collectively through representatives of their own choosing, and to engage in other concerted activities for the purpose of collectively bargaining or other mutual aid or protection." The NLRB was formed to administer and police these § 7 rights: the NLRA applies to all employers whose business affects commerce, although the NLRB can decline to intervene if the effect on commerce is minimal. Today, there is no question that professional sports and the corresponding collective bargaining relationship between players and management falls firmly under the NLRA's protection.

Richie Phillips, former Chief of the Major Leagues Umpires Association (MLUA), sued MLB and everyone else for his demise as chief. He claimed interference with existing and prospective contractual relations and conspiracy—these claims arose from his failed labor negotiation tactic when he suggested a mass resignation, instead of striking. A majority of MLUA's members followed his suggestion, but MLB countered by hiring minor league umpires. Some of Richie's army panicked and withdrew their resignations; and MLB hired back all but 22 of the MLUA umpires. MLUA was not amused with Richie's failed strategy. Another union was formed to compete with MLUA. A new union, represented by Robert Shapiro filed a successful petition with the NLRB to decertify MLUA. Phillips failed to meet his burden that defendants had specific intent to harm him. Additionally, all of defendant's actions, including decertifications, were within their power under the National Labor Relations Act. *Phillips v. Selig,* 2007 WL 711820 (Pa. C.P. 2007).

B. UNIONS AND MANAGEMENT

It was a tough struggle for unions to organize in professional sports: management was especially adamant in the defense of what they considered their personal and private fiefdom. For many years, labor groups were not sufficiently organized to be recognized as unions by the NLRA. Even after recognition, the relationship between unions and management was stormy, with the owners' behavior characterized by a demeanor that was both procrastinating and bullying.

The first question the NLRB must decide when considering if a particular industry is eligible for protection under the NLRA is whether the coverage of the NLRA is broad enough to include that industry. The NLRB answered in the affirmative regarding the sports industry, since the affect of professional sports on commerce is not minimal.

Next, the NLRB must determine the appropriate bargaining unit. In most sports, the unit is determined to be the sport as a whole instead of individual teams or particular positions (e.g., not a union for catchers only). Once a union is recognized it becomes the exclusive bargaining representative for all members of the unit.

In *North American Soccer League v. NLRB*, 613 F.2d 1379 (5th Cir.1980), the court found the bargaining unit to be all professional soccer players on clubs that are based in the United States. The court held that the league and its member clubs are joint employers. The key to the decision was the joint employer status of the individual teams and the league. The court, however, was momentarily swayed by the apparent individuality of each team: "Contrary to our first impression, which was fostered by the knowledge that teams in the League compete against each other on the playing fields and for the hire of the best players, * * *." However, after further consideration, the court agreed with the NLRB that there was a joint employer relationship among the league and its member clubs; they then designated the league as the appropriate bargaining unit.

The NLRB is not required to select the most appropriate bargaining unit, but only to choose an appropriate unit under the circumstances. The NLRB's decision not to exercise jurisdiction over the three Canadian clubs did not undermine its evidentiary base for their finding that there was a joint employer relationship between the league and the clubs.

There is one caveat. The duty to bargain requires that both sides must bargain in good faith. Section 8(d) of the NLRA states that both parties must meet at reasonable times and confer on mandatory subjects of collective bargaining. The failure to do so is an unfair labor practice. This duty to bargain in good faith can be defined as a willingness to enter in negotiations with an open and fair mind and with a sincere desire to find a basis of agreement. The duty to bargain calls for sincerity, not results.

An example of the above process was revealed in *NFLPA v. NLRB*, 503 F.2d 12 (8th Cir.1974). In the case, various National Football League owners and their management council unilaterally promulgated and implemented a rule that provided for an automatic fine against any player who left the bench while there was a brawl or altercation on the playing field. The unilateral enactment of this rule without the benefit of collective bargaining was an unfair labor practice. This rule was an unfair labor practice since it involved a mandatory subject of collective bargaining and should have been sifted through the collective bargaining process. Also, the c.b.a. itself provided that any change in current practices that affect the players' employment conditions shall be negotiated in good faith.

The union has the responsibility to fairly represent all members of the bargaining unit, even those who are not members. This is the duty of fair representation. In order to prove a violation of this duty one must show that the union acted arbitrarily or in bad faith. For example, a union always defends any of its players when they are disciplined for clubhouse brawls, but then the union ignores one particular player who happened to be anti-union. This case would reflect a violation of the duty of fair representation.

C. COLLECTIVE BARGAINING GENERALLY

Collective bargaining is the process under the NLRA where owners and the players' union participate in a give-and-take that produces a document which is called the collective bargaining agreement (c.b.a.). This document establishes the rules and regulations of their relationship. Once they have entered into collective bargaining, they are obliged to bargain in good faith. The failure of either party to bargain in good faith is an unfair labor practice.

The subject matter of collective bargaining, that is, what must be discussed at the bargaining table, includes wages, hours and conditions of employment. There are also permissive subjects of bargaining which include anything other than wages, hours and conditions. The parties must bargain in good faith about mandatory subjects, but they may refuse to bargain about permissive subjects. A party may insist that the other party agree to their proposal on a mandatory subject, even to the point of impasse. If an agreement does not materialize, a party then may resort to economic pressure, i.e., strikes or lock-outs, without risking NLRA §§ 8(a)(5) or 8(b)(3) unfair labor practice charges. This is important because if a strike is an unfair labor practice, it can be enjoined.

D. THE COLLECTIVE BARGAINING AGREEMENT

Collective bargaining agreements express the complete range of relationships between management and their athlete employees. This document will specify the scope of the union—management agreement and will prohibit the use of either strikes or lockouts. Although the collective bargaining agreement will vary with the sport, it will cover at a minimum the following: club discipline, non-injury grievances, commissioner discipline, injury grievances, the SPK, college draft, option clauses, waivers, base salaries, access to personnel files, medical rights, retirement, insurance and the duration of the c.b.a.

In *Garvey v. Roberts*, 203 F.3d 580 (9th Cir.2000), a celebrated former baseball player won a part of the baseball collusion settlement ex post facto. The 9th Circuit ruled on February 10, 2000, that a district court improperly refused to consider former major league baseball all-star Steve Garvey's appeal of an arbitration decision denying him a portion of the settlement fund established as a result of Major League Baseball owner's free agent collusion in the 1980's. In 1986–88, the union filed grievances alleging collective bargaining agreement violations by engaging in collusion in the market for players' free agent services after the 1985–87 seasons. Arbitrators agreed and on December 21, 1990, a settlement agreement was reached that established a $280 million fund that would be distributed to players who were financially damaged as a result of the collusion. A framework was put into place to distribute the funds properly. Garvey claimed he was entitled to a piece of the settlement because the San Diego Padres, for which he had played the prior four seasons, had offered him a $3 million contract extension for the 1988 and 1989 baseball seasons only to withdraw the offer due to the club's collusion. The Ninth Circuit overruled the arbitrator, since he ignored the recently obtained letter from the former Padres' CEO Ballard Smith that substantiated Garvey's allegations. The court found this letter to be credible, whereas Smith's testimony during Garvey's original hearing clearly was not credible.

However, the U.S. Supreme Court in *Major League Baseball Players Ass'n v. Garvey*, 532 U.S. 504 (2001), held that the Court of Appeals erred in reversing the denial of the motion and in directing the arbitration to enter judgment for Garvey. The appellate court usurped the arbitrator's role by resolving the dispute and barring further proceedings, a result at odds with the governing law.

In *Metropolitan Sports Facilities Commission v. Minnesota Twins Partnership*, 638 N.W.2d 214 (Minn.App.2002), the Minnesota Court of Appeals blocked professional baseball's contraction scheme regarding the Minnesota Twins. The Metropolitan Sports Facilities Commission, which operates the Metrodome in downtown Minneapolis, settled its lawsuit against the Minnesota Twins and Major

League Baseball, insuring that the Twins will be playing in that stadium through the 2003 season. Under terms of the settlement, MLB will not contract the team out of baseball during those two seasons. The Twins also agreed to a lease extension to play in the Metrodome through the 2003 season. News leaked out that baseball intended to eliminate two teams. The Commission then brought suit, seeking to enjoin Major League Baseball from rescinding the Twins franchise for the 2002 season on the ground that the team was contractually obligated by its stadium lease to play the 2002 season in the Metrodome. A TRO and then a preliminary injunction was granted. The Minnesota Court of Appeals affirmed and concluded that the team's lease agreement warrants such equitable relief and that the lower court did not abuse its discretion in granting it.

In *White v. NFL*, 899 F.Supp. 410 (D.Minn.1995), (one of many cases under that name issued by Judge Doty, the special master who brokered the stipulation and settlement agreement (SSA) that settled an earlier lawsuit between the National Football League and the National Football League Player's Association), under the NFL collective bargaining agreement, a football player was entitled to become an unrestricted free agent if he had four or more accrued seasons. The c.b.a. further specified that a player was credited with an accrued season if he was on full pay status for six or more regular season games. The special master determined that he was prevented from receiving a fourth accrued season, thereby denying him unrestricted free agency, since his team had a bye week during one of his qualifying weeks. The sole question before the court was whether the bye week, during which the player was on full pay status, counted as a "game" for purposes of defining an accrued season under the c.b.a. provisions. The special master concluded that its clear language provided that a player would only be credited with an accrued season if he was on full pay status for a total of six or more regular season games in a given year and that games played by other terms during a week in which a player's team had a bye did not count toward the calculation of an accrued season. After a de novo review, the court concurred and affirmed the decision.

White v. NFL, 149 F.Supp.2d 858 (D.Minn.2001) (re Kyle Richardson), was a case which arose out of a proceeding commenced by class counsel and the NFLPA regarding the status of Kyle Richardson, a punter for the Baltimore Ravens. Under the Collective Bargaining Agreement, an NFL player is entitled to become an unrestricted Free Agent if he has four or more Accrued Seasons. The CBA further specifies that a player is credited with an Accrued Season if he was on full pay status for six or more regular season games. Richardson has three Accrued Seasons in the NFL apart from his service in 1997. On class counsel's objections to the special master's decision, the court held that games played by other professional football teams during a week in which punter's team had a bye could not count as a "game" for the player for purposes of calculating an "Accrued Season."

The following is a so-called "free-agent glossary" for the National Football League, as of March 2, 2002, when free agency began for 2002:

EXCLUSIVE RIGHTS FREE AGENT—A player whose contract expires at a time when he has fewer than three accrued seasons in the NFL can't market his services to other teams if his former team gives him a minimum salary tender on or before March 1. If the tender is provided, the player can only sign with his old team unless the tender is later withdrawn.

RESTRICTED FREE AGENT—A player whose contract expires when he has three accrued seasons is in this category in a capped year. If his former club provides him with sufficient qualifying offer on or before March 1, it retains the right to either match an offer the player gets from another team or receive draft compensation from the team making the offer.

UNRESTRICTED FREE AGENT—A player whose contract has expired when he has accumulated at least four accrued seasons in a capped year is free to sign with any other team if he does so by the beginning of training camp of the same year. If he does not sign elsewhere, the exclusive rights revert to his former team after that date provided the former team has given him a written tender by June 1, offering to re-sign him for an additional year at a 10 percent increase in salary.

FRANCHISE PLAYER—Each team can designate one player who otherwise would be an unrestricted free agent as a franchise player. The team must tender the franchise player a one-year offer equal to the average of the top five salaries in the league at his position or a 20 percent salary increase, whichever is greater. The former team can match any offer to retain the player or receive two first-round draft picks if it decides not to match.

A TRANSITION PLAYER—A team can elect to use a transition player designation for one free agent instead of using a franchise player designation. If it does so, the team must tender the player a one-year offer equal to the average of the top 10 salaries in the league at his position or at a 20 percent increase, whichever is greater. A transition player can obtain an offer from another team, but his former team can match if it chooses. No drafts choices can be collected as compensation for losing a transition player.

The National Basketball Association and the National Basketball Players Association reached a new collective bargaining agreement that will run through the 2010–11 season. The following is a list of changes from the previous agreement:

- The salary cap was increased from 48.04% of BRI ("Basketball Related Income") to 51% of BRI. Where there was no guarantee in the prior agreement, the players will now be guaranteed 57% of BRI.

- The longest contract that a player can sign with his current team was reduced from 7 years with maximum annual salary increases of 12.5% to 6 years with maximum annual salary increases of 10.5%.

- The longest contract that a player can sign with a new team was reduced from 6 years with maximum annual salary increases of 10% to 5 years with maximum annual salary increases of 8%.

- Luxury tax revenues will be divided equally among all 30 teams instead of only among those teams that did not have to pay the tax.

- The player's escrow tax was reduced from 10% to eight percent.

- Each teams' active roster was expanded from 12 players to 14 players.

- The minimum age for draft eligibility was increased from 18 to 19 years old by the end of the calendar year. Additionally, a domestic player's high school class must have graduated one year earlier.

- The number of guaranteed contract years for rookies was reduced from three years to two years.

- Where the National Basketball Development League (NBDL) previously operated independently, players with less than two years of experience will now be eligible to be assigned to a team in the NBDL.

- Suspensions of 12 games or more by the commissioner for "on-court misconduct" will now be arbitrable.

- Testing for performance-enhancing and recreational drugs will be increased from a single time during training camp to four times per year. The penalties for a positive test of a performance-enhancing drug enhancing drug were increased to 10 games for the first offense, and a lifetime ban for a fourth offense.

- The salary range within which players must be traded for one another was increased from 110% plus $100,000 to 125% plus $100,000.

- The time during which players who have suffered career-ending injuries will count against the salary cap was reduced from two years to one year.

- The minimum salary will be increased. Pensions will be increased with the approval of the IRS.

After losing the 2004–05 season to a lockout, the National Hockey League and the National Hockey League Players Association in July reached a new collective bargaining agreement, which will run through the 2010–11 season. The NHLPA has the right to re-open the agreement after the 2008–2009 season and has an option to extend the agreement for one year at the end of the 2010–11 season. The following is a list of changes from the previous agreement:

- Whereas there was no linkage between revenues and salaries previously, the players will now get 54% of league revenues below $2.2 billion, 55% of league revenues between $2.2 billion and $2.4 billion, 56% of league revenues between $2.4 billion and $2.7, and 57% of league revenues above $2.7 billion.

- A portion of player salaries will be held in an escrow account to reimburse the NHL in the event that the players receive greater than their share of league revenues.

- Whereas there was neither a team payroll floor nor cap previously, there will be a team payroll minimum of $21.5 million and a payroll cap of $39 million for every team during the 2005–06 season.

- Player contracts for the 2004–05 season will be considered eliminated, as if they never existed.

- Player contracts for all other seasons will be reduced by 24%.

- Player contracts will not be eligible for renegotiation during their term.

- Player contracts will be eligible for extensions only during the final year of their term and only within the constraints of the salary cap.

- No individual player will be allowed to earn compensation in any year greater than 20% of the team's salary cap for that year.

- The minimum player salary was increased from $175,000 to $450,000 for the 2005–06 and 2006–

07 seasons, $475,000 for the 2007–08 and 2008–09 seasons, $500,000 for the 2009–10 and 2010–11 seasons, and $525,000 for the 2011–12 season (if the agreement is extended).

- Whereas there was no signing deadline in the prior agreement, restricted free agents who do not sign contracts by December 1st will be ineligible to play for the remainder of that season.

- Players will be eligible for salary arbitration after four years of service in the league, an increase from three years.

- Whereas only players were allowed to elect salary arbitration in the prior agreement, either a player or his team will now be allowed to elect arbitration.

- Whereas there was no authorization for testing for performance-enhancing drugs in their prior agreement, players will be subject to two random tests per year. The penalties for a positive test of a performance-enhancing drug will be 20 games and mandatory referral to the NHL's substance abuse program for the first offense; 60 games for a second offense, and a permanent suspension for a third offense (although a player may apply for reinstatement after 2 years).

- The two sides also agreed that the players would be allowed to participate in the 2006 Olympic Games in Turin, Italy and the 2010 Winter Olympic Games in Vancouver, Canada.

On March 8, 2006, the NFL voted to approve a new labor deal that extends the existing collective bargaining agreement with NFLPA by four years. Some highlights of the deal include:

- The agreement runs for a term of six football years, through the end of the 2011 season, thereby extending the current agreement that would have expired at the end of the 2007 season.

- The salary cap jumps to $102 million for the 2006 season and then to $109 million for the 2007 season, after 2007, the salary cap will be determined by revenue.

- The salary cap will be based on 59.6% of defined revenues.

- Top 15 revenue-generating teams contribute to a revenue pool, with the top five teams giving the most. The bottom 17 teams don't contribute to the pool, which is expected to add between $850 million and $900 million over the life of the contract.

- Players drafted in the 1st round can sign deals exceeding the old five-year limit. Players drafted in rounds 2–7 may sign deals no longer than four years. Such a rule prevents teams from locking up players who prove to be worth more.

- A team using the "franchise" tag for the third consecutive season on the same player must pay that player the average salary of the highest salaried position, even if that is not the player's position. For example, if a team "franchises" a kicker salary for three straight years, the kicker may be paid the average salary of the five highest paid quarterbacks.

- Players must be three years removed from high school in order to qualify for the NFL Draft.

- A club no longer can discipline a player as Philadelphia did Terrell Owens last season. Under the new agreement, the maximum punishment that a team can impose on a player is a suspension without pay for four weeks–in essence, a reversal of the Owens decision of last year. The team can continue to de-activate the player week-to-week, but they cannot remove the player for extended periods of time as a disciplinary measure.

- While there is still no standard language for signing bonuses, there is restrictive language barring clubs from recouping portions of signing bonuses from players guilty of misbehavior. Teams can still write their own language regarding bonuses, but they must keep it within the guidelines of the new agreement.

On October 24, 2006, the Major League Baseball Players Association reached a deal with Major League Baseball to finalize a new 5–year Collective Bargaining Agreement. The new c.b.a. will assure labor peace through 2011. It is unusual because it was negotiated out of the public eye and without and reciprocal threats.

During the period from 1972 to 1995, there were a total of eight work stoppages as a result of stalled or unsuccessful negotiations between the union and ownership. The unrest culminated in 1994 when the MLBPA elected to strike in August, almost two-thirds of the way into the season. The strike led to the cancellation of that year's World Series and a delay in the start of the 1995 season. The new c.b.a. is substantially similar in key respects to the 2002 agreement and reflects the significant economic success the league has enjoyed since the late 1990's. The new deal continues to employ a luxury tax on team payrolls exceeding a threshold level (with that threshold increasing from $136.5 million to $148 million next year), general free agency at the same points in a player's career as before, the amateur draft, and an amended drug policy. Some significant changes that were made include the elimination of free agency deadline, recognition of player-trade demands, as well as a shorter time period in which to sign draftees. The new c.b.a. can be modified, however, and there is some movement to discuss the possible commencement of Human Growth Hormone testing.

E. CONCERTED ACTIONS

The process of collective bargaining only works because of the threat of concerted action that each party can legally invoke if negotiation reaches an impasse. This is especially true in professional sports where the season is only so long and the athlete's career is limited in duration. Even though the history of collective bargaining in professional sports is not very long, there is an almost annual ritual in the major sports of either concerted actions, the threat of concerted actions or accusations of unfair labor practices.

1. Strikes

The NLRA guarantees employees, and thus professional athletes, the right to engage in strikes and in other concerted activities. If collective bargaining reaches an impasse then the players' union is legally allowed to strike. A strike is the failure to report to training camp or to the playing field. The strike is the players' primary weapon in coercing the owners to either adhere to the players' demands, compromise, or at least get back to the bargaining table and continue to negotiate in good faith. All strikes are a double-edged sword with the "winner" being the side that can most easily withstand the economic hardships that concerted actions by nature bring.

This right to strike cannot generally be diminished or thwarted and will receive considerable legal protection. Even though there is a right to strike, the union must still continue to bargain in good faith. The union will also lose their legal right to strike if it agrees to a no-strike clause in the c.b.a., if the players' union engages in an activity that has an unlawful objective or if the union uses improper means. The owners can impose sanctions on the strikers; however, they are still employees and cannot be punished for any unfair labor practices committed by management during a strike.

2. Lockouts

On the other hand, the owners have the ability to lockout the players, that is, to not allow the athletes to report to training camp. The lockout is the owners' primary economic weapon; it is the power to withhold employment. It is used as a means to economically coerce the players to either return to the bargaining table and/or rekindle their desire to continue good faith negotiations. Lockouts are legal as long as bargaining continues in good faith and the lockout occurs only after impasse.

F. ARBITRATION AND MEDIATION

The arbitration and mediation procedures in professional sports are probably the most important result and ingredient in the collective bargaining process. In fact, in baseball, the grievance procedure which began in the 1970 c.b.a. helped to end the reserve clause; and salary arbitration which began in the 1973 c.b.a. is perhaps the greatest additive to the players' quest for higher salaries.

If there is an applicable clause, arbitration will be the exclusive remedy for achieving peace. Courts rarely reverse an arbitrator's decision if the party seeking arbitration makes a claim that on its face is governed by the arbitration provisions of the c.b.a. The basic issue in arbitration is whether the dispute is arbitrable," that is, is it within the range of matters that were intended to be arbitrated through the grievance procedure.

The seminal case of *Kansas City Royals Baseball Corp. v. MLBPA*, 532 F.2d 615 (8th Cir.1976), is a good illustration of how grievance arbitration works in sports. In this case, a major league baseball team brought an action against the players' association to overturn an arbitration award that ruled in favor of two professional baseball players who played out their option years and then sought to be declared free agents. The court's review was limited to the legitimacy of the arbitration process. The court's favorable ruling was predicated on the following: The arbitration provision of the c.b.a. was broad enough to cover the dispute in question; there was nothing in the history of their collective bargaining relationship that showed a strong intent not to arbitrate grievances that involved the reserve clause, that is, there was nothing to overcome the presumption that the question of free agency was arbitrable; that the documents in question (e.g., the c.b.a.) were at least susceptible of the arbitration panel's interpretation; that the decree was not impermissible against other entities that were not party to either the arbitration or the court proceedings; and that the decree was not vague and indefinite as regards the granting of free agency.

In an SPK a party has certain rights. The question becomes how to enforce these rights; the answer generally is arbitration. An agreement to arbitrate is a promise to resolve disputes by non-judicial means. Arbitration is preferred to judicial remedies because it is more informal, less costly and less time-consuming. It is also more private, which is important in an industry which is concerned with its public image and constantly under intense media scrutiny. The parties can pick the person who will hear the case which can guarantee that that person is at least familiar with the peculiarities of the particular sport.

As regards determining what controversies are subject to arbitration, one must look to the actual wording of the SPK. Most sports contracts contain a very broad arbitration clause: it will cover nearly all disputes. However, in most agreements the club will still retain the right to seek judicial redress as regards the players' promise to perform exclusively for that club during the term of the contract. Clubs want the power of an injunction to stop players from club or league jumping.

Matters that are not subject to arbitration include controversies not covered in the agreement, situations when the breaching party waived his arbitration rights (e.g., initiating a law suit instead of proceeding with arbitration) and cases where the court recognizes certain claims that they believe require direct judicial enforcement because of public policy reasons (e.g., equal employment or antitrust).

There are few grounds for vacating an arbitrator's award. A court will set aside awards only in extreme cases; therefore, agents should not approach arbitrations with a cavalier attitude. The rationale behind the "finality" of the award is that the parties have freely bargained away their rights to seek judicial remedies and presumably each party has received something in return. Therefore, the parties should be made to keep their bargain. Also, arbitration is deemed to be a desirable mechanism for dispute resolution and as a result, arbitration decisions should be maintained and honored.

In *Lindland v. U.S. Wrestling Ass'n, Inc.*, 230 F.3d 1036 (7th Cir.2000), an arbitration award directing the United States wrestling association to rerun a wrestling bout, after the original bout had resulted in another wrestler, rather than the grievant, being nominated a member of the United States Olympic wrestling team, entitled the grievant to be nominated for the U.S. team after he won the rematch. The arbitrator "did not order an exhibition match," but instead ordered that the bout was to "be re-wrestled" in accordance with the association's rules, which, in turn stated that its winner would receive its support in going to the Olympic Games as the U.S. representative. The fact that the first nominated wrestler had initiated his own arbitration, thus creating the possibility that the association would be subject to inconsistent awards, did not absolve the association of the duty to implement the original arbitration award. Moreover, the grievant was not required to have named the first nominated wrestler as a party in the earlier arbitration.

1. Grievance

The standard grievance arbitration clause will usually stipulate that all problems that arise out of a dispute or grievance that emanates from an interpretation or misinterpretation of the c.b.a. or SPK must be handled through agreed upon arbitration procedures.

Arbitration procedures are relatively standard in most SPK's and c.b.a.'s. Usually they deal only with grievance or contract disputes, but, as in professional baseball, they can be formulated to deal with other concerns, such as salary disputes.

The grievance arbitration procedure as usually stipulated in the c.b.a. is an extremely practical method for both parties to settle their differences. The purpose of this clause is to provide an orderly and expeditious procedure for the handling and resolving of certain disputes, grievances and complaints. Although it is similar to all other sports, baseball's arbitration procedure specifically excludes the benefit plan, union dues check-off and complaints involving the integrity of the sport.

2. Salary

In baseball, a player or a club is allowed to submit a dispute over a player's salary to binding arbitration without the consent of the other party after a certain number of years in service have been accumulated by the player. (It was two years, then it was three, now, it falls between two and three years; more precisely, as a result of the 1990 lockout, 17% of the two to three year players are eligible for salary arbitration). The technique that is used in this type of arbitration is called "high-low," which means that both parties must submit proposed salary figures to the arbitrator who then must choose only one figure, without modification or compromise. The tool of the arbitrator and also the tool for both the players and owners, is statistics: the player's statistics covering productivity, longevity, potential and comparable worth as compared to like-situated players. Each party will offer statistics in order to prove their contention that their salary figure is most correct. The arbitrator must then decide the significance of mutually contradictory figures and choose the one that he feels is most correct. A major complaint about this type of arbitration is that the arbitrator who is chosen (under mutual agreement by both the union and the owners) is often lacking in the requisite baseball expertise to properly decipher the often confusing statistics.

CHAPTER 5

ANTITRUST

A. GENERALLY

The Sherman Antitrust Act, 15 U.S.C.A. § 1, *et seq.*, makes illegal every combination in the form of a conspiracy that restrains interstate commerce. Every person who monopolizes or combines to monopolize is guilty of a felony. The goal of the antitrust acts is to stop monopolies and protect fair competition.

These laws are the major mechanism available to effect change in sports. That is because the basic leitmotif in organized sports is summarized by the oxymoron of competitive cohesion. In sports one competes in some respects and cooperates in others. Organized sports must have honest competition to be attractive, but to be organized it must establish rules to assure fair play, arrange schedules, punish wrongdoers, etc. "Cooperation" is necessary for the college draft, cable TV, roster limitations, player restraints, preseason games, season tickets, franchise movement and league competition.

The antitrust laws have been used by various groups: e.g., players, owners, colleges, etc. The goal of these antitrust plaintiffs was to achieve some result at the expense of management, whether it was better wages, better conditions, a new location or less control.

The typical situation involves players who contend that they are victims of anti-competitive practices. The thrust of the Sherman Act is to protect the public interest from anti-competitive practices. (Interestingly, these players, or victims of anti-competition, are paid millions a year to play sports.)

Monopolies are deemed to be against public interest: the concern is that a monopolized industry can result in exorbitant prices because it is unchallenged by free competition.

There are two basic ways to interpret an antitrust controversy: either as a "per se" violation or through a rule of reason approach. Professional sports usually will merit the rule of reason analysis rather than a mechanical "per se" review.

The per se approach is most applicable to overt antitrust violations. Throughout the years, the courts have gained enough experience with antitrust problems to identify certain types of agreements that are so consistently unreasonable that they may be deemed to be illegal per se without further inquiry into their purported rationales. Among the practices that are so pernicious that they are illegal per se are group boycotts and concerted refusals to deal. A concerted refusal to deal is an agreement by two or more persons either not to do business with other persons or to do business with them only on particular terms. Group boycotts are refusals to deal or inducements to others not to deal or to have business relations. *Mackey v. NFL*, 543 F.2d 606 (8th Cir.1976).

In the district court's opinion in *Mackey,* which analyzed the legality of the Rozelle Rule (allowing the commissioner, one Pete Rozelle, in his sole opinion, to require the club that acquires a free agent to compensate the free agent's former club in the form of money, players and/or valuable draft picks), the court held that the Rule significantly deterred clubs from negotiating with and signing free agents. Because of the Rule, a club would only sign free agents if it was able to reach an agreement to compensate the player's former team or when it was willing to risk the commissioner's awarding of unknown compensation. The court held that the rule as enforced constituted a group boycott and a concerted refusal to deal and thus a per se violation of the Sherman Act.

The Court of Appeals in *Mackey,* however, acknowledged that it was inappropriate to declare the Rozelle Rule illegal per se without reviewing the purported justifications behind the Rule. The per se approach is typically used with agreements between business competitors in the traditional sense. Professional sports combines aspects of both competition and cooperation; also, the NFL does assume some characteristics of a joint venture in that each member club has a stake in the success of the other teams. That is, no one club is interested in driving any other team out of business, since if the league fails then no one team can survive.

The *Mackey* appellate ruling reviewed the Rozelle Rule under a rule of reason analysis. The focus of inquiry under a rule of reason approach is whether the restraint as imposed is justified by legitimate purposes and it is no more restrictive than necessary. A rule of reason analysis poses the question of whether the restraint is reasonable under all the circumstances.

In *Worldwide Basketball & Sports Tours, Inc. v. NCAA,* 273 F.Supp.2d 933 (S.D. Ohio 2003), the court applied a full rule of reason analysis when it disallowed a permanent injunction prohibiting the NCAA from forcing its "Two in Four Rule." Plaintiff sports promoters sued the NCAA alleging that the "Two in Four Rule" limited Division I college basketball teams from participating in more than two "exempt" tournaments every four seasons. Historically "exempt" tournament participation was not considered in calculating the number of regular season games. The NCAA saw this as a problem. Since its adoption in 1999, the rule has led to a significant decrease in the number of exempt tournament games, number of tournaments, and in the number of basketball games scheduled by Division I teams. The NCAA also increased the maximum number of allowed regular season games. The effect essentially defeated one of the NCAA's jurisdictions: namely, to allow lesser known teams to play in more desirable tournaments. Another justification of limiting the total games was a concern for athlete welfare which was also nullified. The "Two in Four Rule" has a substantially adverse effect on competition in the relevant product market of all Division I college basketball games. The plaintiffs were not able to show that the restraint had significant anti-competitive effects, such as a reduction in output. The court found that the promoters failed to establish a relevant market. Therefore, the court chose not to permanently enjoined the NCAA from enforcing the "Two in Four Rule."

Most of the obvious antitrust infractions, for example, certain onerous player restriction procedures that were a part of the SPK, have now been ameliorated through collective bargaining so that currently these procedures can either pass antitrust examination or they are protected by an exemption to the antitrust laws. However, antitrust actions are still very much part of attempts to regulate and readjust both amateur and professional sports. For example, the NBA salary cap was attacked but found to be legal. *Wood v. NBA*, 602 F.Supp. 525 (S.D.N.Y. 1984). The NCAA violated the antitrust laws by restricting college football broadcasts. *NCAA v. Board of Regents*, 468 U.S. 85 (1984). The NFL violated antitrust laws by restricting franchise movement. *Los Angeles Memorial Coliseum Commission v. NFL*, 726 F.2d 1381 (9th Cir.1984).

In *Toscano v. PGA Tour, Inc.*, 201 F.Supp.2d 1106 (E.D.Cal.2002), senior professional golfer brought action against professional golf association

(PGA) for alleged antitrust violations associated with PGA media rights, conflicting events rules that prevented competition from rival senior professional tours, and eligibility rules that protected PGA player directors and tour members from competition from other senior golfers. PGA filed motion for summary judgment. The District Court held that (1) golfer did not have antitrust standing to challenge media rights and conflicting events rules; PGA's eligibility rules did not have sufficient anticompetitive effect under rule of reason analysis; (3) even if golfer had provided evidence of significant anticompetitive effects associated with PGA eligibility rules for senior professional golf tournaments, rules had sufficient procompeitive justifications to withstand rule of reason analysis; and (4) evidence consisting of extrapolation of golfer's alleged future profits during period of alleged anticompetitive activity was insufficient to support golfer's damages claim in antitrust action against PGA.

In *Kingray, Inc. v. NBA*, 188 F.Supp.2d 1177 (S.D.Cal.2002), purchasers of satellite broadcast of NBA games brought antitrust action against NBA and satellite pay-per-view TV providers in connection with contract between NBA and providers that gave them exclusive right to broadcast out-of-market games; court held that evidence was insufficient to support price fixing or restriction of output claims; also, purchasers waived tying arrangement claim and the purchasers did not have the standing to bring antitrust action for damages against NBA.

B. EXEMPTIONS

Although many of the policies, rules, regulations and procedures of organized sports appear on the surface to violate both the letter and the spirit of the antitrust laws, they are deemed to be legal because they fall under certain exemptions to these laws. Usually, an allegedly underpaid professional athlete claims that league rules have financially disadvantaged him because he cannot achieve free agent status and test the market. Facially, this appears to be an antitrust violation; however, this procedure might be protected by an exemption. In this hypothetical, the exemption used by management would be the non-statutory labor exemption which protects agreements that are a product of good faith union-management negotiation.

1. Baseball

Professional baseball is exempt from the antitrust laws. Baseball's exemption is an anomaly that was categorized by Justice William Douglas as "a derelict in the stream of law." *Flood v. Kuhn*, 407 U.S. 258 (1972) (Douglas, J., dissent). The Supreme Court realized its mistake but preferred for Congress to formulate a solution: "If there is any inconsistency or illogic in all this, it is an inconsistency and illogic of long standing that is to be remedied by the Congress and not by this court."

Baseball's exemption began in 1922 when Justice Holmes declared that professional baseball was not a business that involved interstate commerce. *Fed-*

eral Baseball Club of Baltimore, Inc. v. National League of Professional Baseball Clubs, 259 U.S. 200 (1922). Even though it was freely acknowledged "that *Federal Baseball* was not one of Mr. Holmes happiest days." *Salerno v. American League of Professional Baseball Clubs*, 429 F.2d 1003 (2d Cir. 1970). No court would dare overrule Holmes and a unanimous court. In fact *Federal Baseball* was affirmed in 1953 and again in 1972. *Toolson v. New York Yankees*, 346 U.S. 356 (1953); *Flood v. Kuhn*, 407 U.S. 258 (1972). However, *Piazza v. Major League Baseball*, 831 F.Supp. 420 (E.D.Pa.1993) redefined the exemption to apply solely to baseball's reserve system. *Piazza*, an opinion by the Eastern District of Pennsylvania, has limited precedential merit; it involved an attempt to purchase and relocate the San Francisco Giants.

There is no chance that baseball's exemption will be extended to any other sport. Professional football was specifically denied immunity despite the obvious similarities between the two sports. *Radovich v. NFL*, 352 U.S. 445 (1957). Baseball's exemption then is just "a narrow application of *stare decisis*." *United States v. Shubert*, 348 U.S. 222 (1955).

The Curt Flood Act of 1998, 15 U.S.C.A. § 27, establishes a partial repeal (or retrenchment) of baseball's long-time common law exemption to the antitrust laws. The Act is narrow, it allows for only those issues relating to the employment of major league baseball players and the potential for antitrust scrutiny. This partial repeal specifically does not apply to minor league reserve clauses; the amateur draft; the "Professional Baseball Agreement," franchise relocation, club ownership rules, ownership transfer, and the relationship between commissioner and owners; baseball marketing; the Sports Broadcasting Act of 1961, 15 U.S.C. §§ 1291, *et seq.;* the relationship with umpires; and "persons not in the business of organized professional Major League Baseball." The most interesting narrowing of the application of this retrenchment can be found in § 27(d)(4): "Nothing in this section shall be construed to affect the application to organized professional baseball of the nonstatutory labor exemption from the antitrust laws."

In *Butterworth v. National League of Professional Baseball Clubs*, 644 So.2d 1021 (Fla.1994), the court held that baseball's antitrust exemption only cover matters that concern players and does not protect the business-side of baseball, including sale and relocation of existing franchises. The Curt Flood Act was promulgated in late October 1998; but, it revokes the exemption only for labor relations, not for matters that involve franchise relocation, league expansion, or the minor leagues. But because of the Supreme Court's 1996 decision in the NFL case, *Brown v. Pro Football, Inc.*, 518 U.S. 231 (1996), the Act has limited implications since union members are essentially estopped from seeking antitrust relief on the basis of the numbing effect of the nonstatutory labor exemption to the antitrust laws.

In *Minnesota Twins Partnership v. Minnesota*, 592 N.W.2d 847 (Minn.1999), the proposed sale and relocation of a professional baseball team was an integral part of the business of professional baseball, and thus, fell, within the exemption from antitrust laws, such that the Attorney General could not enforce compliance with Civil Investigative Demands served pursuant to an investigation of potential antitrust violations based on the proposed sale and relocation. This case rejected *Piazza*, *Butterworth*, and *Morsani*, and the validity of baseball's antitrust exemption for franchise relocation cases.

In *Morsani v. Major League Baseball*, 79 F.Supp.2d 1331 (M.D.Fla.1999), state court's granting of summary judgment on antitrust count precluded federal court from asserting jurisdiction on basis of baseball's federal antitrust exemption. *Morsani* applies *Butterworth* and overturns a trial court's decision that dismissed the lawsuit of a rejected prospective buyer who tried to locate a major-league baseball franchise to Tampa Bay.

In *Major League Baseball v. Butterworth*, 181 F.Supp.2d 1316 (N.D.Fla.2001), Major League Baseball's proposed contraction of teams was part of the "business of baseball" exemption from federal and state antitrust laws. The number of clubs allowed to compete was a decision integral to the business of baseball. Thus, the Florida Attorney General was enjoined from issuing Civil Investigative Demands regarding the proposed contraction pursuant to state antitrust laws.

In *Major League Baseball v. Crist,* 331 F.3d 1177 (11th Cir.2003), the Eleventh Circuit considered whether baseball's antitrust exemption extends to the realm of investigation. The controversy arose following Major League Baseball's contradiction decision to eliminate two teams (the Florida Marlins and the Tampa Bay Devil Rays) from the league on November 6, 2001. The Florida State Attorney General issued several civil investigative demands (CIDS) to Major League Baseball pursuant to his authority under Florida's antitrust statute. MLB challenged these CIDS contending that its federal exemption provided a right to be free of both antitrust prosecution and investigation under either federal or state antitrust law. They argued that the "business of baseball" was exempt from both antitrust enforcement and investigation. Additionally, it argued that the Florida antitrust investigation was precluded by the exemption because federal law preempts state antitrust law. The court based its decision on Supreme Court precedent of *Flood v. Kuhn* and the Supremacy Clause. Contraction fell within the "business of baseball," and accordingly, it could not be subject to federal antitrust prosecution.

2. Labor Exemption

The "statutory" labor exemption originated in certain provisions of the Clayton Act (15 U.S.C.A. § 12, *et seq.*) and the Norris–La Guardia Act (29 U.S.C.A. §§ 101–115) in which unions are allowed to enter into agreements, *inter se,* which might eliminate competition from other unions and create monopolies of all union organizational activities. Businesses cannot claim this privilege.

3. NFL Exemptions

Other "minor" exemptions to the antitrust laws in professional sports are those that were specifically created for the National Football League (NFL). One allows agreements between the NFL and the TV networks to pool and sell a unitary video package. 15 U.S.C.A. § 1291. Another allows blackouts of non-local games telecasted into home territories when the home team is playing. It will also permit the blackout of home games in the home territory. 15 U.S.C.A. § 1292. Also, when the two major leagues (NFL and AFL) were merged the merger of their two draft systems was specifically excluded from antitrust scrutiny. 15 U.S.C.A. § 1291.

4. Non–Statutory Labor Exemption

The non-statutory labor exemption is a derivative of the labor exemption that protects union activity from antitrust scrutiny. It is the crux of nearly all antitrust actions in professional sports. Basically, any union-management agreement that was a product of good faith negotiation will receive protection from the antitrust laws.

The goal of this exemption is certainly laudable; however, it is increasingly used by management as a means of legitimating certain agreements that were clearly forced on a weak union. Management attempts to wrap their anti-competitive policies with the mantle of this exemption. This is not the intent of the original Supreme Court decisions.

The non-statutory labor exemption is based on the policy that favors collective bargaining and gives it preference over the antitrust laws. The exemption will apply where the restraint on trade primarily affects only the parties to the collective bargaining agreement; where the restraint concerns a mandatory subject of collective bargaining; and where the agreement that is sought to be exempted is a product of bona fide arms' length bargaining. *Mackey v. NFL*, 543 F.2d 606 (8th Cir.1976).

In *Mackey,* although the Rozelle Rule did not deal with a mandatory subject of collective bargaining on its face, since it was neither wages, hours or conditions of employment; however, since the Rule operated to restrict a player's ability to move from one team to another and thus depress salaries, the court held that the rule constituted a mandatory subject of collective bargaining. *Id.*, at 615.

Regarding the Rozelle Rule in *Mackey,* it was established that there was no bona fide arm's length bargaining over the Rule. The Rozelle Rule imposed significant restraints on player mobility. The form of the Rule was unchanged since it was unilaterally promulgated by management in 1963. Also, there was no evidence to suggest that the players received any benefits from the Rule. Because of this, the Rule did not qualify for an exemption from the antitrust laws.

However, in *McCourt v. California Sports, Inc.*, 600 F.2d 1193 (6th Cir.1979), an action by a professional hockey player challenging the National Hockey League's reserve system, the court held that the nonstatutory labor exemption applied since the reserve system was incorporated into the c.b.a. as a result of good faith, arms' length bargaining. In this case, good faith bargaining was deemed to exist even though one of the parties to the negotiation did not yield on its initial bargaining position. The fact that one party's position on a mandatory subject prevailed unchanged does not necessitate the conclusion that there was no bargaining over the issue. A failure to succeed is not the same thing as a failure to negotiate.

However, recent court decisions which have sought to decipher the National Football League's labor-management imbroglio have expanded the protection of the non-statutory labor exemption to continue not only after the expiration of the c.b.a., but even after the parties have reached an impasse. *Powell v. NFL*, 888 F.2d 559 (8th Cir.1989). In *Powell,* the policies under question were the "free agent" and draft procedures. These policies are protected by the non-statutory labor exemption even though they are actively opposed by the union and its constituents. This opposition exists regardless of the fact that these policies carry an alleged favorable imprimatur by way of an earlier c.b.a. (1982).

At the same time, there have been situations where labor and management have compromised enough to create policies that reflect bona fide, good faith collective bargaining. For example, in *Wood v. NBA*, 602 F.Supp. 525 (S.D.N.Y.1984), a district court analyzed the legality of the NBA's salary cap provision, which limits the total amount that each team can annually pay to their players. This procedure could limit the salary that a particular player could negotiate from his club. But, the cap was agreed to by both labor and management and became a part of their c.b.a. The court held that the cap was exempt from antitrust regulations and that the player in question, Leon Wood, came under the coverage of the agreement even though as a rookie he only entered the bargaining unit after the agreement was negotiated. The exemption was applicable since the salary cap affected only the parties to the c.b.a. (management and players), involved mandatory subjects of bargaining and was the result of bona fide, arms' length negotiations.

In *Brown v. Pro Football, Inc.*, 518 U.S. 231 (1996), professional football players assigned to developmental squads of substitute players brought an antitrust class action against the professional football league challenging the league's unilateral imposition, after bargaining to the point of impasse, of a fixed salary for developmental squad players ($1,000 per week). The Supreme Court held that the league's conduct in unilaterally imposing a fixed salary for developmental squad players fell within the scope of the nonstatutory labor exemption from antitrust liability. That is, the exemption continues after the expiration of the agreement and impasse. Justice Stevens' dissent in *Brown* (at 257) reminded the sports community that exemptions should be construed narrowly; whereas the majority opinion allows for a broad interpretation.

The case of Maurice Clarett and his attempt to opt early for the NFL draft was truly the "case of the century" as regards sports law and media attention to it. *Clarett v. NFL*, 369 F.3d 124 (2d Cir. 2004). Maurice Clarett, star freshman tailback for Ohio State's undefeated 2002 football season, initiated an antitrust challenge to the NFL's rule that limits eligibility for the NFL entry draft to those players who are three full college football seasons removed from high school. Because of disciplinary concerns, he was forced to sit out (at least) what would have been his second year out of high school. He sought to be included in the pool of players eligible for the 2004 NFL draft to be conducted April 24–25, 2004. Judge Scheindlin of the federal district court for the Southern District of New York granted plaintiff's motion for summary judgment on February 5, 2004. She also denied the NFL's motion to stay pending appeal on February 11, 2004. But, the Second Court of Appeals reversed and remanded Judge Scheindlin's summary judgment on May 24, 2004. Judge Scheindlin found for plaintiff opining that the NFL's rule did not fall within the scope of the non-statutory labor exemption on the basis that the rule was not a mandatory subject of collective bargaining. The Court of Appeals found that the rule, since it represented a condition for initial employment, affected the job security of veteran players, and thus had tangible effects on the wages, hours, and working conditions (i.e., mandatory subjects), of current NFL players. Also, the fact that the NFL and the players' union did not bargain over the rule (per se), did not exclude the rule from the scope of the non-statutory labor exemption, since these rules were included in the NFL's Constitution and By–Laws; the union was aware of these rules; and the union generally agreed to waive any challenge to the Constitution and By–Laws.

C. PLAYER RESTRAINTS

The use of antitrust litigation as a means to force change in professional sports historically developed from policies that restrain the movement of the athletes. Player restraint mechanisms limit the player's ability to negotiate the best dollar from the highest bidder and thus restrict the player's commerce; these procedures appear on their face to violate antitrust laws.

For example in *Smith v. Pro Football, Inc.*, 593 F.2d 1173 (D.C.Cir.1978), football's draft of collegiate talent was held to violate the antitrust laws. The draft is a procedure where negotiating rights to graduating college seniors are allocated each year among the NFL teams in reverse order of the club's finish in the previous year. The NFL draft as it existed in 1968 had a severely anticompetitive impact on the market for player's services; also, this type of restraint was not reasonably necessary to accomplish whatever legitimate business purposes that might be asserted as a rationale for a 17–round draft. In short, it was anticompetitive in both its purpose and its effect.

However, many of the earlier player restraint mechanisms have been modified through collective bargaining so that they are no longer considered to be an antitrust violation. As in the NBA salary cap dispute, the current generation of player restraints will now be decided under the purview of the non-statutory labor exemption.

D. FRANCHISE MOVEMENT

Antitrust strategies in professional sports have shifted in recent years. Once the sole domain of relatively underpaid athletes, they are now used by the team owners themselves to gain advantage from the league, usually in the form of attempts to relocate their franchise. Professional sports is a big business; the precise geographical location of a team at a particular moment in time can be essential to that team's economic life or death. Franchise movement, however, is regulated by league regulations.

In *San Francisco Seals, Ltd. v. NHL*, 379 F.Supp. 966 (C.D.Cal.1974), an individual NHL team brought suit against the league when they denied their request to relocate from San Francisco to Vancouver, British Columbia. The court held that the team was not competing economically with the league and the other teams. Because of this, the league's relocation rules did not restrain trade within the relevant market. Also, the Seals did not have standing to sue the league and the other teams for an alleged §2 Sherman Act violation of monopolizing the business of major league hockey, since an individual team was not within the target area with respect to the claimed conspiracy.

However, in *Los Angeles Memorial Coliseum Commission v. NFL*, 726 F.2d 1381 (9th Cir.1984), the applicable league regulation directed that ¾'s of all NFL teams must approve any franchise relocation into the home territory of another team. The court held that the NFL's rule violated antitrust laws as the NFL was not a "single entity" and the regulation was an unreasonable restraint of trade. If it was not a single entity, the NFL could be held liable under a rule of reason analysis for unreasonably restraining the trade of the Oakland Raiders by thwarting their plans to relocate in Los Angeles. However, if the league was viewed as a single entity, it would be immune from suits against it by individual teams.

The NFL was not a single entity since each team had a separate identity independent from the league; the teams competed with the others for revenue and personnel; and each team was independently owned and operated. If the league was a single entity, it would be logically and legally unable to conspire with itself to restrain trade. However, since that is not the case, the league is simply a group of individual competitors whose joint votes on league matters could constitute an illegal group boycott.

In *St. Louis Convention & Visitors Commission v. NFL*, 154 F.3d 851 (8th Cir.1998), a public commission that was charged with the obligation of returning professional football to St. Louis sued the NFL on antitrust grounds. The theory the St. Louis Convention & Visitors Commission (CVC) presented "was that the league's relocation rules and the way they had been applied had created an atmosphere in which teams were unwilling to relocate. It contended that this anti-relocation atmosphere had discouraged interested teams from bidding on the St. Louis lease." As a result, there was a one-buyer market. However, the court held that CVC failed to establish concerted action by the NFL teams simply from the fact that only one team responded to CVC's offer to provide an attractive stadium lease to lure an existing franchise that was willing to relocate; that CVC failed to show a casual connection between league rules that regulated relocation and absence of more than one relocation suitor; and that CVC failed to show an antitrust injury.

In *VKK Corp. v. NFL*, 244 F.3d 114 (2d Cir.2001), a federal district court in New York dismissed an antitrust suit brought by former New England Patriots owner Victor Kiam against the NFL over Kiam's allegations that the NFL illegally conspired to prohibit him from relocating the Patriots. The jury returned a verdict for the NFL on the severed issue of whether the former owner's signing of a condition for obtaining the NFL's approval for his sale of his majority interest to another, was made under economic duress. The release was held dispositive and plaintiff's claims were dismissed.

E. LEAGUE VERSUS LEAGUE

Antitrust conflicts also arise in professional sports when a nascent league claims that the dominant, established league is guilty of unfair competition. There is a cyclical history in professional sports: when it appears that there is money to be made a new league will form to compete against the established league. The end result is either that the older league conquers the new league upstart or they compromise and the two leagues merge as one (e.g., the NFL–AFL merger).

Many of the famous law suits that have shaped the current state of antitrust in professional sports have involved interleague rivalry. *Radovich v. NFL*, 353 U.S. 931 (1957). Radovich involved the blacklisting of a football player by an NFL affiliate for playing with a competing league and held that football is not exempt from antitrust laws.

In *AFL v. NFL*, 323 F.2d 124 (4th Cir.1963), the American Football League (AFL) sued the more established NFL on grounds that the older league monopolized all the best markets. The court found that the older league did not have the power to monopolize the relevant market; and did not attempt a conspiracy to monopolize the market. That is, the court found that any monopoly that the NFL might have possessed over the AFL was a natural monopoly.

A natural monopoly does not violate antitrust laws unless the natural monopoly was misused to gain a competitive advantage. Basically, the NFL acquired markets that the latecomer thought desirable. But, the first league is not required to surrender any, or all, of its advantageous sites to the second league simply to enable the latecomer to compete more effectively with the NFL. However, one must acquire a natural monopoly by means which are neither exclusionary, unfair, nor predatory.

In *USFL v. NFL*, 644 F.Supp. 1040 (S.D.N.Y. 1986), although the USFL won treble damages ($3.00), and attorney fees ($5,515,290.81), years later, the USFL immediately disintegrated. The court held that the NFL's superiority in the bidding war was due to the USFL's poor management and the NFL's natural superiority and not entirely the result of illegal antitrust violations; therefore, the jury award of nominal damages was not in error.

F.   TV PACKAGING

Although antitrust litigation is endemic in professional sports, it has also arisen in amateur sports, especially in the area of the NCAA's packaging of television broadcasts of college football games. In *NCAA v. Board of Regents*, 468 U.S. 85 (1984), the court held that the NCAA's plan of packaging these broadcasts was unlawful under a rule of reason analysis since, *inter alia,* the plan was not intended to equalize competition, it did not regulate the money that the schools spent on their football programs, and it gave control of the packaging to schools that either did not have football programs or would not be affected by the restrictions (i.e., small-time collegiate football).

The NCAA's TV package was an unreasonable restraint of trade since the plan restricted the total number of football games that an NCAA member could televise, and further, the plan did not allow the member schools to sell their TV rights except in accordance with the NCAA's stipulations. By limiting the output and curtailing the big schools' ability to respond to network offers the NCAA was found to restrict the trade of these colleges. The *Board of Regents* decision set the networks free to negotiate TV contracts with the major college football teams; as a result, two large groups of universities were formed under the auspices of the two major television networks. See *Regents of University of California v. ABC*, 747 F.2d 511 (9th Cir.1984).

G. CABLE TV

Sports has become an increasingly noticed phenomenon because of the advent and prosperity of cable TV. During recent years a number of prime time regular season professional football games and the National Hockey League's TV package have shifted from the major TV networks to cable TV, i.e., football to ESPN and hockey to Sportschannel America. Cable TV is limited access TV, in that viewers must pay for the pleasure of enjoying their programming. Many fans who once watched sports programming without payment are now forced to pay for that privilege. ESPN is a basic cable network whereas Sportschannel America costs more than the basic cable rate and thus reaches far less viewers.

There is also the emerging technology of pay-per-view broadcasts of one-of-a-kind sports spectaculars, e.g., the Holyfield–Foreman professional boxing match billed as the "Battle of the Ages". Does this migration of sports programming from the major networks to cable TV violate the antitrust laws? There is a court defined methodology that can deduce whether a package sale of broadcast rights increases or decreases the viewing of sports events. When these agreements diminish viewership, then they will constitute an unreasonable restraint of trade and thus can be enjoined. *NCAA v. Board of Regents of the University of Oklahoma*, 468 U.S. 85 (1984).

These package sales are agreements among individual teams who would otherwise sell their rights to broadcast their own games. Package sales are agreements among competitors and as such will often invoke a per se analysis. However, courts have consistently reaffirmed that the special needs of professional sports leagues demand the more careful analysis of a rule of reason review.

Broadcast rights agreements when analyzed under a rule of reason analysis will be found to be anticompetitive and thus illegal if the prices become higher and the output lower. Cable TV, by definition, increases the costs and reduces the number of potential viewers since not everyone is covered by cable. Therefore, the phenomenon of the transfer of sports broadcasts from the major networks to cable TV may well be determined to be anticompetitive when it comes under judicial analysis.

H. AMATEUR SPORTS

TV packaging is not the only area in which antitrust litigation has arisen in amateur sports. The typical situation involves the National Collegiate Athletic Association (NCAA) as a defendant versus either a college, an athlete or another athletic governing organization. The plaintiffs will claim that NCAA policies and regulations have acted as an illegal restraint on their trade and commerce. Although the court found against the NCAA as regards their television packaging regulations, that is not the case for their eligibility requirements. Neither the NCAA eligibility rules that restrict compensation to athletes nor the enforcement of these rules are violations of the antitrust laws. These eligibility rules are justifiable means of encouraging competition among amateur teams and therefore, are pro-competitive since they enhance public interest in intercollegiate sports. See *United States v. Walters*, 711 F.Supp. 1435 (N.D.Ill.1989).

I. MISCELLANEOUS

Other than the primary arenas of antitrust litigation discussed above, there are also some peripheral areas of litigation. Most of these miscellaneous antitrust actions coalesce around tie-ins, rival sports and business-type problems.

A tie-in is the practice of tying the purchase of preseason tickets to the purchase of season tickets. Fans do not like this practice and have sued on antitrust grounds. This practice is legal since there is no consumer compulsion and there are always individual seats left for all home games. *Laing v. Minnesota Vikings Football Club, Inc.*, 372 F.Supp. 59 (D.Minn.1973).

A corollary of the more famous league versus league suits, are those that involve rival sports. In *North American Soccer League v. NFL*, 505 F.Supp. 659 (S.D.N.Y.1980), a soccer league sued the NFL for its cross-ownership ban which stipulated that an NFL team owner could not own a part of another sports franchise. The court stated that, if there was a limited sub-group of sportsmen/entrepreneurs, then plaintiff had the burden of proving that that somewhat illusory fraternity did indeed exist. A rule of reason analysis was applied with the caveat that not every concerted action of professional sports league members possessed antitrust implications.

In another area, the NFL sued a state for trademark infringement concerning a state lottery that was based on the outcome of NFL games. The state claimed that the NFL's restrictions on trademark usage was violative of the antitrust laws since all NFL licenses were only obtainable through a package arrangement. The state lost, even though the scores, etc., were not property. However, since there was an illusion of sponsorship the state must issue a disclaimer. *NFL v. Governor of Delaware*, 435 F.Supp. 1372 (D.Del.1977).

Business-related antitrust implications also arose when the owner of a controlling partnership in a professional football franchise brought an action against certain banks for allegedly attempting to force a distress sale of the club. This claim failed in part because plaintiff failed to establish that this alleged action by the banks violated the rule of reason. *Tose v. First Pennsylvania Bank, N.A.*, 648 F.2d 879 (3d Cir.1981).

CHAPTER 6

TORTS

A. NEGLIGENCE

The tort action of choice for sports-related injuries is negligence. Negligence is any conduct that falls below the reasonable man standard. In sports, there is a myriad of possible variations of what that standard is as it relates to the varieties of sporting conduct. Negligence is measured against the particular facts and circumstances in each and every case.

The burden is on the plaintiff to show that a negligent act or omission occurred on the part of the defendant and that it was the proximate cause of that injury. That is, there must be an established duty of care, a breach of that duty, a proximate cause between defendant's action and the injury, and damages that resulted from that breach.

Negligence in sports is a relatively new phenomenon. In earlier days, the law was dominated by Justice Cardozo's maxim that "the timorous may stay at home." *Murphy v. Steeplechase Amusement Company*, 250 N.Y. 479, 166 N.E. 173 (1929). Basically, the law did not want to place an unreasonable burden on active participation in sports. One was assumed to voluntarily embrace any danger that might occur in a sporting activity. However, the courts slowly began to understand that athletic competition did not exist in a vacuum; "some other restraints of civilization must accompany every athlete onto the playing field." *Nabozny v. Barnhill*, 31 Ill.App.3d 212, 334 N.E.2d 258 (1975).

1. Duty of Care

The inquiry of whether the defendant owed a duty to the injured party is one of law. Whether that duty has been breached or whether there is a causal connection between breach and injury are questions of fact.

A duty is an expression of the sum total of policy considerations that would lead an adjudicator to find that a particular plaintiff is entitled to some sort of protection. A duty can be created by either common law, statute, contract or policy. If no duty is evident then an action in negligence will be unsuccessful.

A duty of care can also arise through a special relationship. Duty is predicated on the existing relationships between the parties at the relevant times. *Kleinknecht v. Gettysburg College*, 989 F.2d 1360 (3d Cir.1993) held that a recruited lacrosse player who suddenly collapsed and died during practice was owed a duty of care by the college to provide prompt emergency medical service. The special relationship here was the active recruitment of the player.

In *Davidson v. University of North Carolina at Chapel Hill*, 142 N.C.App. 544, 543 S.E.2d 920 (2001), like in *Kleinknecht*, the Court found a special relationship between the injured JV cheerleader and the university in that the defendant voluntarily undertook to educate the cheerleaders on safety, which thus created a separate duty of care as a matter of law.

In *Hills v. Bridgeview Little League Assn.*, 195 Ill.2d 210, 253 Ill.Dec. 632, 745 N.E.2d 1166 (2000), a little league coach was horribly beaten by two rival coaches, the court held that the association did not have an affirmative duty to protect plaintiff from the criminal attack of another coach. Similarly, in *Cutrone v. Monarch Holding Corp.*, 299 A.D.2d 388, 749 N.Y.S.2d 280 (2 Dept. 2002), the owner and operator of a skating rink did not have a duty to protect a spectator from the unexpected and unforeseeable criminal assault by a deranged hockey player.

In *Allen v. Dover Co–Recreational Softball League*, 148 N.H. 407, 807 A.2d 1274 (2002), the team sponsors, field owners, etc., were not responsible for the injury that a softball player suffered from an errant throw. Defendants had no duty to protect player from such an ordinary risk. Infielder did not have a duty to refrain from making errant throws. Team sponsors did not have the duty to conduct game using certain equipment or to enforce male-female ratio on teams. League sponsor and insurer had no duty to warn and instruct league regarding the risk of injury.

However, in *Sanchez v. Hillerich & Bradsby Co.*, 104 Cal.App.4th 703, 128 Cal.Rptr.2d 529 (2002), a college baseball pitcher who brought a negligence action against bat manufacturer and college sports association, for severe brain injuries sustained when he was hit by a baseball was able to withstand summary judgment for the manufacturer on the basis that a genuine issue of material fact existed as to whether the design and use of a newly designed aluminum baseball bat substantially increased the inherent risk the pitcher faced during a baseball game. There was also a genuine issue of material fact as to whether the design and use of a newly designed aluminum baseball bat caused the pitcher's severe brain injury by increasing the speed at which the baseball left the bat compared to other metal and wood bats. Although a defendant owes no duty of care to protect plaintiff against risks inherent in a particular sport voluntarily played by the plaintiff; the defendant does owe a duty to participants not to increase the risk of harm over and above that inherent in the sport.

Korey Stringer, of the Minnesota Vikings, died of heat stroke following training camp practice in 2001. In the two days of practice before he died, he vomited numerous times and collapsed to his knees on several occasions. Fre Zamberletti, coordinator of medical services for the Vikings, and Paul Osterman, an assistant trainer, gave him fluids for hydration. On the second day, Stringer became ill again and was taken to a trailer to cool off. While in the trailer, Stringer began moving his head back and forth for about ten minutes. Osterman called the training room for a golf cart to pick up Stringer, but Stringer was unresponsive. No one took Stringer's temperature or monitored his heart beat. An ambulance was finally called after Stringer's conditioned worsened. Stringer was unconscious at the hospital, his pulse was 148 beats per minute and his blood pressure was undeterminable. Stringer had a body temperature of 108.8 degrees. After many failed attempt to help him, Stringer died at the hospital.

In a wrongful death action, Korey's widow asserted that both Osterman and Zamberletti had a personal duty to protect and care for Korey's health. The Court of Appeals held that both men did owe Stringer a personal duty, but their actions were not grossly negligent as a matter of law. The Minnesota Supreme Court applied the personal duty test. This test indicates that the defendant must take or direct another to take action toward the injured employee and that defendant acted outside the course and scope of employment. As a result of applying the personal duty test, the Supreme Court determined that the defendants did not owe Stringer a personal duty and affirmed the granting of summary judgment to both defendants. See *Stringer v. Minnesota Vikings Football Club, LLC*, 705 N.W.2d 746 (Minn.2005).

2. Standard of Care

The key to discovering a breach of a duty is to determine whether defendant's conduct falls below an applicable standard of care. For example, a violation of a league safety rule could constitute an actionable duty, if that rule is recognized as a standard of care created for the protection of participants.

In some instances a school is held to the same degree of care as the children's parents. The school is *in loco parentis*, and the applicable standard is that of reasonably prudent parents acting under similar and comparable circumstances.

The level of care will vary with the plaintiff's situation. The more foreseeable the injury, the higher the standard. An example of this would be an injured football player who is carried off the field in a stretcher in an unreasonable and dangerous manner. The standard of care for an already injured player is one of extreme caution. An absence of a specific standard of care as created by a safety rule or a physical education standard does not defeat negligence. Without a specific applicable rule, the standard of a reasonable man acting under similar circumstances will be applicable. Established rules and regulations will merely assist the plaintiff in his or her burden of proof.

In *Geiersbach v. Frieje*, 807 N.E.2d 114 (Ind.App. 2004), a university baseball player filed suit against university, coach, and another player for personal injuries sustained during team drill. The Indiana

Court of Appeals held that the standard of care for university sporting events and practices was to avoid reckless or malicious behavior or intentional injury, rather than the reasonable care standard; and that a participant in a sporting event, including any person who was part of the event or practice such as players and coaches, did not have a duty to fellow participants to refrain from conduct which was inherent and foreseeable in the play of the game. A teammate, who did not act recklessly or maliciously, was not liable to player; also coaches were not liable to player, and the university was not vicariously liable to player.

3. Breach of Duty

A breach will occur when there is sufficient evidence for a jury to conclude that defendant breached a duty; and if so whether the jury could reasonably infer that defendant's breach was the proximate cause of the injury. When a duty exists, the question of breach is one for the trier of fact to resolve unless the evidence is so obvious that reasonable minds could not differ in their conclusions. Since the question of breach is one of fact, the determination must be on a case-by-case basis.

4. Proximate Cause

The next factor is whether there is a connection between the negligence and the resulting injury. The question is whether the breach of a duty was the proximate cause of the injury. This is a fact question and must be decided by a jury on a case-by-case basis.

Proximate cause is that cause which in a natural and continuous sequence, unbroken by an efficient intervening cause, produces the injury and without which the injury would not have occurred. In proving proximate cause, the plaintiff is not required to eliminate all of the other potential causes. One needs only to prove a sufficient evidentiary basis from which causation could reasonably be inferred, and the causation must only be a substantial factor in bringing about the injury.

5. Damages

Negligence requires that the plaintiff must suffer some damages. The phenomenon of a sporting activity is such that it is action-oriented and creates a situation in which the participant is extremely prone to injuries as a result of physical contact. Therefore, damage is usually easy to prove. The only requirement is that actual loss or damages must result to the interest of another. Nominal damages alone where no actual loss has occurred will be insufficient. Likewise, the threat of future loss without more is also insufficient.

The question of damages is intertwined with the requirement of proximate cause. If the negligence in question is the proximate cause of the injury then it follows that the resulting damages, if more than nominal, would be sufficient to complete the negligence cause of action.

B. MEDICAL MALPRACTICE

Malpractice is a bad or unskilled practice by a physician or other medical professional. As in other negligence actions, the element of duty is essential to malpractice. Duty is an obligation to conform to a particular standard of conduct towards another. In the medical sports area, this duty can include the duty to disclose, the duty to instruct, the duty to disclose whether the physician is employed by a third party, e.g., a sports team, and a duty to disclose medical negligence. The duty is evaluated by a standard of conduct taking into account the skill and knowledge of the medical community as a whole.

A key element in any suit against a team for potential malpractice is whether the doctor in question was a team physician. The problem is that there is great deal of flexibility and variety among the possible relationships between doctor and team. The problem will usually translate into a question of whether the doctor is an employee of the team or an independent contractor. A doctor-patient relationship requires mutual acceptance between a doctor and an athlete (or an athlete's agent or parents or guardians). When mutual acceptance has occurred, a doctor-patient relationship is established; then consent to treat must be obtained. Consent must come from either the adult patient himself or from the parents of a minor athlete, since a minor is deemed incapable of giving valid consent.

1. Duty of Care

Like in any other negligence action, there must be a duty, breach of duty, causation and damages. The most typical potential for malpractice will come from the medical examination. Examinations, however, are conducted for a variety of purposes with various degrees of thoroughness: for example, pre-participation exams, determination of fitness to participate, and examinations to prevent subsequent injury and to assess rehabilitation status. Since each type of examination calls for a different degree of analysis by the attending physician, it is difficult to establish a precise standard by which a physician's conduct may be evaluated. However, as in all medicine, a physician must act with the skill and knowledge that will be utilized by other doctors acting in similar circumstances.

In analyzing a physician's duty of care for medical examinations, one factor that must be considered is whether this particular physician is acting for the benefit of the team or for the benefit of the athlete. When a team physician acts for the benefit of the athlete, the duty of care owed will also include a duty not to increase the risk of other, foreseeable losses. Therefore, a missed diagnosis would be subject to liability for any lost opportunities that the athlete could prove were resulting losses.

2. Duty to Disclose and Informed Consent

A physician must disclose any material information regarding the athlete's physical condition.

This duty to inform emanates both from the fiduciary nature of the relationship and from the athlete's right to determine the procedures that will be performed on his own body. A failure to disclose any medical information that ultimately results in damages to the athlete will create tort liability for the physician. The duty to disclose includes the duty to inform the athlete that he must seek further medical advice. Since an athlete is expected to perform at his highest obtainable level, a doctor's concealment or failure to disclose might cost the athlete his career through the aggravation of an injury.

A duty to disclose will remain even in the case where the doctor is hired by a party other than the athlete: the duty will exist regardless of who pays or even whether the doctor is paid or has an expectation of payment.

A corollary to the duty to disclose, at least as regards who needs the information to make a well-reasoned decision, is the doctrine of informed consent. A patient's consent to treatment is valid if it is informed. An athlete is informed when the doctor has released an amount of medical information relevant to the proposed treatment and sufficient to allow the athlete to make an intelligent choice as whether he should continue that treatment. This includes the reasonable disclosure of available alternative procedures as well as the dangers that correspond with each and an indication of whatever applicable advantages might ensue. The consent by the athlete should always be in writing and should be clear and understandable in terms and in scope.

Finally, in the world of sports, physicians' disclosure of information relative to the physical or even mental condition of the athlete is unusually important since any disclosure to the media could severely damage an athlete's potential to successfully continue his career. For example, if a team's doctor communicates any information on an athlete's conditions to the media, with or without consent, the doctor may be subject to liability for defamation, invasion of privacy or breach of a confidential relationship. Also, disclosure in the absence of consent may subject that doctor to potential liability if the team relies upon the physician's statement and it is subsequently proved inaccurate.

3. Fraudulent Concealment

The Charlie Krueger case revolved around allegations that the team physicians for his professional football team fraudulently concealed medical information about his injuries, the extent of his injuries and his ability to continue to play. *Krueger v. San Francisco Forty Niners*, 234 Cal.Rptr. 579 (1987). Mr. Krueger was an exemplary defensive lineman for the San Francisco 49ers from 1958 until 1973 when he retired; he missed only parts of two seasons due to injuries. During his career he suffered numerous injuries but continued to play through the pain: for example, a broken arm, broken ring fingers on each hand, numerous broken noses, multiple dislocations of fingers and thumbs on both hands, a blow-out fracture of the right ocular orbit, an eye infection, a sprained right knee and hypertension.

Those injuries, however, were somewhat minor compared to the problems that befell his left knee. It was operated on in college and in 1963 he ruptured his medial collateral ligament; the team operated on it at that time and told him it was in "good repair". He continued to play with the help of rehabilitative therapy from the team trainer and a brace which he wore while playing until 1967. The team physician noted that Krueger's anterior cruciate ligament, which prevents the tibia from shifting forward on the femur, appeared to be absent. An injury like this produces instability in the knee, particularly when combined with other injuries; Krueger was never told of this injury.

His left knee continued to hurt and swell; in 1964, he received further treatment from the team physicians in the form of an aspiration of bloody fluids by syringe and a contemporaneous injection of novocaine and cortisone, a steroid compound. Krueger testified to 50 such treatments in 1964 and a 14 to 20 average per year from 1964 to 1973; through all this he was never informed of the dangers that are associated with steroids: possible rupturing of tendons, weakening of joints and cartilage, and destruction of capillaries and blood vessels. In 1971, he underwent another operation on his left knee by the team doctor to remove "loose bodies" as a result of chronic chondromalacia, thinning and loss of cartilage on the knee cap's undersurface; this condition is fully consistent with steroid abuse. Also, x-rays from 1964 to 1971 revealed degenerative post-traumatic changes in the knee; he was not informed of any of these afflictions by the 49ers medical staff. Added to this, in 1971, Krueger felt a hit on his knee with a resulting feeling that a piece of substance dislodged on the outside of his knee joint; still, he played the five remaining games. During this time period he was never advised by the team doctors that he risked permanent injury by continuing to play without surgery.

Finally, five years after retirement, he was shown x-rays and was advised for the first time that he suffered from a chronic and permanent disability. He now suffers from traumatic arthritis and a crippling degenerative process in the left knee; he cannot stand up for prolonged periods; he cannot run; he is unable to walk up stairs without severe pain; his condition is degenerative and irreversible.

Under the informed consent doctrine an integral part of the physician's overall obligation is to the patient: there is a duty of reasonable disclosure of the available choices with respect to the proposed therapy and of the dangers that are inherently and potentially involved in each procedure. The physician must disclose all information that is necessary to make a knowledgeable decision about the proposed treatment. This duty is imposed so that the patient can meaningfully exercise their right to make decisions that affect their own bodies; therefore, even if the patient rejects the recommended treatment the duty will still continue. The failure to make this type of disclosure not only constitutes negligence, but, where the requisite intent is shown, fraud or concealment can also be established. A physician, especially a team doctor, cannot avoid responsibility for failure to fully disclose simply by claiming that information was not specifically withheld. Krueger was never advised of the adverse effects of the injection of steroids or the continued medical risks that would occur as a result of his continuing in football; therefore, the requisite disclosure was not forthcoming.

Intent also must be established for fraudulent concealment; plaintiff must show that at the time of the concealed information defendant intended to induce the patient to adopt or abandon a course of action. In this case, the intent was to induce Krueger to continue to play despite his injuries. The team in its desire to keep their player on the field consciously failed to make full, meaningful disclosure as to the magnitude of the risk he took in continuing to play a violent contact sport with a profoundly damaged left knee. It is axiomatic in the situation of an athlete and a team doctor that the element of reliance was also present.

In *Strock v. USA Cycling, Inc.*, 2006 WL 1223151 (D.Colo.), two cyclists on the junior team were doped by their coach; apparently, a mixture of cortisone and vitamins. About three years later, the coach told the two plaintiffs that there were rumors circulating about that the coach had doped the junior team; but, they had no reasonable reason to believe the veracity of these rumors. Some five years later, one of the plaintiffs, now in medical school, began to believe for the first time that he had been giving steroids. In medical school, he learned that there was no such thing as an "extract of cortisone." Eight years earlier, the coach gave him a substitute for antibiotics which he assured him was both safe and legal. The coach described it as a mixture of extract of cortisone and vitamins. The coach further informed him that he should not question the good judgment of the coaching staff. Both plaintiffs were thereafter injected many times; the second plaintiff alleged that he was injected 42 to 48 times. Both of them suffered severe medical conditions that have been associated with steroid abuse (parovirus and lung infection). Since the coach concealed his doping of the two athletes, the legal question is whether it was reasonable for them not to know that they had been given steroids. The court thwarted defendants' motion to dismiss on the grounds that genuine issues of material fact existed as to when both plaintiffs knew or should have known the cause of their health issues.

4. Team Physicians

The major conflict inherent in analyzing potential medical malpractice claims in athletics is the role or roles of the team physician. The question is what is the doctor's relationship to the athlete's employer and how does that relationship affect the physician's relationship with the patient, the athlete.

Since most claims against team physicians will be based on negligence, the first hurdle will be to establish a duty and a standard of care. The duty to act will usually be predicated on the existence of a physician-patient relationship. A standard of care, on the other hand, will be based upon society's expectations that physicians act reasonably under the circumstances.

Usually, the existence of a physician-patient relationship is a given; however, it is much more complicated when the physician works for a school or a professional sports team. It is clear that when the primary purpose of the medical service is actual care and treatment, then a relationship will be deemed to exist; however, it is less clear when a doctor is hired for non-therapeutic purposes, for example, a preparticipation physical exam. Traditionally, no duty will exist for non-therapeutic examinations. However, many states currently hold that doctors may owe a duty of care to discover dangerous conditions and then to report these conditions to the athlete, even if the physician is paid by a third party.

There is also the question of the extent to which the medical doctor may limit the scope of his relationship to the athlete/patient. The physician-patient relationship is consensual in nature and as such a doctor may generally limit the scope of his professional involvement at the beginning of said relationship. However, he must inform the athlete of these limitations in advance unless the limitations are reasonably expected based upon common practices or past dealings. This truism is relevant for preparticipation and post-injury physical examinations, especially if the doctor is hired on a one time only basis for school preseason physicals. Even these physicians must be responsible both for conditions that are within the scope of the examination that they knew or should have known and for those conditions that are outside the scope of the examination but which the doctor knew or had reason to know about as a result of the examination.

A standard of care for a team physician can be typically defined as performing to the level of expertise that conforms to a reasonably competent medical practitioner under similar circumstances taking into account all reasonable limitations that are placed on the scope of the doctor's undertaking. However, it appears that sports medicine has reached a specialty status for purposes of establishing a minimal standard of care. In the future, courts will probably elevate sports medicine doctors to a specialist's standard. This standard will be limited to the fundamentals of the sub-field of sports medicine which are known to all practitioners in the field based on the types of athletes with whom the doctor is primarily involved. Traditional specialists, such as orthopedic surgeons, who happen to concentrate in sports medicine, will still be expected to act to the standard of a reasonable orthopedist.

In *Gardner v. Holifield*, 639 So.2d 652 (Fla.App. 1st Dist.1994), decedent mother sued her son's physician for alleged acts of negligence, which contributed to her son's death from Marfan's syndrome at the age of 18. Her son, a scholarship basketball player at Florida A & M University, was examined at the school's clinic for a basketball physical and was diagnosed as possibly suffering from Marfan's by the defendant physician. The suit alleged that the doctor failed to properly identify the extent of his illness or to implement an appropriate course of treatment. The question before the court was whether, at the time of the alleged negligent act, a state-employed physician was acting in the scope of the immunity statute (Fla. Stat. Ann. § 768.28(a)). The question of scope of a state employment statute presents a jury issue when it arises upon disputed facts. It was clear that although the doctor made referrals to other medical specialists, he never referred the decedent to another cardiologist after the initial examination revealed a potential heart condition. The doctor's decision to order and read the EKGs at a regional medical center, considered in light of the matters raised by the plaintiffs experts, leads in the court's view, to competing references that may not properly be resolved in favor of the party moving for summary judgment. A permissible reference from the lack of a referral is that the clinic doctor (who was also a cardiologist) assumed responsibility for the basketball player's condition as a private cardiologist. The doctor's responsibilities as a clinic chief consisted solely of referring the decedent to an appropriate medical specialist outside the school, to advise him of the confirmed diagnosis of Marfan's Syndrome, and to advise the athletic department that he had not been medically cleared to participate in basketball. If the doctor was acting as the athlete's personal cardiologist then he was exceeding his scope of employment (and thus would lose the cloak of immunity). Accordingly, the doctor's motion for summary judgment was denied on appeal.

The types of legal relationships between a doctor and the school or professional team are myriad. In an attempt to establish the type of relationship, the preliminary inquiry goes to the contractual obligations between the parties and the degree of control the doctor retains in his management of the athlete. The duties and obligations of the physician to the team should be delineated by their contract. This is more true with professional teams. It is less the case in the amateur level where the duties are often less well-defined. The physician for an amateur team may be paid little or nothing for his participation, and his ties to the team may be limited solely to preparticipation physicals and treatment of specific injuries on a referral basis as opposed to the plethora of duties that a team physician to a professional sports enterprise will generally contract for (e.g., preparticipation, injury treatment, attending practices and games, referrals, rehabilitation, certification of fitness, etc.).

The next question is the degree to which the school or professional team controls the doctor's treatment of the athlete/patient. If the doctor maintains autonomy in his therapeutic decision-making, then he will usually be deemed to be an independent contractor. If that is the case, then the doctrine of respondeat superior will be inapplicable and the team or school as the employer will not be vicariously liable for any negligent acts. of the physician.

A team physician is usually deemed to be an independent contractor; however, in some cases a professional sports franchise will be found vicariously liable for the physician's tortious conduct. In one such case, a team physician detailed a story that alleged that a particular player had a fatal disease and then released that story to the media. The physician was liable for the intentional infliction of emotional distress and the team was liable under the doctrine of respondeat superior. *Chuy v. Philadelphia Eagles Football Club*, 431 F.Supp. 254 (E.D.Pa.1977). Also, a school district was held vicariously liable for the negligence of both the football coach and the team doctor who exhibited improper techniques in the removal from the playing field of an injured player who was suspected to have suffered a fractured neck; this improper removal technique exacerbated the existing injury. *Welch v.*

Dunsmuir Joint Union High School District, 326 P.2d 633 (Cal.App. 3 Dist.1958).

5. Failure to Refer and Vicarious Liability

To establish vicarious liability the team must have the power to select, control and dismiss the doctor. Also, there must be responsibility by the team to supervise; the doctor's services must be part of the services rendered by the team; the services supplied by the doctor must assist the purposes of the team; and there must be at least a certain amount of control asserted by the team over the doctor in the carrying out of his or her work.

A physician may also be liable when she identifies the problem or potential problem; fails to warn the patient of the nature of that problem; and then fails to recommend further care or treatment pursuant to a solution that will ameliorate those medical problems. However, courts have distinguished between the liability of the doctor and the liability of the team for failure to refer. Whether a team can be liable has turned on the degree of control that the team has over the doctor and whether the doctor served the interests of the athlete or those of the team when he allowed the athlete to play without informing him of the conditions that warranted a referral.

C. PRODUCT'S LIABILITY

Actions in product's liability are associated with tort actions that involve defective items that are used in sports. These items would include football helmets, golf carts, lawn darts, etc. An equipment manufacturer must meet state regulated standards of safety and care in the product's design, manufacture, and use; the supplier and seller may likewise be liable for negligence if they fail to exercise reasonable care. A manufacturer must adhere to the standard of reasonable care in the manufacture and design of sports equipment. The manufacturer must assure that the product is reasonably safe when used for the intended purpose and in the intended matter.

When the product is dangerous, e.g., a golf cart, then even if properly used a manufacturer will still have a duty to warn of potential hazards. Sellers or retailers of sports equipment will be liable if they know that the equipment is dangerous and fail to warn an otherwise oblivious purchaser. A seller may also have a duty to inspect if she knows that the product may be dangerous. Similarly, advertisers may also have the duty to warn about the dangers associated with the product. Suppliers or wholesalers of equipment must also use reasonable care to make the product safe. However, warnings are not required when the danger is obvious or when the user already knows of the product's dangerous propensities.

Product warnings must be adequate to perform the intended function of risk reduction. A warning will be inadequate if it does not particularize the risk presented by the product, if it is inconsistent with how the product will be used, if it does not provide the reason for the warning, or if the warning was not designed so as to reach the foreseeable user.

In *Ludwig v. Dick Martin Sports, Inc.,*, 2003 WL 22736591 (Mich.App.2003), a middle school student, Jacqueline Ludwig, suffered a serious eye injury while jumping rope with two other students during an open gym period at school. Jacqueline's friends were twirling the jump rope while Jacqueline was preparing to enter the arc of the rope. When Jacqueline turned around to face the rope, one end of the rope flew loose and the rope struck Jacqueline in the eye.

Jacqueline was transported to the hospital and treated for an ocular laceration and severe ocular trauma, necessitating the removal of the lens of the eye. She has a permanent loss of vision in the eye. Subsequent inspection of the jump rope indicated that it was composed of plastic segments strung on nylon rope that had been knotted together, and numerous segments were cracked or broken. Evidence indicated that the damage to Jacqueline's eye was likely caused by one of the broken pieces on the jump rope.

Plaintiffs filed this action against several companies involved in the manufacture, distribution or sale of the jump rope, the two other students involved, the school, and school personnel. This appeal involves the granting of summary disposition in favor of defendant Dimmer-Warren, the seller of the jump rope, and defendants Beebe and Wilson, physical education teachers at Imlay Community School District Middle School, where the injury occurred.

In its opinion granting summary disposition for Dimmer-Warren, the trial court framed plaintiffs' claim as a design defect claim "that the ropes were made from breakable plastic segments, which made them dangerous to use when the segments become splintered." The trial court concluded that plaintiffs failed to go beyond the mere allegations in the pleadings to show that a design defect existed in the ropes at the time of sale. However, plaintiffs' claim against Dimmer-Warren was premised on a failure to warn. Considering the affidavits, pleadings, depositions, admissions, and other evidence in the light most favorable to plaintiffs, the Appeals Court concluded that summary disposition of plaintiffs' failure to warn claim was improper.

Additionally, given the legal predicate of plaintiffs' claim of failure to warn, the trial court erred in granting summary disposition on the ground that plaintiffs failed to go beyond the mere pleadings to show that a design defect existed in the ropes at the time of sale. Plaintiffs submitted sufficient evidence to survive Dimmer-Warren's motion for summary disposition.

D. STRICT LIABILITY

Strict liability is liability without fault. Athletic equipment suppliers will be liable if they sell an unreasonably dangerous piece of sporting equipment which is harmful as a result of a defective condition. The manufacturer will be liable to the ultimate consumer for injuries suffered provided that the seller is in the business of selling that product and the product has not been substantially changed or altered.

Plaintiff has the burden of proving that the defect existed when the product left defendant and that the defect caused injury to a reasonably foreseeable user. However, plaintiff does not have to prove the negligence of the manufacturer. To prove that the equipment is defective will require more than the mere showing that the product caused injury. Defects can be the result of the manufacturing process or it can be in the design.

Regarding design, factors that should be weighed to determine if a particular piece of equipment is reasonably safe include the gravity of the danger posed by the design defect, the likelihood that danger will occur, the mechanical feasibility of a safer design, the cost of an improved design and the adverse consequences to the product and to the consumer that might result from an alternative design. *Everett v. Bucky Warren, Inc.*, 376 Mass. 280, 380 N.E.2d 653 (1978).

Strict liability is imposed by operation of law for public policy reasons and the protection of the public. A product is defective if it is not reasonably fit for the purposes for which it is sold. This is important in sports since each piece of protective equipment is specifically geared for a particular function. The seller may avoid liability by proper instructions and warnings which if followed properly would avoid injury. The seller can also assume that the athlete will read and follow these admonitions. With strict liability the defense of contributory negligence is generally unavailable although assumption of risk still applies.

Father of 15–year-old who was injured while jumping on trampoline brought premises liability claim on her behalf against owner of property on which trampoline was located and strict liability claim against manufacturer. The Supreme Court of Illinois held that a reasonable 15–year-old teenager would appreciate the danger of rocket jumping on a recreational trampoline, and thus, manufacturer of trampoline had no duty to warn the minor of the danger of two or more jumpers jumping on a trampoline. Neither the distraction exception nor the deliberate-encounter exception applied to require owner to warn of obvious danger. The owner had no duty to warn of obvious risk, and there was no duty to supervise or a duty to prevent use of the trampoline. See *Sollami v. Eaton*, 201 Ill.2d 1, 265 Ill.Dec. 177, 772 N.E.2d 215 (2002).

In *Mohr v. St. Paul Fire & Marine Ins. Co.*, 269 Wis.2d 302, 674 N.W.2d 576 (App.2003), a student, who was injured while practicing racing starts from an 18–inch starting platform at shallow end of high school swimming pool sued manufacturer of platform, state athletic association, and national association of state athletic associations. The court held that:

(1) the manufacturer could raise sophisticated user defense;

(2) a genuine issue of material fact also precluded summary judgment for manufacturer on strict product liability claim; and

(3) a genuine issue of material fact as to whether state athletic association exercised reasonable care in adopting rule regarding starting platforms precluded summary judgment for association.

E. WARRANTY LIABILITY

Breach of warranty is another theory of recovery under product's liability. Warranty liability is based on a breach of contract. A warranty is akin to a promise that concerns the quality and condition of the product. If the product fails to meet the expectations of the promise then the warranty is broken and the seller is liable under contract law for the resulting damage.

There are two types of warranties under the Uniform Commercial Code (UCC), express and implied. Express warranties are those warranties that are made by statements or conduct on the part of the manufacturer or seller; these warranties exist if a reasonable person would take the seller's actions or conduct to be a promise or representation of fact concerning the quality or condition of the product.

There is also an implied warranty of merchantability. Merchantability means fitness for ordinary use. There will be a breach of the implied warranty of merchantability when a specific piece of sporting equipment does not meet the representations that are made on its label; and therefore, it is not fit for the ordinary use for which it was sold.

Privity may be required to maintain an action for breach of warranty. Privity is the direct line that goes from the manufacturer to the buyer. It is a relation between parties that is sufficiently close and direct to support a legal claim on behalf of the plaintiff against the other person with whom this relationship exists. UCC § 2–318 waives the requirement of privity if a purchase is made by a member of the victim's immediate family.

F.   FACILITY LIABILITY

1.   Status of Injured Party

A large portion of sports negligence suits are against stadium owners and operators. The question in these suits is the status of the injured party who has entered the premises. Is that person an invitee, licensee or trespasser? With each category there is a different standard of care on the part of the facility owner or operator.

The infamous "Snowball" game at Giants Stadium on December 23, 1995, in which fans tossed snow and ice that had accumulated under the seats and in the aisles, among themselves and onto the field, produced a case, *O'Connell v. New Jersey Sports & Exposition Authority and the New York Giants*, 337 N.J.Super. 122, 766 A.2d 786 (App.Div. 2001), that determined that a fan who slipped and fell on ice in the stands during this melee has the right to sue the Giants for his injuries.

2. Invitees

Generally, participants and spectators are business invitees. The occupier is not an insurer of the invitee's safety. The duty to an invitee is one of ordinary and reasonable care including protection from negligence and reasonably discoverable hazards created by a third party and an obligation to inspect premises and make them safe for a visit. There is also a duty to warn of known, unsafe conditions.

For example, a health spa patron is a business invitee and the owner-operator owes a duty to keep the premises in a reasonably safe condition for his protection. This duty will include the detection of reasonably discoverable conditions on the premises which might be unreasonably dangerous and the correction of these conditions or warnings to the invitee of the danger. Examples would be the need to shut down a faulty stairmaster that might injure a shin and/or the need to post a warning that one should stop exercising when dizziness occurs.

The invitor/owner/operator also has the duty to furnish reasonable security and protection against the possibility of injury; and to refrain from negligent or careless acts which might make the premises hazardous to invitees. This duty to an invitee does have realistic boundaries and practical ramifications. For example, a ball park owner who screens in the home plate area where the danger of being struck by a foul ball is the greatest was deemed to have provided sufficient protection for as many invitees who could reasonably be expected to desire screened seating. In this situation, the proprietor fulfilled his duty of care and could not be held liable in negligence for injury to a spectator from a foul ball. *Akins v. Glens Falls City School District*, 53 N.Y.2d 325, 441 N.Y.S.2d 644, 424 N.E.2d 531 (1981).

3. Minors

The standard of care will change with the type of invitee, e.g., if the invited person is a minor, invalid or senior citizen. Health spa operators have a duty to keep their premises in a reasonably safe condition for the protection of a patron. In negligence actions against spas the court will consider the type of person entering the establishment: for example, whether the customer was someone who joined the club for treatment of a physical infirmity.

Where minors are involved, one question is whether the minor is capable of appreciating the risk involved in either watching or participating in the sport. For an eight-year old who was struck by a foul ball, the factual question presented to the court was the boy's ability to appreciate the risk of occupying the place that he occupied and whether the design of the screening was negligent since it ignored the high risk area of a picnic grounds adjacent to the right field foul line. *Atlanta v. Merritt*, 172 Ga.App. 470, 323 S.E.2d 680 (1984). The key is the foreseeability of the injury. However, even with children all the elements of negligence must be present.

4. Unreasonably Hazardous Conditions

An owner will be liable in negligence when he has prior knowledge of unreasonably hazardous conditions. The proprietor's duty of reasonable and ordinary care to an invitee includes the detection of reasonably discoverable conditions which may be unreasonably dangerous and the correction of them or at least a warning of their danger. When there is a question of whether the condition is unreasonably dangerous or not, the court may look at prior events. In a case where a high school student crashed through a glass panel located near a gymnasium, the court found negligence because a similar act had occurred several years earlier when a visiting coach walked into that panel. The school authorities should have known of the hazard that this situation created and then have taken steps to either ameliorate or warn of the potential of the danger. *Wilkinson v. Hartford Accident and Indemnity Company*, 411 So.2d 22 (La.1982). However, recovery will not be allowed for obvious dangers.

5. Design, Construction, Maintenance and Repair

Owners of premises will be liable for the negligent design, construction, maintenance or repair of their sports facilities. The preeminent example is when the negligent design and construction of screening at a baseball stadium allegedly causes injury to a spectator from a foul ball.

Another typical case from baseball is when a player slides into an unprotected spike at a base and then alleges that the injury was a result of the negligent design, construction, maintenance or repair of the base. The question will be whether the alleged negligent design of the base and the spike was the cause of the runner's injury. Still, there must be an applicable duty. When a player fractured his ankle while sliding into third base and alleged that the field was negligently packed and the infield dirt too hard, the court found that plaintiff failed to state a claim from which relief would be granted since the player did not allege that the defendant had any duty to maintain the infield dirt in any particular manner or that there was any owed duty. *Blancher v. Metropolitan Dade County*, 436 So.2d 1077 (Fla.App. 3 Dist.1983).

G. PROFESSIONAL SPORTS

In professional sports, a participant can now sue another participant (see chapter seven, § D). The appropriate standard for the intentional striking of an opposing player during a professional football game is one of recklessness.

CHAPTER 7

PARTICIPANT INJURIES

A. GENERALLY

Historically, participants could not recover for injuries that occurred on the playing field. The defense of assumption of risk would block all attempts at recovery. Today, as a general rule, participants assume the risk of unintentional injuries but will not assume injuries that are intentionally inflicted or result from a disregard for safety.

The injured participant might also face the defenses of consent and contributory negligence. Also, an injured participant cannot recover from another participant if the latter did not breach a recognized duty of care.

Liability was found when a basketball player struck an unprovoked blow to an opponent whose back was turned. *Griggas v. Clauson*, 6 Ill.App.2d 412, 128 N.E.2d 363 (2 Dist.1955). Liability was also found when a player violated a safety rule by kicking a soccer goal keeper in a penalty area. *Nabozny v. Barnhill*, 31 Ill.App.3d 212, 334 N.E.2d 258 (1975). Another example of liability was when a base runner deliberately ran into a second baseman who was five feet from the bag. *Bourque v.*

Duplechin, 331 So.2d 40 (La.App. 3 Cir.1976). Liability was found when a catcher deliberately and without warning struck a batter. *Averill v. Luttrell*, 44 Tenn.App. 56, 311 S.W.2d 812 (1957).

Recovery was denied when a second baseman was injured as an unintended consequence of an opposing player's slide into the base. *Tavernier v. Maes*, 242 Cal.App.2d 532, 51 Cal.Rptr. 575 (1 Dist.1966). Liability was likewise denied when a bat slipped out of the hands of a batter and struck another player. *Gaspard v. Grain Dealers Mut. Ins. Co.*, 131 So.2d 831 (La.App. 3 Cir.1961). Recovery was also denied when a basketball player was accidentally struck by an opposing player. *Thomas v. Barlow*, 5 N.J.Misc. 764, 138 A. 208 (1927).

Other cases illustrate the difficulty that participants have in recovering for athletic injuries inflicted through contact with another participant. In *Keller v. Mols*, 156 Ill.App.3d 235, 108 Ill.Dec. 888, 509 N.E.2d 584 (1 Dist.1987), a minor was injured while playing goalie in a floor hockey game. Recovery was disallowed on the grounds that participation in contact sports precluded recovery in negligence if the players were organized and coached; the shooting of plastics pucks in an attempt to score was not viewed as either willful or wanton conduct. Similarly, in a 1986 Louisiana case which involved a softball player injured in a collision with a second softball player, the court found that defendant was neither reckless nor unsportsmanlike while running to first; therefore, the risk of collision between defendant and plaintiff/first baseman was a reasonable risk and one that the player assumed. *Novak v. Lamar Ins. Co.*, 488 So.2d 739 (La.App. 2 Cir. 1986).

In *Niemczyk v. Burleson*, 538 S.W.2d 737 (Mo. App.1976), an action was based on injuries sustained when defendant shortstop in a softball game ran across the infield and collided with plaintiff/base runner as she was running from first to second base. A sports participant accepts reasonable dangers that are inherent to the sport; but only to the point that they are obvious and a usual incident to that sport. Material factors that can be used in determining if a participant's conduct which causes injury to another constitutes actionable negligence include the specific game involved, ages and physical attributes of the participants, their respective skills at the game, their knowledge of its rules and customs, their status as amateurs or professionals, the type of risks which are inherent to the game and those which are outside the realm of reasonable anticipation, the presence or absence of protective uniforms or equipment and the degree of enthusiasm with which the game is played. In *Niemczyk,* the plaintiff sufficiently stated a claim on which relief could be granted on the grounds of negligence.

B. VIOLATION OF SAFETY RULES

A participant can avoid the defenses of assumption of risk and contributory negligence by basing his cause of action on defendant's violation of a safety rule. In *Nabozny v. Barnhill,* 31 Ill.App.3d 212, 334 N.E.2d 258 (1975), plaintiff, a soccer goal keeper, was allowed recovery for being kicked in the head while holding the ball in the penalty area. It was a clear rule violation for the defendant to make contact with the goal keeper in this manner. Safety rules charge participants with a legal duty, breach of which produces actionable negligence. Each player is charged with a legal duty to every other player on the field to refrain from conduct proscribed by a safety rule.

In a 1980 Illinois case, *Nabozny* was interpreted to reflect that a violation of the rules of the National Federation of High School Associations was alone insufficient to establish negligence, since liability for injuries based on a breach of safety rules cannot be predicated on ordinary negligence. A rule violation only establishes a duty if the conduct was more than ordinary negligence; either deliberate or willful conduct or conduct with a reckless disregard for the safety of others. *Oswald v. Township High School District,* 84 Ill.App.3d 723, 40 Ill.Dec. 456, 406 N.E.2d 157 (1 Dist.1980).

C. UNSPORTSMANLIKE CONDUCT

Recovery may be allowed when a plaintiff was injured through defendant's unsportsmanlike conduct. In the case of *Bourque v. Duplechin,* 331 So.2d 40 (La.App. 3 Cir.1976), defendant base runner in a softball game charged the plaintiff who was five feet from second base, with the result that plaintiff suffered substantial damages. Defendant was under a duty to play softball in an ordinary fashion without unsportsmanlike conduct or attempting wanton injury to fellow participants. Defendant breached this duty. A player on the other hand, will most likely assume the risk of injuries from standing on a base and being spiked by someone sliding into that base, which is common in softball.

Participants assume all the ordinary and foreseeable risks incidental to that particular sport. However, they do not assume the risk from fellow participants who act in an unexpected or unsportsmanlike manner with a reckless lack of concern for other players.

D. PROFESSIONAL SPORTS

At one time, recovery for participant injuries was extremely unusual in professional contact sports such as football, due to the defense of assumption of the risk. This ended with *Hackbart v. Cincinnati Bengals, Inc.,* 435 F.Supp. 352 (D.Colo.1977). In *Hackbart,* one Booby Clark, a member of defendant's team, ran a pass pattern during which the ball was intercepted by the opposing team. Plaintiff Hackbart was a defensive back. After the interception, Hackbart and Clark both ended up on the ground near each other and were watching the progress of the play as it transpired up field. Clark, acting out of anger and frustration but without a specific intent to injure, struck a blow with his right forearm to the back of the kneeling Hackbart's head and neck. Neither player complained during the game. Clark testified that his frustration was brought about by the fact that his team was losing. Although there were no protests or any fouls called by the officials, the game film clearly showed that the incident had occurred. Plaintiff later suffered great pain which ultimately forced him out of the game. The injury was eventually diagnosed as a serious neck fracture.

The question was whether in a regular season professional football game an injury which is inflicted by one professional player on an opposing player could give rise to liability in tort when the injury was inflicted by the intentional striking of a blow during a game. The district court ruled in favor of defendant on the grounds that conventional standards of tort liability cannot apply to professional football, since it is a business which is violent by its very nature.

The Court of Appeals, however, reversed and brought professional football back into the standard orbit of recovery for negligent injuries. The Court of Appeals stated that principles of law governing the infliction of injuries must not be disregarded simply because an individual's injury occurred during a professional football game. The alternative would be to admit that the only available option left to the injured football player would be retaliation. The court determined that the instigating player acted impulsively and in the heat of combat in intentionally striking an opposing player in the back of the head during a professional football game. The appropriate standard was recklessness, since Clark intended to inflict serious injury.

Probably the most famous incident in professional sports violence occurred during a National Basketball Association game in 1977 when Kermit Washington of the L.A. Lakers punched Rudy Tomjanovich of the Houston Rockets; Rudy was acting as a peace maker when Kermit saw a red jersey coming at him and landed with a right that caused a concussion, broken nose, broken jaw, skull fractures, facial lacerations, loss of blood, and leakage of brain cavity spinal fluid. Tomjanovich won a substantial jury award (nearly $3 million) in a suit for civil damages against the Lakers, as Washington's employer. His theory was that the Lakers were vicariously liable for his actions since they knew about and even encouraged his dangerous tendencies and reputation as evidenced by a front page *Sports Illustrated* cover that proclaimed him as one of the league's enforcers.

E. CONTACT SPORTS

Contact sports are different from other sports in regard to potential for recovery. In contact sports a certain amount of contact between participants is not only expected but even required.

In *Kabella v. Bouschelle*, 100 N.M. 461, 672 P.2d 290 (App.1983), a minor sued another minor in an attempt to gain damages for injuries sustained in an informal game of tackle football. Plaintiff did not have a negligence cause of action. Voluntary participation in a sport like football constitutes an implied consent to the normal risks that attend permissible bodily contact. But, participation in football still does not constitute consent to contact prohibited by rules which are designed to protect participants and not merely to control the game's flow.

Keller v. Mols, 156 Ill.App.3d 235, 108 Ill.Dec. 888, 509 N.E.2d 584 (1 Dist.1987), involved a minor who was injured while acting as a goalie in an informal game of floor hockey on a friend's patio. The court held that the inquiry should be whether floor hockey was a contact sport and not whether the participants were organized or coached. After they decided that floor hockey was a contact sport, the court established that the standard for contact sports is that mere negligence is insufficient to establish a cause of action. However, willful and wanton behavior will be sufficient to establish a participant negligence suit. Willful and wanton contact is an intentional or reckless disregard for the safety of others. The defendant's action in this case was neither willful nor wanton. Anything normal in the game will not rise to the level of willful or wanton conduct and thus will be insufficient to support an action in negligence.

The contract sports exception to negligence, which provides that participants in a contact sport are only liable for willful and wanton conduct, was applicable to a hockey league, a hockey officials organization, and an amateur hockey association, for purposes of the negligence claims that were brought against them by a father of a minor player who was injured when he was checked from behind at a hockey game by the opposing players. In an issue of first impression, the Illinois Supreme Court noted that while the father alleged that the defendants failed to adequately enforce the rule against bodychecking from behind, rules violations were inevitable in contact sports and are generally considered an inherent risk of playing the game. Additionally, the Court noted that the rules in an organized contact sport directly affect the way in which the sport is played and that imposing too strict of a standard of liability on the enforcement of those rules would have a chilling effect on vigorous participation in sport. *Karas v. Strevell*, 227 Ill.2d 440, 318 Ill.Dec. 567, 884 N.E.2d 122 (2008).

F.   THIRD PERSONS

Another aspect of participant injuries is the interaction of participants with non-participants: spectators or other third persons, such as, referees, coaches, camera men, facility operators, etc.   There is also the phenomenon of spectator abuse. Spectator abuse may take various forms: from a bottle thrown at an outfielder to a mob scene involving an umpire. The key to any evaluation lies in deciding who is responsible for the injuries. A bottle thrower who is caught will obviously be responsible for the consequences of his acts. However, the more difficult situation is when there is no clear cut correlation between injury and the person allegedly responsible. In *Toone v. Adams*, 262 N.C. 403, 137 S.E.2d 132 (1964), an umpire was injured after a call during a minor league baseball game. The umpire contended that fan reaction began and was inspired by the manager of the home team. The court dismissed this claim on the grounds that the injury was not contemporaneous with the manager's antics nor could the manager be held responsible for the acts of the fans.

Some participant injuries stem from the negligent acts of third persons. Many of these types of injuries are created by the conduct of coaches. Courts have imposed tort liability when an athlete was required to compete after sustaining a previous injury, when a coach or a team failed to render medical assistance, when a coach failed to provide proper equipment and when there was negligent instruction. Another third party, in this case, a wrestling referee, was liable for injuries suffered by a participant because of the referee's negligent supervision in not detecting an illegal hold. *Carabba v. Anacortes School District*, 72 Wash.2d 939, 435 P.2d 936 (1967).

In a softball injury case, a player alleged that his fractured ankle which he suffered while sliding into third base, was due to the negligence of the owner of the field who was responsible for the negligent maintenance and packing of the infield dirt in a way that made it too hard. However, the court held that there was neither a duty to maintain the infield dirt in any particular manner nor was there a breach of an owed duty. *Blancher v. Metropolitan Dade County*, 436 So.2d 1077 (Fla.App. 3 Dist. 1983).

CHAPTER 8

SPECTATOR INJURIES

A. GENERALLY

Like participants, spectators run the risk of injury while observing a sport. These injuries can come from foul balls, errant pucks, out of control halfbacks, etc. Spectators, however, will not recover for injuries that result from ordinary and foreseeable risks that are inherent to that particular sport. This is true because they have legally assumed those risks. However, they will not assume the risk of intentional harm, nonforeseeable injury or the negligent acts of a participant. Spectators will also not assume the risk of an arena operator who fails to meet his duty of care.

Although filled with exceptions in most jurisdictions, the doctrine of assumption of risk remains a viable defense in the area of spectator injury, especially baseball spectators. The classic example of an unassumed risk is the outfielder who charges into the stands and assaults a heckler. Under certain circumstances, ordinary negligence is sufficient to establish a participant's liability for injuries to a spectator.

Also, spectators do not assume the risk of an arena operator's failure to meet his duty of care.

155

The owners or operators are business invitors and as a result are liable for conditions which cause harm to invitees, if they knew or should have known that a condition existed which posed an unreasonable risk to the spectators, the spectators could not have discovered and protected themselves against this risk, and the owners failed to exercise reasonable care for the spectator's protection. Arena operators have a duty to maintain the premises in a reasonably safe condition and to supervise the conduct of those on the premises so as to prevent injury. Therefore, spectators may assume that the operators exercised reasonable care to make the arena safe for the purposes of the invitation. The operator is not an insurer of the spectator's safety. The spectator must prove that the acts were a breach of the duty of care and that the breach was the proximate cause of the injury.

B. BASEBALL

Baseball has traditionally been America's number one pastime. Cases of foul ball injuries have received numerous judicial reviews throughout the years. However, the general rule is that a spectator cannot recover for ordinary risks inherent in the sport; and in baseball, foul balls are viewed as an ordinary risk. In *Schentzel v. Philadelphia National League Club*, 173 Pa.Super. 179, 96 A.2d 181 (1953), a female spectator was hit by a foul ball at Philadelphia's Shibe Park. Although she had watched televised broadcasts and had viewed foul balls that went into grandstands, this was her first visit to a ball park. She claimed that defendant had a legal duty to extend the screen protection to encompass all the women patrons, many of whom were both ignorant of the game and lured there by special invitations, such as free admissions. Although plaintiff did not expressly consent to the foul ball injury, the court found that stray balls were a matter of common everyday practical knowledge. As a matter of law the plaintiff had impliedly assumed the normal and ordinary risk incident to attendance at a baseball game. As long as the risks were ordinary, the mere fact of plaintiff's attendance signified that she had assumed those risks.

However, in *Jones v. Three Rivers Management Corporation*, 483 Pa. 75, 394 A.2d 546 (1978), the court argued that the no-duty rule applies only to common, frequent and expected risks, and in no way affects the duty of a sports facility to protect patrons from foreseeably dangerous conditions not inherent in the amusement activity. *Jones* involved a patron who was injured when she was hit by a batting practice foul ball while standing in the interior walkway of a stadium concourse. One who attends a baseball game as a spectator cannot properly be charged with anticipating as inherent to baseball the risk of being struck by a baseball while properly using an interior walkway. The court held that concourse openings are simply not a part of the spectator sport of baseball. As a result, the no-duty rule did not apply and plaintiff was not barred from recovery.

An owner fulfills his duty of ordinary care when there is sufficient screening to provide adequate protection for as many spectators as may reasonably be expected to desire this type of seating. The stadium owner or operator does not have a duty to inform their patrons of the availability of protected seats because their existence is obvious. *Dent v. Texas Rangers*, 764 S.W.2d 345 (Tex.App.—Fort Worth 1989). Assumption of risk to spectators has also been extended to include errant softballs. *Arnold v. City of Cedar Rapids*, 443 N.W.2d 332 (Iowa 1989). As in baseball, the court held that the owner discharged their duty to protect spectators when they supplied sufficient screened seats. The owner could not be held liable for those who chose to sit elsewhere.

In *Clark v. Goshen Sunday Morning Softball League*, 129 Misc.2d 401, 493 N.Y.S.2d 262 (Sup. 1985), a father who brought his son to a pregame softball practice was struck by a warm-up pitch as he stood around the infield as a bystander. The court held that it was inconsequential that the injury occurred during warm up because the father was a spectator as a matter of law and neither the league nor the player who threw the pitch had a duty to warn him of that danger. Whether or not the umpire actually called "play ball" did not minimize the dangers to spectators who are present during warm up prior to the game. When a ball is thrown from point A to point B, its arrival at the last point is not guaranteed in the normal course of baseball. Even after reasonable care, there is some risk of being struck and injured by thrown balls. Interestingly, the father was viewed as a spectator since he was not a casual passerby on the sidewalk. He elected to come specifically into the ballpark thereby placing himself in the zone of danger subject to all the known and inherent risks that are a part of attendance at a ballpark, including casually standing around the infield.

In *Hawley v. Binghamton Mets Baseball Club, Inc.*, 262 A.D.2d 729, 691 N.Y.S.2d 626 (1999), a spectator was struck in the eye during a fly ball catching contest held during the game; the court found for the defendant and held that the fan was aware of and assumed the unique risks inherent in attempting to catch fly balls and that the pitching machine operator did not enhance risks by firing balls at varying trajectories and that neither team nor sponsor has the duty to provide protective eyewear or warn fans.

In *Benejam v. Detroit Tigers*, 246 Mich.App. 645, 635 N.W.2d 219 (2001), Michigan Court of Appeals was asked to determine whether it should adopt, as a matter of Michigan law, the "limited duty" law rule that other jurisdictions have applied with respect to spectator injuries at baseball games. Under that rule, a baseball stadium owner is not liable for injuries to spectators that result from projectiles leaving the field during play if safety screening has been provided behind the home plate and there are a sufficient number of protected seats to meet ordinary demand. The Court concluded that the limited duty doctrine should be adopted as a matter of Michigan law and there is no evidence that defendants failed to meet that duty. There is no duty to warn spectators at a baseball game of the well-known possibility that a bat or ball might leave the field. This is so even though the injured plaintiff was a minor and was struck when a player's bat broke and a fragment of it curved around the net.

The following are brief summaries of baseball spectator injury cases: Infant struck by batting practice ball, defendant supplied sufficient screening and was, therefore, not liable. *Sparks v. Sterling Doubleday Enterprises, LP*, 300 A.D.2d 467, 752 N.Y.S.2d 79 (2002). Spectator suffered permanent brain damage from foul injury; again, no liability since protective screening was adequate. *Hobby v. City of Durham*, 152 N.C.App. 234, 569 S.E.2d 1 (2002). Softball spectator hit by bat thrown in frustration after final out that struck plaintiff by penetrating chain link fence was able to recover on the grounds that she did not assume this type of risk as a spectator. *Larkin v. United States of America*, 2002 WL 31553993 (E.D.La.2002). Spectator struck while returning from restroom assumed risk. *Alwin v. St. Paul Saints Baseball Club*, 672 N.W.2d 570 (Minn.App.2003). Spectator struck while behind dugout assumed risk. *Ray v. Hudson Valley Stadium Corp.*, 306 A.D.2d 264, 760 N.Y.S.2d 232 (2003). Spectator struck by baseball thrown into grandstands by player assumed the risk of injury. *Dalton v. Jones*, 260 Ga.App. 791, 581 S.E.2d 360 (2003). In *Thurmond v. Prince William Professional Baseball*

Club Inc., 265 Va. 59, 574 S.E.2d 246 (2003), the Supreme Court of Virginia upheld the *Schentzel* assumption of risk for foul balls axiom, by rejecting plaintiff's argument that the minor league field's lighting was deficient and that the dimensions of the field were less than standard.

Spectator assumed the risk while standing at concession stand which faced bullpen. *Procopio v. Town of Saugerties*, 20 A.D.3d 860, 799 N.Y.S.2d 316 (3d Dep't 2005), leave to appeal denied, 807 N.Y.S.2d 17, 840 N.E.2d 1031 (2005). Similarly, after a Phillies game, spectator assumed the risk when the centerfielder threw a ball into the stands after final out. This is deemed to be an inherent risk of the game. *Loughran v. The Phillies,* 2005 Pa. Super. 396, 888 A.2d 872 (2005).

Plaintiffs walked towards exit and stopped to speak with a friend. While on the sidewalk with her view of the field obscured by a promotional deck, she was struck by a foul ball between the eyes. As a spectator she assumed the risk. *Neal v. Team Kalamazoo, L.L.C.,* 2006 WL 2380966 (Mich.App.).

Spectator struck in the testicles by an errantly thrown baseball before the baseball game. He was unable to recover since the stadium met its' limited duty, possibility of injury was open and obvious, and stadium adequately warned spectators of the danger of thrown or batted balls. *Teixiera v. New Britain Baseball Club, Inc.,* 2006 WL 2413839 (Conn. Super.).

Even though spectator was distracted by a mascot, here the Famous San Diego chicken, the court held that the claim was barred under the doctrine of primary assumption of the risk. *Harting v. Dayton Dragons Professional Baseball Club, L.L.C.*, 171 Ohio App.3d 319, 870 N.E.2d 766 (2 Dist.2007).

Plaintiff injured by long toss warm-up from centerfield to near dugout between innings, assumed the risk of being struck in the face. *Mauro v. Trenton Thunder Baseball Club,* 2007 WL 776763 (N.J. Super. A.D.).

Spectator was struck and injured by baseball while located in right field pavilion area, brought negligence action against operator of stadium. Summary judgment failed since the limited-duty rule only applies to injuries that occur in the stands, and a genuine issue of material fact existed as to whether the risk of foul ball into right field pavilion was open and obvious danger. *Mantovani v. Yale University,* 44 Conn.L.Rptr. 13, 2007 WL 2318331 (Conn.Super.Ct.2007).

Concession vendor brought negligence action against professional baseball team for injuries sustained when he was caused to fall when he was struck by a fan who was diving for a shirt that was launched into stands by team. Team moved for summary judgment. The court held that the vendor assumed the risk of being injured by a fan. *Cohen v. Sterling Mets, L.P.*, 17 Misc.3d 218, 840 N.Y.S.2d 527 (Sup.2007).

Spectator, who was injured when foul ball struck her in the face as she sat in baseball stadium's concession area, which had no protective screen surrounding it, brought negligence and emotional distress claims against minor league baseball team. The Supreme Court of Nevada held that the "limited duty rule" establishes the totality of the duty owed by baseball stadium owners and operators to protect spectators from foul balls within the confines of the stadium, and that spectator failed to show that concessions area posed an unduly high risk of injury under the limited duty rule. *Turner v. Mandalay Sports Entertainment, LLC.,* 180 P.3d 1172 (Nev.2008).

C. GOLF

Unlike baseball where there is some predictability to the flight of a foul ball; there is far less predictability when one improperly strikes a golf ball. In order to avoid possible liability, golfing sponsors and owners must meet standard safety requirements. Golf spectators assume the inherent dangers and risks involved with the sport. However, golf courses and sponsors still must provide reasonably safe premises for spectators. For example, in *Duffy v. Midlothian Country Club*, 135 Ill.App.3d 429, 90 Ill.Dec. 237, 481 N.E.2d 1037 (1 Dist.1985), a golfball struck a spectator's eye causing total blindness during a tournament while in a roped off concession area. The court held that the sponsors had a duty of reasonable care towards the spectators as business invitees. In a similar case, *Grisim v. TapeMark Charity Pro–Am Golf Tournament*, 394 N.W.2d 261 (Minn.App.1986), plaintiff alleged that there was a negligent failure to provide adequate safety to spectators and cited the fact that she was forced to sit on the ground because of a lack of space in the stands. Even golf tournaments have minimal safety requirements as established by various golf associations; these standards usually include the use of barricades and marshals, neither of which were provided for during this particular tournament.

The landowner does not have to protect the invitee from known or obvious dangers unless the landowner anticipates the possibility of harm. Golf exhibitions, however, do carry a certain amount of risk. The key is whether the defendant has reason to expect harm to the plaintiff from an obvious risk in circumstances where the plaintiff's attention might be distracted from the risk, causing him to forget to protect himself against that harm. *Baker v. Mid Maine Medical Center*, 499 A.2d 464 (Me. 1985).

D.   HOCKEY, CAR RACES AND WRESTLING

Inherently dangerous sports tend to define the legal parameters that control spectator injuries. However, the crux is still whether a plaintiff clearly knows and understands the risk that has occurred and, if so, whether that choice is entirely free and voluntary.

A knowing and voluntary assumption of risk is especially important in ice hockey, automobile racing and professional wrestling. Spectators assume all risks that are matters of common knowledge. Spectators assume the risk of injury from these potential harms as a matter of law. However, what is common knowledge at one time may not have been common knowledge at an earlier time. In a 1952 Pennsylvania case, *Schwilm v. Pennsylvania Sports*, 84 Pa. D. & C. 603 (Pa.Com.Pl.1952), a female hockey fan was deemed not to have the requisite knowledge to understand that the area behind the hockey net was dangerous. Defendants breached their duty to her by improperly screening the goal area; however, they did not breach their duty to her husband, who was a co-plaintiff and an experienced hockey buff who knew the danger and assumed the risk of sitting near the goal. Arguably this case might be decided differently now because of the widespread popularity that hockey currently enjoys.

It is the duty of management to exercise ordinary care for the safety of spectators at hockey games. Courts often contrast knowingly encountered danger with a negligently encountered risk. In the first example, plaintiff consents to the possibility of harm, whereas in the second example plaintiff fails to accurately assess the possible results of his or her own actions. Hockey clubs are not insurers of the safety of their spectators. But they do have a duty to use reasonable care. The clubs should eliminate or warn of hazards which they ought to know of and which are not reasonably expected by patrons.

Hockey spectator hit in head by a puck that entered the stands during warm-up, withstood summary judgment on basis that issue of material fact existed as to whether defendant took appropriate steps to protect spectators from, or warn them about, the special dangers inherent in warm-up activities. *Sciarrotta v. Global Spectrum,* 392 N.J.Super. 403, 920 A.2d 777 (App.Div.2007).

In professional wrestling and automobile racing, the operators must also exercise reasonable care for the safety of their patrons. But, like in all other sporting endeavors, they are not insurers and are likewise not liable unless they fail to act reasonably. For example, in one professional wrestling match (which is by definition noisy and undignified), an unknown person threw a whiskey bottle into the crowd. The court held that the operator was not negligent because there was no showing that the facility breached its duty of care. *Whitfield v. Cox*, 189 Va. 219, 52 S.E.2d 72 (1949). But a spectator at a automobile racing event should expect the same type of screened protection that is required at a baseball park. For example, an operator would be negligent if he failed to provide sufficient protection in the form of fencing between the pit and the area where the spectator is seated near the edge of the track.

E. MINORS

The capability of a person to assume a risk is extremely important. This is especially true for minors. The nature of the risk that may be assumed is not conclusive as to whether it has been assumed. The plaintiff must know and understand the risk that he incurs. Also, the choice to incur that risk must be free and voluntary. With minor spectators, the question is whether they can assume the risks that are inherent in the activity. In *Brosko v. Hetherington*, 16 Pa. D. & C. 761 (Pa. Com.Pl.1931), an eleven year-old caddy in the first day of service recovered damages when a defendant negligently struck a golf ball that injured him, without warning of the potential danger. The defendant had a duty to observe if anyone was in the area where the ball could possibly travel if sliced (i.e., hit to the side) and had a duty to warn anyone in that area in order that they might protect themselves. In golf it is customary to give a warning when driving a ball from the tee under certain circumstances.

It is not customary to give a warning in a baseball game for each ball that is either pitched or batted. When an eight year-old was struck in the face by a foul ball during a game in which he and his parents attended in an inadequately screened picnic area directly adjacent to the right field foul-line, the court observed that spectators at a baseball game are presumed to be aware of the dangers inherent in that sport. However, whether a child's assumption of that risk bans recovery is a question for the jury unless the facts are so plain that they demand a finding by the court as a matter of law. The court found nothing which demanded the conclusion that the eight year-old plaintiff understood the risk of occupying the place he occupied or that he assumed the inherent risks. Because of his age, the lack of evidence in the records concerning his ability to appreciate the risk and his actual understanding of the risk, the court held that the child did not as a matter of law assume the risk of the injury that he sustained. To recover, the child must not possess the ability to appreciate the risk of occupying the place that he occupies and must not understand the risk involved. *Atlanta v. Merritt*, 172 Ga.App. 470, 323 S.E.2d 680 (1984).

However, in a similar Texas case where an eleven year-old baseball spectator was injured by a foul ball the court held that the stadium had no duty to warn the spectator of the danger of being hit by a foul ball while in the area behind the first base dug out. *Friedman v. Houston Sports Association*, 731 S.W.2d 572 (Tex.App.—Houston 1st Dist.1987). The operator met his duty by providing an adequately screened area for those that desire it, although the spectator chose to sit elsewhere. The court concluded that it would have been absurd and no doubt resented by many patrons if the ticket seller had warned each person entering the park that there was a danger of vagrant baseballs in unscreened areas. The fact of the child's age did not alter the fact that the stadium operator had fulfilled his duty to provide adequately screened seats for those who desire them. Under the circumstances, the operator met his duty to exercise reasonable care to protect patrons against injury.

F.　FACILITIES

Spectators will not assume the risk of an arena operator who fails to meet his or her duty of care. Operators are business invitors and will be liable for conditions which cause harm to invitees, if 1) the operators know or should have known that the conditions existed, 2) the conditions imposed an unreasonable risk to spectators which they could not discover or protect themselves against, and 3) if the operators failed to exercise reasonable care for their protection. Operators have a duty to maintain premises in a reasonably safe condition and to supervise the conduct of those on the premises so as to prevent injury. Spectators can assume that operators have exercised reasonable care to make arenas safe for the purposes of the invitation. But, operators are not insurers of the spectator's safety, therefore, the spectator must prove that the acts were a breach of the duty of care and that the breach was the proximate cause of the injury.

The proprietor's duty of reasonable and ordinary care to an invitee includes the duty to detect reasonably discoverable conditions which may be unreasonably dangerous. In deciding whether a condition is unreasonably hazardous a court may look at prior events. One significant question is what constitutes prior knowledge of a dangerous condition. Courts typically deny recovery for obvious dangers.

CHAPTER 9

SCHOOL LIABILITY

A. NEGLIGENCE

In the past, courts were reluctant to hold school systems liable in ordinary negligence because the courts felt that a teacher could not give personal attention to every student all of the time. There were also a number of powerful defenses at the service of the school districts and this helped to create a dearth of actions against schools; these defenses included sovereign immunity, assumption of the risk, etc. Today, there are many negligence actions against schools, school employees, school districts and school boards. A majority of these actions involve either participant injuries in interscholastic sports or injuries that occur while participating in mandatory physical education courses. These actions center on the following acts of alleged negligence on the part of various school officials: failure to warn, failure to instruct, failure to supervise, failure to hire and train competent coaches and staff, and the failure to provide adequate equipment and safe facilities.

The key for recovery against school districts is the determination of whether a duty exists. Along with the duty, there must be some causal connection or proximate cause between the alleged negligence and the injury, without which recovery will not be allowed. Generally, there are several factors that bear on a school's potential liability. For example, public schools are liable for tortious conduct when under the circumstances they owe a duty of ordinary care to participants and spectators in athletic events. The duty owed an athlete takes the form of adequate instruction, proper equipment, reasonable matching of participants, nonnegligent supervision and proper post injury procedures. Also, there is a duty of the school to take reasonable protective precautions for spectators; this will extend to those injured by players, those injured because of rowdyism where it is reasonably anticipated and those who are injured as a result of inadequate grandstands. A basic issue is whether the school district fulfilled its duty of care owed to the injured person and more importantly whether recovery was barred by assumption of risk or contributory negligence.

The school district may be liable for negligent supervision by a person not an employee of the district where the school district encouraged the athletic activity and had a duty to provide nonnegligent supervision. The school district is also liable when an injury to an invitee occurs in an athletic event as the result of a defect in the premises.

A school district can also be liable for injuries that occur during a non-sponsored athletic event if the event is conducted by the student body under school district auspices, is encouraged by the district and is held on school property. Questions of contributory negligence are always for the jury, whereas assumption of the risk has been disposed of as a matter of law in a number of cases.

In *White v. Averill Park Central School District*, 195 Misc.2d 409, 759 N.Y.S.2d 641 (Sup.2003), an action was brought against a school district, board of education, head football coach, assistant football coach, athletic director, principal, school district superintendent, and assistant superintendent arising from a student-on-student hazing incident. Athletic hazing appears to be on the rise in both high school and college campuses. Generally , the offending student-athletes are prosecuted under state anti-hazing statutes, and the institutions are held responsible for the care of their students under the doctrine of vicarious liability.

An injured high school football player brought a personal injury action against the school district. The court held that the school district was not liable for injuries sustained by the varsity football player during practice, since the player assumed the risk of injury by participating in varsity football practice and that he was an experienced football player. *Serrell v. Connetquot Cent. School Dist. of Islip*, 19 A.D.3d 683, 798 N.Y.S.2d 493 (2d Dept. 2005).

Referee who allegedly was injured when he was punched by student during basketball tournament that was organized by non-profit organization and held at high school sued student and school district to recover for his injuries The court held that the school district had no duty to supervise student and that the absence of a special relationship between school district and referee precluded school district's liability for referee's injuries. *Curcio v. Watervliet City School District,* 21 A.D.3d 666, 800 N.Y.S.2d 466 (3d Dept.2005).

Suit was brought on behalf of eighth-grade student against archdiocese and other private school defendants to recover for injuries student sustained in attack by another student during basketball practice. The court held that school defendants exercised reasonable supervision and were not responsible for unforeseen and spontaneous attack by older student and recent graduate who kicked the eighth-grader in the face while at practice to assist coach. *McCollin v. Roman Catholic Archdiocese of New York,* 45 A.D.3d 478, 846 N.Y.S.2d 158 (1st Dept. 2007).

B.   VICARIOUS LIABILITY

Lawsuits against school districts are usually predicated on the negligence of the school district's employees.   Schools, on the other hand, attempt to avoid negligence by claiming that they are not responsible for their actions or that the events are not school sponsored.   However, an employer is vicariously liable for the wrongful acts of his servants and a principal for those of his agent, when the acts are performed within the scope of their employment. Vicarious liability is used to bring the liability of the coach, referee, trainer or groundskeeper under the school board's insurance coverage.

Typically, coaches, aides, teachers, janitors, principals, administrators, groundskeepers, referees, trainers, etc., are viewed as agents of the school district. Without specific statutory immunity the school board will be vicariously liable for their actions. The school board will be liable for the negligent actions of their employees if alleged negligence occurs during the course of employment.

There also is the question of individuals who are not actual employees, but act as quasi-employees, for example, volunteers. The school board may be liable for the actions of the quasi-employee under the principle of vicarious liability. The end result will depend on the amount and quality of the indices that connect the volunteer and his actions to the school board.

In *Kavanagh v. Trustees of Boston University*, 440 Mass. 195, 795 N.E.2d 1170 (2003), a basketball player brought vicarious liability action against university and coach of opposing basketball player who punched him in a basketball game. The court held that opposing basketball player was not an agent or servant of the university for purposes of respondeat superior; and that the university and coach did not have a special relationship with basketball player for purposes of determining whether they had a duty to protect him from the assault and battery.

The court further held that the assault and battery by the opposing basketball player was not reasonably foreseeable. The attacking player was a scholarship athlete, but the lack of reasonable forseeability negated *Kleinknecht*-type duty. Also, his status as a scholarship athlete does not transform the student-university relationship into any form of employment relationship for purposes of respondeat superior.

However, in matter of *State v. Hoshijo*, 102 Hawai'i 307, 76 P.3d 550 (2003), the student-manager of a state university basketball team was deemed to be an agent of the university while interacting with the public. The court held that student manager's actions in shouting racial slurs and threats at spectator fell within the scope of his authority as an agent of the university. Furthermore, the racial slurs and threats were not protected speech within the scope of First Amendment.

The personal representative of a high school athlete's estate brought a wrongful death action against county Board of Education and individual school employees after athlete collapsed during football practice and died from complications due to heatstroke. The court held that the dismissal of wrongful death claims against the individual employees on the merits precluded any vicarious liability for wrongful death against school board. *Draughon v. Harnett County Bd. of Educ.*, 166 N.C.App. 464, 602 S.E.2d 721 (2004).

Mother on behalf of her minor daughter, commenced two actions against various defendants that subsequently were consolidated, seeking damages for injuries sustained by her daughter when she was struck by an automobile owned by youth basketball coach and driven by an assistant coach, who was a high school age student. In the first action, mother specifically alleged that church Diocese was negligent in training, supervising, and instructing basketball coach, and that is was thus vicariously liable under the doctrine of respondeat superior for the alleged negligence of coach in entrusting his automobile. In the second action, mother alleged that church Diocese was negligent in supervising, hiring, assigning, and retaining coach. The Court held that the Diocese was not negligent in training, instructing, supervising, hiring, assigning, and retaining coach, but there was a genuine issue of material fact which precluded summary judgment on the issue of whether coach could be considered a servant of the church as a volunteer, and whether coach was acting within the scope of his duties. *Robinson v. Downs,* 39 A.D.3d 1250, 834 N.Y.S.2d 770 (4 Dept.2007).

College was vicariously liable for injuries suffered by baseball player who traveled with team to Florida baseball tournament and was paralyzed when he dove into a wave and hit the ocean floor at the beach next to the team's hotel. Plaintiff recovered under the college's catastrophic athletic insurance policy on the basis that he was not violating any team rules while on the beach. *Regan v. Mutual of*

Omaha Ins. Co., 375 Ill.App.3d 956, 314 Ill.Dec. 336, 874 N.E.2d 246 (1st Dist.2007).

C. FAILURE TO WARN

One basis of liability under negligence is a failure to warn. Coaches have a duty to warn of both unforeseeable risks and those risks that although not completely unforeseeable are still not entirely and fully understood.

D. FAILURE TO INSTRUCT

Another basis for liability is the failure to properly instruct. In these cases it must be shown that the coaches' or teachers' failure to instruct the student in a proper manner, or no way at all, is the proximate cause of the student's injuries.

E. FAILURE TO HIRE COMPETENT COACHES

Schools may also be liable for the negligent hiring of employees if that negligence is the proximate cause of the athlete's injuries. The school has a duty to hire a coach of reasonable ability whose competence, experience and training is comparable to other similarly situated coaches.

F. FAILURE TO PROPERLY SUPERVISE

The most important duty of a coach or instructor is the supervision of students. School officials cannot be absent from their appointed places at the appointed times if students injure themselves during that period. In those cases, plaintiff will only have to show that the injury was reasonably foreseeable and that proper supervision would have prevented the harm. However, the lack of supervision must be the proximate cause of the injury. Liability would not lie if the injury would have occurred notwithstanding the presence of the school official. Where the gravity of harm increases, then the degree of supervision must also correspondingly increase. In certain activities, continuous and constant supervision is demanded by the nature of the activity. An example would be *Carabba v. Anacortes School District*, 72 Wash.2d 939, 435 P.2d 936 (1967), where a high school wrestler was severely injured when the referee looked away while an illegal hold was applied to the plaintiff. Negligence was found on the failure to adequately supervise the match due to his attention being diverted. The failure to break the hold was the proximate cause of the injury.

However, supervisors do not have the duty to supervise every student every second in every possible area. For example, when a student was injured by rocks thrown in a playground, it was held that there was no liability on the part of the school district. See *Fagan v. Summers*, 498 P.2d 1227 (Wyo.1972); and *Hampton v. Orleans Parish School Board*, 422 So.2d 202 (La.App. 4 Cir.1982). Even though there is a requirement that there must be reasonable supervision by school officials at a playground; there is no requirement that supervisors have every child under direct, constant and continual supervision.

A school district's duty to supervise is best served when supervision is constant and consistent. The lack of direct supervision of activities that are foreseeably dangerous and failure to continually supervise potentially harmful activities are unwise procedures as regards the range of possible personal injury suits that might develop from any injury.

G. FAILURE TO MAINTAIN EQUIPMENT AND FACILITIES

Schools have a duty to provide proper and safe equipment and facilities. To their students, they owe a duty to use reasonable care to inspect and maintain equipment and to protect the students from an unreasonable risk of harm. Schools must maintain reasonably safe facilities for both participants and spectators. A breach of the school's duties to provide and maintain equipment or to provide and maintain reasonably safe facilities will be actionable if it is the proximate cause of plaintiff's injuries.

Certain sports demand a very particular type of protective equipment, for example, football and hockey. It will be a breach of duty if the schools do not provide and maintain appropriate protective equipment. Schools also have a duty to inspect and maintain the equipment that they already possess. In fact, there is a duty of reasonable care to protect students from unreasonable risks even when that harm was a prevailing custom if that custom fell below the reasonable care standard. (*Tiemann v. Independent School District*, 331 N.W.2d 250 (Minn. 1983); student injured during physical education gymnastics instruction on a pommel horse with exposed holes.)

Owners and operators are required to show ordinary care and diligence in maintaining both premises and equipment in a reasonably safe manner. Included in this duty is the establishment of a cleaning, inspection and maintenance schedule. The frequency of inspection will depend on the potential harm anticipated, e.g., scuba diving equipment by its very nature demands almost constant inspection. Owners and operators do not have to possess actual knowledge of a dangerous condition, only that they either knew or should have known of its existence. School employees have a duty of reasonable care to inspect the premises for hidden and lurking dangers. School districts will be liable for harm caused by dangers that coaches discovered or should have detected and failed to warn. However, they are not liable for unconcealed dangers that are known or should be obvious to participants.

CHAPTER 10

COACH LIABILITY

A. GENERALLY

Coaches must use reasonable care to avoid the creation of foreseeable risks to the athlete under their supervision. The standard of reasonableness will change from sport to sport. That degree of care will increase if the activity involves a contact sport. Generally, coaches have a duty to exercise reasonable care for the safety of their players.

Coaches may also be liable for the breach of certain duties. Coaches have a duty to instruct their athletes regarding safety procedures and methods to minimize injuries. Coaches have a duty to provide safe and effective protective equipment. Also, they cannot force their athletes to participate when those athletes have already sustained injuries, if there is a risk that further participation will only aggravate the original injury. Coaches must also take reasonable steps to provide medical assistance when and if it is necessary. Liability has been found when a coach failed to summon medical aid in a timely fashion when a player showed symptoms of heat stroke. *Mogabgab v. Orleans Parish School Board*, 239 So.2d 456 (La.App. 4 Cir.1970).

Negligence will not lie if the coach has fulfilled his duty to exercise reasonable care for athletes under his supervision. This duty will be satisfied by providing proper instructions and explaining to the athlete how to play the game and also by showing due concern that the athlete is in proper physical condition. This duty of care will be satisfied if the coach takes all reasonable steps to minimize the possibility of injury. Although the player must have proper and sufficient instruction, the coach will only be liable if he fails to exercise reasonable care for the protection of his players and that the injury was a result of that failure.

In a New Jersey trial decision, a novice player, a track star who was recruited for football solely for his speed as a receiver, was severely injured while tackling an opposing player on an interception. The player contended that his injury was a result of the negligence of the coaching staff who failed to provide sufficient training, conditioning, equipment and supervision. Specifically, he only had one practice session on tackling. Expert testimony averred that tackling is an extremely dangerous aspect of the sport and that the correct technique and manner, including keeping the head elevated which plaintiff did not do, must be reinforced by repeated practice. The experts agreed that one practice session was insufficient. Plaintiff also contended that he was not provided with sufficient preseason training, including weight training, to strengthen neck muscles which experts contended was essential and the absence of which contributed to the incident.

The jury found the head coach 40% negligent and the interior line coach 60% negligent; they then awarded 6.5 million dollars. The jury was presented with an array of coaching techniques which could be viewed as an indifference to the player's health. The jury emphasized that the plaintiff was a senior who was trained in track and did not receive extensive training in his first year of football; this lack of training only reinforced their view that this was a coaching staff who stressed victory over safety. This inference was reinforced by the deposition testimony of the interior line coach who indicated that the plaintiff was only a name to him. *Woodson v. Irvington Board of Education* (1987), Coburn, J., 3 *Natl. Jury Verdict Rev. & Anal.* 10 (No. 8, 1988).

To determine negligence, some states apply the so-called locality rule which is comparable to the one used to establish applicable standards in medical malpractice cases: this requires that the coach will be held to the standard of other coaches in that specific geographical area. For example, coaches in rural areas might not be expected to possess the expertise that their big city colleagues undoubtedly possess.

Coaches are judged by regional rather than a state or national standard. The locality rule was originated at a time when new coaching techniques were not expected to travel to the more obscure rural areas in America. However, in these days, in an era of coaching clinics, videos, consumer education, instructional pamphlets and coaching magazines, the rationale for a locality rule may no longer be legitimate.

B. QUALIFICATIONS

There is a movement in amateur sports that would demand a basic minimum in education and experience before one could become certified as a coach. Also, coaches would be obliged to take a certain amount of continuing education to maintain certification. In *Everett v. Bucky Warren, Inc.*, 376 Mass. 280, 380 N.E.2d 653 (1978), an injured school hockey player sued his coach and a helmet manufacturer for injuries received when a puck struck him in the head causing severe injuries. The helmet in question was a three-piece helmet which allowed for gaps that under the wrong circumstances allowed enough space for a puck to squeeze through and cause injury. At the time there was another type of helmet available which was a single piece and would have prevented the injury. This single piece design was known to all parties and was available at the time of the accident but at a slightly higher price than the three-piece helmet. The coach was negligent in supplying the helmet: he should have known that the three-piece design was faulty and that another more safely designed helmet was also readily available. The coach who had substantial experience in hockey, could be held to a higher standard of care and knowledge than the average person as it relates to the ordering of the unsafe hockey helmet. Coaches are expected to possess a minimum of education and experience that is thought to be generally prevalent within the industry as a whole. The coach in *Everett* went below that standard.

Coach certification is the key. Approximately half of the physical education departments in institutions of higher learning provide professional training in coaching. As an example, the American Alliance for Health, Physical Education, Recreation and Dance recommends that a minor in coaching should include the following courses: Medical Aspects of Coaching, Problems of Coaching, Theory and Techniques, and Kinesiological and Physiological foundations.

However, the majority of the states still require only teacher certification, regardless of the subject area, as a prerequisite for coaching. If you are certified to teach you are also qualified to coach. In *Stehn v. Bernarr McFadden Foundations, Inc.*, 434 F.2d 811 (6th Cir. 1970), a student was injured during a wrestling program supervised by a faculty member who had only a small amount of wrestling or coaching experience. This so-called coach was supervising two matches at once. The hold that allegedly caused plaintiff's injury was one that the coach had learned while in the service. However, the coach failed to explain a method of escape and a defense to that hold. The plaintiff's case was built on the failure of the coach to supervise and his lack of qualifications in coaching wrestling.

Since one has to be certified to teach, arguably the school districts should require additional training and education as a prerequisite for coaching. This would be a logical step since coaching does provide extra monetary income. This extra preparation should require courses in physical conditioning, the learning and performance of physical skills, first aid, theory and techniques of coaching, and the legal aspects of coaching. Additionally, a minimum of three to five years experience in coaching should be a prerequisite to a head coaching position. School boards should support this trend since they are the ones who will usually be responsible for the acts and omissions of their coaching staffs.

Another aspect of the qualification issue is the training and preparation of assistants and assistant coaches. Under the doctrine of respondeat superior, it is possible that coaches will be responsible for the actions of their assistants whether paid or voluntary, whether student or non-student, and whether or not they were student teaching. Generally, coaches have a duty to warn their athletes of any hidden dangers known to them and then instruct them in methods to avoid these hazards. If the instruction is negligent because of the lack of training of the assistants then the coach would be responsible.

In *Brahatcek v. Millard School District*, 202 Neb. 86, 273 N.W.2d 680 (1979), plaintiff's decedent was a fourteen year-old junior high school student who was injured during mandatory golf instruction when he walked into the back swing of a fellow student who he had asked for instruction. The deceased had never had a golf lesson prior to the accident. His actual instructor was busy instructing another student and thus unable to supervise the decedent. This instructor was actually a student teacher, who only had five weeks experience; the regular teacher was absent that day. Although he had helped with golf instruction in four to six classes on the previous two days, this was his first class as an instructor. In this case the inexperience of the student teacher was found to be the proximate cause of the injury.

C. PREPARATION OF PARTICIPANTS

It is obvious that every athlete must be prepared before he enters the playing field. It is the responsibility of the coach to make sure that the athletes under his charge are ready and prepared to participate. This preparation should consist of the following specific duties: instruction, physical preparation, providing proper equipment, maintenance of equipment and issuance of warnings. Coaches have a duty to prepare; a failure of which could lead to liability based on negligence.

A coach has the responsibility to minimize serious injuries. One way of accomplishing this goal is to provide competent and thorough instruction in the sport's technical aspects and their corresponding safety rules. In *Vendrell v. School District*, 233 Or. 1, 376 P.2d 406 (1962), no negligence was found when football coaches provided adequate, standard instruction and practice without negligently omitting any detail. The program in *Vendrell* contained a daily calisthenic "bull-neck" exercise which was designed to strengthen the neck muscles and thus help to prevent neck injuries. The *Vendrell* court averred that the player had a duty to ask questions on matters to which he was unclear. Since there were no questions, the coaches could have assumed that he was aware of the possibility of injury that could have occurred from using his head as a battering ram.

Another aspect of preparation is the physical preparation of the athlete. This includes weight training, calisthenics, coordination drills, stretching exercises, etc. The requirement here is to prove that this lack of training was the proximate cause of the injury.

It is also expected that the athlete will be furnished with the proper protective and safety equipment which is appropriate for the sport especially if it is a contact sport. Added to that, the athlete must be properly instructed as to the appropriate use of this equipment; also, the equipment must be properly maintained so that its effectiveness is maximized. In *Hemphill v. Sayers*, 552 F.Supp. 685 (S.D.Ill.1982), the coaches were potentially liable for the negligent failure to warn the football player of the danger inherent in the use of a football helmet.

When one defends against these types of charges, the school can protect themselves by having enough equipment brochures and equipment specifications available so as to show a conscious effort to choose the best available equipment. Equipment manufacturers will generally provide fitting and maintenance instructions with their equipment at the time of purchase and will usually supply additional copies upon request. Coaches should read, understand and file these instructions; distribute copies to players and make sure they comprehend the instructions; and retain extra copies so they can maintain a permanent library of information. Coaches should also follow the manufacturer's recommended instructions for periodic inspection and maintenance. These programs of inspection, maintenance and proper repair must be documented. For example, there must be a maintenance history for each helmet.

Coaches can never be totally free from the fear of potential liability. However, one way to decrease potential liability is to check the equipment before the contest and to develop enough expertise in the field so that the equipment that is available is state of the art.

In *Thomas v. Chicago Board of Education*, 77 Ill.2d 165, 32 Ill.Dec. 308, 395 N.E.2d 538 (1979), a coach was protected from suit on basis of sovereign immunity since his conduct was neither willful nor wanton. The conduct in *Thomas* was furnishing but failing to inspect defective football equipment. This conduct was held to be ordinary negligence as it related to injuries that resulted from defective equipment.

In many jurisdictions a coach's act of ordinary negligence is protected by sovereign immunity. However, wanton or gross negligence in the supplying of faulty equipment will still usually expose the coach to liability.

The preparation of the athlete by the coach also includes appropriate warnings about certain types of dangers, potential injuries, conduct, and techniques before the athlete actually participates. Failure to warn exists if the coach fails to specifically warn the student about the potential dangers of using one's head as a battering ram in football; moreover, the student should also be warned that using the head in this way could cause permanent paralysis. In football, each helmet has a written warning explaining the dangers of using a helmet as a ram. However, it would be beneficial to the coach to reinforce this warning orally: if possible, prior to each game or practice.

The duty to warn is the last defense that the coach should use in his preparation of the athlete before participation; however, it relates only to dangers that are non-obvious to the coaches. This applies to all potential dangers including equipment use, proper techniques, and the quality and consistency of the playing field.

The preparation of the participants may appear to be harsh on coaches, but they are usually in the position to give the last piece of advice and check the athlete one more time immediately prior to the athlete's entering onto the playing field. Also, many coaches are in a semi-paternal position to their athletes: the students trust their coaches and rely on their expertise.

D. SUPERVISION

Coaches also have a responsibility to properly supervise the athletes under their charge. This duty is not an absolute but varies with the danger of the activity and the age and maturity of the participant. Coaches are not insurers of the actions of the students under their supervision. An instructor, was not negligent when a student in a physical education class was injured when she and her classmates decided to run a race in the foyer of the gymnasium. The plaintiff, while running at full speed, crashed into a glass wall; the coach was not negligent since he had exercised proper supervision over the class. *Wilkinson v. Hartford Accident and Indemnity Co.*, 411 So.2d 22 (La.1982).

In *Nydegger v. Don Bosco Preparatory High School*, 202 N.J.Super. 535, 495 A.2d 485 (Law Div.1985), a high school soccer player was injured and brought an action against the opposing coach for failure to supervise his players and for teaching them to compete in an aggressive and intense way and to believe that victory was all important. The court held that in the absence of instruction by the coach to one of his players to specifically commit a wrongful act or his instructing the player in procedures that would increase the risk of harm to opposing players, the coach would not be responsible to the injured player. There was no proximate cause, and the aggressive athlete was not an agent of his coach.

Ignoring a potentially dangerous activity might be sufficient to act as a breach of that coach's duty to supervise. This rationale would apply to supervising a spectator's contact with players, leaving children unattended at a swimming pool or not correcting an athlete's faulty maneuver during play. A coach has to use reasonable care in the supervision of athletes under his control so as to avoid the unreasonable risk of harm to the athletes and those associated with the activity.

In *Draughon v. Harnett County Board of Education*, 158 N.C.App. 705, 582 S.E.2d 343 (2003), the personal representative of deceased student's estate brought wrongful death suit against county Board of Education, and several school employees, including coach, based on student's death from a heat stroke while at football practice. The coach was not liable for wrongful death since coach neither prohibited student from getting water while directing him to run wind sprints, nor failed to recognize symptoms of heatstroke, exhibited prior to student's collapse; therefore, coach was not liable for death of athlete, where coach denied he refused water or failed to notice symptoms, and denial was supported by testimony of others.

In *Koffman v. Garnett*, 265 Va. 12, 574 S.E.2d 258 (2003), a middle school football player, who was injured when football coach thrust his arms around player's body, lifted him off his feet and slammed him to the ground while explaining proper tackling technique, brought negligence, assault, and battery claims against coach. The Supreme Court of Virginia held that player consented to physical contact with players of like age and experience, but that he did not expect or consent to his participation in aggressive contact tackling by adult football coaches, stated cause of action of the tort of battery.

The parents of a student who was injured when he was pushed into a pool by another student in swimming class brought negligence claims against the pool's owners, the instructor, the other student, and the other student's parents. The court held that the owners did not have reason to know that the handrail in the pool posed a latent hazard and that they did not breach their duty to inspect the pool or to have it inspected. To the extent that the handrail posed any risks to patrons, it was an open and obvious danger. Even if the 1 to 50 instructor to student ratio was too high to be considered safe, that unsafe ratio did not establish that the owners of the pool were negligent. The instructor's failure to prevent the student from being pushed into the pool did not constitute negligence and the instructor was not negligent when she had the students position themselves on the deck of the pool above the handrail. Similarly, the other student's act of pushing the student into the pool did not amount to reckless and intentional behavior. *Thompson v. Park River Corp.*, 161 Ohio App.3d 502, 830 N.E.2d 1252 (1st Dist. Hamilton County 2005).

CHAPTER 11

REFEREE LIABILITY

Many referees and officials are now finding themselves named as defendants in personal injury suits for alleged acts of negligence. Although they are usually not found personally liable, these suits are still an inconvenience.

To counteract what is viewed as an alarming trend, some states have promulgated laws that eliminate suits against referees and umpires unless they are grossly negligent. For example, New Jersey passed a law that provides partial immunity for volunteer referees from civil suits for damages that result from acts or omissions during the ordinary course of their supervision. N.J.Stat.Ann. 2A:62 A–6.

It is a referee's duty to properly supervise an athletic contest. For example, a wrestling referee was held to be negligent for not properly supervising a match; while the referee's attention was diverted one wrestler used an illegal hold to the other wrestler which resulted in permanent paralysis below the neck. The referee was negligent in that he breached his duty to non-negligently supervise conduct. The referee's standard is one of an ordinarily prudent referee under similar circumstances. The injured athlete will not assume that risk since one cannot assume another's negligence or incompetence. *Carabba v. Anacortes School District*, 72 Wash.2d 939, 435 P.2d 936 (1967).

When the standard of care is met, recovery will not be allowed. In *Pape v. State*, 90 A.D.2d 904, 456 N.Y.S.2d 863 (3 Dept.1982), personal injuries were sustained during a college intramural floor hockey game when plaintiff attacked an opponent. Plaintiff alleged that the injuries were attributable to a lack of proper supervision and training by the referee. The referee's alleged inexperience was argued to be the proximate cause of plaintiff's cervical spine fracture. The court held that the duty owed by the referee to plaintiff was the duty to exercise reasonable care under the circumstances to prevent injuries. The court concluded that the duty had been met.

A. DUTY TO ENFORCE RULES

The referee has a duty to enforce the rules of the sport and to prevent illegal holds or actions. The standard is one of an ordinarily prudent referee. Id. Although referees have a duty to enforce the rules of the game, there is no separate referee malpractice for bad calls. Referees cannot prevent all rule violations, and they only have a duty to use reasonable care to see that the rules of the game, including safety rules, are followed. Reasonable care consists of advising the participants of adverse conditions and illegal maneuvers, showing due diligence in detecting rule violations, penalizing the rule breakers, etc.

B. DUTY TO PROTECT PARTICIPANTS

As a part of a referee's duty to provide non-negligent supervision there is also an implied duty to protect and warn participants. However, like coaches, referees are not insurers of the safety of participants. In *Pape v. State*, 90 A.D.2d 904, 456 N.Y.S.2d 863 (3 Dept.1982), where plaintiff was injured in a floor hockey game, the court found that there was no connection or proximate cause between the referee's alleged negligence and the injuries. The referee cannot guarantee the safety of each participant; moreover, the court found that the plaintiff's injury occurred while using his own initiative to attack his opponent. Therefore, the injury could not be attributed to a lack of supervision or training on the part of the referee. The duty owed to the plaintiff only required that the referee exercise reasonable care under the circumstances to prevent injury; the referee did not have a duty to protect the plaintiff from the danger that was inherent in a maneuver that was initiated and controlled by the plaintiff himself.

C. DUTY TO WARN

There is an implied duty on the part of the referee to warn participants of possible dangers. For example, it is the duty of a wrestling referee to

warn participants of the consequences and dangers
of an illegal maneuver. *Carabba v. Anacortes
School District*, 72 Wash.2d 939, 435 P.2d 936
(1967). This duty can arguably be expanded to
include the referee's responsibility of controlling the
game as regards hazardous conditions and inclem-
ent weather. For example, ceasing play during the
following circumstances: a lightning storm or an
overly oiled basketball court or inadequate lighting
for a baseball game. It also includes protecting
participants from more aggressive players by penalizing or warning athletes of their inappropriate
conduct.

D. ANTICIPATING REASONABLY FORESEEABLE DANGERS

Comparable to the duty of the referee to protect
and warn participants is his duty to anticipate
reasonably foreseeable dangers. Before the contest
and while the game is in progress, it is the responsibility of the referee to determine that the playing
conditions are safe. This could reasonably include
checking for the following: glass on the running
track, holes on the field in football, metal stakes
protruding from the dirt in a baseball diamond,
loosely secured bases in softball, etc. Officials have
an obligation to inspect field conditions. In basketball, the safety rules provide that a referee must
ascertain whether there are loose basketballs in the
vicinity of the court, whether the padding at the
basket supports is secure and continuous around

the entire pole, and whether the area surrounding the court is clear for the players.

Another group of reasonably foreseeable dangers that the referee ought to anticipate are adverse weather and overall unsafe playing conditions. Before the game, it is the referee's responsibility to decide whether the game should start. His first duty is to inspect the overall playability of the playing surface. It is conceivable that a referee could be held liable for allowing play to continue if a football field is overly muddy and correspondingly unsafe. The crux of this issue is the referee's reasonable judgment: the responsibility to call a game will rest solely on the shoulders of the referee.

E. FAILURE TO CONTROL GAME

One other potential area for referee liability is the failure to control and properly supervise the flow of the game. *Carabba v. Anacortes School District*, 72 Wash.2d 939, 435 P.2d 936 (1967). It is the duty of the official to detect and control the use of illegal and dangerous maneuvers. The standard of care is one of an ordinarily prudent referee.

However, the duty to supervise and control only requires that the referee exercises reasonable care under the circumstances to prevent injury. It is clear that the referee has the duty to stop the match if it appears that an opponent is in serious danger of injury. This is especially true in the dangerous contact sports of boxing and wrestling.

Most of the cases to date have revolved around actions against referees for personal injuries to participants. There are many other conceivable tort cases that could be brought against referees. The most probable would be actions based on "blown calls". However, absent corruption or bad faith, no independent tort exists for "referee malpractice". There has been no court yet that has recognized a viable cause of action against an official for either an honest error in judgment or a misapplication of a game rule. The rulings of an umpire or referee are presumptively correct.

CHAPTER 12

DEFAMATION

Sports is an established part of the American existence, and because of that sports figures and people involved in the sports industry are constantly commented on in various ways. The business of sports journalism is to create controversy through opinions and accusations about the problems of different athletes. Therefore, there is a great possibility that sports figures will be defamed by journalists or newscasters. The question is whether journalistic tirades are defamatory and, if so, are they also actionable. Statements will be defamatory if they are published, false and cause damage to one's reputation. Defamation is the taking from one's reputation: it is defamatory if it tends to diminish the esteem, respect, goodwill or confidence in which the plaintiff was held, or, if the remarks excite adverse, derogatory or unpleasant opinions.

In *Montefusco v. ESPN, Inc.*, 47 Fed.Appx. 124 (3d Cir.2002), former major league baseball player, Jon "the Count of" Montefusco filed action against television network for defamation and false light invasion of privacy. Under New Jersey law, sports news broadcast describing criminal proceedings against former major league baseball player based on domestic violence charges by his ex-wife was not defamatory, despite comparison between player and another ex-athlete accused of domestic violence, where comparison and all statements related to criminal charges against Montefusco were factually accurate and not misleading.

On July 15, 2005, a three-judge panel of the U.S. Court of Appeals for the Eleventh Circuit remanded Mike Price's defamation lawsuit against Time, Inc., for further depositions to identify a confidential source. The court held that the defendants are not protected by Alabama's reporter shield law. However, since Price has not yet exhausted all reasonable efforts to discover the source's identity, the court required further depositions before compelling the defendants to reveal their confidential source.

In December 2002, the University of Alabama ("Alabama") agreed to pay $10 million over seven years for Price to coach the Crimson Tide football team. Four months later, Price attended a pro-am golf tournament in Pensacola, Florida. While at the tournament, Price visited a club known as "Artey's Angels." Subsequently, a *Sports Illustrated* article cited a confidential source as alleging that Price had sex with two women from the club in his hotel room. Price denied any sexual encounter, but Alabama still fired him soon afterward. On June 20, 2003, Price filed a $20 million lawsuit for defamation. In response to Price's interrogatories, Time asserted Alabama's reporter shield statute and the First Amendment's qualified reporter privilege as grounds for refusing to identify its confidential source. See Ala. Code § 12–21–142.

However, the Eleventh Circuit panel unanimously agreed with the district court. Regarding Alabama's reporter shield law, the court observed that the plain and unambiguous language of the statute protects persons "connected with or employed on any newspaper, radio broadcasting station or television station." Since *Sports Illustrated* is a magazine, the court reasoned that it is not included. As for the First Amendment's qualified reporter privilege, the court believed that Price's own testimony under oath constituted substantial evidence that the challenged statement is untrue, and the identity of the source is necessary to the presentation of the case. However, the court also noted that Price could still depose four more individuals in an effort to discover the source's identity. As such, the court concluded that he had not exhausted all reasonable efforts as required by the First Amendment. Therefore, the court remanded the case for the dispositions to occur before it compelled the defendants' disclosure.

On October 7, 2005, a settlement was reached between Price and Time, Inc. However, the following week Time filed a motion with the district court alleging that Price statements, as well as those of his lawyers, regarding the settlement breached its confidentiality provisions. The motion requested that the settlement be thrown out, the case be dismissed, and sanctions be imposed upon Price and his lawyer. *Price v. Time,* 416 F.3d 1327 (11th Cir.2005), as modified on denial of reh'g, 425 F.3d 1292 (11th Cir.2005).

A. SPORTSWRITERS

The usual source of defamation in sports is the sportswriter, sports journalist or radio sports personality. These people are paid to create as much controversy as possible concerning sports heroes. It is their job and they do it well. They are also protected in a majority of the cases by the privilege of fair comment: their analyses are deemed opinions and are thus protected by the First Amendment. But, a "mixed opinion" that is capable of implying an underlying defamatory fact is actionable. *Milkovich v. Lorain Journal Co.,* 497 U.S. 1 (1990).

In one instance a television sports commentator called a soccer player a quitter and then at the end of the broadcast took a photograph of the athlete and drew a mustache and a beard on it, spat on the photograph, laid it on the floor and jumped on it, and then threw it off the set. The question is whether these antics are defamatory. The Colorado Court of Appeals said they were not and that the commentator's comments were merely opinions and thus constitutionally protected. These comments were not deliberate or reckless falsehoods, since the athlete did decide not to play for the team in question during playoffs. Therefore, these comments were not capable of defamatory meaning. *Brooks v. Paige*, 773 P.2d 1098 (Colo.App.1988).

B. PER SE

There are two forms of defamatory publication, libel and slander. Publication is a necessary element of the tort and is the means of communication of the defamatory statement to a third party. The tort of libel originally referred to the written or printed work whereas slander was oral. The distinction is that libel must have some embodiment in some permanent physical form. The slandered plaintiff must prove actual damages as opposed to libel where the damages are assumed to be greater because the language is in a more permanent form.

There are four exceptions to a plaintiff's requirement of proof in a slander action. A statement that imputes one of the four exceptions is slander per se or slander which is actionable per se. These instances are so egregious that no actual proof of damages is necessary to support an actionable slander claim. Slander per se occurs when one imputes a crime, imputes a loathsome disease, adversely affects the plaintiff in his trade, business or profession, or imputes unchastity to a woman. Therefore, if one accuses an athlete of suffering from AIDS or states that a coach lacks good sportsmanship and is a rowdy drunk, then these comments may be per se defamatory.

Many courts apply this rule: a libelous statement that imputes one of the exceptions is libel per se and any other libel is libel per quod. Under libel per quod the plaintiff must prove damages. Some decisions, however, accept the proposition that any libel is actionable because it is more permanent than the spoken word and is accordingly more circulated.

Other courts use the term "defamation per se," that is, defamation on its face, which is thereby actionable. In *Fawcett Publications, Inc. v. Morris*, 377 P.2d 42 (Okla.1962), the plaintiff was a member of the 1956 Oklahoma University football team and was allegedly defamed in a 1958 *True Magazine* article entitled "The Pill that can Kill Sports" in which that Oklahoma team was alleged to have used amphetamines. The court found that the article was defamatory on its face and was libel per se, in that it exposed the entire football team to a public hatred and contempt and tended to deprive the team and its members of any public confidence they might have earned. The reader was unequivocally informed that members of the team had illegally used drugs.

This case also stood for another principle: that as a member of the team, plaintiff could sue even though he was not specifically named in the libelous article. The court's view was that since it was libelous per se and since the suggestion of drug use is both criminal and adverse to plaintiff's professional and business standing, it libeled every member of the team including plaintiff even though he was not specifically named. Moreover, the court felt that the average reader would identify the player as a subject to these accusations since he was a starting player and thus not a changing element within the defamed group.

In *Sprewell v. NYP Holdings, Inc.*, 1 Misc.3d 847, 772 N.Y.S.2d 188 (2003), a professional basketball player, Latrell Sprewell, brought action against newspaper publisher and journalist for allegedly libeling him in a series of articles. The Court held that fact that average sports reader would already have been aware of previous incident in which player allegedly choked his former coach during practice did not, as a matter of law, preclude finding that later series of newspaper articles allegedly imputing the crimes of assault and/or battery to player further damaged his reputation. Additionally, statements about player in newspaper articles could be read as imputing crime or attempted assault to player, which, in light of prior publicity of incident in which player allegedly attempted to choke his former coach, was sufficiently serious to be actionable as libel per se without proof of special damages. Also, statements in newspaper articles implying that player delayed in reporting his injury from an alleged altercation to team management, whether implying that such delay was deliberate or merely negligent, defamed player in his business or profession, and were thus actionable as libel per se without proof of special damages. However, the N.Y. Supreme Court Appellate Division reversed and held that Sprewell could not recover damages for defamation (11 Misc.3d 1091(A), 819 N.Y.S.2d 851

(N.Y. Sup. Cty. 2006), rev'd 43 A.D.3d 16, 841 N.Y.S.2d 7 (N.Y.A.D. 1 Dept. 2007)).

C. PUBLIC FIGURES

Certain people must meet a heightened burden of proof of actual malice before they can maintain a successful libel suit. These certain individuals would include public officials and public figures. Public figures are people who by reason of their notoriety or success or their achievements or the manner in which they seek the public's attention are categorized as public personalities.

The first remedy of a defamatory victim is self-help, that is, using available opportunities to offset the lie or correct the error and thereby minimize its adverse impact on his or her reputation. Public officials and public figures enjoy significantly greater access to channels of communications and, therefore, have a much more realistic opportunity to counter false statements than a private individual would enjoy. Private individuals are more vulnerable to injury and the state's interest is correspondingly greater. More important is the likelihood that private individuals will lack the opportunity to rebut. Consequently, the press is allowed more room for error with public figures since the stars have greater access to the press for rebuttals than a truly private person.

Usually public figures want to be one, that is, they obtain that status and purposely assume roles of special prominence in the affairs of society.

Some occupy a position of such pervasive power and influence that they are public figures for all purposes; more commonly, however, public figures have thrust themselves to the forefront of a particular public controversy in order to influence the resolution of the issues involved. In either event, they invite attention and comment. Thus, not only can one be a public figure if he thrusts himself to the forefront of a public controversy but he also can be a public figure for a limited purpose.

The media is entitled to act on the assumption that public people have voluntarily exposed themselves to an increased risk of defamatory falsehood. Courts have focused on whether the libel plaintiff has voluntarily sought media attention in determining whether he or she is a public figure. Several courts have even held that individuals by entering certain lines of work have voluntarily exposed themselves to media attention. Entertainers and professional athletes in major sports are considered to be public figures. This presumption of a public figure is also applicable to coaches who share the limelight with their athletes. Player disagreements, coaching philosophy or just plain personality problems will always be given great attention by the media. Therefore, an individual who manages a professional sports team or who is involved with the management has voluntarily stepped into the public eye. Since the organization that he works for attracts and courts media attention, he is a public figure at least for the limited purpose of stories that relate to his job.

Athletes are usually deemed to be limited public figures. In sports, there are many personal factors in an athlete's life which may affect his career but which may not be the proper subject of unlimited publication.

It may be hypothetically possible for someone to become a public figure through no purposeful action of his own, but the instances of truly involuntary public figure status are exceedingly rare. One can be a public figure if one thrusts himself into the forefront of a public controversy like Bucky Woy, the sports agent who during a contract dispute with one of his athletes used the media (through press conferences) to help make his point. *Woy v. Turner*, 573 F.Supp. 35 (N.D.Ga.1983).

But in *Time, Inc. v. Firestone*, 424 U.S. 448 (1976), the court held that the spouse of a millionaire was not transformed into a public figure by filing for divorce. She had no less of a public forum than filing to assert her rights; she did not freely choose to publicize issues as to the propriety of her married life. She was compelled to seek the court by the State in order to obtain release from the bonds of matrimony.

In a 1980 case the court found that a football player and his wife, an ex-movie star, were limited public figures. *Brewer v. Memphis Pub. Co.*, 626 F.2d 1238 (5th Cir.1980); see also *Chuy v. Philadelphia Eagles Football Club,* 595 F.2d 1265 (3d Cir. 1979).

Every story that is related to a public career is
controlled by the *New York Times* standard. *New
York Times Co. v. Sullivan*, 376 U.S. 254 (1964).
That standard is that public officials and public
figures must demonstrate that the statements were
made with actual malice. In *Nussbaumer v. Time,
Inc.*, 1986 WL 12640 (Ohio App. 8 Dist.1986), the
plaintiff was in a high profile job with an organization, the Cleveland Browns, that sought and thrived
on media and public attention. Nussbaumer, an
official with the team, was viewed as a public figure
in a controversy where an article five years after
the event characterized him as "spying" on a team
meeting. A professional football team is a business
whose product is sold by having people purchase
tickets or watch the games on television. Media
attention is a critical tool to attract and keep the
public's interest. During the football season the
local daily paper carried at least one story on that
team every day; in fact, part of Nussbaumer's job
was to help this coverage by informing the media
about things that affected the club's performance.
The managing of a professional club attracts intense media coverage. Decisions that control what
a player will do on the field, coaching, and general
management philosophy are all publicized and
much discussed by the public. News conferences
are frequently held to announce changes that affect
the team. When Nussbaumer accepted a front office job with the Cleveland Browns, he stepped into
the public eye. He was in charge of player selection, and he helped arrange player trades with

other clubs, select possible choices in the college player draft, and negotiated contracts with players on the team. All of these chores directly affected who would be playing for the team; hence, these activities attracted continuing media coverage. Since the article in *Nussbaumer* dealt solely with the management of his team, Nussbaumer was required to demonstrate actual malice on the part of the defendant even though the article stated that he was spying on the head coach for the front office.

Plaintiff, a sportscaster, sued another sportscaster and a radio station alleging defamation, conspiracy, tort of outrage, and invasion of privacy. The Court held that defendant sportscaster's on-air statement that compared a conversation he had heard between plaintiff and another male participant on plaintiff's program to "oral sex" did not give rise to liability for defamation, tort of outrage, or invasion of privacy. Plaintiff/sportscaster was a public figure. A public figure cannot recover for defamation unless he proves by clear and convincing evidence that the defendant published the defamatory statement with actual malice, i.e., with knowledge that it was false or with reckless disregard of whether it was false or not. The most repulsive speech enjoys immunity against defamation liability provided it falls short of a deliberate or reckless untruth. *Finebaum v. Coulter,* 854 So.2d 1120 (Ala.2003).

A high school athlete brought defamation action against newspaper publisher for repeating rumors that he had exposed himself after championship basketball game. The Court held that the athlete was not a public figure. *Wilson v. Daily Gazette Co.,* 214 W.Va. 208, 588 S.E.2d 197 (2003). This high school athlete, although outstanding in both football and basketball, and the son of former professional football player Otis Wilson, was certainly not an all-purpose public figure. Additionally, the Court held that he was neither a limited purpose public figure nor an involuntary public figure.

The Supreme Court of Alabama in *Cottrell v. NCAA* held that former assistant football coaches at the University of Alabama who had been charged by the NCAA with recruiting violations, were limited purpose figures as regards their defamation claims asserted against the NCAA for their allegedly false statements in its penalty summary report.

However, assistant coach who served as recruiting coordinator was a private person in his defamation claim against independent recruiting scout who alleged that his coach stole money and videotapes. *Cottrell v. NCAA,* 975 So.2d 306 (Ala.2007).

Plaintiff was collegiate head football coach for seven years prior to being fired. He filed a complaint against the athletic director after a tense exchange with her. The athletic director confronted him about kicking a football towards trainers and a player during practice. A day after receiving a written memo memorializing these conversations, he was fired. After he was fired an article appeared in the local newspaper that states several incidents had led to his firing, which included information from anonymous university sources. After the article was published two university officials met with the parents of the players and implied that the coach had committed immoral acts. He sued the university for defamation. The court denied his motion to compel depositions of the reporters because the coach was a limited purpose public figure and the statements were a matter of public interest. The court also dismissed the claims because he could not show malice on the part of any of the university officials. *McGarry v. University of San Diego,* 154 Cal.App.4th 97, 64 Cal.Rptr.3d 467 (4th Dist.2007).

D. RULE OF REPOSE

Hypothetically, after one attains public status, he might possibly slip back into the veil of privacy. This is called the rule of repose. But this is difficult in sports since sports heroes are in many ways larger than life and therefore, their public image will last. A sports personality will usually always be a sports personality. However, there can be exceptions. One case in this area involved Jack Dempsey, the great heavyweight boxing champion. The champion was defamed 45 years after the alleged event occurred when in a *Sports Illustrated* article his manager claimed that he had loaded the champion's boxing gloves with plaster-of-paris. This was too much for even a sports icon, that is, to reach back almost 50 years to discuss non-noteworthy tactics. The court averred that reaching back that far is not within the purview of the *New York Times* standard; therefore, the glove loading was not cloaked with the veil of privilege. *Dempsey v. Time Inc.*, 43 Misc.2d 754, 252 N.Y.S.2d 186 (N.Y.Sup.1964).

However, *Johnston v. Time, Inc.*, 321 F.Supp. 837 (M.D.N.C.1970), a former professional basketball player sued a sports magazine for publishing an allegedly defamatory article by a professional basketball coach who described him as being "destroyed" by another player. This article was published 12 years after the event and nine years after plaintiff's retirement. At the time of publication, plaintiff was an assistant basketball coach at a university. There is no question that plaintiff was a public figure in his days as a basketball player, but this article was 12 years later. The lower court acknowledged that the rule of repose could apply. At the time of the publication of the article, the plaintiff did not command a continuing public interest nor did he have access to the means of a counter argument. The Court of Appeals, however, held that plaintiff was still a public figure since he remained in basketball.

Public officials will also usually continue their role as a public person after retirement. In Ohio, the retirement of a public school superintendent did not diminish his status as a public official concerning his alleged perjury at a high school athletic association hearing regarding a fracas which had occurred at a wrestling match and was related to his former position. In short, he was still a public figure for purposes of a defamation action. *Scott v. News–Herald*, 25 Ohio St.3d 243, 496 N.E.2d 699 (1986).

E. INVASION OF PRIVACY

Related to defamation is the right to protect one's privacy. The right to privacy will compensate the athlete for the distress created by the public exposure to accurate but private facts. Privacy is the right to be left alone and to live one's own life as one may choose, free from assault, intrusion or invasion except what can be justified by the clear needs of the community living under governmental law. However, to the extent the athlete is a public figure, the actual malice standard of *New York Times Co. v. Sullivan*, 376 U.S. 254 (1964), will still apply, since to recover one must prove that the defendant published the report with the knowledge of its falseness or in reckless disregard of the truth. In the absence of malice, invasion of privacy suits must deal with an athlete's private life as opposed to his athletic pursuits.

The test for determining whether information on the star's private life is newsworthy and thus privileged under the first amendment, or non-privileged and an invasion of privacy, is to discover if the information is the type that the public is entitled to or just a morbid and sensational delving into the private lives of people for some prurient machination.

In *Spahn v. Julian Messner, Inc.*, 18 N.Y.2d 324, 274 N.Y.S.2d 877, 221 N.E.2d 543 (1966), a publication of a fictitious biography of the Hall of Fame pitcher, Warren Spahn, was found to constitute an unauthorized exploitation of his personality for purposes of trade. Although Spahn gave away his rights to his public privacy, he still maintained the right to secure his privacy in his personal, nonpublic life.

Comparable to the right of privacy is the athlete's right to his commercial representation. The right of publicity recognizes the commercial value of a non-newsworthy pictorial representation and protects the propriety interests in the profitability of his public image. In *Ali v. Playgirl, Inc.*, 447 F.Supp. 723 (S.D.N.Y.1978), an unauthorized pictorial representation of Muhammed Ali was used for commercial purposes. The portrait depicted a nude black man sitting in a corner of a boxing ring and was claimed to be unmistakably recognizable as Muhammed Ali. The court upheld his right to the commercial value of this photograph. In *Zacchini v. Scripps–Howard Broadcasting Co.*, 433 U.S. 562 (1977), the court gave the entertainer, in this case, the "human cannonball," the power to protect his publicity rights in that it did not immunize the television station from liability for televising Zacchini's entire act.

On January 12, 2004, the United States Supreme Court "rejected without comment" an appeal from "Spawn" comic book creator Todd McFarlane, who argued that his comic depiction of NHL tough-guy Tony Twist as a mafia thug was free speech protected by the First Amendment. Twist is now free to pursue a second trial, which is the result of the reversal of a jury verdict in Twist's favor in 2000. Circuit Court Judge Robert H. Dierker, Jr., granted McFarlane's motion for judgment notwithstanding the verdict in an en banc decision, thus negating a $24.5 million St. Louis jury verdict for Twist. In the event Judge Dierker's verdict was overturned on appeal, his ruling provided for a new trial. *Doe v. TCI Cablevision of Missouri,* 30 Media L. Rep. (BNA) 2409, 2002 WL 1610972 (Mo.App.E.D.2002), transferred to Mo. S. Ct., 110 S.W.3d 363, 31 Media L. Rep. (BNA) 2025, 67 U.S.P.Q.2d (BNA) 1604 (Mo.2003) (judgment not withstanding the verdict reversed; judgment granting new trial affirmed), cert. denied, 540 U.S. 1106, 124 S.Ct. 1058, 157 L.Ed.2d 892 (2004).

The right of publicity and free speech issues at hand stem from the introduction of a character named "Anthony 'Tony Twist' Twistelli" to the Spawn comic in 1993. The fictional character, Tony Twist, is a mob guy who engages in murder and mayhem. The real life Tony Twist was an NHL hockey player known both for his "enforcer" abilities on the ice and his involvement with children's charities and the community. In 1997, Twist found out about the "Tony Twist" character when he was asked by children to autograph Spawn trading cards. In October 1997, Twist filed suit, seeking an injunction and damages for misappropriation of name and defamation. The defamation claim was dismissed. McFarlane defended against the misappropriation claim on First Amendment grounds. The Missouri Supreme Court ordered a new trial. Twist argued that the Spawn character, Anthony (Tony) Twistelli, damaged his image and cost him endorsement opportunities. The Missouri Supreme Court found the misappropriation of name claim to actually be a right of publicity claim and analyzed it under the following elements: (1) defendant used plaintiff's name as a symbol of his identity (2) without consent (3) and with the intent to obtain a commercial advantage. While elements (1) and (3) were both the subject of argument, the judgment notwithstanding the verdict was due to the belief that the latter had not been proved.

In *Doe v. McFarlane*, on remand to the Circuit Court, the court awarded $15 million. On appeal, the court affirmed and held that the creator's use of the hockey player's name was not protected speech. Additionally, the creator's admission in a magazine article that he named comic book character after hockey player, was not relevant to right-of-publicity claim.

F.   DEFENSES

Even though certain statements about athletes can certainly appear to be defamatory in their content, they may still be non-actionable if there are defenses that are available to the defendant, for example, truth, fair comment or privilege. Truth is a defense to any civil action for libel or slander; also, it is a defense that the comment was substantially true. For example, in *Nussbaumer v. Time, Inc.*, 1986 WL 12640 (Ohio App. 8 Dist.1986), defendant claimed that plaintiff spied on a team meeting after a loss to the Los Angeles Rams, but instead it occurred after a loss to the San Diego Chargers. The defendant's claim was substantially true.

Another way for a sportswriter to avoid defamation is the doctrine of fair comment. Everyone has a right to comment on matters of public interest if it is done fairly and with an honest purpose. Public individuals, especially those who engage in sports, must expect critical reviews, but they may not complain unless they are in fact falsely accused of wrong-doing. The *New York Times* standard requires that false comments about public figures must be knowing and in reckless disregard of the truth to be actionable. Reckless disregard means that the defendant entertained serious doubts as to the statement's truth before publication.

The corollary to fair comment is the first amendment right to express an opinion. Sports columns are usually opinions and thus protected. An Ohio Supreme Court case discussed the parameters of a sports columnist's right to express opinions. The key here was the determination of whether an alleged defamatory statement was an opinion or an assertion of fact; this determination is a question of law. *Scott v. News–Herald*, 25 Ohio St.3d 243, 496 N.E.2d 699 (1986). The standard to be applied is totality of the circumstances which will include specific language, whether the statement is verifiable, the general context of the statement, and the broader context in which the statement appears. Sports columns are traditionally the home of hyperbole and invective. Columns can be protected when the headlines of these captions show in some way that the statements are protected opinions (e.g., "in my opinion," etc.). When a column is prefaced with an opinion-like statement, then it is highly suggestive that it is indeed the opinion of the author; however, such language is not always dispositive, particularly in view of the potential for abuse.

In *Stepien v. Franklin*, 39 Ohio App.3d 47, 528 N.E.2d 1324 (1988), the former owner of the NBA Cleveland Cavaliers was verbally attacked by a radio sports talk show host. He was described as stupid, dumb, buffoon, nincompoop, scum, a cancer, an obscenity, gutless liar, unmitigated liar, pathological liar, egomaniac, nut, crazy, irrational and suicidal. Nevertheless, these attacks were viewed as opinions and thus constitutionally protected. The first amendment protects unrestricted debate on issues of concern to the public including what may well be viewed as vehement, caustic and unpleasant attacks. Public figures like the owner of this basketball team have thrust themselves in the public eye, and because of that they cannot later prevent others from criticizing their actions. Opinions are not capable of defamatory content; assertions of fact on the other hand are unprotected and thus capable of a defamatory meaning.

Sportswriters can also sue for defamation. In *Falls v. Sporting News Publ. Co.*, 834 F.2d 611 (6th Cir.1987), a long time columnist was terminated by his employer, who issued uncomplimentary remarks that categorized the writer as less energetic than other sportswriters and out of touch with the current sports scene and implied that plaintiff was on a "down swing." The court observed that certain opinions of public concern could qualify as forms of privileged criticism which are protected in the name of fair comment. There are three kinds of expressions of opinion. First, simple expression of opinion which occurs when the comment maker states the facts on which he bases his opinion and then expresses a comment as to the plaintiff's conduct, qualifications or character. The statement of facts and the expression of opinion are treated separately at common law in the sense that either or both could be defamatory. Secondly, a pure type of opinion may occur when the maker of the comment does not express the facts on which he bases an opinion but both parties of the communication know the facts or assume their existence and the comment is clearly based on those facts and does not imply the existence of other facts in order to justify that comment. The privilege of fair comment is said to apply to the pure type of opinion. Thirdly, the mixed type of opinion, while an opinion in form, is apparently based on facts regarding the plaintiff that have not been stated by the defendant or assumed to exist by the parties to the communication. The expression of the opinion gives rise to the inference that there are undisclosed facts which justify the forming of the opinion.

The Supreme Court, in *Gertz v. Robert Welch, Inc.*, 418 U.S. 323 (1974), determined that the common law rule that an opinion of the pure type may be a basis of an action for defamation offends the first amendment guarantee of freedom of speech. However, the mixed type of expression of opinion may still be the basis of defamation since it could imply undisclosed defamatory facts as the basis of the opinion. It is the court's responsibility to determine whether opinion can reasonably imply the assertion of undisclosed facts, and it is the responsibility of the jury to determine if this meaning was attributed by the recipient of the communication.

In *Falls,* the defendant's "on the down swing" comment, was held to be capable of a defamatory meaning since the jury could reasonably find that the defendant knew of undisclosed facts that could justify such an opinion. For example, the plaintiff's writing and reasoning ability might have deteriorated or the quality of his work might have declined to the point that other people had to rewrite or cover for him. Similarly, defendant's implication that plaintiff was inferior to his replacements could create a reasonable inference that the comment was also justified by the existence of other undisclosed facts, for example, the plaintiff did not work hard, etc.

CHAPTER 13

TORT DEFENSES

A. GENERALLY

There are many defenses that the stadium owner or team owner or school district can use in their attempts to avoid liability. The preeminent defenses are assumption of risk, contributory negligence and comparative negligence.

B. ASSUMPTION OF RISK

Assumption of risk can be defined as a voluntary assumption, expressed or implied, of a known and appreciated risk. A participant or a spectator who assumes the risk created by the conduct of another cannot recover when harm in fact occurs.

In sports or recreational activities, the plaintiff will assume the ordinary risks of the game; however, he does not assume the risk of injury from a violation of a duty owed him by the promoter or stadium operator and thus is not precluded from recovery for injury that results from their negligence. This duty will include reasonable care in the construction, maintenance and management of the facility and reasonable care with regards to the character of the exhibition and the customary con-

225

duct of invited patrons. But the operator is not an insurer of the safety of the plaintiff. For recovery for injuries sustained in a sports facility, the participant or spectator must prove both that specific acts or omissions constituted a breach of defendant's duty of care and that the breach was the proximate cause of the injury.

Professional baseball park operators are required to provide seats protected by screens for as large a number of patrons as may reasonably be expected to call for such seats on an ordinary day of attendance. A breach of this duty may constitute negligence which would make the operator liable to injured spectators. It is generally held that a spectator who has knowledge of the game and takes an unprotected seat will assume the risk of injuries from thrown or batted balls and thus cannot recover for those injuries when they occur.

Assumption of risk was once an impenetrable and monolithic defense. This, however, has markedly changed in recent years. Recovery is now allowed for injuries which result from safety violations. *Nabozny v. Barnhill*, 31 Ill.App.3d 212, 334 N.E.2d 258 (1975). Plaintiff can also recover for the intentional misconduct of another participant. *Bourque v. Duplechin*, 331 So.2d 40 (La.App. 3 Cir.1976). Participants also might recover when the injury was caused by the negligent acts of third persons, usually coaches or referees. *Nabozny* and *Bourque* both involved participants, as opposed to spectators. Voluntary participants usually are viewed to assume all risks that are incident to the contest which are also obvious and foreseeable.

Spectators assume the risk of hazards incident to the game. Spectators assume the risks that are a matter of common knowledge. Courts have allowed recovery where the risk of the sport was not considered common knowledge. Spectators will assume only the ordinary and inherent risks of attending sports activities. For example, a swinging gate at a baseball game and a baseball flying into an interior corridor are not ordinary risks and thus will not preclude recovery.

Spectators will also not assume the risk of unreasonable conduct by participants, e.g., a ball player who intentionally throws his bat into the stands. Assumption of risk will not apply as a complete bar when there is either a direct dereliction of a duty by the defendant or a lack of knowledge of the risk on the part of the plaintiff.

There may be a question of whether plaintiff had actual knowledge of the specific danger involved. This knowledge must include not only a general knowledge of the danger but also knowledge of the particular danger and the magnitude of the risk involved. Actual knowledge of the risk may be inferred from the circumstances.

For plaintiff to assume risk, he must knowingly and voluntarily encounter those risks which cause harm: he must also understand and appreciate the risks involved and accept the risk as well as the inherent possibility of the danger which can result from that risk.

The necessary ingredient for plaintiff to assume risk is knowledge: there must be a knowing assumption of risk which means that the plaintiff has actual knowledge of the risk involved or that knowledge is imputed because of certain observations and from that he should have reasonably known that the risk was involved.

For example, coaches can assume that a football player knows he may get hurt if he uses his head as a battering ram. The high school football player has a duty to ask his football coach questions concerning any matter on which he is not clear; and coaches have a right to assume that their players possess the intelligence and stock of information of a normal young man interested in sports. Therefore, it has been held that coaches can assume that a player knew of the possibility of injury that comes to the player who uses his head as a battering ram.

It has been held that voluntary participation in football games constitutes an implied consent to the normal risks that go with the bodily contact that is permitted by the rules of football. However, participants involved in contact sports do not automatically consent to contacts which are prohibited by the rules or customs of that sport, if those rules are designed for protection rather than the control of the mode of play.

1. Expressed

The injured spectator or participant may expressly assume the risk and waive his right to be free from those bodily contacts inherent in the sport, that is, he takes his chances and is therefore barred from recovery. The doctrine of expressed assumption of risk includes expressed covenants not to sue and situations of actual consent (such as voluntary participation in contact sports) which will create a complete bar to plaintiff's recovery against the negligent defendant.

In the determination of whether a plaintiff who is injured in a contact sport subjectively appreciates the risk giving rise to the injury, it is within the power of the jury to review all evidence as to what plaintiff really expected while participating in that sport. If plaintiff is found to have recognized the risk and continued participation in the face of danger, then the defendant can raise the defense of expressed assumption of risk.

2. Implied

An injured spectator or plaintiff may also impliedly assume the risk of injury. This situation will arise when the plaintiff is aware of the risk created by defendant's negligence but continues to voluntarily proceed. Plaintiff's consent is implied from the continuation of the activity in that he goes forward although aware of the risk. Plaintiff's actions in assuming the risk may be unreasonable or reasonable, however, if the conduct is unreasonable then it is no different from contributory negligence.

Some states have abolished the doctrine of implied assumption of risk by statute. In other states the defense is still applicable.

Under the doctrine of primary implied assumption of risk, in *Foronda ex rel. Estate of Foronda v. Hawaii International Boxing Club*, 96 Hawai'i 51, 25 P.3d 826 (2001), a boxer assumed all risks that contributed to his death. As regards whether defendants created or enhanced risk beyond that inherent to the sport by failing to utilize two spacer ties, properly tied, on each side of the ring; there was no evidence that the ring was otherwise unsafe or substandard; in fact, it appeared that the coach, in renovating and maintaining the ring, reduced rather than increased the inherent risks.

3. Jockeys and Car Racers

Assumption of risk is more intransigent as a doctrine in the ultra-hazardous sports of horse racing and race car driving. Where a horse racing jockey is injured in an accident and sues a fellow jockey to recover for injuries sustained as a result of the other jockey's alleged negligence; barring a specific intent to injure on the part of the fellow jockey there can be no recovery for injuries which the jockey sustained as a result of jockey error or careless riding.

In a case where a jockey was thrown and injured during a race as a result of the closing of two other horses, it was held that reasonable implied assumption of risk remained a viable defense in the absence of comparative fault since the jockey assumed the risk of injury as a result of the negligence of another jockey even though the second jockey was in violation of the rules as long as that jockey's conduct was not reckless. *Ordway v. Superior Court*, 198 Cal.App.3d 98, 243 Cal.Rptr. 536 (1988).

Thoroughbred horse racing by its very nature is a sport that poses great peril to its participants. It is a situation where up to a dozen horses each weighing up to 1200 pounds break from a starting point and attempt to gain a preferred position at the rail as the first turn approaches. On these charging horses moving at full speed are persons weighing approximately 100 pounds; these jockeys also drive for position.

In this attempt to acquire the best position, due to both jockey error and the difficulties in controlling a sensitive thoroughbred horse, contacts and collisions are common place which occasionally result in spills that create injuries. These dangers are inherent to the sport of horse racing and are well known to the jockeys especially those who have significant experience in riding professionally.

Although a participant in a horse race does relieve his fellow participants of the duty of care in respect to those dangers that are normally associated with the sport, he does not relieve them of the duty to refrain from reckless, wanton or intentionally injurious conduct. A jockey also does not have to assume the risk brought about by the negligence of others.

A jockey was injured when his horse veered across the track towards a negligently placed exit gap; he then brought a negligence action against the race track alleging that the accident resulted from the negligent placing of the exit gap. The jockey was deemed not to have assumed the risk of the negligent placement of the gap in the race track which was also determined to be the proximate cause of his injuries. *Ashcroft v. Calder Race Course, Inc.*, 492 So.2d 1309 (Fla.1986).

Even more obvious is the application of assumption of risk to the race car driver. When a race car driver has actual knowledge of the presence of a disabled automobile off the drag strip and several hundred feet beyond the finish line, he will be held to know the conditions of the track. Since he knew of the inherent danger, he actually and subjectively comprehended the risk of undertaking the trial run under the existing conditions including proceeding in the face of a known danger by voluntarily racing his car and knowingly assuming the risk of injuring himself. *Robillard v. P & R Racetracks, Inc.*, 405 So.2d 1203 (La.App. 1 Cir.1981).

A race car driver, whether he signs a release or not, assumes the risks of known, inherent dangers by simply entering the race. When an oil slick developed on the surface of a race track during the course of a race, it constituted a development over which the defendant had no control. Yet when an accident occurred as a natural result of the slick, it was held to be among the type of risks which were assumed by the plaintiff in taking part in the race. *Seymour v. New Bremen Speedway, Inc.*, 31 Ohio App.2d 141, 287 N.E.2d 111 (1971).

4. Skiing, Golf and Baseball

Assumption of risk is also applicable to skiing, golf and baseball spectator injuries. Skiers are business invitees. The operators owe the skiers the duty to exercise reasonable care to keep the premises in a safe condition so that skiers are not unnecessarily or unreasonably exposed to danger. A skiing operator not only owes the duty to protect the skier from known dangers but is also required to exercise reasonable care in locating unknown dangers which pose a potential threat to skiers. Whether the duty to exercise reasonable care has been discharged is the key issue in ski injury litigation.

Often the issue of reasonable care is not reached in a ski injury suit, because the skier assumes the risk inherent in that sport. For a skier to assume the risk, the defendant must show that plaintiff knew the risk, appreciated the extent of those risks and accepted those risks voluntarily. Thus, where ski areas have changed the nature of the sport by improving slope grooving and maintenance, one can argue that these improvements make it questionable that the hazards encountered by skiers are currently obvious and necessary to the sport and therefore, they might be viewed as no longer inherent to that sport.

Since skiing may be a large part of a particular local or state economy, many state legislatures have enacted statutes protecting resorts. Some statutes have created presumptions that skiers, rather than resorts, are responsible for collisions occurring between skiers and other individuals and for injuries not incurred on improved trails or slopes.

Generally, courts have held that skiers assume the risk of dangers that are obvious, necessary or inherent in skiing. Courts have held that the hazards presented by the presence of a tree stump or a metal pole used for ski lift supports, snow making or other utilities are obvious, necessary or inherent to the sport and thus assumed by participants. A skier who collides with a pole subsequent to a collision with another skier is required to demonstrate that the pole constituted a hazard capable of producing liability on the part of the resort independent of the initial collision.

Courts generally reject plaintiff's argument that skiing is an activity to which a standard greater than reasonable ordinary care applies. Ski resorts will also protect themselves through releases on the back of lift tickets which waive the skier's right to bring an action against the resort.

Ski resorts must use at least reasonable care in the marking of trails and taking other precautions to assure that skiers do not stray from the designated trails. Liability, may be imposed on a ski area for selling its service in such a manner that allows persons on toboggans access to the same hill used by beginning skiers. Likewise, the variation of the terrain of a slope, a loose bush and an unmarked rock outcropping have been found to be hazards for which ski areas may be held liable.

In golf, golfers assume only some of the risks of the game. It is negligent for a golfer to drive another ball without warning when his prior drive is already on the fairway: he has a duty to warn under those circumstances. Also, when a golfer allows another party to play through and is struck by a golf ball, assumption of the risk will bar recovery even though the defendant did not yell "fore" since plaintiff voluntarily placed himself in the orbit of the shot of the person behind him. Plaintiff purposely requested the defendant to shoot; therefore, he certainly had notice that defendant would indeed shoot. This notice obviated defendant's duty to warn.

As regards to baseball spectators, the spectator assumes the foreseeable and known risks of a baseball game. For example, he would assume the risk of a foul ball at a evening baseball game. However, spectators do not assume injuries from baseballs that are projected into the stands by non-normal means. Also, a spectator does not assume the risk of a foul ball while she was walking in the inner corridor of a baseball stadium. *Jones v. Three Rivers Management Corp.*, 483 Pa. 75, 394 A.2d 546 (1978).

5. Minors

Assumption of risk takes a slightly different variation when the injured person is a minor. A young child need not conform to the behavioral standard which is reasonable as an adult, that is, his conduct is to be judged by the standards that are expected from a child of a like age, intelligence and experience. However, when a minor was injured when a baseball bat flew from the hands of another minor, evidence failed to establish defendant's negligence. The minor plaintiff voluntarily participated in the game and thus assumed the risk of injury. *Gaspard v. Grain Dealers Mut. Ins. Co.*, 131 So.2d 831 (La.App. 3 Cir.1961).

C. CONTRIBUTORY NEGLIGENCE

If an athlete or spectator with knowledge of conditions goes into danger then he or she assumes the consequences of that danger even though there might be negligence on the part of another; if his or her negligence is the proximate cause of the injury then he or she is barred from recovery. This is contributory negligence.

In a health spa slip and fall case, a spa member who allegedly slipped and fell on a foreign substance in the shower was contributorily negligent where she had used the spa facilities on several occasions and had heard that the showers were slippery, filthy and dirty. She exposed herself to the risk without ever protesting the danger and without ascertaining the condition of the showers on that day.

Contributory negligence is a question for determination by the jury, but when the evidence admits but to one reasonable inference then it becomes a matter of law for determination by the court. There will be no recovery for negligently inflicted injuries if the injured person proximately contributed to his own injury.

Contributory negligence is conduct that falls below the standards which a plaintiff should meet for his own protection and which is a contributing cause of his injuries. It frequently involves plaintiff's inadequate failure to notice and appreciate danger; however, absent notice to the contrary, a spectator can usually assume that the premises are reasonably safe. Plaintiff's contributory negligence is a complete bar to recovery even if the plaintiff was only slightly negligent and defendant was primarily so.

At common law, a plaintiff who had negligently contributed to his own injury was barred from recovering damages. This situation imposes a duty for his acts or omissions towards others with a similar obligation existing as regards his own safety. Therefore, if a plaintiff does not use reasonable care for his own safety and his lack of care is a substantial factor in causing his own injury, a defendant may raise plaintiff's contribution in defense of his own acts. Under this theory, the existence of contributory negligence on the part of the plaintiff is sufficient to preclude recovery.

For minors, contributory negligence involves three distinct issues: the existence of capacity on the part of the child, the standard of care to be applied and conformance by that child to the applicable standard of care. Courts have recognized the general rule that the ultimate determination of a child's capacity to be contributorily negligent is a question of fact, and some courts have specifically held that children within a certain age group as a matter of law may not be contributorily negligent. Generally, children over five may or may not be contributorily negligent depending upon the circumstances.

Where a young golfer was struck by the ball hit by a mature golfer, the older golfer must be aware that young children possess limited judgment and are likely at times to forget the dangers and behave in a thoughtless manner. The negligence of a child golfer in standing on the fairway or raising his head from safety into danger when the mature golfer drove a golf ball at his general direction was not contributory negligence which would bar recovery for injuries. A nine-year old may be capable of contributory negligence but like a 12–year old, he is not held to the adult standards of comprehending danger and the duty of self care. *Outlaw v. Bituminous Ins. Co.*, 357 So.2d 1350 (La.App. 4 Cir.1978).

A youth football coach's contributory negligence outweighed any negligence on the part of a football team or league in setting up football games on adjacent fields without any sideline distance between them. The coach was coaching his own team when players from the game behind him ran into his leg and caused a knee injury. The coach was familiar with the risks involved in youth football games, had seen countless youth football games, and was fully aware that the players who injured him were playing in a game directly behind him. Sideline areas, including the area in which the coach stood, were in zone of danger. Thus, the coach's own contributory negligence in standing in that area precluded recovery for his negligence. *Shain v. Racine Raiders Football Club, Inc.,* 297 Wis.2d 869, 726 N.W.2d 346 (App.2006).

D. COMPARATIVE NEGLIGENCE

Many states have responded to the onerous effects of assumption of risk and contributory negligence by creating comparative negligence as an alternative. Comparative negligence compares the fault of defendant to that of plaintiff. Although each state may have a different version of comparative negligence, the essential principle is that plaintiff will be allowed to recover at least a proportion of the damages sustained if plaintiff's negligence was proportionally less than the negligence of defendant.

Also, assumption of risk is not necessarily merged into the defense of contributory negligence under principles of comparative negligence. For example, an experienced skater who intentionally and voluntarily chose to perform an unsupervised traverse on a ramp while holding a ski pole in either hand will assume the risk of injury. *Gary v. Party Time Co.,* 434 So.2d 338 (Fla.App. 3 Dist.1983).

E. WARNINGS

Courts favor warnings. Warnings explain the inherent dangers that are involved in a certain activity as opposed to a release which by means of an agreement releases the defendant from all potential liability that might accrue from injuries to participants.

Participants must be warned about inherent risks in a sport. The more dangerous the sport, the more important the warnings. It is preferable to place warnings in writing and to read through the written warnings with players and parents, if the sport is a particularly hazardous one and the players are minors. A signed, written warning, dated and understood by players and parents, will assist the coach in his attempt to defend himself against liability.

Certain types of sports equipment, e.g., football helmets or trampolines should also contain general warnings that explain the hazards that are associated with that product. Each warning should contain a description of the demands and stresses that the sport places on the human body. It is especially important that the description include any potential cardiac stress so that the players can appreciate the physiological demands that are a part of the sport.

On the other hand, it has been held that a stadium owner did not have the duty to warn an injured spectator of the danger of the possibility of being hit by a foul ball while in the area behind the first base dugout; the stadium owner met his duty to provide adequately screened seats for those desiring them even though spectators chose to sit elsewhere. *Friedman v. Houston Sports Association*, 731 S.W.2d 572 (Tex.App.—Hous. 1 Dist. 1987).

An owner or occupier of premises owes a duty to invitees to exercise reasonable care such as inspecting the premises for any latent defects and making safe any defects or providing an adequate warning about those defects.

In practice, warning sometimes merge with waivers. There are usually both warnings and waivers on the back of a baseball ticket. There are also statements on the back of season passes that acknowledge the hazards that exist in skiing and that specifically waive injury from the carelessness or negligence of fellow skiers. However, in a suit against a ski area for injuries when plaintiff collided with a metal pole after a collision with another skier, the court analyzed that type of warning and waiver, and since the document was ambiguous, the court decided against the drawer of that document. *Rosen v. LTV Recreational Development, Inc.*, 569 F.2d 1117 (10th Cir.1978).

F. WAIVERS

The main feature of all exculpatory agreements is to relieve one party of all or part of his responsibility to another. A waiver is simply one form of an exculpatory agreement. A waiver is a contract and presents a conflict between two fundamental legal axioms: one in contracts where all persons are free to contract as they desire, and one in negligence where one is responsible for negligent acts which cause injury to others. Although exculpatory clauses are valid in certain circumstances, they are not favored in the law. Any clause which exonerates a party from liability will be strictly construed against the party that benefits. If the clause is ambiguous in scope or purports to release the benefiting party from liability for intentional, willful or wanton acts, it will not be enforced. Waivers, to be valid, must be nonambiguous, particular as to the wording regarding liability, not against public policy, not intimate condemnation of gross negligence, and not allow results that would indicate a large disparity in bargaining power.

The most significant aspect of a release is the particular words that are used. For example, when the injured plaintiff is an expert in a particular sport, the failure of the release to include the word "negligence" does not preclude other language which may have the same effect. The release will be enforceable as long as the release agreement is sufficiently clear to show the party's intent that defendant is to be held harmless for any injury that is caused by his own negligence.

A waiver will be valid if it does not contravene any policy of law and does not involve a quasi-public entity that supports or supplies essential services, but rather relates to the private affairs of individuals.

If there is no ambiguity and the contract is not one of adhesion, the exculpatory clause will not violate public policy. Ambiguity will not be an issue if the clause simply purports to exonerate a facility owner from liability for acts of negligence and for negligence only. However, where a contract is drafted unilaterally by a business enterprise and forced on an unwilling and often unknowing public for services that cannot readily be obtained elsewhere then that contract is an "adhesion contract", that is, a contract that is generally not bargained for but one that is imposed on the other party on a take it or leave it basis.

However, this view will not apply to health club memberships when there is no disparity in bargaining power and no evidence that the services were necessary or that the services could not be obtained elsewhere. Since the services were not essential, suitable for public regulation or of such great importance as to be clearly a necessity for some members of the public, then the waiver clause did not violate public policy.

However, it is universally held that a waiver will not bar a claim for gross negligence. This is correct even though the same exculpatory clause would bar an action for simple negligence. Similarly, a disclaimer is against public policy if it is inconspicuous.

Where a release was obtained only from racing participants and those choosing to be in the pit area of a race track, the exculpatory clause was held unenforceable as regards protecting the race track owner against possible dram shop liability. The exculpatory agreement did not release the defendant from dram shop liability, because if it did it would be against public policy. *Scheff v. Homestretch, Inc.*, 60 Ill.App.3d 424, 18 Ill.Dec. 152, 377 N.E.2d 305 (1978).

Waivers that public school students are required to sign as a prerequisite for participation in high school sports which release the school district from the consequences of all future school district negligence are invalid because they are a violation of public policy. *Wagenblast v. Odessa School District*, 110 Wash.2d 845, 758 P.2d 968 (1988).

The factors that are essential in a determination of whether a release will violate public policy include the following: whether the agreement concerns the type of business that is generally thought suitable for public regulation; whether the party seeking the waiver is engaged in performing services of great importance to the public; whether the party holds itself out as willing to perform these services for any member of the public; whether the party invoking exculpation possesses the decisive advantage and bargaining strength; whether the party thus invoking confronts the public with a standardized adhesion contract; and whether as a result of this contract the purchaser is placed under the control of the seller and, therefore, subject to the risk of carelessness by the seller.

1. Foot Races

An integral part of any jogger's routine is to scrutinize the ubiquitous waiver on the form for road race participation. A waiver of this sort will not release the defendant from all types of liability. The question is when and under what circumstances this release will be applicable.

The leading case in this area involves a young law student who was gravely injured while participating in a 10,000 meter event in Atlanta, Georgia, in July. The young man accused the organizer of being negligent by failing to adequately warn that he could suffer serious injuries from participation in the extreme heat and humidity; also, that defendant failed to provide liquids and medical facilities along the race and failed to ascertain whether all entrants were physically capable of completing the race. However, the plaintiff not only signed but understood the waiver agreement.

Each participant was required to pay a fee and sign a very specific and particular application form that described the race and the physical conditioning necessary in a very specific manner, along with a particular description of the type of heat and humidity that would be expected. The application form added that all of this made it "a grueling ten thousand meter race." *Williams v. Cox Enterprises, Inc.*, 159 Ga.App. 333, 283 S.E.2d 367 (1981).

Regardless of the explicit warning, the law student, as a result of extreme exertion in the exact conditions that were described in the waiver, succumbed to heat prostration which resulted in a permanent impairment of some motor functions. It was decided that this waiver was not against public policy. There was no disparity in bargaining position. Plaintiff alleged that road racing had become so popular and this race in particular was one of a kind, that he and other participants were under enormous pressure to enter it under whatever terms were offered to them. The court saw this argument as "ludicrous." The court also determined that recovery was precluded under assumption of risk because the waiver was described in extremely particular terms and the plaintiff agreed that he read the waiver and was already aware of the danger. Because of this, any injury that resulted from over heating and dehydration could not reasonably be construed to have emanated from any breach of duty on the part of the defendant.

2. Car Races

Releases also will usually be allowed in ultra-hazardous sporting activities such as race car driving, especially when the signed waiver is voluntary and a product of knowledgeable agreement. Waivers for participation in a vehicular racing event will especially be upheld where there is valuable consideration as an exchange for a signed released. The valuable consideration deemed important in law is the right to participate in the event with the hope of winning prize money. In this situation, the waiver constitutes a full defense to any claim for damages except those due to wanton or willful negligence. However, willful negligence does not occur, for example, when an oil slick develops on the surface of the race track during the course of the race and as a result creates an accident which causes injury to plaintiff.　*Seymour v. New Bremen Speedway, Inc.*, 31 Ohio App.2d 141, 287 N.E.2d 111 (1971).

Even a race car driving release, however, will not waive liability for defendant's gross negligence. Similarly, it will not always act as a bar to an action by decedent's spouse on the grounds of loss of consortium (the courts are split).　Nor will a waiver release a defendant for liability under the state's dram shop act, since that type of waiver even under the conditions of a car race would violate public policy.　Another question is, who is included under a waiver which stipulated that both "participants" and "advertisers" were released from liability;　it was held that the tire distributor and tire manufacturer respectively, were included in those descriptions.　*Kircos v. Goodyear Tire and Rubber Co.*, 108 Mich.App. 781, 311 N.W.2d 139 (1981).

3.　Minors

Generally when a minor is involved with a release, the law will not bind him to it.　This is correct whether he signs it or whether it's signed by his parents or any combination thereof.　A minor who was injured while attending an ice hockey clinic was not bound by the fact that his father had signed a release on behalf of his son which purported to exempt the city and the hockey league for injuries.　Also, since the father's cause of action was derivative to his child, the father's waiver was not barred by the waiver that involved his child.

The father's cause of action was derivative to his son's and drew its life from the existence of the cause of action which inured to the benefit of the infant. A parent cannot release a child's cause of action. *Doyle v. Bowdoin College*, 403 A.2d 1206 (Me.1979).

A minor's waiver is unenforceable because a child does not have the capacity to contract; the traditional rule for minors is that they can disaffirm a contract unless it involves life's necessities. Since recreation is not a necessity then an exculpatory contract signed by a minor is usually voidable. This is true even when a minor misrepresents his age.

G. SOVEREIGN IMMUNITY

Another way for tortfeasors to avoid liability for sports-related injuries is to plead immunity based on the fact that the particular activity was protected from liability. These immunities are designated as either sovereign or charitable. Recently, however, courts and legislatures have made broad-based attacks against these doctrines so that in many jurisdictions, public, private and charitable institutions receive the same status as most other tortfeasors, that is, they must compensate those who are injured by their wrongful acts.

Broadly, sovereign immunity provides that a state or its instrumentalities shall not be subject to suit without its consent. This immunity relies on several policy considerations including that as a sovereign entity the state can do no wrong, that public agencies have limited funds and can expend them only for public purposes, that public bodies cannot be responsible for the torts of their employees, and that public bodies do not possess the authority to commit torts. Immunity in its purest form will protect actions of all public bodies, including school districts, their employees, school boards, racing commissions, board members of a state university, etc., in as much as they are agents or instrumentalities of the state itself.

Although sovereign immunity once provided a broad umbrella of protection to state and state-related agencies, consent to suit has been provided by the legislatures in many states in a variety of ways. Where such consent is not allowed, courts in several jurisdictions have responded to the criticism of sovereign immunity by abrogating it through judicial action.

When trying to understand sovereign immunity, it is important to distinguish between state and municipal entities. Municipal corporations have a duality which have influenced their tort liabilities. These corporations are entities that perform both governmental functions and subdivisions with special local interests which are comparable to those of a private corporation and not shared by the state. The doctrine of sovereign immunity has attempted to respond to this duality. Immunities are provided for the acts of the municipal corporation while in its governmental posture, but not when its in a corporate posture. Political or governmental functions can be described as those which are necessary to the well-being of the community. Therefore, public education and protecting public health are governmental functions while mere amusement or entertainment is not.

An example of the governmental-private duality is provided by cases that turned on the status of the party which is utilizing a public owned stadium for sporting events. When a public school is using the stadium, courts have generally found that the contests are a part of the state's educational responsibility and thus are governmental functions to which sovereign immunity would apply. However, if a public school leases its stadium, courts have held that through that process the school has conducted a proprietary activity and will be liable for injuries sustained as a result of negligent facility maintenance. One convenient standard in determining whether an event is governmental or private is the charging of a fee; but usually that is viewed as only one factor in reaching a determination.

In a Michigan case, when an injured football player brought suit against both his football coach and a helmet manufacturer for damages which left him a quadriplegic, the court held that football coaches were entitled to governmental immunity. The court stated that a public school in the operation of its athletic program will include the administration and supervision of football and, thus, is entitled to governmental immunity. Teachers and their supervisors are entitled to immunity when their duties are performed within the scope of their employment. The argument is that a physical education program, as either part of a general curriculum or as an extracurricular activity, is in furtherance of and an integral part of the total public education provided to students. Football is a part of these day-to-day operations and is therefore immune. *Churilla v. School District*, 105 Mich.App. 32, 306 N.W.2d 381 (1981).

Similarly, in Illinois, a high school varsity football player brought an action against the board of education and his coach for injuries sustained in football. The court held that the coaches were immune under the school code from liability for ordinary negligence as it relates to a player's injuries due to allegedly defective equipment. Absent willful and wanton conduct in the course of their supervision, which encompasses inspecting and supplying students with appropriate equipment, coaches will be immune from liability for alleged negligence under the Illinois school code.

1. Discretionary Acts

The doctrine of discretionary immunity allows state officials and their employees to receive partial immunity but usually only for discretionary duties as opposed to ministerial duties. Under the doctrine of discretionary immunity, state officials are not absolutely immune from suit, but ordinarily will be liable only in the performance of ministerial duties. The question is what type of activities are properly construed as ministerial as opposed to discretionary. Discretionary duties are those which call for the exercise of the public official's judgment or discretion; for these types of activities, he will not be personally liable to an individual for damages unless he is guilty of a willful or malicious wrong. A ministerial duty is one in which nothing is left to discretion, that is, a simple, definite duty arising under and because of stated conditions as imposed by law. An official duty is ministerial when it is absolute, certain and imperative, involving only the execution of a specific duty arising from fixed and designated facts.

The determination of what is discretionary as opposed to ministerial is often a difficult one. The distinction is nebulous and abstruse because almost any act involves some aspects of both freedom of choice and perfunctory execution. Generally, the answer will be decided after evaluating the nature, quality and the complexity of the decision-making process involved in that particular responsibility. The question is deciding whether a teacher's performance in a physical education course is a discretionary or ministerial function. If it is discretionary then defendant is protected by the doctrine of discretionary immunity. Applicability of this doctrine is not dependent upon whether a person's duty requires some degree of judgment and discretion. The crucial analysis centers on the nature of the act undertaken. Decisions intended to be protected by discretionary immunity are those made on the planning level of conduct.

The doctrine of discretionary immunity is intended to protect public officials or employees whose policy making duties include choosing between various alternatives even if one of the options is to do nothing. If a teacher never engages in the type of decision making that is relevant to developing and administering a physical education curriculum, then his negligence will not involve decision-making on the planning level. Therefore, the teacher's activities would be construed as ministerial rather than discretionary.

2. Policy Considerations

Traditionally the crown could do no wrong and hence suit against the crown was not allowed. The primary policy consideration behind this view was that for governmental officials to do their job they must be free from the fear of suit.

At direct conflict with this idea is the equitable principle that every plaintiff must have his day to plead his case when an alleged negligent action produces injury. This is especially true in sports where robust activity is coupled with the possibility of catastrophic injury. Although the strength of the immunity doctrine has been decreased by both the governmental/proprietary distinction and the ministerial/discretionary question, this relic still survives. Therefore, it is imperative that the first step for plaintiff's attorney is to evaluate the status of the immunity doctrine in the relevant jurisdiction before evaluating a sports injury case that involves a governmental or charitable institution.

H. CHARITABLE IMMUNITY

Like sovereign immunity, charitable immunity, if applicable, will provide an umbrella from suits against charitable institutions that is comparable to that provided governmental institutions. Like governmental immunity, the bases of charitable immunity are large and diverse. The most prevalent is the concept of a trust fund in which charitable funds are held in trust for charitable purposes and may not be diverted for other uses. Another theory is that charities are immune from the doctrine of respondeat superior and therefore are not responsible for the injury-causing actions of their employees since no profit is derived from their work. Under this theory liability can result only from the acts of the charity itself.

However, even where this doctrine is still applicable it has exceptions and distinctions which neutralize it to a great extent. One distinction is that charities may be liable to strangers but cannot be liable to their beneficiaries, that is, to the recipients of their charity. Another distinction has been drawn between employees and non-employees, with only employees allowed to recover from that charitable organization. Finally, charities have been held liable for activities which involve non-charitable aspects: e.g., when admission fees are charged or for those activities that constitute a nuisance.

I. RECREATIONAL USE STATUTES

A recent addition to the immunity umbrella is the so-called Recreational Use Statutes (R.U.S.). Although they vary from state to state, the basic principle is that landowners who allow free recreational use of their property, owe no duty of care to keep their premises in safe condition or warn of dangerous or hazardous conditions. However, if a fee is paid for use, then the statute will not apply. As with sovereign immunity, these statutes offer some protection from suit for those entities (either public or private) that perform a "state-like" function, namely, providing the means and opportunities for the masses to satiate their recreational and sporting needs.

CHAPTER 14

WORKERS' COMPENSATION

Usually, the first step in recovering for an injured athlete is to sue in tort. However, there is a parallel universe created by state statutes that provides for employees to secure compensation for employment-related injuries. This alternate form of recovery is workers' compensation. The relevant statutes will differ from state to state. Even though a singular description does not exist, the following is an overview of the basic attributes of the various state laws.

A. PROFESSIONAL SPORTS

Professional athletes and other employees of professional teams will usually come under the protection of their particular state's workers' compensation statutes. However, there are certain states that specifically exclude professional athletes from coverage.

As a general caveat, the basic requirements for any workers' compensation statutes is usually that the person must be an employee who was injured by an accident while involved in a job-related function. Workers' compensation will also generally be the exclusive remedy against the employer for that injury if the injury is covered under the statute; if that is true then the employee will not have the option to bring a judicial action against either his employer or his co-workers for injuries that result from the same accident.

For injuries to professional athletes, it must be determined whether the injured person is an employee. For an injury to a horse jockey it was held that because he was employed and paid by the job as an independent contractor, he did not come under the control of the owner or trainer and thus was not an employee. Since he was not an employee he was not covered under workers' compensation. *Munday v. Churchill Downs, Inc.*, 600 S.W.2d 487 (Ky.App.1980).

Another obstacle for the professional athlete is whether the event that created the injury was an accident. This can be an interesting question in physical sports such as football. Where the injury occurred to an offensive guard while blocking, that event could not be construed to be an accident under the applicable workers' compensation statutes. That was because the relevant statute only protected against injuries that were the result of an accident, that is, trauma from unexpected or unforeseen events in the usual course of the employee's occupation. This statute did not contemplate that the deliberate collision between human beings during a professional football game was an accident, or that the injury, in the usual course of his occupation was caused by an unexpected event. *Palmer v. Kansas City Chiefs Football Club*, 621 S.W.2d 350 (Mo.App.W.D.1981).

In *Bayless v. Philadelphia National League Club*, 472 F.Supp. 625 (E.D.Pa.1979), a former pitcher brought an action against a professional baseball team seeking damages for mental illness allegedly caused by the team's administration of drugs following complaints of severe back pain. Plaintiff based his claims on a breach of defendant's contractual duty to provide him with sound medical care in the event that his skills were impaired by injury. The court held that the pitcher's exclusive remedy was workers' compensation. In the athlete's complaint, he averred that his injury was caused by the club's failure to provide medical care thus placing himself within the ambit of the Pennsylvania Workmen's Compensation Act.

The pitcher then attempted to skirt coverage of the Act by placing his injury in the same category as an exception for exposure to diseases whose gradual progression would not constitute an accident. However, the court disagreed on the grounds that the pitcher's complaint established that the onset of mental illness was directly traceable to treatment received from the club and not a gradual progression of a disease that preexisted the club's administration of the drugs. The court also held that the Act applies equally to high paid professional athletes as well as lower paid athletes; it applies to all athletes regardless of their earnings.

B.   COLLEGIATE SPORTS

In professional sports the injured athlete is an employee of the team.   A more ambiguous situation occurs when the injured athlete is a member of a college sports team.   The question then is whether the injured athlete is an employee for purposes of workers' compensation.   If the athlete was a walk-on and had no financial relationship with the school, the courts will not view that person as an employee for workers' compensation purposes. However, some courts will view the athlete as an employee if the athlete is paid in anyway whatsoever for his participation.   For scholarship athletes, the general view is that if there is a contract to pay for the athlete's participation, then there is a relationship on which to base compensation coverage. If there is a continued receipt of a job, free meals or money, and it is contingent upon the athlete's continued participation in a sport, then a contract to play that sport has been created.   Since there is a contract of employment, then compensation coverage will exist for student-athletes who are injured in accidents during the course of their employment as an "athlete."

C.   EMPLOYER–BASED SPORTS

Another frequently used category of sports compensation plaintiffs covers those that are injured in employment-related sports, such as team softball or bowling leagues.   Employment-related sporting activities that have been brought under the coverage of workers' compensation include those which occur on the jobsite during job hours, those which are controlled by the employer who furnishes uniforms, league fees, equipment and encourages participation; and those that the employer will receive direct benefit from, such as advertisement, public relations or improved customer relations.

The key to coverage is whether the employer has brought this sporting activity within the course of employment. If there are few or no indices that bring the activity under the course of employment, workers' compensation will not be applicable. This includes those sports-related activities that are significantly employee-generated, have little contact with the employer and are basically an ad hoc employee recreational activity. However, the opposite is true in those situations when the employer actively encourages and provides for participation in the sporting enterprise.

The more indices that show that the activity is within the course of employment then there is more of a chance that the court will find that coverage applies. Indices can include that the team was entered in an industrial league and played against teams of other employers who were involved in a similar occupation as defendant employer; that a championship trophy is displayed on the employer's premises; that the employer paid the entrance fee to the league; that the employer required bats, balls, and other equipment to be kept on the company's premises; that equipment is paid for by the employer and that the name of the company was displayed on the uniforms of the athletes; and that the uniforms were paid for by the employer and/or that the employer paid towards the costs of each uniform. Other indices would be that the umpires of each game were paid for by the employer; that a raffle was allowed to be held in cooperation with the employer and the members of the team on the employer's premises during working hours in order to help gain more financial support for the team; that schedules were passed out at the plant, copies of which were given to the employer; and that when the employer withdrew support from the team, it resulted in the disbanding of the team for lack of support. All these factors are the type which will be used in the determination of whether the activity falls within the course of employment. *Scott v. Workmen's Compensation Appeal Board*, 113 Pa.Cmwlth. 80, 536 A.2d 492 (1988).

D. NON–PARTICIPANTS

There is always the possibility that coaches, physical education teachers, team managers, stadium attendants, trainers, umpires, referees, and similar athletic personnel will also be employees and because of that fall under the coverage of workers' compensation statutes for job-related injuries. Because of their proximity to the field of action, trainers, referees and coaches are the most likely nonathletic personnel to be injured and thus apply for coverage.

Trainers and referees are usually not viewed as employees but instead as independent contractors who are not covered under the applicable workers' compensation statute. The question is who has the right to control the details of another's performance. If there is control of the details of the performance of the referee or the trainer, then that could be used to show the necessary indices to prove employee-status.

Coaches, on the other hand, are usually employees of the school district or team. However, in those situations where the coach is not a salaried employee per se, it must be determined what type of relationship exists between the coach and the supervising authority.

CHAPTER 15

CRIMINAL LIABILITY

A. VIOLENCE IN SPORTS

There is no question that some degree of violence is a part of sports. This is especially true in contact sports. This is even more true in the extreme contact sports, like football and hockey. There is some degree of violent contact that is unavoidable in any contact sport. However, arguably there is an unnecessary amount of violence in today's professional sports. This excessive violence has spilled over to amateur sports.

One attempt to deter unnecessary violence is through league and disciplinary rules in professional sports. Each team and league through their SPK and their collective bargaining agreement (c.b.a.) have established rules and procedures to penalize and control violence that is deemed to be unnecessary and not an inherent part of the sport. These procedures include an independent arbitrator to decide if there is a conflict between the player and league as regards disciplinary disputes. But, these documents contain ambiguous terminology which does not precisely reflect the degree that violent behavior cannot exceed. For example, the standard language is "contrary to the best interests of the game." Subjective language of this type does not clearly define the parameters of acceptable behavior.

Another way to curb violence is civil actions for injuries that occur through participant contact. These tort cases are few and far between, and they usually revolve around principles of negligence and/or assault and battery. They have not effectively decreased the amount of unnecessary violence that is evident today in professional sports.

A third way to deter violence is to punish the offenders criminally. Criminal sanctions might be useful in this endeavor if one accepts that the rationale behind criminal punishment is deterrence. As an example, other athletes would be on notice that incidents of that type will no longer be tolerated or unpunished. The trial of a professional athlete would be a highly publicized media event which would be both embarrassing to all parties and expensive. The time lost through litigation and possibly a jail sentence would be irretrievable. The end result is that the athlete's career might be significantly altered or even destroyed.

The threshold question that arises when one contemplates criminal sanctions for violent conduct is to determine if the facts require the imposition of criminal sanctions, i.e., if the particular penal laws in question are intended to be applied to conduct in sporting events. Next, one needs to concentrate on the elements of the particular crime, for example, assault and battery, or manslaughter, and then to ascertain if these elements were present at the time of the incident. It must be determined if the accused had a defense. The standard defense is that the injured person consented to the injury by voluntary engagement in that sport. Also, if the conduct was provoked, a self-defense argument might arise.

In *City of Cleveland v. Swiecicki*, 149 Ohio App.3d 77, 775 N.E.2d 899 (2002), defendant was convicted of disorderly conduct and resisting arrest in connection with his heckling of a professional baseball player. The Court held that words uttered by defendant to professional baseball player did not rise to level of criminal disorderly conduct, and defendant's heckling did not provide a reasonable police officer basis to believe that it constituted a criminal offense, as was required to convict defendant of resisting arrest.

Of course, the major "sporting event" in 2004 was the brawl that occurred during an NBA game between the Indiana Pacers and the Detroit Pistons on November 19, 2004. One Pacer, Ron Artest ran into the stands after he was pelted with ice and liquid. Commissioner Stern levied the harshest penalties ever and some players and fans were charged with assault and battery.

B. CRIMINAL ACTION GENERALLY

The philosophy behind criminal law is based on society's need to be free from harmful conduct. Criminal law defines criminal contact and prescribes the punishment to be imposed on persons convicted of that proscribed conduct. Violence and possibly criminal conduct, however, is looked on differently when that violence occurs in a sporting or recreational event. That is because the harm and violence are confined to the participants who obviously know and assume the risks that are inherent to the game. Also the innocent public is not subjected to that risk of physical harm. The question becomes whether the violent conduct is accidental or within the rules of the particular sport or criminal conduct. The crux is that certain sports are extremely physical and violent physical conduct is part of the sport. For battery to be a crime, there must be illegality. Yet, that element is to some extent negated in conventional sports. However, arguably the most onerous and heinous acts that occur in contact sports such as football, hockey and basketball extend beyond any possible justification that is built within the scope of the game.

The criminal defendant will use consent and self-defense as defenses in a criminal prosecution that accrues from sports violence. Consent usually is not a defense to a criminal act since one cannot consent to be a victim. In the crime of battery, consent of the victim is not an element, but in certain battery cases, the unlawful force application element is not present because of consent. Consent to application of force per se is not unlawful. The difficult problem with the consent defense is establishing a demarcation between reasonably foreseeable hazards that one can consent to and unreasonably foreseeable hazards to which one cannot consent. One can knowingly consent to the normal violence associated with a sport, whereas, one cannot knowingly consent to non-normal physical contact. To use the consent defense in this context, one must ascertain for each particular sport the type of violence that is foreseeable and thus capable of consent.

C. INHERENTLY VIOLENT SPORTS

In inherently violent sports, the question is to what type of violent conduct is consent a defense. Consent is arguably a defense to criminal charges that arise from injury so long as it is a reasonably foreseeable hazard of that sport and not a result of intentional conduct that is not reasonably related to that particular sport. Although there is no direct American authority on point, the situation where consent would not be a defense is arguably the type of unforeseeable and unexpected punching incident that occurs every once in a while in professional basketball. An athlete would arguably be criminally responsible for an intentional and reckless act. As regards the consent defense, an athlete would not be deemed to consent to intentional or reckless acts that are not reasonably related to the conduct of the particular sport.

A certain degree of consent to violent behavior and contact is expected in professional contact sports. Consent is an effective defense to conduct that does not threaten or cause serious injury or to reasonably foreseeable conduct that results in reasonably foreseeable harm. Therefore, in the attempt to prove that plaintiff did not consent to defendant's violent conduct, one must prove that defendant's behavior was not or could not have been reasonably foreseeable by the plaintiff. There is a difficulty in distinguishing between reasonably foreseeable conduct and injurious non-foreseeable harmful conduct; this difficulty as a rule will discourage athletes from seeking criminal charges against fellow participants and has added to the dearth of criminal prosecutions in sports cases. If criminal prosecutions are going to be regularly pursued in sports that have an inherently violent nature drawn into their very existence, like football and hockey, it is essential to define and ascertain the acts that will incur criminal penalty. Currently, there are no neat and predictable lines as to when a certain act will go beyond the parameters of the game and the rules and be eligible for criminal sanctions.

D.   BATTERY

Battery is the criminal offense that is most usually applicable in cases of sports violence. A battery is an unlawful application of force to the person of another that results in bodily injury. Battery possesses an element of unlawfulness and that is the key to the question of whether battery is relevant or not in the sports arena. Society and the criminal codes have made sports violence an exception from criminal laws by treating it as lawful. The type of

activity that is unlawful on a city street might be
entirely lawful when used in a professional football
game. The elements of battery are a guilty state of
mind, an act, a physical touching of a victim and
causation. Battery's state of mind does not require
actual intent. Criminal negligence or a conscious
disregard of known and serious risks will be sufficient. Both states of mind allow for aggravated
battery and will punish battery as a felony when
the use of a deadly weapon or the causing of serious
bodily injury is a part of the criminal act. Deadly
objects can be ordinary objects if they are used in a
way that may cause death. For example, hockey
sticks or baseball bats, under certain circumstances,
could easily qualify as deadly objects.

In *Goff v. Clarke*, 302 A.D.2d 725, 755 N.Y.S.2d
493 (2003), a varsity basketball player brought personal injury action against high school basketball
coach, alleging he was hurt during an altercation
that occurred while the two were waiting for practice to begin. The Court held that triable issue of
fact as to whether contact between high school
basketball coach and varsity basketball player during physical altercation that occurred while the two
were waiting for practice to begin was offensive or
whether it was jovial in nature, precluding summary judgment.

E.   THE CANADIAN APPROACH

American courts have been very hesitant to cross
the line between physical contact that is a part of

violent sports and that type of contact that is deemed to be criminal behavior. However, in Canada, criminal prosecutors have used criminal laws much more frequently against athletes accused of violent contact towards fellow players. This is especially true in hockey because of its popularity and the dangerousness that is inherent in the use of ice skates and hockey sticks. There have been numerous criminal convictions for offenses that involve player to player violence in Canada, as opposed to a near absolute dearth of reported cases in the United States.

As in the United States, the major problem that Canadian courts have faced is the status of the consent defense. The statutory definition of assault in Canada specifies that the intentional application of force to the person of another must be without that person's consent; a finding that there was consent will negate a necessary element of this offense. Three issues have evolved in the consent defense in reported Canadian cases: consent implied by participation, consent implied by specific acts and a public policy limitation on ones' ability to consent.

Self-defense is also a tool that is commonly used by defendants in Canadian criminal prosecutions for assault and battery. A defendant may use whatever force is reasonably necessary to repel an attack; this is especially logical in the sport of hockey where one is attacking with a hockey stick while his opponent is using his stick to parry blows and thrusts.

In the case of *Regina v. Maki,* 14 D.L.R.3d 164 (1970) and *Regina v. Green,* 16 D.L.R.3d 137 (1970), defendants were able to successfully assert the defense of self-defense in hockey injury prosecutions. In *Green,* the court found that plaintiff did indeed consent to being hit with a glove during a hockey match. An incident of this type was found to be a common occurrence in that sport. The court, however, brushed over the consent defense and justified defendant's action by the use of a self-defense explanation which ended with the court's conclusion that defendant did nothing "more in the circumstances than protecting himself."

For a successful assertion of self-defense, defendant must show that he was not the aggressor. This creates a problem in sports injury cases since the athlete will often fail to qualify as a nonaggressor. Therefore, self-defense will be unavailable in the majority of sports violence cases.

In the Canadian case of *Regina v. Ahmed (Bobby)* 2001 WL 31397586 (CA (Crim Div) 2002), defendant/soccer player initially was involved in a scuffle with the opposing goalkeeper and trouble broke out involving both teams. During that initial trouble the defendant punched the goalkeeper in the face. He broke the goalkeeper's nose and caused it to bleed profusely. The referee then intervened. He sent the defendant off the pitch and in doing so held up a red card. With the red card aloft, the defendant punched the referee in the face. The referee contended that was done with a fist, but the defendant said it was with an open hand. In any event, he caused bruising and soreness to the referee's left check. That act constituted common assault.

The defendant then left the pitch. There was approximately a 30 second intermission. He walked around behind the goal where the goalkeeper was receiving treatment for his broken nose. The defendant then moved quickly towards the goalkeeper and kicked him with force in the face.

The goalkeeper's injuries were serious. He spent three nights in a hospital, where he was treated for a broken jaw, a broken eye socket and the broken nose. His jaws were wired together and three metal plates and 13 screws were inserted. When arrested some three months later the defendant admitted pushing the referee. He denied kicking the goalkeeper. The referee did not consent to any form of physical contact, and in this particular case he was particularly defenseless, having one arm raised in the air with a red card in it. So far as the goalkeeper is concerned, the more violent of the two blows was inflicted when he was off the field of play, lying on the ground completely defenseless behind the goal. If there is some lesser penalty applicable to those who are actually engaged in sports, it would not be available here for this defendant. Defendant has been violent and unruly on numerous occasions in the past; accordingly, his appeal was denied and his conviction for causing grievous bodily harm was affirmed.

CHAPTER 16

AMATEUR SPORTS

A. GENERALLY

The term, "amateur athlete," is a true oxymoron. Amateurism was at one time a pure recreational outlet for the upper class. Today, all amateur sports are tinged with some shadings of professionalism. The distinction between amateur and professional athletes is ambiguous and uncertain. Amateur athletes of the past did not expect remuneration in any form for their athletic endeavors. However, this is certainly different today: for example, many college athletes are supported by scholarships. Also, many college athletic programs are a grooming ground for professional sports. The student athlete is subject to rigid rules, requirements and restrictions.

B. ADMINISTRATION

Amateur sports can be divided into two basic forms: restricted competition and unrestricted competition.

Restricted competition includes high school and collegiate competition. It means that competition is restricted to essentially the same groups at different levels. Administratively, competition is controlled and organized by athletic conferences or associations or leagues which encompass high schools and colleges. These entities establish rules of competition and organize the means of scheduling competition within these groups. Part of their function is to ascertain and establish participant eligibility. These entities are established to insure that their members comply with the pertinent rules and regulations; they will determine if inappropriate conduct has occurred. They will also impose sanctions if applicable to either the individual athlete or the school.

Unrestricted competition, on the other hand, is open to all athletes. An example would be Olympic competition, which in the United States is controlled by the United States Olympic Committee (USOC). This type of competition allows competition among all types of people and groups and is not restricted by age or college or other restrictive criterion.

C.　STATUS OF ATHLETE

What is amateur sports turns on the status of the amateur athlete. If one is an amateur then one cannot by definition also be a professional. But the applicable categorizations are ambivalent, especially in the context of collegiate sports where a well known amateur athlete can also be a quasi-professional since he is under scholarship and perhaps creating revenue in other ways. The definition of an amateur is defined by the governing body of that particular sport and for that particular athlete. The definition of an amateur athlete may change from one organization to another. For example, it is possible that an individual can be viewed as an amateur under the rules of the USOC but not recognized as an amateur under NCAA rules.

D. RULE-MAKING

The courts are generally reluctant to overrule the rules, regulations and restrictions of the athletic associations as regards eligibility, participation and discipline of their members. Generally, courts will not interfere with the internal affairs of voluntary associations. Unless there is mistake, fraud, collusion or arbitrariness, the decisions and the rules of the governing body will be accepted by the courts as conclusive.

Voluntary associations may adopt reasonable by-laws, rules and regulations which will be valid and binding on their members unless their rules violate law or public policy. Courts eschew the responsibility of inquiring into the expediency, practicability or wisdom of these rules and regulations. Courts will not substitute their interpretation of an association's rules and regulations for those interpretations that are placed on these rules by the association itself, so long as the association's interpretations are fair and reasonable.

E. NCAA

The NCAA is only one of a very large number of groups of governing bodies that control athletic participation in amateur sports; however, regarding college sports, it is easily the most important one and perhaps it is the most important governing body in sports of any type at any level. The NCAA is controversial in that many critics view it as paternalistic. There has been much debate, for example, on the various propositions (e.g., proposition 42, proposition 48 and proposition 16) which limit academic eligibility based on achievement on standardized tests and high school grade point averages in core courses.

The NCAA was founded in the early 1900's and throughout the years has offered championships in a variety of sports. It eventually obtained football television contracts, and accordingly, greatly increased its financial and regulatory powers. It is a voluntary, unincorporated association of colleges of which approximately 50 percent are state supported. At the present, the NCAA is composed of more than 1300 member schools; all schools that are accredited by a recognized academic accrediting agency will meet NCAA standards and may become a member. Not only does it sponsor national championships but it also possesses the authority to make and enforce rules and regulations. The purpose of the NCAA is to formulate policy and regulations that in essence govern almost all aspects of intercollegiate athletic participation.

The NCAA is governed by a large and detailed compendium of rules and regulations. This compendium, or manual, contains the constitution and bylaws, as established at the annual convention of its members; it also contains interpretations and executive actions that emanate from these conventions. In between the annual conventions, NCAA affairs are controlled by a council, its executive committee and a paid staff. The interpretation and enforcement of the large body of NCAA rules, regulations and precedents are interpreted, enforced, and reviewed by legislative assistants and enforcement personnel; attorneys are involved when and if litigation occurs.

The NCAA general policies were formally promulgated at their annual convention. However, it is no longer one school, one vote. The governing structure is changed so that policy is now implemented through a series of levels (see enclosed chart for the procedures that make up the process for approving legislation). It has a professional staff with headquarters in Indianapolis. When the convention is not taking place, policy is established, controlled, and directed by the NCAA council which is elected by the entire membership at the annual meeting.

In *NCAA v. Lasege*, 53 S.W.3d 77 (Ky.2001), the university and student athlete who had been declared ineligible to compete in intercollegiate basketball by NCAA, sought a temporary injunction requiring the NCAA to reinstate the student's athletic eligibility. The Circuit Court entered the injunction and banned the association from imposing future restitution sanctions if the injunction was subsequently reversed. The Supreme Court of Kentucky, however, held that the injunction was an abuse of discretion and the trial court could not enjoin NCAA from imposing restitutionary sanctions pursuant to bylaw which university agreed to abide by.

In *Bloom v. NCAA*, 93 P.3d 621 (Colo.App.2004), a state college football player and professional skier sought preliminary relief, enjoining college and NCAA from application of its bylaws, which restricted him from engaging in paid entertainment and commercial endorsement work in connection with his skiing career. The Court held that football player had standing as a third-party beneficiary to challenge bylaws, but he was not entitled to injunctive relief, as he failed to demonstrate that there was a reasonable possibility of success on the merits.

In *NCAA v. Yeo*, 114 S.W.3d 584 (Tex.App.— Austin 2003), an intercollegiate swimmer and former Olympian from Singapore who transferred from Cal–Berkeley to the University of Texas ran afoul of the NCAA transfer rules. The Court, however, found that the swimmer was denied due process. The Court held that she had a constitutionally protected property interest in her athletic reputation as an Olympian swimmer, which was formed prior to her enrollment at Cal–Berkeley. Joscelin

Yeo had an established liberty interest in her reputation as an athlete and was thus entitled to due process. The University of Texas, as a state actor, had an obligation to protect that liberty interest; the university breached this duty by failing to provide notice (of the problems with her eligibility) to Yeo.

On January10, 2005, the NCAA Division I Board of Directors adopted a new academic reform structure, the Academic Performance Program, which will impose "contemporaneous penalties" on Division I college sports teams whose athletes' performance in the classroom falls below a new minimum standard. The Board approved use of the Academic Progress Rate, which is based on individual academic performance and retention over a five-year period and will apply to all Division I men's and women's sports starting in the 2005–06 school year. If a team's APR falls below the minimum cut score of 925, roughly equivalent to an expected fifty percent graduation rate, the NCAA will penalize the offending team by reducing its available scholarships by up to ten percent. Currently, the NCAA estimates that 7.4% of all Division I sports teams, including 30.7% of football, 23.9% of baseball, and 20.1% of men's basketball teams do not meet the APR cut score of 925. The NCAA also estimates that 51.2% of the 325 Division I schools have at least one team that does not currently meet the standard. The Committee on Academic performance is drafting the second phase of the program, "historical penalties," which will be more severe and directed at schools with ongoing noncompliance.

In the appendix, we have included the Knight Foundation Commission on Inter–Collegiate Athletics. It sets the standards that should be effectuated if there's any hope to bring any real change to big-time collegiate athletics.

NCAA Division I Legislative Process

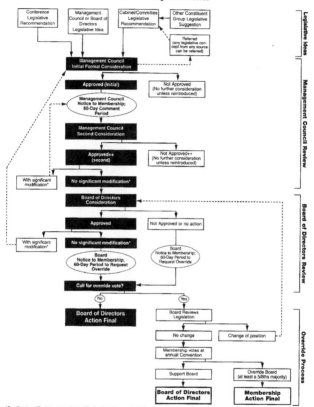

*Significant modification = a greater modification from the current rule than the original proposal.
++On a topic for which the Management Council has been delegated final authority by the Board of Directors; the override process begins at this point.
Note: During the Management Council's first and third meetings of each calendar year (e.g., January and July meetings), the Management Council shall be authorized to adopt only emergency, noncontroversial legislation, subject to approval by the Division I Board of Directors.

CHAPTER 17

ELIGIBILITY

A. GENERALLY

The key to amateur sports is the question of eligibility. Eligibility is the decision by the athletic governing body of whether a particular athlete or team is eligible to participate in a specific sport or a specific event. Establishing eligibility under a particular rule or bylaw is the province of the applicable governing association. The question is whether a denial of eligibility is a violation of that participant's constitutional or civil rights. An athlete's right to participate may be protected by the constitutional guarantees of due process and equal protection.

B. SCOPE OF ELIGIBILITY RULES

Eligibility rules cover all of the possible requirements and rules that might control a potential athlete including age, years of participation and academic standards. They range from grade point average to length of hair, transfer rules, red shirting rules, the number of semesters enrolled in school and married status. All these elements are used as a means to restrict an athlete's eligibility to participate. Whatever the regulation, it still has the same common objectives: the protection of the athlete, the promotion of education and the continuation of amateurism. A further objective is the control and regulation of a system of fair competition between the various schools and their athletes.

C. PARTICIPATION AS A RIGHT OR PRIVILEGE

The threshold question in an analysis of the eligibility of the student athlete to participate is whether that individual has a right or privilege to participate. When there is a right, then the relationship between the athlete and the governing body which administers the competition will be on a much different legal status than if the participation is viewed as a mere privilege. The question becomes whether an athlete in a public institution has a sufficiently important interest in participation so as to require due process safeguards. If the questioned interest is a right, then due process will apply. To receive due process protection, the constitutionally guaranteed right must be either a liberty or property interest.

There is a great difference in the way that high school and intercollegiate sports can be analyzed. For example, a high school athlete will receive no present economic benefit from participation; his only benefit is the possibility of the receipt of an offer of a college scholarship. This possibility is too speculative to be recognized as a property right.

However, a college athlete can receive a scholarship of substantial monetary value. Scholarships often cover the complete cost of attending a school; therefore, for a college athlete the right to participate is not a mere speculative interest but a property right of some present economic value. *Gulf South Conference v. Boyd*, 369 So.2d 553 (Ala.1979).

One federal district court case has also recognized an athlete's limited property interest in being allowed to participate in intercollegiate sports. *Hall v. University of Minnesota*, 530 F.Supp. 104 (D.Minn.1982). In this case, procedural due process was ignored when a basketball player (who had the requisite g.p.a. to continue in school but did not have sufficient credits for a particular program) was disallowed the opportunity to participate further in intercollegiate basketball. The court held that he had a sufficient property interest in the continuation of his basketball career to warrant constitutional protection since it was a distinct possibility that this lack of playing time would affect his ability to be drafted by a professional basketball league and earn a livelihood as a basketball player.

Yet, in a Court of Appeals case, the court found that the interest of student athletes including scholarship athletes to participate in intercollegiate hockey did not rise to the level of any right that would earn due process protection in connection with the NCAA's imposition of sanctions against the school for failure to declare several of its players ineligible. *Colorado Seminary v. NCAA*, 570 F.2d

320 (10th Cir.1978). The court found no difference between high school and collegiate athletes. The court did concede that though other courts may aver that scholarships create a distinction between high school and collegiate sports, that type of distinction is more of a difference in degree. The court observed that the fundamental positions of these athletes are the same and the goals and issues are the same. Since the same relations exist between the primary academic functions of both colleges and high schools, it was held that the degree of difference does not lead to a different result.

In high school sports, the courts rarely find that a right to participate exists. In the Texas no pass, no play case, for example, the court held that fundamental rights are born in the express and implied protection of personal liberties as recognized in federal and state constitutions. Therefore, a student's so-called right to participate in extracurricular activities does not rise to the same level as the right to free speech or religion both of which have long been recognized as fundamental rights. *Spring Branch I.S.D. v. Stamos*, 695 S.W.2d 556 (Tex.1985).

Although the opportunity to participate in extracurricular activities is not by itself a property interest, under certain circumstances a high school student can establish an entitlement to due process in connection with his suspension and exclusion from high school athletics. *Tiffany v. Arizona Interscholastic Association, Inc.*, 151 Ariz. 134, 726 P.2d 231

(App.1986); and *Boyd v. Board of Directors of McGehee School District*, 612 F.Supp. 86 (E.D.Ark. 1985).

D. STATE ACTORS

In a determination of the eligibility of an athlete, it is essential that one ascertains if the association's regulation is deemed to be state action. Generally, the protections of the 14th Amendment, due process and equal protection, will not extend to private conduct that abridges only individual rights. The question is whether the actions of the governing body are state action or fall under the color of state action. This question is extremely important as regards the actions of the NCAA. At one time, this was a fairly close question. However, a 1988 Supreme Court case suggests that NCAA eligibility regulations may no longer be viewed as state action. *NCAA v. Tarkanian*, 488 U.S. 179 (1988).

Tarkanian is a narrowly drawn opinion that establishes that the NCAA did not assume the role of the state when it directed a state university to initiate certain particular actions against one of its employees. This case, however, does not definitively settle the question of whether the NCAA can *ever* be a state actor. The court observed that the action of removing a coach from a state institution is a state action. However, in *Tarkanian* the NCAA did not take part in that particular action.

Even after *Tarkanian*, state action nonetheless might lie if a university by embracing the NCAA's rules transforms them into state rules and thereby arguably transforms the NCAA into a state actor. Some states, e.g., Texas, have passed legislation that provides for liability for violation of an NCAA rule. Vernon's Texas Statutes and Codes; Civil Practice & Remedies Code § 131. With legislation of this type the NCAA's regulations will arguably be deemed to represent state action.

On the other hand, all actions by a state high school athletic association will usually be viewed as state action for constitutional purposes. An example is the action of a state high school association that declares a high school must forfeit football games when an ineligible player suited up; this action is construed to be state action for constitutional purposes. *Florida High School Activities Association, Inc. v. Bradshaw*, 369 So.2d 398 (Fla.App. 2 Dist.1979). Also, a state athletic association, which is a purely voluntary group with a membership made up of 85% public schools, has sufficient public character to confer state action status on the activities of the association. *Griffin High School v. Illinois High School Association*, 822 F.2d 671 (7th Cir.1987).

In *Brentwood Academy v. Tennessee Secondary School Athletic Association*, 531 U.S. 288 (2001), plaintiff sued the Association alleging, *inter alia,* violation of its First Amendment rights and its 14th Amendments rights of substantive and procedural due process, and sought a permanent injunction barring the TSSAA from enforcing its recruitment rule. The rule prohibits "use of undue influence. . . to secure or retain a student for athletic purposes." The claims against Brentwood included providing free game tickets to a middle-school team, impermissible off-season practice, and urging students who have already agreed to play at Brentwood to attend spring football practice. The TSSAA found the school guilty with penalties that included fines, probation, no postseason play, and finding certain athletes ineligible. The appeals court found for TSSAA on the grounds that it is not a state actor; the United States Supreme Court, however, in 2001, reversed and remanded.

The state action question has been reviewed in the context of evaluating the legality of a mandatory drug testing program for high school athletes. In that case, a public school district, as opposed to a state athletic association, established the requirement that all varsity athletes must consent to submit to random urine analysis drug testing as a prerequisite to interscholastic athletic participation. This regulation was viewed as an action that was initiated under the color of state law. *Schaill v. Tippecanoe County School Corporation*, 864 F.2d 1309 (7th Cir. 1988).

E. DUE PROCESS AND EQUAL PROTECTION

After determining whether a regulation is state action, one must review it for purposes of equal protection. Although it is acceptable to classify per se, it is not acceptable to differentiate among classes when the purposes behind classification are not constitutionally permissible. Permissibility is determined by applying either the permissive or strict standard of review. If the standard is the permissive one, all that is required is that there must be a reasonable relation to the stated purpose. The strict standard, however, requires that classifications be precise and substantially justified. The strict standard will be applied whenever a classification touches on a fundamental interest, e.g., freedom of religion, or is based on a suspect criteria, e.g., race or national origin. When a suspect criteria is involved, constitutional permissibility will be determined by whether the classification promotes a compelling interest of the governing body. Usually, participation in sports is not a fundamental right; and therefore, eligibility is not entitled to a strict standard of review. However, a strict standard of review might still be applied if the classification is based upon suspect criteria.

Equal protection will only require a rational relation to a legitimate state interest if the regulation does not infringe upon fundamental rights and does not burden an inherently suspect class. In a Texas Appeals case it was held that a regulation that prohibits married high school students from participation in sports was a violation of the equal protection clause. There was no logical basis for the married student rule since the right to marry is a basic and fundamental right; therefore, the no marriage rule established a classification of individuals that was treated differently than other students without promoting a compelling state interest. *Bell v. Lone Oak Independent School District*, 507 S.W.2d 636 (Tex.Civ.App.—Texarkana 1974).

In *Jones v. West Virginia State Board of Education*, 218 W.Va. 52, 622 S.E.2d 289 (2005), the West Virginia Supreme Court for Appeals decided that the home-schooled children can be excluded from sports. Aaron Jones was home schooled. In order for Aaron to participate on a middle school wrestling team, he must get approval from the West Virginia Secondary School Activities Commission (WVSSAC). But he also must be enrolled full-time in a WVSSAC participating school. Jones filed a complaint against the school officials seeking declatory, equitable and injunctive relief. Surprisingly, the circuit court entered a preliminary injunction permitting Aaron to immediately participate based on its findings that school official inter alia violated the home-schooled student's right to equal protection. The appellate court reversed, finding that the circuit court erred on the equal protection claim, since prohibiting home-schooled children from participating in interscholastic athletics does not violate equal protections under West Virginia's state constitution. In short, the court found that the WVSSAC did not exceed its statutory authority in promulgating a rule pertaining to the eligibility requirements for home-schooled children to participate in interscholastic athletics.

However, in another Texas case, a summer camp rule was found to be constitutional. This rule did not allow students to participate in interscholastic sports if they attended a same sport summer camp. The compelling state interest was that the rule sought to achieve a balance in interscholastic athletics. This interest outweighed a parent's freedom of choice in family matters as regards the student's participation in summer activities. *Kite v. Marshall*, 661 F.2d 1027 (5th Cir.1981).

In a 1981 Texas Supreme Court case, a state's sports association's non-transfer rule which declared all non-seniors ineligible for varsity football and basketball competition for one year following their transfer to a new school was held to be unconstitutional on equal protection grounds. The court stressed the over-inclusiveness of the rule in light of its intended purpose of discouraging the recruitment of student athletes and the irrebuttable presumption created by that rule. In light of these two factors, the court declared the rule not rationally related to its intended purpose. *Sullivan v. University Interscholastic League*, 616 S.W.2d 170 (Tex. 1981).

However, in the Texas no pass, no play case, the rule provided a strong incentive to participate in extracurricular activities and to maintain a minimal level of performance. In view of the rule's objective to promote and improve scholastic performance, the court found that the rule was rationally related to a legitimate state interest of creating quality education. *Spring Branch I.S.D. v. Stamos*, 695 S.W.2d 556 (Tex.1985).

The next basic area of review is whether due process exists. Due process is used to eliminate regulations which are overbroad in application or those that overlook more reasonable alternatives, which are less restrictive of protected liberties. Procedural due process will only apply where a state or federal action is involved, the aggrieved party is a person, and an interest in life, liberty or property is threatened.

Due process as a whole is flexible and calls for such procedural protections as the particular situation might demand. Where a student asked for a hardship waiver from an athletic association's rule that limited eligibility to those 19 years old or younger, the court recognized that the student did not have a constitutional right to participate in high school sports, but concluded that the executive board of the association was unreasonable, capricious and arbitrary when it failed to exercise its discretion in even considering the student's request for a hardship waiver from this rule. *Tiffany v. Arizona Interscholastic Association, Inc.*, 151 Ariz. 134, 726 P.2d 231 (App.1986).

F. TYPES OF RULES

There are many rules, but they all possess the same theme of attempting to control the way in which an individual will be deemed to be eligible to participate in high school sports. Usually these rules involve around such broad concepts as the "no transfer" rule, the anti-marriage rule, rules that relate eligibility to grade point average, no-agent rules and anti-red shirting rules.

1. Red Shirting

The concept of "red shirting" is a tendency of some schools to hold students back academically so they can develop their bodies and playing abilities in the hope of increasing their potential for athletic success. In an attempt to stop this practice, some associations have devised eligibility rules to prevent red shirting. These rules can be classified as four year rules, eight semester rules or age rules. All these regulations have in common the goal of restricting eligibility to a certain time period and thus thwarting attempts to red shirt. With these so-called anti-red shirting regulations, plaintiffs will usually lose. When an athlete challenges an anti-red shirting rule, he will usually argue that the rule violates the 14th Amendment due process right. He will also argue that he has a constitutional right to participate in interscholastic sports. However, the courts will generally hold that a student does not have a constitutionally protected right to participate. The courts will not interfere with these regulations unless the action complained of is fraudulent, an invasion of a property right, capricious or an arbitrary instance of discrimination.

The rationale for supporting a regulation of this type is that the classification made by the athletic association rule (for example, that beginning with sixth grade a student that repeats any grade which he has passed shall lose his fourth year of eligibility in high school), is neither inherently suspect nor an encroachment on a fundamental right but rather is reasonably related to the legitimate state interest of defeating the anti-academic tendency of red shirting. However, due process will usually require that the association at least allow the student a chance to argue hardship as a means to circumvent the eligibility rule.

2. No Transfer Rules

The "no transfer rule" was created to thwart the negative effect of recruiting athletes from one district or one school to another as a means to enhance the athletic ability of the team to which the athlete was recruited. This rule is usually viewed as rationally related to a legitimate state purpose of preventing school shopping by athletes and the prevention of their recruitment by coaches. This type of regulation will usually not violate equal protection.

However, in one case, a transfer rule did not pass constitutional analysis. *Sullivan v. University Interscholastic League*, 616 S.W.2d 170 (Tex.1981). This particular rule provided that a student who represented any high school other than his present school in either football or basketball was ineligible for a calendar year after moving to another district to participate in the same sport in the new school. This rule was not rationally related to the purpose of thwarting recruitment of high school athletes and, therefore, was violative of equal protection. It was not rationally related to the purpose of stopping such recruitment because it was overly broad and punished those students, for example, who moved with their parents from one state to another because of economic hardship.

3. Anti-marriage

While transfer rules and red shirting rules usually will pass analysis under constitutional standards, eligibility rules that infringe on a fundamental right will not pass constitutional analysis. The classic example of such a rule is the no-marriage rule, which prohibits married high school students from participating in high school sports. This rule is violative of equal protection since the school board has the burden of proving that the regulation that prohibits married students from participation promotes a compelling state interest. Since there is no compelling state interest and since the rule treats two classes in a different way, the discrimination is unconstitutional. *Bell v. Lone Oak Independent School District*, 507 S.W.2d 636 (Tex.Civ.App.—Texarkana 1974).

4. "No-agent" Rule

Another cluster of restrictions to eligibility are those created by the NCAA. Most of their rules tend to restrict eligibility either for incoming freshmen or continuing students. However, the so-called "no-agent" rules are designed to terminate eligibility when an athlete instigates any step towards a professional career.

These two rules are contained in a section of the NCAA rules entitled "Amateurism." The first rule (no. 12.2.4) states that an athlete will lose his eligibility to participate in a particular sport once the athlete requests to be included in the pool of players that are eligible to be chosen in the annual professional draft of collegiate athletes. The second rule (no. 12.3) renders an athlete ineligible once that athlete agrees to be represented by an agent.

The combination of these two rules will clarify the line of demarcation between professional and amateur athletes. An example of how these rules tend to operate and their affect on a student-athlete's attempts to maintain his eligibility can be shown in the case of Braxston Lee Banks. *Banks v. NCAA*, 746 F.Supp. 850 (N.D.Ind.1990). Mr. Banks filed a class action suit against the NCAA alleging that these two rules were violative of the antitrust laws. Banks was a talented Notre Dame football player who had been injured throughout his collegiate career; at the end of the 1989 football season, he had a year of eligibility remaining. Banks originally wanted to use this remaining year of eligibility; however, he changed his mind between the conclusion of the 1989 season and the 1990 NFL college draft. His plan was to test the waters as regards his marketability. Accordingly, he petitioned the NFL for eligibility and retained an attorney to advise and represent him. The NFL approved his petition and invited him to a league-wide scouting combine. His plans failed in that a bad knee reduced interest in him, and as a result he was neither drafted nor offered a free agent contract. At that time, Banks decided to return to college, complete his eligibility, and prove to the NFL scouts that his knee was rehabilitated; however, his college refused to reinstate him.

To test the waters, Banks had to petition the NFL; the NFL will only invite players to their combine that have either exhausted their eligibility or renounced their remaining eligibility by requesting to be included in the draft. However, this process of petitioning and obtaining legal counsel violated the NCAA's so-called no-agent rules and thus automatically eliminated his remaining year of eligibility. It made no difference that Banks did not receive an offer to contract with any team or that he received any monies from his agent.

Banks filed suit. He was denied a preliminary injunction to enjoin Notre Dame from enforcing the rules that prevented him from playing football during the 1990 season. In the court's ruling on a subsequent motion to dismiss, it held that the NCAA's rules produced significant pro-competitive effects and that Banks failed to show that the rules produced an adverse market impact on either college players or NCAA member schools. Banks alleged that the rules created a group boycott by restricting the football labor market; however, the court held that the rules did not have a non-competitive impact on any identifiable market.

G. PROPOSITION 48 AND PROGENY

Proposition 48 and other proposed NCAA propositions create academic requirements as a barrier for incoming freshmen who desire to participate in interscholastic athletics. These requirements relate to the prospective athlete's academic performance in high school and in certain standardized tests. An earlier rule, the 1.600 rule, required that NCAA schools grant athletic scholarships only to prospective athletes with whom they could predict through high school grades, class rank or scores in standardized tests, a minimum of a 1.6 g.p.a. during the freshmen year. This rule passed constitutional analysis since the classification was reasonably related to the purposes for which the rule was created, that is, the maintenance of academic excellence. *Associated Students, Inc. of California State University–Sacramento v. NCAA*, 493 F.2d 1251 (9th Cir. 1974). The 1.600 rule was rationally related to a legitimate state purpose and the privilege of participation was deemed outside the protection of the law.

Proposition 48 strengthened the old rules by requiring a combination of required high school g.p.a. and a minimum score on standardized tests as a prerequisite to freshman eligibility. When Proposition 48 was promulgated, the effect was immediate; a great deal of major college football and basketball recruits were ineligible in the first year of the rule. During 1989, a great furor was created when the NCAA discussed the possibility of Proposition 42.

Proposition 42 called for tighter restrictions on borderline students. Proposition 42 would have eliminated the possibility that a partial qualifier, either a 2.0 or a passing score on a standardized test, of the Proposition 48 standards, could still receive an athletic scholarship in his freshman year. To qualify, both were required.

Proposition 48 has been viewed by many experts as arguably racist in that a disproportionate percentage of minorities are affected by the results of the rule. In the final analysis, the NCAA's propositions will probably pass constitutional muster. Since the NCAA's bylaws will not be construed as state action, it appears that most NCAA regulations and propositions will also be construed as not state action; and because of that, due process protection will be inapplicable. Replacing Proposition 48, Proposition 16 requires a minimum g.p.a. in 13 core courses with a corresponding minimum score on one of the standardized tests. This was declared invalid as a violation of Title VI of the Civil Rights Act by a federal district judge. *Cureton v. NCAA*, 37 F.Supp.2d 687 (E.D.Pa.1999). However, the NCAA was granted a stay on March 30, 1999, re-establishing the Proposition 16 standards.

H. NO PASS, NO PLAY STATUTES

An integral part of many states' attempts to improve the educational potentiality of their students is the enactment of legislation that keys eligibility to play high school sports to the participant's ability to achieve certain academic grades. This type of legislation is generally called, "no pass, no play." The basic format of this legislation will demand that no student can participate in an extra-curricular activity for a certain period if he or she fails any course during the preceding period other than the last grading period before the summer break. There are variations to these statutes in that some grant the power to specify the criteria to counties while some grant the power to a state's athletic association. Also, in Texas, for example, this statute applies to all extracurricular activities, however, in West Virginia it applies only to "non-academic" extracurricular activities (sports and cheerleading). But all have one thing in common: they tie high school athletic eligibility directly to the student's previous academic achievement.

An equal protection analysis is the first question that arises as regard to the constitutionality of no pass statutes. One can argue that the state illegal-ly discriminates against those who participate in extracurricular activities as opposed to those who do not. However, it is well established that partic-ipation in activities is not usually a fundamental right. Because no pass neither infringes funda-mental rights nor burdens any inherently suspect class, it is not subject to strict or heightened scruti-ny. Usually, when the state's regulatory classifica-tion scheme neither infringes on fundamental rights nor burdens an inherently suspect class, then the equal protection analysis requires only that the classification be rationally related to a legitimate state interest. For example, since providing a quality education to Texas public school students is a legitimate state interest, then the no pass rule has only to be rationally related to that interest. *Spring Branch I.S.D. v. Stamos*, 695 S.W.2d 556 (Tex.1985).

Other states have analyzed similar no pass statutes in similar ways. In *State, ex rel. Bartmess v. Board of Trustees of School Dist. No. 1*, 223 Mont. 269, 726 P.2d 801 (1986), the Montana Supreme Court was forced to deal with a school district rule that required a student to maintain a 2.0 (or "C") grade average for the preceding 9–week period as a prerequisite to participation in any extracurricular activities in the following 9–week period. This school district rule was even more stringent than the requirements of the Montana High School Association which required only a 1.0 (or "D") average for participation. However, the court held that this rule had a rational relationship to the state's legitimate goal in that the rule was an incentive for those students who wished to enjoy extracurricular activities and would also promote adequate time to study for those students who have not maintained a 2.0 g.p.a. In a strong dissent, Justice Sheehy opined that there was no rational relation between the rule and the goal and that the rule was overbroad.

It appears that all judicial reviews of comparable no pass statutes will conclude that a rational relation to a legitimate state purpose exists. In *Bailey v. Truby,* 174 W.Va. 8, 321 S.E.2d 302 (1984), the West Virginia Supreme Court reviewed a rule that required students to maintain a "C" g.p.a. in order to participate in extracurricular activities. The court held that this rule was a legitimate exercise of the State Board of Education's general supervision power over the educational goal of academic excellence. The rule did not violate the student's rights to procedural due process, substantive due process or equal protection. The rule in *Bailey,* however, differentiated between academic extracurricular (theater, debate, school newspaper, 4–H, band, etc.) and nonacademic extracurricular activities on the basis that the academic extracurricular activities were too closely related to identifiable academic courses and served to complement those courses. In dissent, Justice Harshberger recommended that if a student satisfies the State Board's academic and attendance requirements for graduation with his class, then all programs should be open to that student. He also viewed the rule as violating a common sense penumbra to equal protection in that it placed a higher duty to achieve academically on those students who participated in extracurricular activities than is required of those students that loiter at malls. He further noted as to the distinction between academic and non-academic extracurriculars: "My brothers would let a flutist flunk without forfeiting his or her flute. But pity the poor punter who did not pass."

CHAPTER 18

THE DISABLED ATHLETE

A. GENERALLY

There are many ways in which eligibility to participate can be restricted; one way is through a person's alleged disability whether it is physical or emotional. Eligibility is restricted by rules that are based on paternalism and disallow individuals who are viewed as disabled from participation in interscholastic sports. Many schools, colleges, athletic associations and school districts have such rules.

Guidelines that bar students from participation are often based on rules provided by the American Medical Association (AMA), which recommend that students with particular types of disabilities be disqualified from participation in certain recreational activities. When a student challenges a disqualification to participate based on these rules, courts will usually defer to the judgment of the school and uphold the disqualification unless the school's actions are arbitrary or capricious.

However, in recent years disabled students have used § 504 of the Rehabilitation Act to establish a right for disabled athletes to participate in interscholastic sports, if they are otherwise qualified. 29

U.S.C.A. § 794. The act provides in pertinent part that no otherwise "qualified handicapped individual * * * shall, solely by reason of his handicap, be excluded from the participation in * * * or be subjected to discrimination under any program * * * receiving federal financial assistance." A handicapped individual is described as any person who "has a physical or mental impairment which substantially limits one or more of such person's major life activities, * * * has a record of * * * impairment or * * * is regarded as having * * * an impairment." 29 U.S.C.A. § 706. This law is further refined in 45 CFR § 84.37(C)(1), in which disabled students are specifically given the right to participate in organized sports: "in providing physical education courses * * * a recipient * * * may not discriminate on the basis of handicap. A recipient that offers physical education courses or that operates * * * interscholastic, club or intramural athletics, shall provide to qualified handicapped students an equal opportunity for participation * * *."

For example, an outstanding high school athlete was precluded from playing his last year of football because he possessed only one kidney; he then won an injunction on the ground that he was discriminated against in violation of § 504 of the Rehabilitation Act of 1973. *Grube v. Bethlehem Area School District*, 550 F.Supp. 418 (E.D.Pa.1982).

B.   ELIGIBILITY TO PARTICIPATE

As mentioned above, disabled athletes were regularly restricted under a paternalistic attitude. Even after medical assurance that athletic participation would not harm the individual, school boards would still restrict participation. Courts usually supported the school board's decision that the athlete was not qualified to participate. For example, an individual who was blind in one eye was precluded from participation in contact sports because of medical testimony that indicated that continuation in that sport would result in a high risk of injury to his good eye. *Kampmeier v. Nyquist*, 553 F.2d 296 (2d Cir.1977).

Courts progressed to a point where a person who is otherwise qualified would not be excluded from participation in a federally funded program solely by reason of disability. The mere possession of a disability is insufficient to assume that there is a corresponding inability to function in an appropriate manner in a particular sport. Otherwise qualified individuals are people who are able to meet all the program requirements in spite of their handicap. *Southeastern Community College v. Davis*, 442 U.S. 397 (1979). A disabled athlete must have the opportunity to participate for inclusion in a sports team. An example is the person who only has one kidney but still wants to participate in a contact sport such as interscholastic wrestling. In *Poole v. South Plainfield Board of Education*, 490 F.Supp. 948 (D.N.J.1980), plaintiff and his parents were well aware of the risk involved in his participation and were prepared to sign a waiver that would release the school from all liability. The court held that the school's only duty was to advise the family of the risk and not to impose a paternalistic view of the proper course of action for the family.

The courts are now beginning to recognize that under the legal definition of a disabled individual the more subtly handicapped such as the emotionally disturbed or the learning disabled have the same rights as other more overtly disabled students. A disabled student who was learning disabled, sought an injunction against the high school athletic association to preclude it from enforcing their transfer rule that would prohibit him from participation for a year after transferring from a private religious school to a public school.

This individual was a certified disabled student under the Education of the Handicapped Act, 20 U.S.C.A. § 1400, *et seq.*; the association discriminated against the student by prohibiting participation by failing to grant a special hardship exception to the transfer rule. The student was granted a preliminary injunction of the athletic association's rule; the association was similarly precluded from punishing the high school by forcing them to forfeit games in which the student participated pursuant to a federal court order. *Crocker v. Tennessee Secondary School Athletic Association*, 735 F.Supp. 753 (M.D.Tenn.1990). See also *Crocker v. Tennessee*

Secondary School Athletic Association, 873 F.2d 933 (6th Cir.1989).

High School wheelchair athlete was denied opportunity to compete against able-bodied athletes in state-qualifying meet. *Badgett ex rel. Badgett v. Alabama High School Athletic Ass'n,* 2007 WL 2461928 (N.D.Ala.2007). Similarly, another high school wheelchair athelete was not entitled to preliminary injunction to force state educational officials to allow her to earn points for her team in state-wide track and field competition. *McFadden v. Grasmick,* 485 F.Supp.2d 642 (D.Md.2007).

On May 16, 2008, the Court of Arbitration for Sport (CAS) ruled that the previous decision of International Association of Athletics Federations "fell short of the high standards that the international sporting community is entitled to expect" when the IAAF denied South African dual amputee quarter-miler Oscar Pistorius who runs on two carbon-fiber blades a chance to run in the Summer Olympic Games. Unfortunately, Pistorius was unable to lower his time enough to qualify in 2008; so he may have to wait until the 2012 Games in London. The CAS said that there was not enough evidence to prove that his j-shaped blades which attach to below his knees gave him an unfair advantage; the court said he should be able to compete with able-bodied athletes. *Pistorius v. IAAF.* CAS 2008/A/1480, CAS, May 16, 2008, rev'g IAAF No. 2008/01 (Jan. 14, 2008).

C.   SECTION 504 OF THE REHABILITATION ACT

In § 504 of the Rehabilitation Act, the prohibition of discrimination against otherwise qualified handicapped individuals in a federally funded program creates a private course of action for monetary as well as injunctive relief.   Typically, where the school board is aware of the parents' knowledge of the dangers involved in their handicapped son's continued athletic participation and the school board knows of the parents' encouragement then the school board will have neither the duty nor the right under § 504 to deny the student's right to participate.   See *Poole v. South Plainfield Board of Education*, 490 F.Supp. 948 (D.N.J.1980).   See also *Neeld v. National Hockey League*, 594 F.2d 1297 (9th Cir.1979).

Under § 504, a high school student with one kidney must be allowed to play football if his parents sign a waiver.   *Grube v. Bethlehem Area School District*, 550 F.Supp. 418 (E.D.Pa.1982).   In a case where a college student with vision in one eye wanted to play football, the university claimed that § 504 was not applicable to the football program because the program itself did not receive federal funds.   However, the court noted that under the regulations, a recipient of funds was defined as "any public or private agency * * * to which federal financial assistance is extended directly or through another recipient * * *" 45 CFR § 84.3(F).   The court then concluded that federal funds need not go to the football program specifically to bring that program within the protection of § 504. The court averred that, even if the football program was not a recipient per se, the decision to prohibit the athlete from participation was ultimately made by the school itself and not the program. Therefore, the school was a direct recipient of funds. *Wright v. Columbia University*, 520 F.Supp. 789 (E.D.Pa. 1981).

As regards § 504, school districts must now consider the needs of each handicapped student and devise a program which will enable each individual handicapped student to receive an appropriate and free public education. A part of this education is the right for all otherwise qualified individuals to participate in the complete array of extracurricular activities. This right will pertain to a facially constitutional regulation (e.g., a rule that prohibits students from transferring to different schools in an attempt to stop the development of super-teams) when the impact of the rule would disallow a handicapped student the chance to participate if the basis of the decision involves his handicap.

For example, an emotionally disturbed student moved in with his grandparents and was urged by his therapist to play football at the school in which his grandparents were located as opposed to the school district in which his parents lived. The therapist felt that it was necessary for the student's emotional health. However, this transfer was a violation of the league's non-transfer rule. The rule stated that a student who changes schools to a school district in which his parents do not reside will be ineligible for varsity contests. Also, a student living with a guardian is ineligible if the guardianship is of a one-year duration and both parents are still alive. The league generally did not acknowledge the existence of legal guardianships. This was to prevent athletes from shopping around for a school or a coach. However, the result of this rule still violated § 504. The court concluded that if the student was denied the opportunity to participate in football, there would be a corresponding devastating effect on his emotional stability. *Doe v. Marshall*, 459 F.Supp. 1190 (S.D.Tex.1978).

D. AMERICANS WITH DISABILITIES ACT

To improve the conditions of the disabled, the massive Americans with Disabilities Act was enacted. This act, the ADA, is § 504 of the Rehabilitation Act with teeth (42 U.S.C.A. § 12101, *et seq.*). The ADA extends its coverage to most employers other than the smallest and thus covers professional athletic teams and probably college teams (in that most scholarship athletes are usually deemed to be employees). The act prohibits employment discrimination against individuals with real or perceived disabilities; it also prohibits discrimination in employment against associates of the disabled. This includes an employer who might refuse to hire a relative of an individual suffering with an illness such as AIDS based on the fear that this relative might contact the illness or that he or she might miss too much work due to the illness of the other person.

The ADA, like § 504 of the Rehabilitation Act, requires employers to make reasonable accommodations for otherwise qualified disabled individuals. An accommodation would not be reasonable under the ADA if it would impose an undue hardship on the employer's business. Undue hardship can be defined to be an action that requires significant difficulty or expense.

In *PGA Tour, Inc. v. Martin*, 532 U.S. 661 (2001), a disabled golfer, unable to walk a course due to significant leg atrophy as a result of Klippel–Trenaunay–Weber Syndrome, challenged the PGA's "no cart" rule which precludes players from using carts during the third stage of the PGA qualifying tour and the tour itself. By not providing a cart, the PGA violated the ADA by failing to make the tournaments accessible to the disabled.

Under the ADA, a qualified individual with a disability is one, with or without reasonable accommodation, who can perform the essential functions of the particular job. However, the ADA provides that a disabled person is not qualified if he poses a direct threat to the health or safety of other individuals in the work area. But, absent an actual threat, an employer cannot refuse to hire a disabled person based on fears relating to safety; for example, an athlete with AIDS, a disease which is not transmitted by casual contact will not fall within the safety exception and thus will be protected from employment discrimination under the ADA.

Under the ADA, the term "qualified disabled person" will not include those currently using illegal drugs so long as their employer acts on the basis of such use. However, rehabilitated drug users are protected from employment discrimination under the ADA. Although the act allows employers to adopt policies, including drug testing, to ensure that their employees no longer use illegal drugs; this is applicable to the professional athlete.

In a strengthening of § 504 of the Rehabilitation Act, Title III of the ADA also prohibits discrimination against the disabled in all places of public accommodation, including privately operated stadiums, auditoriums, convention centers and places of exercise or recreation (e.g., gymnasiums, health spas, bowling alleys, golf courses, aerobic facilities, etc.). Unlike the definition of the term employer under the ADA, the definition of the term places of public accommodation is not limited to entities of a certain size or having a certain number of employees. All places of public accommodation are now forced to comply with Title III accessibility requirements.

In *Costello v. University of North Carolina at Greensboro,* plaintiff, a scholarship golf player on the school's team was diagnosed with Obsessive–Compulsive Disorder. He notified his coach of his disorder and told the coach that he would have to see a psychologist weekly. Ultimately, the coach

dismissed plaintiff from the team for missed practices. Plaintiff lost his athletic scholarship. He
brought a disability discrimination suit alleging violations of the Fourteenth Amendment, Title III of
the Americans with Disabilities Act of 1990, Section
504 of the Rehabilitation Act of 1973, and a constitutional claim under Section 1983.

As regards his ADA claim, the court found that
neither the privilege to play collegiate sports nor
the benefit of receiving a scholarship, rose to the
level of a fundamental right based on the Eleventh
Amendment. The plaintiff's constitutional claims
were also denied because the Fourteenth Amendment created no cause of action and because the
university was not a public entity, it was not subject
to plaintiff's ADA claims. Plaintiff's Rehabilitation
Act claim did survive because he met the pleading
requirements in federal courts by alleging that with
or without reasonable accommodations he met the
necessary requirements to participate in the university's golf program. *Costello v. University of North
Carolina at Greensboro,* 394 F.Supp.2d 752
(M.D.N.C.2005).

In *Miller v. California Speedway Corp.*, the plaintiff, who was disabled and uses a wheelchair, attended three to six NASCAR races a year from 1997
to 2006 at the California Speedway, which has
wheelchair spaces located in the upper level. The
plaintiff claimed the Speedway violated the Americans with Disabilities Act because he could not see
the track when other spectators stood up. The De-

partment of Justice's original interpretation of the ADA did not mention sight lines in regards to standing spectators, but a subsequent interpretation stated that wheelchair locations should provide a line of sight over standing spectators. But, the second interpretation was adopted without the required notice and comment period. *Miller v. California Speedway Corp.,* 453 F.Supp.2d 1193 (C.D.Cal. 2006).

High School student-athlete, who used a wheelchair, sued state educational officials and their agents and designees, claiming they unlawfully discriminated against her, in violation of the Rehabilitation Act (ADA) and § 1983, because their rules and protocols for assigning team points in statewide track and field competition precluded her from earning points for her team. Student moved for a preliminary injunction, but the court held that the student was not entitled to preliminary injunctive relief. *McFadden v. Grasmick,* 485 F.Supp.2d 642 (D.Md.2007).

Owners and operators of places of public accommodation must allow the disabled to participate in an equal way or to benefit in an equal manner from the goods, services and accommodations provided by the establishment. These owners and operators must make reasonable modifications in their practices or policies. Likewise, the owners and operators must remove structural and architectural barriers where such removal is readily achievable.

CHAPTER 19

COLLEGE SCHOLARSHIPS

A. THE NATURE OF SCHOLARSHIPS

A major problem inherent in most cases that pertain to collegiate athletics is the phenomenon of the scholarship athlete. Scholarships are ways for colleges to get athletes into their schools to play sports. The problem is that a scholarship really is not defined in any neat or comprehensible manner. The question is whether the scholarship is a contract or just some sort of informal arrangement which does not require duties, responsibilities or obligations on each party.

By accepting a scholarship, an athlete enters into a relationship with the university which grants the award to the athlete. A relationship of this sort will typically require the athlete to maintain certain grade levels and to perform as an athlete for the school in return for tuition, books and certain other educational expenses. The question is whether a scholarship athlete is an employee of that school. This is important for ascertaining whether the athlete will be covered under workers' compensation laws if he is injured, and whether that scholarship is taxable as income.

315

Arguably, the better policy might be to accept college athletes as entertainers and treat athletes as employees. This makes sense since the big college football powerhouses recruit quasi-professionals to play in collegiate athletics. Yet, schools have been reluctant to acknowledge that the relationship between universities and their athletes is one that can be characterized as a business relationship. This in turn leads to a reluctance to recognize scholarships as contracts and the athletes as the college's employees. To do this would be to legally recognize the rights and responsibilities that are owed to the athlete as part of the contractual relationship in which the athlete must perform for that particular sports team. These institutions have benefited from the talents of their athletes: sometimes financially, sometimes to the detriment of the student-athlete. If there is a bargained-for exchange that is legally universally recognized between the institution and the athlete, then there will be significant consequences for both the student-athlete and the school in terms of the athlete's status as an amateur, as an employee, or as one who receives taxable income in the form of a scholarship.

When and if the schools admit that their athletes are indeed employees and the scholarship is an employment contract, then it may be necessary to compensate the athletes beyond the value of the scholarship; and with those students who genuinely desire to earn a degree, part of their compensation package might include tuition, room and board and other fees.

B. SCHOLARSHIPS AS CONTRACTS

Some courts have viewed the relationship between the scholarship athlete and the university as contractual. The university requires the student to meet certain requirements, e.g., maintain academic eligibility, attend practices, compete in games and follow the rules and regulations of the institution, the conference and the NCAA. In return the athlete receives the benefits of the scholarship. If an integral part of an agreement is not fulfilled or if one or both parties are unable to comply with the agreement, then the courts have allowed the college to rescind or revoke the scholarship.

A contract is enforceable because of the interplay among offer, acceptance and consideration. When a college extends a scholarship offer to an athlete, the athlete who chooses to attend that college accepts the offer. The receipt of the scholarship is the athlete's consideration, and it is in exchange for his participation in sports which is the college's consideration. With the presence of offer, acceptance and consideration an enforceable contract is deemed to exist.

The NCAA requires that before the student signs a letter of intent that will form a relationship between the student and the college, the college must provide him with a statement that will list the terms and conditions, including amount and duration, of the student's financial aid packet. When the student signs this financial aid agreement, both parties have consented to be bound by the amount of the grant. Although each college will draft its own financial aid statement, some clauses are uniform, e.g., the athlete agrees to abide by the school's rules and regulations, the rules and regulations of the conference, and the rules of the team and the coaching staff. This type of clause is standard. The athlete also agrees to maintain athletic eligibility.

If the student does not meet any of the obligations as outlined in the agreement, the college often will reserve the right to revoke the student's athletic scholarship. The national letter of intent and the financial agreement combine to impose a series of obligations that the athlete will owe to the institution, obligations that exceed those imposed upon the average college student.

In *Taylor v. Wake Forest University*, 16 N.C.App. 117, 191 S.E.2d 379 (1972), the university terminated an athlete's scholarship when that athlete refused to continue in football practice. Because of the contractual nature of the obligations between the athlete and the school, the court decided that the student was obliged to participate in the football program as an agreed upon exchange for his scholarship.

A federal trial court in *Begley v. Corporation of Mercer University*, 367 F.Supp. 908 (E.D.Tenn. 1973), also used contract law to determine the rights of both the athlete and the school. In *Begley,* the school sought to terminate an agreement for an athlete's scholarship when it discovered that the entering student did not have the required high school grade point average. The court found that because the student did not meet one of the conditions of the contractual agreement, he could not expect the university to perform its part of the contract by allowing him to keep the athletic scholarship.

The contractual nature of the scholarship was further explored in dictum in a 1979 Alabama case where the court noted that the relationship between a college athlete who accepts a scholarship and the school which awards that scholarship is contractual in nature: the athlete agrees to participate and the school in return agrees to give assistance to that athlete. *Gulf South Conference v. Boyd*, 369 So.2d 553 (Ala.1979).

However, a different result was reached by the Indiana Supreme Court. The court had to decide whether a scholarship athlete who injured himself playing football was eligible for workers' compensation. The Indiana Court of Appeals found that the athlete was an employee and noted that the University had conceded that some form of contract did indeed exist between the school and the athlete. The Court of Appeals then found that there was a contract between the athlete and the school to play football.

This decision, however, was unanimously reversed by the Indiana Supreme Court. Although it agreed that the determination of whether an employee/employer relationship existed between the athlete and the school was indeed complex and involved many factors, the court held that as regards whether a contract of employment, either expressed or implied existed, the primary consideration must be intent. The court found that there was no intent to enter into an employee/employer relationship at the time the parties entered into the agreement. The court found the financial aid that was received was not considered by the parties to be payable income; it was not given to the athlete in return for playing football anymore than academic scholarships are given to other students for their high scores in standardized tests.

The court found that in both cases, whether academic or athletic scholarships, the students will receive benefits based on their past demonstrated ability in various areas which will enable them to pursue opportunities for higher education as well as to progress further in their own field of endeavor. Scholarship recipients then are students that seek advance education opportunities and are not professional athletes, musicians or artists that are employed by the school for their skills in their respective areas. *Rensing v. Indiana State University Board of Trustees*, 437 N.E.2d 78 (Ind.App. 4 Dist. 1982).

After *Rensing,* there is a real possibility that the scholarship agreements will not be viewed as an employment contract. Accordingly, it should follow that there is no contractual obligation between the athlete and the school. However, it is obvious that athletes are obligated to perform under the tenets of at least a quasi-contractual relationship. These schools may later deny that a contract existed in order to avoid extending the protection and the benefits of a contractual relationship to athletes. This will give the school an advantage, however, the issues as presented in *Rensing* are still far from being completely settled.

C. WORKERS' COMPENSATION

The status of amateur athletes and the evaluation of college scholarships has mainly occurred in workers' compensation cases. Typically an injured collegiate athlete on an athletic scholarship seeks workers' compensation coverage for that injury. The crux of the problem usually is whether that athlete is or is not an employee for purposes of the particular workers' compensation statute. If that individual is viewed as an independent contractor or a person of some other status, rather than an employee, then that person would not be included under workers' compensation coverage. These cases that interpret the eligibility of workers' compensation coverage for athletes on scholarships are important because they ascertain whether and under what circumstances collegiate athletes on scholarships will be viewed as employees.

Although there are numerous cases that hold that a scholarship athlete is eligible as an employee for workers' compensation purposes, the case of *Rensing v. Indiana State University Board of Trustees*,

444 N.E.2d 1170 (Ind.1983) (discussed *supra*), arguably is currently the standard. In that case, the Indiana Supreme Court denied workers' compensation benefits and held that an individual on an athletic scholarship is not an employee of the particular school.

It must be noted, however, that pre-*Rensing* cases have indeed decided that a scholarship athlete is an employee of the school; that a contractual relationship exists between the scholarship athlete and the school; and that the athlete who is injured during competition should be awarded workers' compensation. See *Van Horn v. Industrial Accident Commission*, 219 Cal.App.2d 457, 33 Cal.Rptr. 169 (2 Dist. 1963); *University of Denver v. Nemeth*, 127 Colo. 385, 257 P.2d 423 (1953); *Taylor v. Wake Forest University*, 16 N.C.App. 117, 191 S.E.2d 379 (1972); and *Begley v. Corporation of Mercer University*, 367 F.Supp. 908 (E.D.Tenn.1973). The more indices of employment that are present the more of a chance that the athlete will be deemed an employee for workers' compensation purposes. The Colorado Supreme Court has stated that simply performing for the school's athletic team does not confer the status of an employee upon the athlete for purposes of workers' compensation. However, if the athlete receives a financial benefit in exchange for and conditioned upon participation in that university's athletic program, then the athlete will be construed as an employee of that school for purposes of workers' compensation coverage. *State Compensation*

Insurance Fund v. Industrial Commission, 135 Colo. 570, 314 P.2d 288 (1957).

In *Rensing* where the Indiana Supreme Court reviewed the issue of whether the requisite employer/employee relationship existed between plaintiff and the school, the court found that the claimant failed to establish that a contract of employment existed between the parties. Plaintiff's failure to demonstrate the existence of this essential element precluded the possibility of the court finding him to be an employee for workers' compensation purposes. However, *Rensing* did not specifically disagree with the earlier decisions that found that a scholarship athlete is an employee for workers' compensation purposes; rather, *Rensing* turned on the question of whether sufficient proof was proffered as regards the existence of a contract of employment. *Rensing v. Indiana State University Board of Trustees*, 437 N.E.2d 78 (Ind.App. 4 Dist. 1982).

D. TAXATION

Courts have also reviewed whether athletic scholarships are contracts and whether the athletes are employees in the context of the taxability of scholarships. The question is whether scholarship athletes are university employees and, if they are, should they be taxed on their scholarship income. Usually the scholarship is not includable within a person's taxable gross income. The athlete will not be taxed for all services, accommodations, and amounts that cover expenses for travel and equipment, as long as they are incident to the scholarship and expended for that purpose. However, this exclusion from taxation will not apply to amounts received by a student athlete which represents payment for the rendering of services for part-time employment as a condition of the receipt of the award. To qualify as non-taxable, the scholarship must be in the nature of a disinterested educational grant without the requirement of any substantial *quid pro quo* from the student athlete.

If the factual circumstances indicate that the athlete received the scholarship in consideration for his athletic participation, then the award will not be within the exclusion from taxability for scholarships because of the *quid pro quo* arrangement. The scholarship grant will be taxable. *Taylor v. Wake Forest University*, 16 N.C.App. 117, 191 S.E.2d 379 (1972).

If the relationship is a "pay for play" arrangement between the athlete and the school, the scholarship income will be taxable. The IRS will use certain tests to determine the taxability of an athletic scholarship. Some courts have used a primary purpose test. The court will inquire whether the amount was given to benefit the grantor or the grantee; if the scholarship primarily benefits the grantor, then it is not an excludable scholarship. This test requires a scrutiny of the grantor's motives since they relate to the purpose of the grant itself. This test has generally given way to the *quid pro quo* analysis.

The *quid pro quo* analysis involves an appraisal of whether the grant results from a bargained for relationship as opposed to an endowment or no strings grant. Only those grants which lack a *quid pro quo* will be tax free. However, athletic scholarships usually involve a *quid pro quo*. Accordingly, it is important to go to the language of the scholarship grant itself. Also applicable to the *quid pro quo* inquiry is the type and nature of the negotiations that led to the awarding of the scholarship. If the grant is a result of a bargained for arrangement, then the scholarship will not withstand § 117 scrutiny. Recruiting is very elaborate and coaches visit high schools and bring prospective athletes to their colleges. This tends to imply the existence of negotiation: the give and take of trying to recruit a scholarship athlete and trying to sign scholarship athletes indicate a bargained for arrangement to receive the scholarship. This is further proven by the National Letter of Intent Program in which a student certifies that he intends to attend a particular school.

The last factor in the determination of the *quid pro quo* is the evidence of a present contractual obligation. The finding of consideration to support a contract will parallel to some extent the finding of a *quid pro quo* to establish taxation. Therefore, if one ascertains that a contract does indeed exist, this fact will support the existence of a *quid pro quo*.

As a caveat, a *quid pro quo* will be established when an athlete loses a scholarship if he withdraws for any reason other than a physical injury.

E. EMPLOYEE STATUS

The discussion of taxation, workers' compensation, and contractual position all relate to the question of the status of the scholarship athlete as a possible employee. If a scholarship athlete is deemed to be an employee, then he or she will be covered under workers' compensation; however, that income will also be taxable.

In the *Rensing* case, the Indiana Supreme Court concluded that plaintiff did not receive pay for playing football within the meaning of the applicable act. Because of that, an essential element of the employer/employee relationship was lacking. *Rensing v. Indiana State University Board of Trustees*, 444 N.E.2d 1170 (Ind.1983).

However, in *University of Denver v. Nemeth*, 127 Colo. 385, 257 P.2d 423 (1953), the court found that the college athlete was an employee of the school. The consideration received by plaintiff was actually an exchange for his participation in football even though the consideration was directed to him through his salary for cleaning the tennis courts. His financial gain was an exchange for playing football. Since the compensation was conditioned upon football participation, the court decided that he was an employee of the school and his participation was the form of his employment.

CHAPTER 20

INTERNATIONAL SPORTS

Sports is international in scope, not only with the Olympics, but also with international leagues in different sports. American sports are becoming more and more international in their own outreach. All the major leagues now have some teams with foreign venues and some sports, for example, football and basketball, are actively courting foreign markets. Under international law, a Court of Arbitration (CAS) for sport and specialized tribunals help resolve sports-related disputes that transcend national boundaries.

A. OLYMPICS

International competition generally involves open competition among amateur and professional athletes. The United States Olympic Committee (USOC) has governed American participation in the Olympic and Pan American games and has operated under a federal charter since 1950. 64 Stat. 902, 36 U.S.C.A. §§ 371–383. The United States Olympics Committee is the sole organization in the United States that is recognized by the international governing board of the Olympics, the International Olympics Committee (IOC). The USOC contains more than 200 amateur groups, but under the IOC rules its voting control lies in the groups which are recognized by the international sports federation for those particular sports which are a part of Olympic competition. The USOC has a constitution and bylaws which govern its administrative functions. For example, pursuant to the Amateur Sports Act of 1978, 36 U.S.C.A. § 391, the Athletic Congress (TAC) was designated as the national governing body for track and field athletes in the United States. TAC established a trust program that enables its member athletes to receive athletic participation funds and sponsorship payments without losing their Olympic and international eligibility.

Under public international law, the IOC is registered under Swiss laws as a non-profit, private society with legal status under both national and international law. Switzerland has also given it special status under tax and labor laws because of its international character. Under its own charter, the IOC has a legal status under international law and a perpetual succession. The Olympic Charter serves as the best evidence of international custom in governing international competition and related disputes. The Charter forms the basis of international sports law.

B. OLYMPIC AND AMATEUR SPORTS ACT

As a response to the report of the President's Commission on Olympic sports, the Amateur Sports

Act of 1978 (as it was then called) was created. 36
U.S.C.A. §§ 371–396, *et seq.* (It is now called the
"Ted Stevens Olympic and Amateur Sports Act," 36
U.S.C.A. §§ 220501 *et seq.*). The Act was established to coordinate amateur athletic activity; to
recognize certain rights that belong to amateur
athletes; and to provide for the resolution of disputes involving national governing bodies. The Act
amends the statutory provisions that relate to the
United States Olympic Committee. It also established that the USOC is authorized (for any sport
which is included in the Olympic or Pan–Am games)
to recognize as a National Governing Body (NGB)
any amateur sport group, which files an application
and is eligible for recognition. However, only one
NGB is recognized for each sport for which an
application is approved. Prior to recognition, the
USOC holds a hearing on the application which is
open to the public. It also must publish notice as
regards the hearing. An amateur sports organization will be eligible to be recognized as an NGB only
if it, *inter alia,* is incorporated as a domestic, non-
profit corporation with the purpose of advancing
"amateur" athletic competition (the distinction between "amateur" and professional is no longer a
sharp one); submits an application for recognition;
agrees to submit to binding arbitration; demonstrates that it is autonomous in its governance of
the sport; demonstrates open membership; provides equal opportunity to amateur athletes and
coaches without discrimination; is governed by a
Board of Directors who are selected without regard

to race, color, religion, national origin or sex except
in sports where there are separate male and female
programs; demonstrates that the Board of Directors includes among its voters individuals who
are actively engaged in amateur athletic competition in that sport; provides for reasonable direct
representation of the sport for any amateur sports
organization for which recognition is sought; con-
ducts national programs; demonstrates that none
of its officers have conflicts of interest with other
national governing bodies; provides procedures for
prompt equitable resolution of grievances; does not
have eligibility criteria relating to amateur status
which would be more restrictive than those of the
appropriate international sports group; and demonstrates that it is prepared to meet the obligations
imposed on an NGB. 36 U.S.C.A. § 391(A). The
USOC will recommend and support an NGB to the
appropriate international sports group as a representative of the United States for that sport.

The Amateur Sports Act of 1978 is very detailed
regarding specification of the duties of an NGB and
establishes a guide which relates to the competition
of amateur athletes and events sponsored by other
organizations. 36 U.S.C.A. § 392(B). The Act also
provides that any amateur sports group which is
eligible to belong to an NGB may seek to require
the NGB to comply with its responsibilities under
the act, by filing a written complaint with the
USOC; but only after exhausting all remedies within the appropriate NGB for correcting the problems
(unless it can be proven that those remedies would

have resulted in unnecessary delay). 36 U.S.C.A. § 395(A). The Act also provides that amateur sports groups may seek to replace an NGB under certain circumstances. 36 U.S.C.A. § 395(B). Disputes may be arbitrated by the American Arbitration Association or under rules of international sports federations, by the CAS or other special tribunals. 36 U.S.C.A. § 395(c). Also, there are provisions which are designed to protect the opportunity of amateur athletes to compete. 36 U.S.C.A. §§ 374(8), 382(B).

On June 19, 2003, the Independent Commission on Reform of the United States Olympic Committee issued its recommendations for changing the structure of the United States Olympic Committee. The commission, appointed by USOC at the request of U.S. Senators McCain, Stevens, and Campbell, recommended the following changes in USOC governance:

The business and operations of the USOC be governed by an elected nine-person Board of Directors. The Board would include five independent directors, two elected from individuals proposed by the Athletes Advisory Council ("AAC"), and two elected from individuals proposed by the National Governing Bodies Council ("NGB Council"). The terms of Board members would be limited to six years on a staggered basis. The Board will be led by a Chair of its own selection.

An Assembly be created to represent the volunteer core of the U.S. Olympic Movement. Participants will include the National Governing Bodies ("NGBs"), the athletes, community based organizations ("CBOs"), education-based organizations ("EBOs"), disabled-athlete sports organizations ("DSOs"), and other groups, Olympian alumni and the American public. The assembly will provide a forum for all of these groups and a device through which the Board will have the opportunity to exchange information and interact with those constituencies.

The USOC be required to report annually to the United States Congress, the constituent groups, and the American public on its finances and work done.

The Board of the USOC be required to establish financial and ethical whistleblower procedures for the receipt of complaints by USOC employees and volunteers and procedures prohibiting retaliation against USOC volunteers and employees who provide whistleblower information.

In 2013 and every ten years thereafter, an outside independent commission be appointed to review whether the governance structure remains appropriate for the current Olympic movement in the United States.

It is the hope of Senator McCain, the chair of the Senate Commerce Committee, that these changes can be incorporated into amendments to the Amateur Sports Act.

C.   BOYCOTTS

Boycotts of Olympic sports occasionally occur by countries, who attempt to make political gains through not participating.   An example is the boycott of the United States from the 1980 Olympics as a protest to the activities of the USSR in Afghanistan.   The 1980 games were set to occur in Moscow, and the Soviet Union then correspondingly boycotted the 1984 games in Los Angeles.   Usually these boycotts are based on political motivation (e.g., a protest in the 1980s against South Africa's apartheid).   Boycotts are clearly illegal when their purpose is to induce conflict or to engage in measures of coercion that would violate the United Nations Charter.   Similarly, they are also illegal when their purpose is to confirm diplomatic non-recognition in violation of governing international rules.   Under some circumstances, boycotts can fall within a protected range of retaliatory sanctions.   To be within this range the boycott must not violate provisions of the United Nations Charter or other binding instruments, it must conform to state practice, and it must not violate general principles of law.   Also, otherwise illegal boycotts may be acceptable in some circumstances, if they are a reprisal measure against an illegal act of another state.

As regards the American boycott of the 1980 Moscow Olympics, a federal district court held that the USOC has the authority to decide not to send a team to the summer Olympics even if that plan was based on reasons not directly related to sports considerations, e.g., political considerations. While reaching this decision, the court rejected an argument that the provisions of the Amateur Sports Act of 1978 which relate to athletes' rights supersede the USOC's authority. Also, it held that there was no private cause of action under this act to enforce a right to compete in the Olympics in the face of a ruling by the USOC not to compete. *DeFrantz v. United States Olympic Committee*, 492 F.Supp. 1181 (D.D.C.1980).

What has reconfigured the legal process in sports is the rapidly growing role of international sports law as a distinct regime governing international and, to a lesser extent, domestic sports activity. Until the 1990's the principal focus within this process was on political issues, such as boycotts of the Olympic Games or competition involving athletes from apartheid South Africa, and on issues of player eligibility, given a now passé distinction between professionals and amateurs. Today, the focus of international sports law has shifted toward organizing and judging of competition, doping of athletes, violence in sports, and commercialization of the sports arena and athletes.

The nongovernmental foundation of international sports law is unusual. It is noteworthy that the constituent organizations of the Olympic Movement, such as the International Olympic Committee (IOC) and international sports federations(IF's) for each sport, are nongovernmental organizations with international legal personality whose normative instruments such as the Olympic Charter have binding force. The development of this process is striking insofar as the constituent organizations were intended to be not only strictly nongovernmental but also limited to the staging of specific events exclusively for amateurs. As the events became the peak of aspiration for young athletes and as open competition blurred the distinction between professional and amateur athletes, however, the process of international sports law rooted in the Olympic Movement began to influence professional athletes and purely domestic competition.

National legal systems have strengthened this process. For example, United States courts have normally refused to review decisions of nongovernmental sports bodies and have characterized the Olympic Charter as a binding international agreement. Moreover, the Amateur Sports Act designates the United Olympic Committee and constituent national bodies for each sport to govern Olympic, Pan American and Paralympic competition in the United States, participation of United States athletes in international competition, and their solution of related disputes. The Act applies to all participants in designated competition regardless of their earnings from sport, thereby extending the process of international sports law far beyond such competition so as to regulate athletes and athletic activity, at least minimally, in all sports that are fully recognized by the IOC. Even sports that have not been fully recognized by the IOC, such as golf and North American-style football, are influenced by such aspects of the emerging regime as uniform testing procedures and sanctions related to doping of athletes.

The resolution of sports-related disputes is complex, involving administrative facilities within sports associations and IFs, national and international arbitration, and courts of law. The Court of Arbitration for Sport, headquartered in Lausanne, Switzerland, is a particularly effective tribunal of both first instance and last resort. Its jurisdiction extends, for example, to competing claims for accreditation of sports bodies, Olympic judging controversies, commercial and intellectual property right disputes, and appeals from anti-doping sanctions.

Doping of athletes (and horses in equestrian events) has been a particularly troublesome issue. Until recently, efforts to provide a level playing field of competition by sanctioning and excluding abusers suffered from a lack of uniformity among both national regulatory systems and different sports. Now, however, the World Anti-Doping Authority (WADA), assisted by constituent national organizations, has established uniform rules, sanctions, and testing procedures.

Regional Law, particularly within the European Union, has played an increasingly important role in shaping sports activity at both international and domestic levels. For example, the European Court of Justice instituted new rules for free agency of football (soccer) players and imposed restrictions on national formulas for the constitution of football (soccer) teams. Similarly, boycotts by the Supreme Council for Sports in Africa encouraged the elimination of apartheid in South Africa.

D. DRUG TESTING

In the Olympic Charter and the constitutions and bylaws of international sports federations, it is made clear that the use of drugs contravenes the spirit of fair play in sports. The use of drugs is forbidden in all Olympic competitions, and the competitors will be liable to medical control and examination that are carried out in conformity with the rules of the IOC medical commission. There are a long list of procedures for more than 300 banned substances. Individual violators and teams that benefit from the use of drugs will be subjected to disqualification and exclusion under the Olympic rules.

To enforce the ban on certain drugs, the International Olympic Committee requires that each competition site have adequate testing facilities and that each competitor also agree to submit to a possible medical examination at the risk of exclusion. Any competitor who refuses to submit to an examination or is found using a drug must be excluded from competition. If this athlete is also a team member, the competition in which the infringement occurred will be forfeited by that team. Penalties will vary according to whether use was deliberate or accidental or whether the use constituted a first or a second offense. Any offense during competition would lead minimally to suspension from the games and forfeiture of all medals won during that competition.

Although not related to drug testing per se, another similar problem is the practice of blood doping. This is a technique in which an athlete's blood is drawn from his body during training and then returned to his body just before competition. This technique is used in sports that require endurance such as cycling or cross-country skiing. These transfusions are banned by international rules.

In addition to IOC regulations against drug usage, there also are individual agreements between the various Olympic committees of the various countries that are established to ensure drug testing procedures. For example, the now dated United States Olympic Committee (USOC) Olympic Committee of the Soviet Union (SOC) doping control agreement which committed their organizations to work together to eliminate blood doping and the use of performance enhancing drugs (steroids) in athletes under their control. The CAS has, however, upheld more drastic decisions of sports bodies including exclusion of athletes from competition for life.

In ruling on a longstanding dispute between the international and American track federations, a panel of the Court for Arbitration for Sports concluded that USA Track & Field did not have to disclose the results of drug tests of 13 athletes because of its and the athletes' reliance on a confidentiality policy it had maintained, despite rules by the International Amateur Athletic Federation (IAAF) requiring such disclosure.

Typically, a participant in Olympic competition will test positive for a banned substance and have their case heard in front of the Court of Arbitration for Sport. Such was the case in *Australian Olympic Comm. v. Federation Internationale de Bobsleigh et de Toboganning,* CAS ad hoc Division (O.G. Turin OG) 010, award of Feb. 20, 2006, where the Brazilian and New Zealand four man bobsled teams qualified for the Olympic Games by finishing first and second in the North American Challenge Cup. The Australian team finished third. However, the Olympic Committee conducted tests, in which one bobsledder tested positive for nandrolone. The result was announced to the press and the bobsledder was sent home. The Australians appealed to CAS to declare Brazil ineligible, and allow Australia to qualify. However, because the positive result was announced without confirmatory analysis, it was considered an adverse analytical finding and not a doping violation per se. Therefore, the Brazilian team was not disqualified since there was no doping violation.

A new global code against drugs in sports was approved by the IOC. The World Anti-Doping Code (WADA), adopted in March 2003 by sports bodies and governments, sets out uniform rules and sanctions for all sports and countries and was approved on the final day of the IOC general assembly. It is the first international policy against banned performance-enhancing substances and calls for a two-year suspension for steroid or other serious drug offenses. The Code adopts uniform testing procedures and standard punishments for violations. Athletes will be subject to random, out-of-competition testing for everything from ephedrine to steroids to marijuana. The Code calls for a two-year suspension for a first offense and a lifetime ban thereafter.

E. COURT OF ARBITRATION FOR SPORT

The Court of Arbitration for Sport (CAS) was created and formally established in 1984 by the IOC for resolving disputes related to international sports. Its headquarters are in Lausanne, Switzerland. The CAS also maintains offices in Sydney and New York to facilitate its work. The purpose of the CAS is to provide a central specialized authority to decide sports-related disputes. Its jurisdictions is broad and extends to all sports activities that are not otherwise provided for by the Olympic Charter.

The Charter itself provides that "any dispute arising on the occasion of, or in connection with, the Olympic Games" must be submitted exclusively to the CAS. Olympic Charter, Rule 74. According to the CAS Rules of Procedure, the applicable law to decide a dispute is that chosen by the parties or, in the absence of such a choice, Swiss law. In the instance, of a dispute between an athlete and an IF where the parties have not chosen the governing law, Swiss choice-of-law rules will refer to the statutes and regulations of the IF. The parties may also authorize both written and oral arguments.

The CAS does not resolve technical questions such as those related to the technical rules of the game, scheduling of competition, or prescribed dimensions of the playing field or ball court. The CAS addresses such issues as the eligibility and suspension of athletes, the adequacy of protections for individual athletes during drug testing, breaches of contract between an athlete and a sports club, the validity of contracts for the sale of sports equipment, television rights, licensing, sponsorship, and the nationality of athletes for purposes of competition. Basically, the CAS hears three kinds of disputes: disciplinary, eligibility-related, and commercial.

The CAS arbitrates disputes brought by individual athletes as well as by IFs and national governing bodies. The CAS is empowered to review decisions of an IF if any of the following are at issue: the IF's constitution, its powers over an individual athlete's person or property, its adherence to the principles of good faith and general contract law, or its compliance with procedural fairness. Advisory Opinion at the request of the Australian Olympic Committee, CAS 2000/c/267 ACO (2000).

The advantages of the CAS arbitral procedures have been described as confidentiality, specialization, flexibility, and simplicity of the procedure, speed, reduced costs and international effectiveness of the arbitration award. CAS awards are final and binding on the parties. They can be enforced internationally by the New York Convention on the Recognition and Enforcement of Foreign Arbitral Awards. Convention on the Recognition and Enforcement of Foreign Arbitral Awards, June 10, 1958, 330 U.N.T.S#3.

The CAS instituted the 1994 reforms and also restructured the CAS by creating two principal arbitration divisions: an Ordinary Arbitration Division and Appeals Arbitration Division so as to distinguish disputes of the first instance from those arising on appeal of decisions by sports bodies, including IFs. In addition to the two arbitration divisions to hear contentious cases, the Code's Procedural Rules provide for advisory opinions. Constituents of the Olympic Movement may also request consultation proceedings concerning any legal issue with respect to the practice or development of sports or any activity related to sports. Since 1999 the CAS also offers a mediation procedure, but it excludes doping and disciplinary disputes on the premise that an athlete should not be allowed to negotiate a settlement of those issues. It follows the parties' own stipulations; failing, the CAS mediator determines the appropriate procedure.

Beginning with the Atlanta Games in 1994, the CAS has maintained on-site arbitration to render expeditious decisions on issues that arise in major competition. Since 1996, the decisions from these ad hoc proceedings have arbitrated numerous issues at all the Olympic Games, the Commonwealth Games, and the European football championships. The special rules for the ad hoc proceedings provide for applicable regulations, general principles of law, and rules of law.

The CAS allowed South African double amputee quarter-miler Oscar Pistorious who runs on two carbon-fiber blades to compete against able-bodied athletes. The court ruled that the decision by the International Association of Athletics Federations "fell short of the high standards that the international sporting community is entitled to expect." *Pistorious v. IAFF,* CAS 2008/A/1480 (May 16, 2008).

CHAPTER 21

DISCIPLINE AND PENALTIES

A. POWER TO DISCIPLINE AND PENALIZE GENERALLY

A major attribute of any amateur sports association is its power to discipline and penalize its members. The power to discipline and penalize is an essential and important aspect of the ability to determine if a particular athlete is eligible to participate. Rule enforcement by athletic organizations can include investigations, prosecutions and adjudication. If there is a potential problem, the organization will investigate the institution and, if applicable, the individual player. Usually, the athletic regulatory group must provide enforcement through fair, reasonable and constitutional procedures.

Enforcement must adhere to procedural due process. Due process will be determined by a judicial evaluation of the particular circumstances of each case. Due process comes to play when the act in question is a state action and infringes on a property right, i.e., when the plaintiff can show a legitimate claim of entitlement to the benefit which is sought to be protected.

If the incident is subject to due process, then it must be determined what type of process is due.

The courts will balance the interest of parties including the importance of the interest, the type of proceeding in which the interest is reviewed, the appropriateness of the procedure required to prevent any deprivation of the protected interest and the cost of the procedure. Another consideration is the seriousness of the possible sanction that may be imposed. Due process requires that before an action is taken the person who is to be affected must be given a fair hearing which will include notice and a hearing.

B. NCAA

1. Power to Sanction

The National Collegiate Athletic Association (NCAA) is the regulatory board in collegiate athletics. Their preeminent function is to penalize and discipline. After *NCAA v. Tarkanian*, 488 U.S. 179 (1988), their disciplinary measures will not be deemed to be state action. The NCAA was not required to protect Tarkanian's constitutional rights because the NCAA is a private organization which acted independently of the state supported University of Nevada, Las Vegas (UNLV), when that school sought to discipline its coach. Tarkanian argued that UNLV had delegated its disciplinary power to the NCAA, and, because of that, the NCAA acted under the color of state law. However, the Supreme Court did not agree. The Supreme Court held that the NCAA is in actuality an agent of its member institutions, which as competitors of

UNLV, have an interest in the even-handed enforcement of the NCAA's recruitment and disciplinary standards.

There is no question that the NCAA has significant power to invoke sanctions against a university's athletic program, but a few states have added power legislatively to enhance preexisting sanctions for any NCAA-imposed violations. Texas, for example, enacted legislation that stipulates that anyone that is shown to have violated the NCAA rules can be liable for monetary damages resulting from the sanctions that were enforced against the school. These damages can include ticket or television revenue that were lost because of probation or suspension by the NCAA against that university.

2. Death Penalty

The most onerous sanction that the NCAA can enforce against a school is the "death penalty". The death penalty, basically, will not allow a school to participate in a particular sport for up to two years. The only school to be assessed this penalty in football is Southern Methodist University. After the imposition of the death penalty, it was disclosed that boosters and officials had been implicated in numerous violations. As a response, Texas enacted legislation that made it a civil offense to violate NCAA rules. Vernon's Texas Statutes and Codes; Civil Practice & Remedies Code § 131.

The death penalty is only for repeated violations, that is, if after a major violation another major violation is found within the five-year period following the starting date of the first violation. Basically, the penalty prohibits the coaching staff and the team from being involved in that sport, either directly or indirectly, for a two-year period and includes the elimination of all scholarship and recruiting activities. The price is severe and its effect can last for more than a one year period; with SMU, the end result was that the football team was disbanded for two years. The death penalty is specifically reserved for repeat offenders, with the goal of having a chilling effect on the prospect of future offenses and assisting in the self-policing by member universities.

C. HIGH SCHOOL SPORTS

Penalties and discipline in high school sports usually take the form of a denial of eligibility to participate in a particular sport. Courts usually will not interfere with eligibility determinations made by a voluntary state high school athletic association. Unless there is fraud or the defendant acted in an unreasonable manner, the athletic association will usually be permitted to enforce its rules without interference by the judicial system.

Although high school students are not completely denied their constitutional protections, determinations of these rights is different in public schools than in other environments. Courts will not substitute their interpretation of the bylaws of a voluntary athletic association for an association's interpretation of those rules, so long as the association's interpretation is fair and reasonable. If high school associations do not act arbitrarily in applying a law which punishes, disciplines or permits the eligibility of an athlete, then there is no improper influence. An example would be an association's rule that limits eligibility for those who transfer without a change in the residence of their parents; this rule is not based on any suspect classification and does not represent an improper discrimination against a particular group. Therefore, it is constitutionally correct. Participation in high school sports is not a constitutionally protected right, even though the athlete may loose the opportunity to play in tournaments or to compete for scholarships at the collegiate level.

D. PROFESSIONAL SPORTS

In professional sports, the athlete-employer relationship is based on consent and defined by agreements such as the SPK and the c.b.a. These agreements along with some principles of antitrust law define the boundaries that the employer must address as regards disciplining or penalizing athletes for various infractions, e.g., gambling, referee arguments or drugs. Those who punish are the club and the league, and those who receive the punishment are the athletes. The power to discipline emanates from the consent of the player himself.

The basic foundation of this power emanates from the SPK which is an agreement between the employer and the athlete. The SPK, however, is extremely broad and simply secures a player's agreement to abide by the rules which the team or league may ultimately develop. A typical SPK will only outline that the club has the power to establish rules that will govern the conduct of the player, and in return, will require the player's express agreement that he will abide by those rules and regulations. Penalties can be in the form of fines, suspensions, expulsion or a termination of the contract. The SPK will stipulate the procedural rights that the player will be protected under; usually they will be in the form of notice and review by the league's commissioner. The SPK will also establish that the commissioner will have independent disciplinary authority. The question is whether the player has consented to be bound by the particular disciplinary rules. The answer will depend on the interpretation of the penalty clause in the SPK and an analysis of the breadth of the discretion which the league has to define and punish what they have determined to be inappropriate behavior.

Since it is controlled by both contract and the collective bargaining agreement, the authority to discipline in professional sports is not as broad as in amateur sports. The league's commissioner cannot use his disciplinary power solely to enhance the league's economic position or to restrict the competitive opportunities of a player.

One example of misbehavior in professional sports is gambling. Professional sports have always viewed gambling as contrary to the goal of maintaining the competitiveness and credibility in the sport. Gambling will diminish the fans' belief in the honesty of the games. When players gamble on the outcome, there is no guarantee that any real competition exists. Leagues have a strong interest in assuring that the contest is one of pure athletic skill and not influenced by the participant's desire to have their team perform in relationship to the views of oddsmakers. In *Molinas v. NBA*, 190 F.Supp. 241 (S.D.N.Y.1961) (see also *Molinas v. Podoloff*, 133 N.Y.S.2d 743 (N.Y.Sup.1954)), a professional basketball player was suspended for life because he gambled on the outcome of a game. The court concluded that a rule in a contract such as this was necessary for the survival of the league and a rule invoked against gambling is as reasonable as could be imagined.

As a result of the highly publicized brawl involving players and fans during the November 14, 2004 NBA game between the Indiana Pacers and Detroit Pistons in Auburn Hills, Michigan, NBA Commissioner David Stern handed down suspensions for nine players, some of them unprecedented in their length. Stern suspended the Pacers' Ron Artest for the remainder of the season (73 games plus the playoffs), Stephen Jackson for 30 games, Jermaine O'Neal for 25 games, and guard Anthony Johnson for five games. The Pistons' Wallace was also suspended for six games. For leaving the bench during the brawl, Pacers guard Reggie Miller and Pistons center Elden Campbell, forward Derrick Coleman, and guard Chauncey Billups were each suspended for one game.

Although the collective bargaining agreement expressly provides that discipline for on court conduct is exclusive and unappealable within the Commissioner's authority, the union filed an appeal in early December with the designated grievance arbitrator, Roger Kaplan, claiming that the brawl was not "on the playing court" within the meaning of the bargaining agreement, and the impartial arbitrator. Kaplan initially ruled in early December that he did not have the authority to decide whether he has jurisdiction over the case. Before the hearing on both the jurisdictional and substantive issues, the NBA filed a lawsuit in federal district court in Manhattan, claiming that Kaplan did not have jurisdiction to hear the appeal, but it did not seek a preliminary injunction to bar Kaplan from holding a hearing on the issue of whether he had jurisdiction to determine his own jurisdiction.

The NBA also did not participate in the December 9 hearing, after which Kaplan ruled on December 22 that (a) he did have jurisdiction because the incident was "obviously not on the playing court," and (b) that the Commissioner had just cause for all of the disciplinary actions except for the suspension of Jermaine O'Neal, which Kaplan reduced to 15 games. The union then immediately sought a court order in the Southern District of New York enforcing the arbitral decision as to O'Neal so as to prevent the league from extending

O'Neal's suspension beyond 15 games. An order enforcing the arbitral award was entered by Judge George B. Daniels on December 23, allowing O'Neal to resume play on Christmas Day. The NBA's suit filed earlier to declare that the arbitrator did not have jurisdiction continued, but on January 3, 2005, Judge Daniels upheld the arbitrator's ruling that he had jurisdiction and dismissed the NBA's case. The NBA had not appealed the merits of Kaplan's ruling reducing O'Neal's suspension, so the court did not have to review that. See *National Basketball Ass'n v. National Basketball Players Ass'n.* 176 L.R.R.M. (BNA) 2487, 2005 WL 22869 (S.D.N.Y.2005).

On another legal front, Oakland County (Michigan) District Attorney David Gorcyca on December 7, 2004 filed misdemeanor assault and battery charges against five of the Pacers involved in the brawl: Ron Artest, David Harrison, Stephen Jackson, Anthony Johnson (all of whom were charged with one count), and Jermaine O'Neal (who was charged with two counts). No Pistons were charged. In addition, misdemeanor charges have also been filed against seven fans who were involved; two for going onto the playing court during a game, two with counts of assault and battery, and three with one count of assault and battery. One of the fans was also charged with felony assault for throwing a chair at Artest during the melee.

An arbitrator upheld the Philadelphia Eagles' four games suspension and indefinite deactivation of wide receiver Terrell Owens for conduct detrimental to the team. He held that the team's disciplinary action was based upon clear and convincing evidence of misconduct and the team's discretionary action did not violate the NFL's collective bargaining agreement. Owens was originally suspended on November 5, 2005 for one game after he criticized Eagles quarterback Donovan McNabb, called the team "classless" for not recognizing a career milestone, and fought with popular Eagles player Hugh Douglas. Two days later, the Eagles increased the suspension to four games and indicated that it intended to deactivate Owens with pay for the remainder of the season. The arbitrator Bloch found that the four-game suspension was for just cause because the record was full of facts demonstrating that the team had taken progressive discipline for Owens' repeated detrimental conduct towards team. *In re Arbitration of Terrell Owens*, Nov. 23, 2005, arbitrator, Richard Bloch.

Antonio Bryant played for the NFL's San Francisco 49ers until the team terminated his contract on March 1, 2007. Despite this termination, the NFL required Bryant to continue submitting to random drug tests. Additionally the league told him that as discipline for not complying with the tests, he would be sanctioned as though he had failed a test. The NFL also told teams that if they signed Bryant, he would be suspended. Bryant sued for tortious interference with prospective contractual relations and filed a motion for a temporary restraining order. The court denied the temporary restraining order because Bryant failed to show that he is at risk of suffering an immediate injury. Although the NFL has disclosed the results of past tests to prospective NFL teams, there is nothing that shows the NFL will disclose information in the future. *Bryant v. NFL,* 2007 WL 3054985 (D.Colo. 2007).

The year of 2007 has become the year of sports misbehavior, most notably "Pacman" Jones, Michael Vick, and that NBA referee (Tom Donaghy). NFL Commissioner Roger Goodell has initiated a crackdown of what he perceives to be a "crime wave." Goodell was concerned about Tennessee Titans cornerback Pacman Jones strip-club misadventure during the N.B.A. All–Star week-end in Las Vegas where Jones had showered more than 40 strippers on stage with cash (about $81,000) that was intended to be a "visual effect." NFL Commissioner Goodell said that he expected to begin disciplining players who were tainting the league with their misbehavior under a new personal conduct policy. He threatened to punish repeat offenders with one-year suspensions and teams with fines and the loss of draft picks. Pacman Jones was suspended for the 2007 season without pay. The NBA referee resigned and is the target of an FBI investigation that he bet on games. And, of course, Michael Vick pled guilty on charges of interstate dog fighting charges. The N.F.L. suspended Vick indefinitely without pay on August 24, 2007, after he admitted that he paid for dog fighting bets and helped kill underperforming dogs. Vick was out for the 2007 and 2008 season and maybe longer.

Finally, some good news for Michael Vick, although he was sentenced to 23 months in prison, and one cannot help but wonder why education, fines, and community service would not have better served the interest of society as opposed to incarceration? But the United States District Court for Minnesota found that Atlanta Falcons could not recover roster bonuses of $22.5 million paid to Michael Vick because 9(c) of the 2006 C.B.A. precluded the forfeiture of those bonuses. The court also found that the CBA protected those bonuses from forfeiture on any other legal or equitable theory. *White v. NFL*, (In re Michael Vick), 533 F.Supp.2d 929 (D.Minn.2008).

There are many other ways in which players can receive penalties. In the NFL, for example, penalties will accrue for being overweight, for being ejected from a game, for failing to properly report an injury, for damaging club equipment, and for any contact which is viewed to be detrimental to the club. "Detrimental to the club" is the all encompassing phrase under which a player can be disciplined for associating with undesirables or involving themselves in criminal activities off the field or acts which in any way might exhibit qualities that could be viewed as "anti-social." Finally, it should be noted that since the league is judge and jury, there is always the possibility of bias in the disciplinary process.

CHAPTER 22

DRUG TESTING

A. GENERALLY

There are many different policies in the various sports that are promulgated to restrict drug usage by their players. These policies cover the entire range of policing activities from statutory requirements for mandatory drug testing to voluntary programs. The more dangerous sports, for example, boxing and horse racing, have had drug testing and drug testing requirements as a part of their sport for many years.

Although there are numerous policies and programs that detect and punish drug usage in sports, there are limits to the range and breadth of these various drug testing programs. These limits are established by the Constitution.

B. PROFESSIONAL SPORTS

Every professional sport has a plan to evaluate and monitor drug usage. These programs are usually developed through collective bargaining, with a system that progressively punishes drug usage in a step-by-step program, according to the amount of repeat offenses. In these processes, elements of review and due process are made a part of the procedures.

As regards the heavily regulated sports; for example, in *Shoemaker v. Handel*, 795 F.2d 1136 (3d Cir.1986), there was a challenge to prevailing regulations which directed jockeys to submit to testing for drug usage. In upholding these regulations, the court emphasized the nature of horse racing, which is highly regulated with people wagering on the outcome. Drug abuse by jockeys could affect public confidence in the integrity and legality of the sport.

However, the Seventh Circuit Court of Appeals enjoined a state racing board from substance abuse rules that provided for random drug testing and probable cause testing for all racing licensees whether outriders, starters, jockeys, etc. The court held that the racing board's interest in safety and integrity were insufficient to outweigh the invasion of privacy through an otherwise unconstitutional random urinalysis. The court found that urine testing possessed limited use for those purposes since it could not measure plaintiff's present impairment, and instead, only revealed that drug usage had previously occurred at some earlier time. *Dimeo v. Griffin*, 924 F.2d 664 (7th Cir.1991).

The seriously regulated sports, however, will usually be allowed to maintain mandatory random drug testing. Those programs that have developed through a collective bargaining agreement in the less regulated sports, e.g., football, baseball and basketball, combine potential redemption with punishment. Their aim is education and treatment, and if that fails, punishment. These collectively bargained for agreements usually provide for some sort of amnesty for those players who voluntarily seek treatment. However, there is a heightened schedule of punishment which usually leads to a life banishment if the abuse continues.

Millions of dollars in cash payments by California-based BALCO Labs are the focus of a federal Bay Area grand jury investigation that could link more than 100 athletes to the use of a newly detectable "designer" performance-enhancing steroid known as THG. BALCO produced THG, a substance undetected by testing until recently by a lab at UCLA under contract with the US Anti–Doping Agency. Many athletes, Americans and non-Americans, amateur and professional, are expected to be called to testify before the grand jury. On February 12, 2004, four men were indicted on charges of illegally distributing steroids and other performance-enhancing drugs to professional athletes in football, baseball, and track and field. The indictments were announced at a press conference in Washington, D.C., by Attorney General John Ashcroft. However, the names of the athletes supplied with steroids have not been revealed to the public. The Internal Revenue Service has stated that everyone involved, including the athletes, knew about the illegal conduct. IRS agents found e-mails showing BALCO communication with athletes and coaches about steroids.

In response to BALCO, Major League Baseball increased punishments for steroid use that includes year-round random testing: first positive test—10–day suspension without pay; second positive test—30–day suspension without pay; third positive test 60–day suspension without pay; fourth positive test—one-year suspension without pay; fifth positive test—discipline to be determined by the commissioner.

On June 2, 2006, Barry Bonds requested that his lawsuit against two *San Francisco Chronicle* reporters be dismissed. The suit was dismissed without prejudice. The suit was filed in March 2006, after two reporters published a book entitled *Game of Shadows* claiming that Bonds used steroids and other performance-enhancing drugs. The book included descriptions of the testimony that Bonds gave to the grand jury, quotes from Bonds' trainer Greg Anderson, and references to supposedly-confidential grand jury documents pertaining to steroid-use allegations. Bonds' attorneys also requested that the federal judge hearing the four criminal prosecutions of the BALCO conspiracy, issue an order of contempt against the reporters for publishing the grand jury proceedings and information.

In *United States v. Comprehensive Drug Testing, Inc.,* 473 F.3d 915 (9th Cir.2006), w/drawn & superseded, 513 F.3d 1085 (9th Cir.2008), as a part of an ongoing BALCO investigation, the government sought drug testing information from Major League Baseball for eleven players with connections to

BALCO. MLB said that it did not have the information. The government then subpoenaed two drug testing companies to turn over the drug testing information for all MLB players. The MLB Players Association filed a motion to quash the subpoenas. The government then applied for search warrants for the two drug testing facilities. The district court ordered the government to return seized property and quashed the government's subpoenas. The government appealed. The appellate court reversed and remanded because the searches were reasonable. The government did not have to return the evidence immediately, but it did need to sort through the evidence and return the evidence that was not needed. The appellate court also found it was abuse of discretion for the district court to quash the subpoenas. In short, issuance of subpoena, which sought drug testing records and specimens for all professional baseball players who tested positive for steroids, and contemporaneous execution of related search warrants, as to part of government's ongoing grand jury investigation into illegal steroid use by professional athletes, was reasonable.

Major League Baseball and the Major League Baseball Players Association agreed to a more comprehensive steroid-testing program that features year round tests and stricter penalties than previously. The new agreement was announced on January 13, 2005. The new program has been ratified by all 30 clubs and approved by the players. The agreement will extend through the 2008 season. Previously, testing occurred only from the first day of spring training through the end of regular season. Players faced a single mandatory test, and there was no automatic suspension for first time offenders. The new agreement requires every player on each team's 40–man roster to take at least one unannounced test during the season. In addition, random tests can occur during both the regular season and the off-season regardless of a players country of residence, and there is no specific limit on additional random tests to which a player can be subjected. The list of the banned substances includes not only steroids but also steroid precursors and designer steroids such as tetrehydrogestrinone (THG), masking agents, and diueretics. Amphetamines, however, are not included in the new agreement. A single positive test will carry an automatic 10–day suspension. Second and third positive tests will carry 30 and 60–day suspensions. A fourth positive test will result in a one-year suspension and any further positive tests will be punished at the discretion of the Commissioner. All suspensions will be without pay.

On January 24, 2007, the National Football League and the NFL Players Association reached an agreement that will toughen the league's steroid testing policy. The league and the union agreed on a series of substantial changes to its program, the modifications include a 40% increase in the number of players who are randomly tested, so that up to ten players from every team can now be tested each week. This means more than 12,000 tests will be given to 1,800 players each season. The NFL will also use the sophisticated carbon-isotope test with greater frequency, which, due its high costs, was previously only used to confirm positive tests. The NFL also becomes the first professional sports league in the U.S. to add stamina-increasing drug erythropoietin (EPO) to its list of banned substances. In addition, the new policy will carry greater financial penalties for violations. Players who are suspended for steroid use will now forfeit not only their salaries for the games missed, but also the prorated portion of their previously guaranteed signing bonuses attributable to those games, which can be larger than their actual salaries.

George Bush himself initiated the war on steroid use in his 2004 State of the Union Address; "To help children make right choices, they need good examples. Athletics play such an important role in our society, but, unfortunately, some in professional sports are not setting much of an example. The use of performing enhancing drugs...is dangerous, and it sends the wrong message..." State of the Union Address, Jan. 20, 2004, http://www.whitehouse/gov. news/releases/2004/01/20040:20–t.html.

Former Senator, George Mitchell, was the chairman of the special commission ("the Mitchell Report") established to examine the use of performance enhancing drugs in Major League Baseball. (See App.) He had asked a number of active players to appear before the commission, this was a move that represented a major turning point in what was then a yearlong investigation. However, Barry Bonds, declined to speak to the panel on the grounds that he might risk incriminating himself. Bonds, of course, was already under federal investigation; but Bond's decision to invoke his constitutional rights only reinforced the public's belief that he must have been guilty of something. This investigation left baseball in the uncomfortable position of trying to decide how to celebrate the magic moment when Bonds broke the home run record.

Brian McNamee was Roger Clemens' trainer and later an informant; Clemens, of course, was prominently displayed in the Mitchell Report; here, McNamee's motion to disqualify Clemen's attorney Rusty Hardin is denied. The facts surrounding McNamee's Motion are essentially uncontested. According to Plaintiff William Roger Clemens and his attorney, Rusty Hardin, on December 5, 2007, Hardin received a phone call from sports agent, Randy Hendricks, who represented both Clemens and Andy Pettitte, a professional baseball player who is not a party to this lawsuit. During this phone call, Hardin learned that McNamee had alleged to Senator George Mitchell and others, during a private investigation commissioned by Major League Baseball, that both Clemens and Pettitte had used performance enhancing drugs, and that the two baseball players might be interested in retaining Hardin to help defend them against the allegations. Neither Hardin nor his firm had an dealings with either Clemens nor Pettitte prior to this phone call.

On December 7, 2007, Hardin and other members met with Hendricks to review a copy of a tape recorded phone conversation between McNamee and one of Hendricks; colleagues in which McNamee discussed his allegations. On December 9, 2007, Hardin and other firm members met with Clemens and Pettitte in person and proceeded to interview each separately, first speaking with Clemens, then Pettitte. According to Hardin, each individual was interviewed outside the presence of the other.

On December 12, 2007, the firm sent two investigators to speak with McNamee in person about his allegations. The investigators arrived bearing two documents, signed by Clemens and Pettitte, respectively, each stating, "This is to confirm that [the investigators] work for the law firm that represents me." The investigators spoke to McNamee for several hours, and later that evening they debriefed Hardin and Clemens as to the details of their discussion.

On December 13, 2007 Senator Mitchell released his report, which included McNamee's allegations about Clemens and Pettitte. The same day, Hardin held a press conference at which he announced that he had been retained to represent Clemens, but not Pettitte. Subsequently, Pettitte confirmed McNamee's allegations about him; Clemens denied them and filed this lawsuit alleging defamation. Shortly thereafter, McNamee filed an instant motion, arguing that Hardin's prior joint representation of both

Clemens and Pettitte created a conflict of interest requiring the disqualification of Hardin and his law firm. Pettitte ultimately retained his own counsel; his public testimony regarding Clemens' use of performance enhancing drugs has been subject to various conflicting interpretations, and is likely to be central to this lawsuit. Pettitte has neither consented nor objected to Hardin representing Clemens, although McNamee's attorney has submitted a sworn declaration stating that, according to Pettitte's current attorney, Pettitte will not waive any attorney-client privilege that attaches to his communications with Hardin. See *Clemens v. McNamee,* 2008 WL 1969315 (S.D.Tex.2008).

C. AMATEUR SPORTS

The NCAA requires that all athletes annually sign a consent to drug testing as part of their statement pertaining to eligibility, recruitment, financial aid, amateur status and involvement in organized gambling activities. Failure to adhere to this statement will result in the student's ineligibility to participate. The NCAA also has a random, mandatory drug testing program in connection with post-season intercollegiate athletic activities.

A student found to be on a substance which is included in the list of banned drugs will be ineligible for post- and regular season competition for a minimum loss of one season of competition or its equivalent. If the student-athlete tests positive for the use of any drug, other than a "street drug," he/she shall lose all remaining regular-season and post season eligibility in all sports. If the student-athlete tests positive for a street drug after restoration of eligibility, the student shall be charged with the loss of a minimum of one additional season of competition in all sports.

In 1990, a California Court of Appeals granted a permanent injunction against the NCAA prohibiting testing student athletes on the grounds that their right to privacy under the California Constitution was violated. The court averred that the NCAA did not show a compelling interest which would justify an invasion of an athlete's right to keep their urine private and the right to maintain the privacy of medical history, e.g., use of birth control pills. The NCAA program was overly broad and produced results whose accuracy was doubtful. Also, the court found that other alternatives to testing that were less intrusive to a student's right to privacy were not considered by the NCAA as possible alternatives. *Hill v. NCAA*, 273 Cal.Rptr. 402 (1990) (*Hill I*). However, the California Supreme Court reversed *Hill* in 1994. *Hill v. NCAA* (*Hill II*).

After *Hill II* the NCAA's program of consent to drug testing appears to be legal. The program demands that every athlete must annually sign a statement as regards a consent to be tested. If they do not, they can be declared ineligible. The standard seems to be that the NCAA's use of monitoring urine testing to enforce drug testing is not an unreasonable infringement on a student athlete's expectation to privacy. See *O'Halloran v. University of Washington*, 679 F.Supp. 997 (W.D.Wash. 1988).

In a seminal 7th Circuit case dealing with a program which appears on its face consistent with NCAA policies, the court held that a high school consent program of urinalysis of prospective athletes was legal. *Schaill v. Tippecanoe County School Corporation*, 864 F.2d 1309 (7th Cir. 1988). This case dealt with an athlete who had to sign a consent form for urinalysis before he could be eligible for participation. Although the process of safeguarding confidentially is important, the court held that a consent program, such as this, is still legal. The court stressed that there was a lessened expectation of privacy because of the general locker room ambience. The court also averred that urine samples in that particular school were already a part of the pre-participation medical examination and, thus, were established prerequisites to athletic participation. In short, participation in high school athletics is a privilege rather than a right; because of this, limited drug testing is an acceptable way to foster an important state interest. See *Vernonia School District 47J v. Acton*, 515 U.S. 646 (1995).

Drug testing is also important to the United States Olympic Committee. Its concern is not only with street drugs, but also with performance enhancing drugs, that is, drugs taken by athletes to increase their athletic powers, e.g., steroids. The USOC's drug program has been in place since 1983 and provides for both informal and formal testing at Olympic trials. The USOC's policy stipulates that all Olympic athletes shall be drug tested at the trials and at least be disqualified from joining the Olympic team if found to be positive. In this program, there are a variety of legal considerations: for example, the list of banned drugs, informed consent, prevention of a false positive, prevention of a false negative, confidentiality, accurate information and appeal. However, this program in its application is arguably constitutional, and it is not the subject of protest at this time.

In *Board of Education of Independent School Dist. No. 92 v. Earls*, 536 U.S. 822 (2002), the U.S. Supreme Court allowed drug testing of those students who participated in extracurricular activities on the grounds that the policy did not constitute an unreasonable search because it reasonably served the board's important interest in detecting and preventing drug use among its students.

D. RIGHT OF PRIVACY

The question is whether an individual has a right to privacy as regards to urinalysis. An expectation of privacy must be one that society is prepared to recognize as legitimate. In *Schaill v. Tippecanoe County School Corporation*, 864 F.2d 1309 (7th Cir. 1988), the court held that the students did not have a legitimate right of privacy or an expectation of privacy in a situation where high school students were forced to sign a consent form which would allow random urinalysis as a prerequisite to athletic participation.

The California Court of Appeals in *Hill v. NCAA*, 273 Cal.Rptr. 402 (Cal.App. 6 Dist. 1990) (*Hill I*), held that the NCAA did not show a compelling interest to substantiate an invasion of a student athlete's right to keep their urine private and to maintain privacy of medical records in a situation where the court viewed the program as overly broad and capable of producing results whose accuracy are doubtful. However, the California Supreme Court reversed in *Hill II*. Even though a policy may violate some privacy rights, it will still stand if it promotes a compelling state interest. However, the California Supreme Court used the less rigorous, legitimate interest standard with the NCAA, a private, nongovernmental entity. The NCAA's interests were sufficiently legitimate to overcome the athletes' privacy rights. *Hill v. NCAA*, 865 P.2d 633 (Cal.1994) (*Hill II*). Like the California Supreme Court in *Hill II*, the United States Supreme Court in *Vernonia School District 47J v. Acton*, for high school students, concluded that student-athletes have a diminished privacy expectation, the so-called locker room mentality, for purposes of determining the reasonableness of drug urinalysis as a "search." *Vernonia School District 47J v. Acton*, 515 U.S. 646 (1995).

Urine is a private thing. One's urine product is not normally intended to be inspected or examined by anyone other than the donor. An individual's privacy rights will vary with the context. In certain situations an individual's expectation of privacy will be diminished by a past history of significant governmental regulations. But, the governmental interest furthered by a particular search must be weighty and generally of such a nature that alternate, less intrusive means of detection would not sufficiently serve the government's ends.

E.   REASONABLENESS OF SEARCH

The legality of a urinalysis will depend on the reasonableness of the search, under all the circumstances. Reasonableness is determined by whether it is justified at the beginning of the search; and whether the search as conducted was reasonably related in scope to the circumstances that justified the search in the first place. The standard for determining the legality of the asserted force of intrusion is reasonableness. *Shoemaker v. Handel*, 795 F.2d 1136 (3d Cir.1986). The courts must balance the intrusiveness of the search and an individual's fourth amendment interest against a legitimate governmental interest. The test is vague and gives the courts a great deal of discretion in this matter. Before determining reasonableness, the athlete must show that he is entitled to protection; after this, the legality of the search is determined in light of fourth amendment reasonableness.

F. DUE PROCESS AND EQUAL PROTECTION

In all programs that involve drug testing, questions arise as regards the athlete's privacy, due process and equal protection rights. The 14th Amendment protection of due process and equal protection will not extend to private contacts that abridge only individual rights. Only state action can be challenged under the 14th Amendment. It must be determined whether the action in question is either state action or comes under the color of state action. Under *NCAA v. Tarkanian*, 488 U.S. 179 (1988), at the college level it appears that the NCAA's actions will not be construed to be state action.

In high schools, there is no fundamental right to play football. It is more privilege than right and since it is not a fundamental right, the strict scrutiny test will not apply in an equal protection claim. The relevant standard is minimal rationality. This rational basis or minimal rationality test only calls for a rational relationship between the program and a compelling state interest. In *Schaill v. Tippecanoe County School Corporation*, 864 F.2d 1309 (7th Cir. 1988), the compelling interest was control of drugs in high school which is certainly a positive goal. All that was required was a rational basis or connection between the state's interest and the drug testing program. Whether this was the best way to achieve the interest, or whether there were other appropriate alternatives was not the question.

The constitutionality of the drug testing program did not rest on whether the program was the best choice of alternatives, but only on whether it was a reasonable choice. See *Vernonia School District 47J v. Acton*, 515 U.S. 646 (1995).

In the context of due process in drug testing, it would be a violation of a high school athlete's due process right, if, for example, he was forced to strip in public and urinate every hour. But as in *Schaill,* if the urine sampling is done in a discrete and confidential way, it usually will be held to be constitutional. Due process is provided for if there is multiple testing to assure the accuracy of the test, protection of confidentiality, the availability of an appeal of the determination at the school level, a limiting of the sanction to suspension from athletic competition and the availability of an appeal to the judiciary.

CHAPTER 23

CIVIL RIGHTS

A. GENERALLY

The Civil Rights Act of 1964 is a comprehensive legislative plan to prohibit discrimination. The goal of the Civil Rights Act of 1964 was to eliminate discrimination and to create disincentives to discriminate (42 U.S.C.A. §§ 1981, 1983, 1985, & 2000). The Civil Rights Act prohibits discrimination in employment practices (§ 2000e); discrimination in places of public accommodation (§ 2000a); and discrimination by persons acting under color of state law (§ 1983). In addition, the Civil Rights Act of 1866, which ended slavery, also bars racially motivated and intentionally discriminatory acts in the making and enforcement of private contracts (42 U.S.C.A. § 1981).

1. Title VII

Section 2000e (Title VII of the Civil Rights Act of 1964) applies to employers with 15 or more employees who work at least 20 weeks per year, and whose business impacts interstate commerce. Title VII makes it unlawful for an employer to discriminate against an employee on the basis of color, religion, sex, or national origin (42 U.S.C.A. § 2000e–2(a)).

Title VII expressly excludes private clubs from its scope and provides that the term "employer" does not include a bona fide membership club (other than a labor organization) that is exempt from taxation under section 501(c) of the Internal Revenue Code of 1954 (42 U.S.C.A. § 2000e(b)). Thus private golf and country clubs would not be considered "employers" under Title VII if they are indeed a bona fide private membership club. The EEOC has promulgated a three-part inquiry for assessing whether an organization qualifies as a private club pursuant to § 2000e(b). An organization is a bona fide private club if: (1) it is a club in the ordinary and common meaning of that word; (2) it is private; and (3) it requires meaningful conditions of limited membership. *EEOC v. The Chicago Club,* 86 F.3d 1423 (7th Cir.1996).

2. Title II

Section 2000a (Title II of the Civil Rights Act of 1964) prohibits discrimination based on race, color, religion, or national origin in places of public accommodation affecting interstate commerce. It is important to know that discrimination on the basis of gender is not prohibited under Title II. An establishment is a place of public accommodation under Title II if its operations affect commerce and it is one of four categories of establishments that serve the public.

Private golf clubs are considered places of exhibition or entertainment since most private golf clubs provide activities either in the form of direct participation or through viewing sports activities as spectators. Once an organization is covered by one of the four categories in section 2000a, the next question is whether the activities affect interstate commerce. The commerce requirement has been easily satisfied with regard to golf and country clubs due to golf outings with out-of-state professionals, guest memberships, snack bars open to the general public, out-of-state golf teams playing on the course, and service contracts fulfilled by out-of-state contractors. Thus, since private golf clubs are places of public accommodation and affect interstate commerce, they are subject to the act unless they qualify for an exemption. *U.S. v. Lansdowne Swim Club,* 713 F.Supp. 785 (E.D.Pa.1989).

3. Section 1981

Section 1981 prohibits certain racially motivated acts, that are intentionally discriminatory including the making and enforcement of private contracts (42 U.S.C.A. § 1981). This prohibition applies to both private and state actors. A private golf club and country club is subject to the statutory mandate. A person is aggrieved by a violation of this statute must show: (1) that he/she was a member of a racial minority; (2) the defendant's intent to discriminate on the basis of race: and (3) the discrimination concerned the making or enforcement of a contract. *Gibbs-Alfano v. The Ossining Boat & Canoe Club, Inc.,* 47 F.Supp.2d 506 (S.D.N.Y.1999). In *Gibbs-Alfano,* the plaintiffs were members of the Ossining Boat & Canoe Club. Gibbs–Alfano was expelled from the club for allegedly using foul language. She contends that other members of the club who were white also used foul language but were not expelled. She and her husband further contended that her expulsion interfered with their contractual rights.

4. Section 1983

Section 1983 prohibits a person acting under color of law from depriving any citizen of the United States of any rights, privileges, or immunities secured by the Constitution and law of the United States. It is clear that Section 1983 only applies to persons acting on behalf of a governmental entity. Thus, all public recreation clubs, resorts, or areas would be covered by the statute; however, private clubs do not come under the statute's mandate. Public recreation clubs, resorts, or areas affected could include public golf courses, parks, lakes, camping areas, college and university facilities, or any other area owned, operated, or maintained by a governmental entity. While a private club would have no direct responsibility for a violation of Section 1983, it could expose a city, county, or state to liability if the governmental entity is involved in a close relationship with the private club. For example, where a city grants licenses or leases in order for a private club owner to operate, the private club can be deemed to be acting under color of state law if it deprives someone of membership privileges. The courts will examine the relationship to determine whether a mutually beneficial relationship exists between the private club and the city; and whether the private club appears to be performing a public function.

B. STATE AND CITY CIVIL AND HUMAN RIGHTS ACT

The U.S. Constitution provides no protection from discrimination. Similarly, federal civil rights statutes only provide prosecution to a limited class of persons in a limited number of situations. However, the scope of state antidiscrimination statutes generally exceed the scope of federal statutes as to both the classes of individuals they protect and the type of organizations governed. For example, many state public accommodation statutes not only prohibit discrimination on the basis of race, religion, and national origin, but also prohibit discrimination on the basis of gender, sex orientation, age, disability, personal appearance, marital status and familial status.

C. RACISM IN SPORTS

Racial discrimination in the United States in sports has deep historical roots. African American athletes were not able to participate at many universities until after World War II. Jackie Robinson did not break the color barrier in professional baseball until 1947. However now African–American athletes dominate Division IA basketball and football; that is, those sports that are revenue producing for colleges and universities. One can certainly argue that African–American athletes are in actuality taken advantage of and exploited for financial reasons. These large revenues generated by African American athletes are then used for purposes other than supporting the educational development of these athletes. This too, is exploitation in a manner that is at best ironic. The new assertion that African Americans now have a natural superiority in sports, acts as a negative and racist counter-balance to the implied assertion that these athletes are correspondingly intellectually or ethically inferior.

1. Discrimination Generally

In *Dambrot v. Central Michigan University,* 55 F.3d 1177 (6th Cir.1995), the head basketball coach was fired for violating the University Discrimination Harassment Policy. He successfully argued that his words were protected by First Amendment. In *Dambrot,* a basketball coach called his players "niggers" just to motivate them. The plaintiff coach was fired. In essence, he was disciplined because he violated his school's discrimination policy.

1. The Rooney Rule

It can also be said that racism exists in the roster construction in professional sports teams. Title VII of the Civil Rights Act of 1964 (U.S.C.A. § 2000e) is the most significant tool in shaping the legal and political discourse on the practical application of equality. All of America's major professional leagues (e.g., basketball, hockey, football, and baseball) have a history of racial discrimination and either actual or implied Title VII violations and concerns. For example, after the collapse of the "Caucasian" Boston Red Sox to the much more integrated New York Mets in the 1986 World Series, there developed a riot by white students against anything deemed to be associated with the Mets. This ugly riot, which was pursued by approximately 3,000 students implied racism as it was directed not only against the "African American–Oriented" Mets, but also the African–American students at the University of Massachusetts at Amherst, who may or may not have been Mets fans. The riot was peppered with racial invective including beating and injuring students. Even if this was an "isolated incident," it was one that was clearly inspired by racism, and the inherent racism and the racist duality that lies at the heart of racism in sports.

Just as roster-construction was racist, so to was the lack of African–American management hirings in professional sports. An attempt to alleviate the situation was brokered by Johnnie Cochran and Cyrus Mehri in a report entitled, *Black Coaches in the National Football League: Superior Performance, Inferior Opportuni*tes, which became the basis for the Rooney Rule. The Rooney Rule requires every NFL team to interview at least one minority candidate when there are head coaching vacancies or else suffer the imposition of a significant fine. Impetus to ameliorate what was coined an "unconscious bias," was ignited by racist assertions regarding the management capabilities of African–American coaches and former athletes. These ideals were most infamously asserted by Los Angeles Dodgers executive Al Campanis and Cincinnati Reds owner Marge Schott. Irrespective of good intentions, the question unfortunately becomes whether the Rooney Rule has resulted in the mandating of tokenism.

2.   Jackie Robinson and The Color Barrier

2007 marked that 60th anniversary of Jackie Robinson's breaking the color barrier and playing professional baseball. It coincided with the racially insensitive remarks of radio personality Don Imus who disparaged the women's basketball team of Rutgers University. In 1964, 20% of all baseball players were African–Americans. In 2007, only 8% of major league players are African–Americans, and only 3% of players on NCAA Division I teams. One reason may be that baseball holds little current interest in the imagination of young African–Americans; baseball is a game of nostalgia. It sells itself through the memory of being taken to a game by your father when you were a child. But for African–Americans, going into baseball's past means recalling the Jim Crow era, where there was "White Baseball" and "Black Baseball"–with the inevitable knowledge that the Negro League Baseball was meant to exist under conditions that were inferior to the white version. Even the breaking of the color barrier by Jackie Robinson only serves to remind African–Americans that their institutions were weak and eventually abandoned. It is at best, a bitter sweet recollection of the different ways that Americans look at African–American institutions. African–American athletes who broke or distorted the sanctity of the color barrier were the victim of death threats and racial antagonism similar to the threats O.J. Simpson received as a result of his victory in the "trial of the century."

3. The Dual Consciousness of the African–American Athlete

Johnnie Cochran's book, *A Lawyer's Life*, "is dedicated to all those lawyers, past, present, and future, who spend their lives seeking justice for others, especially those who have used the law to change society for the better." Johnnie Cochran, however, was very much aware of the "racial split personality." He understood how an African–American in America could, literally, be with it, but not of it—even as a lawyer; even as a football icon. In his book, Johnnie Cochran paraphrased from W.E.B. Dubois' *The Souls of Black Folks* and explained that African–Americans have a dual consciousness. "It is...inevitable...that the Simpson case would be...a metaphor for the seemingly intractable problem of race in America."

2. Sexual Discrimination and Harassment

Anucha Sanders worked as a marketing executive for Madison Square Garden from 2000 to 2006. Up until 2004, she received favorable job reviews; however, beginning in 2004 she began having problems

with Isaiah Thomas, the President of Basketball
Operations for the New York Knicks, and Kevin
Layden, the President and General Manager of the
Knicks. She was fired because she complained that
she was sexually harassed by Thomas and for investigating the possible sexual harassment of other
female employees within the organization. Defendants claimed that Sanders was fired because of her
poor job performance, but it has also issued an
internal report that recommended Thomas receive
sensitivity training because he occasionally raised
his voice, used profanity, and had on occasion greet-
ed Sanders with a hug and a kiss; the report also
indicated that Sander had numerous business disagreements, demonstrated poor job performance,
and should be terminated. However, the garden's
chairman stated during a deposition that he would
not have terminated Sanders even though her job
performance was poor. Sanders sued for sexual discrimination and retaliation; the court, however, denied summary judgment because there was a question of fact as to why Sanders was fired. *Sanders v.
Madison Square Garden, L.P.*, 2007 WL 2254698
(S.D.N.Y. 2007), opin. w/drawn in part or reconsid.
525 F.Supp.2d 364 (S.D.N.Y.2007).

3. Native American Team Nicknames and Mascots

In August 2005, the NCAA Executive Committee
implemented a policy that applied to UND and 17
other schools because the NCAA Executive Committee found that some schools' American Indian

nicknames were "hostile and abusive." This policy prohibits these schools from hosting NCAA championship events and from displaying Native Americans nickname logos at their facilities or on their uniforms during NCAA sponsored events. North Dakota alleges that the NCAA has breached its contract because, according to the NCAA Constitution and Bylaws, the Executive Committee has no power to legislate such a policy. Also, North Dakota claims that the NCAA has failed to implement an adequate appeals process of clear standard in determining whether a Native American nickname is "hostile or abusive," thus breaching an implied covenant of good faith. Finally, the state alleges that the policy violates N.D.C.C. § 51–08.1–02 as an unreasonable and unlawful restraint of trade or commerce. Thus, the state seeks a preliminary, and then a permanent, injunction against the NCAA's policy, unspecified financial damages, and attorney's fees.

On October 6, 2006, the state of North Dakota filed a lawsuit against the NCAA for breach of contract, breach of good faith and fair dealing, and unlawful restraint of trade. The state challenges the NCAA's rule that bars the University of North Dakota from hosting any post-season NCAA tournament events as long as it uses its Fighting Sioux nickname.

CHAPTER 24

SEX DISCRIMINATION

A. DISCRIMINATION GENERALLY

Sexism can occur in almost every aspect of sports, including different rules in girls sports and less opportunities for girls to participate in amateur sports. Men historically have felt that women are too frail to meaningfully participate in sports.

The most vital aspect of sex discrimination is the limiting of athletic opportunities for girls. Ways in which opportunities can be curtailed cover the gamut, from school regulations which exclude girls from participation in athletic programs to rules which are not per se discriminatory but discriminate in the method by which they are applied. Another form of discrimination is the failure to provide equal funding, facilities or opportunities for female athletes, their coaches and managers.

In an attempt to solve or at least ameliorate these problems, there are three basic types of athletic programs: separate but equal, mixed competition and the component approach. All the other programs which have been experimented with are variations of these approaches.

A separate but equal type of program arguably appears to be the perfect solution to the problem of discrimination. However, these programs are often not equal, especially in their application which will disclose gross inequalities. Women lack coaching, sports selection, equipment, scheduling and access to facilities which men and boys take for granted. Funding and the type of available competition also make the separate programs unequal. For example, a boy's program may have state wide competition and championships while the girls' program may not.

Another approach is to allow mixed competition in all sports that do not involve physical contact. The only criteria for participation would be the person's ability to play. Here, the outstanding female athlete would have the opportunity to participate at the most competitive level. However, this type of program has its drawbacks because females have traditionally had poor experiences in sports training; therefore, the males would be likely to dominate every sport. The end result would be that few females would be selected and participate in the particular sporting program.

The last approach would be that each school would provide a single team which could be made up of components. Each component would contribute to the success of or failure of the team in competition with other schools. The teams would win or lose based on the total score of their components. This component program has the effect of · making recognition of one component contingent on the performance of another component.

All these programs have flaws that in some way may enhance discrimination. Yet they all have something to offer which would could be positive and beneficial to the interests of female athletes. The best system is one that enables the greatest number of participants to compete against those of comparable ability.

B. SEPARATE BUT EQUAL

A typical situation is one where a college has failed to provide equally between its men's and women's athletic programs. An institution can provide separate programs for men and women. The question is not so much the separateness of the separate programs but rather the equality of the different programs. Programs must exist for both sexes; there also must be opportunity to participate in intercollegiate sports.

One way in which to examine the distinctions between programs is to analyze the revenue producing capability of each program. The courts recognize that some athletic programs are intended to be revenue generating and that the monies that are produced from an individual sport will affect the financial support of the program. Still, these discrepancies must have a basis in fact.

In an attempt to ascertain if a school's action would result in a disparate effect on one sex at the expense of the other sex, one must analyze the amount of funding that is budgeted for the various female athletic endeavors as compared to the monies budgeted for the men. Another aspect of the comparison is the amount of money spent on equipment, facilities and programs. If the differences are blatant, then no other evidence is necessary to show that disparate treatment exists between the programs. In short, equal money for both male and female collegiate sports; or, to use the rallying cry of the 90s, "gender equity."

C. CONTACT AND NON-CONTACT SPORTS

Courts have traditionally differentiated between contact and non-contact sports as regards the level and commitment of participation for girls in sports.

In the majority of cases that involve non-contact sports where no women's team is available, the courts usually allow the women to participate on the men's team. If there is not a team sponsored for one sex in a particular sport and the excluded sex has had a history of limited opportunity, then the excluded sex must be permitted to try out for that team. The pertinent Health, Education and Welfare regulations, 45 CFR § 86.41 (1979), contain a general prohibition against sex-based discrimination in any school-sponsored athletic program.

When there is ample opportunity for women to compete on their own, courts appear less apt to allow them to compete with men in contact sports. (See also discussion of Title IX *infra*). The Health, Education and Welfare Regulations under Title IX permit an athletic department which receives federal funds to maintain separate teams if selection for those teams is based on competitive skill or if the sport involved is a contact sport. 45 CFR § 86.41(b).

Finally, the exception that provides for competitive skill applies to most programs, because sports and the competition thereof, is ultimately based on individual skills. Therefore, separate teams are permissible for most sports, contact or non-contact, if they are available.

D. TITLE IX

Under Title IX of the 1972 Education Amendments (discussed *infra*), contact sports include boxing, wrestling, rugby, ice hockey, football, basketball and other sports in which the purpose or preeminent activity involves bodily contact. Some courts, however, have also included baseball and soccer as contact sports.

In order to win on a constitutional claim of gender discrimination, plaintiff must show that state action was involved in the denial of a request to participate. However, if the college shows that there is potential physical harm to the female athlete due to the nature of that particular contact sport, it is constitutional to limit participation in that sport. The state must demonstrate that the preeminent concern is for the average differences between males and females and that its concern is for the health and safety of the athletes. The criteria that will be used to justify the potential harm (which the state must both allege and prove) are intimidation, safety and displacement.

1. Application

The sexual discrimination in academics called for an answer which was created in the form of Title IX of the 1972 Education Amendments, which provided that no person shall on the basis of sex be excluded from participation in, be denied the benefits of or be discriminated against, in any education program that receives federal financial assistance. 20 U.S.C.A. § 1681, *et seq.* This act prohibited any federally funded educational program from discrimination and intended to curtail discrimination in any program, organization or agency that received federal funds.

Title IX clearly applies to primary and secondary schools. Title IX has been viewed as an illustration of congressional intent and policy against discrimination based on stereotypical characterizations of the sexes. It was an attempt to end misguided paternalism. The objective was to give women an equal opportunity to develop the skills that they hoped to develop and to apply those skills in the way they had hoped.

Facts and situations as enforced by the Department of Health, Education, and Welfare (HEW) are limited to discrimination against participants in federally funded educational programs. Title IX applies to the admissions policies of these institutions, whether they are vocational, professional, graduate or undergraduate in nature. It also applies to policies and practices other than admissions in all educational programs, which will include athletic programs, that also receive federal funds.

Title IX protection does not cover, however, educational institutions that traditionally admit members of only one sex, institutions that train individuals for the military, and institutions under the control of religious groups whose compliance with Title IX would violate their religious beliefs.

Even though the statute and the regulations appear to be rather clear, problems have arisen regarding the scope of the act's application. The issue is whether the term "federal financial assistance" encompasses indirect federal aid, and if so, what constitutes a program or activity funded for the purposes of regulation and fund termination under § 902 of the act, the enforcement arm of Title IX. HEW regulations from 1975 determined that "federal financial assistance" include funds received indirectly by a school, including grants and loans paid directly to students but which ultimately are received by the school. 34 CFR § 106.2(G)(1)(ii). Under this analysis, indirect benefits that emanate from federal funding will be sufficient in certain cases to allow athletic departments to be characterized as Title IX recipients.

In *NCAA v. Smith*, 525 U.S. 459 (1999), the U.S. Supreme Court held that the NCAA is not subject to the requirements of Title IX on the grounds that it receives dues from its members, which receive federal financial assistance. Renee Smith sued the NCAA alleging that the NCAA's enforcement of a by-law that prohibited students from participating in athletics while enrolled in graduate programs other that her undergraduate institution violated Title IX.

In *Mercer v. Duke University*, 190 F.3d 643 (4th Cir.1999), the court held that the plaintiff/female kicker stated a claim under Title IX on the basis that the university was prohibited from discriminating against the student-athlete on the basis of her sex once it allowed her to try out for its football team. A federal jury awarded her 2 million dollars in punitive damages which she ultimately lost, but she was still able to keep 80% of her attorney fees. *Mercer v. Duke University*, 301 F.Supp.2d 454 (M.D.N.C.2004).

A closely divided Supreme Court (5–4) ruled that a coach who claims sexual discrimination on behalf of others is protected from firing under Title IX. This decision expands the scope of Title IX gender equity law to protect whistle-blowers as well as direct victims. It means that school officials, regardless of their gender, may sue when they suffer retaliation for complaining about discrimination. Justice Sandra Day O'Connor, writing for the majority, said Alabama high school girls' basketball coach Roderick Jackson was entitled to pursue a Title IX lawsuit after he was fired for complaining that the boys' team received better treatment. *Jack-*

son v. Birmingham Bd. of Educ., 544 U.S. 167 (2005).

2. Grove City and Civil Rights Restoration Act of 1987

The authors of Title IX arguably intended the benefits of their reforms to reach all federally funded programs; and thus athletic participation would also receive the umbrella protection of Title IX. However, the United States Supreme Court in *Grove City College v. Bell*, 687 F.2d 684 (3d Cir. 1982), ruled that only those programs within an institution that receive direct financial aid from the federal government would be subjected to Title IX protection.

This case obviously limited the affect that Title IX would have in general, and more particularly, the affect that Title IX would have on female athletic participation. The issue here was whether Title IX applied only to specific departments that received direct funding or whether it extended to any department within an institution that benefit from financial aid. The Supreme Court saw Title IX as program specific.

The Supreme Court was unwilling to hold that the receipt of basic education opportunity grants (BEOG's) by particular college students subjected the entire institution to coverage under Title IX. The Supreme Court's rationale was that in order for the entire institution to be subjected to regulation there must be evidence that the college used federal funds in areas other than the college's own financial aid program. However, the Supreme Court did hold that the colleges' financial aid program was covered under the program-specific requirements of Title IX. In short, the court held that Title IX applied only to individual programs that received federal funding at an institution of higher education and not the entire institution itself.

The ruling in *Grove City College,* however, was not the intent that Congress had in mind when they established Title IX. This ruling was a narrow approach and not intended by the Title IX creators; therefore, they did the very unusual step of rewriting *Grove City College* through a federal statute: the Civil Rights Restoration Act of 1987. 29 U.S.C.A. § 1687. This act extended the definition of "program" or "activity" to include the entire program, for example, the college, as opposed to the program specific approach as established in *Grove City College.*

Haffer v. Temple University, 524 F.Supp. 531 (E.D.Pa.1981), is arguably the most important Title IX case to be reviewed after the passage of the Civil Rights Restoration Act. It was alleged that the school, Temple University, failed to afford women an equal opportunity to participate in interscholastic sports. The female athletes claimed that disparities existed in the resources that were distributed to the women's athletic programs and that applicable financial aid was unequally distributed among male and female athletes. The *Haffer* plaintiffs also asserted violations of the federal equal protection clause and Pennsylvania's ERA.

In 1988, the parties in *Haffer* reached a settlement agreement that followed the court's decision in which the court ruled in favor of a reconsideration of plaintiff's claims and denied summary judgment for the defendant. The settlement, *inter alia,* contained changes in Temple's athletic program that included proportional scholarships, increased athletic opportunities, and increased budget stipends for the female programs. The agreement only applied to this school; however, it has been viewed by many as the outline for collegiate compliance with Title IX.

In this case, for example, the cost of the expensive men's football and basketball teams were included in the overall sports budget; also, the school agreed that the money spent on the female teams would be within ten percentage points of the amount spent on the men's teams. The school was required to monitor participation in the women's sports programs to guarantee that their participation to financial aid figures are proportionate to the agreed upon ratio in the men's sports programs.

E.   EQUAL PROTECTION

When one brings an action founded on the equal protection clause of the 14th Amendment, there must be a finding that state action is involved. After state action is determined the next step is to ascertain whether the athletic program's provisions or the enforcement of its prohibitions violate the equal protection clause of the 14th Amendment.

When the equal protection clause was first applied to sexually discriminatory sports rules, the standard was one of a "rational relationship." *Brenden v. Independent School District*, 342 F.Supp. 1224 (D.Minn.1972). The Supreme Court has since held that the applicable standard of review for sex-based classification is one in which classification based on gender must serve an important governmental objective and also be substantially related to the achievement of those objectives. *Craig v. Boren*, 429 U.S. 190 (1976).

This standard was followed in *Dodson v. Arkansas Activities Association*, 468 F.Supp. 394 (E.D.Ark.1979), where the difference of rules for girls and boys basketball was found to deprive the girls of equal protection since these changes were not justified by an important governmental objective.

In *Dodson,* a suit was brought to challenge the constitutionality of different rules for girls' and boys' high school basketball, basically, the difference was that there was full-court basketball for the boys and half-court basketball for the girls. The court held that the difference in the rules deprived the girls of their equal protection rights. The association's rationale behind the different rules was based solely on tradition. Tradition alone without some supporting substantive gender-based reason is insufficient to justify the rule variations in light of the fact that those rules placed Arkansas girl athletes at a substantial disadvantage in comparison to their male counterparts.

Sex-based classifications will be held to violate equal protection unless they are shown to rest upon a convincing factual basis that goes beyond archaic, over broad, and paternalistic generalizations about the differences between males and females. When equal protection requirements are not met, the remedy will be to allow the complainant to participate or try out for a particular athletic team. Courts have not required that new teams be created but that the existing teams be open to all qualified people.

Under equal protection the ultimate test becomes one's ability without regard to sex. Equal protection claims can be combined with a Title IX action and also a state ERA claim. In an equal protection claim in sports sex discrimination, courts have considered elements that include demonstrations that show an adverse affect by the state action and that the disparate impact was a result of an invidious intent. This test is difficult since it requires the court to guess as regards the motives behind the choices made by the school, since schools usually do not document the intent behind their regulations.

In an equal protection claim, the courts will also consider whether the sport is or is not a contact sport. Women can be excluded from a men's team as long as there is a women's team in the same sport. If there is no female equivalent, the courts are divided; however, the state's interest here is

usually expressed as the protection of the participants' health and safety. Some courts, however,
hold that total exclusion when there is no separate
program is overly inclusive since it is based on the
assumption that females are relationally fragile.
However, in noncontact sports, where there is no
health or safety risks, and likewise no separate
female team, then the courts will hold that total
exclusion violates equal protection.

The last element that courts will consider as
regards equal opportunity is the requirement of
separate teams or opportunities to try out for the
only available team. The courts have allowed a
"separate but equal" policy when there is a separate girl's team. When a separate but equal policy
is upheld, the court's next determination is to ascertain if the teams are truly equal in all levels of
funding, coaching and support. The court then will
evaluate the intangibles as regards the quality of
the resources that are provided to the women's
teams.

In summary, courts will apply an intermediate
standard of review in their evaluation of the constitutionality of sex-based classifications. Sex-based
classifications will only be allowed if they are substantially related to an important governmental objective. This test is somewhat subjective; and, as a
result, each court's analysis can produce different
or mixed results.

F. STATE ERA'S

Another route to attack alleged sex discrimination in athletics is through that particular state's Equal Rights Amendment (ERA). Not all states have passed ERA's (as of 2009, 35 states have passed E.R.A.'s). There is no federal constitutional amendment that is enacted at this time that prohibits sexual discrimination. Thus ERA's impact athletics at the state level for the particular state but not at the federal level. If there is an applicable state ERA, it is often helpful and may be crucial to the success of sex discrimination cases.

For example, in *Blair v. Washington State University*, 108 Wash.2d 558, 740 P.2d 1379 (1987), a class action was brought under the Washington ERA. It was held that there was a substantive cause of action for victims of sex-based discrimination in intercollegiate sports, that is, Washington's ERA prohibited sex-based classifications altogether. *Blair* illustrates that state ERA's can be instrumental in overcoming discriminatory rules and practices which exclude or deny females the opportunity to participate in sports.

An outstanding female high school golfer, brought a claim of gender discrimination against the Massachusetts Interscholastic Athletic Association claiming she was denied the opportunity to play in the boys' state championship even though she participated on a mixed-gender team during the school year. A bylaw required male and female players on mixed-gender teams to compete in their own gender's state tournaments. The association offered spring seasons, but only offered a spring championship to female golfers. She claimed that fall tournaments offered a higher level of competition, a greater attendance of college coaches and recruiters, and a better stage for her to showcase her talents. The court found that the Association put the female players whose school decided to play in the fall season at a disadvantage by holding two boy's tournaments and one girls' tournament. Therefore, the court found that the bylaw violated the Massachusetts Equal Rights Amendment and enjoined enforcement of the bylaws against any female golfers. *Thomka v. Massachusetts Interscholastic Athletic Ass'n, Inc.,* 2007 WL 867084 (Mass.Super.Ct.2007).

An important advantage of the ERA approach is that state courts can now determine under state law whether gender classifications are suspect and thus warrant strict scrutiny as a standard of review. School rules will pass this standard if the gender classification is deemed necessary to achieve a compelling state's interest. Strict scrutiny will enhance the female athlete's opportunities for success since the school must prove that the classification has a direct relationship to the purpose of the regulation and that this purpose cannot be achieved by less restrictive means.

CHAPTER 25

INTELLECTUAL PROPERTY

A. GENERALLY

Intellectual property law encompasses ideas and subjects such as patents, trademarks, copyrights, trade secrets, trade dress as well as other subjects that relate to topics such as publicity rights, misappropriation, false advertising and unfair competition.

B. THE NATURE OF MARKETING

The marketing of both the athlete and sports in general deal directly with the laws of intellectual property. Sports marketing has become a huge industry in the United States and in the international community. The business of sports has become a billion-dollar industry. The growth of sports has exposed millions of people to sports every day in one form or another. Licensed sports merchandise sales totaled $13.9 billion in the United States in 2006. The National Football League has consistently been the leader in sports merchandise sales in the United States.

Sports licensing and marketing agreements are now commonplace in the business of sports and are

found in many different forms. Corporate sponsor-
ships are popular ways for a company to promote
company identification and product through the
purchasing of television time, etc. Corporations understand that sports has a universal appeal and
they attempt to use that to their advantage to assist
them in expanding their presence in a global fashion. Licensing sports properties and corporate sponsorship has become commonplace in the sports
world today.

The Super Bowl is the essence of sports marketing. Every year corporate behemoths vie for the
right to advertise their products on commercials
during the Super Bowl.

C. ATHLETES AS ENTERTAINERS

Sports has become a part of the huge entertainment landscape in America. Sports is thought of as
entertainment. Athletes have become associated
with the entertainment business in many different
fashions ranging from the movie industry to television appearances. Athletes have always been somewhat associated with the entertainment industry
(think Johnny Weismuller). In the 1970's, such
noted athletes as Jim Brown, O.J. Simpson, Fred
Dryer and Merlin Olsen have had notable movie
and television careers. More athletes are now appearing in movies and on television. LeBron James,
Michael Jordan, Dennis Rodman, Shaquille O'Neal,
and Dwayne "The Rock" Johnson have been the
most recent entries as cross-over athletes into the

movie arena. Athletes are now appearing in movies and television on a regular basis as endorsers for major corporations.

D. PATENTS

Patent law is governed by the Federal Patent Act. 35 U.S.C.A. § 1, *et seq.* (1995). If an individual discovers or invents any new machine, process, manufacture or composition of matter they may apply to obtain a patent. An individual can secure a patent by filing an application with the United States Patent and Trademark office (PTO).

The patent act defines a potential patent as any "new and useful process, machine, manufacture, or composition of matter" which includes mechanical, chemical, and electrical structures and processes. In order for an invention to be patentable, it must meet four requirements. An invention must be (1) in a subject matter category, (2) useful, (3) novel in relation to the prior art, and (4) obvious from the prior art to a person of ordinary skill in the art at the time the invention was made.

A patent confers on the owner the right to exclude others from selling or using the process or product. A patent owner may sue those individuals who directly infringe upon the patent by using or selling the invention without the proper authority to do so. A patent lasts 20 years from the date of the filing of the patent application with the PTO.

Patent law is involved in the sports industry in many different forms from golfing gizmos to football helmets to skates to rackets to lawn darts, etc.

E.   COPYRIGHTS

Copyright law protects original works of authorship embodied in a tangible medium of expression. See the Copyright Act, 17 U.S.C.A. §§ 101, *et seq.* (1998). Subject matter that may be copyrighted include music, drama, computer programs, sound recordings and the visual arts. Copyright protects the original expression of ideas, not the ideas themselves. A work may fall into more than one category. Copyright law gives exclusive rights to produce the work, to prepare derivative works based on the work, to distribute copies or photo records of the work and to publicly display or perform such work. A copyright term extends for the life of the author plus 70 years after the author's death. There are three basic conditions. A work must be within the constitutional and statutory definitions of a work of authorship; the work must be in a tangible medium of expression and it must be original.

There are a myriad of copyright concerns that entangle the sporting universe from autobiographies to instructional videos to TV broadcasts and re-broadcasts, etc. A typical and increasingly frequent example of a modern sports copyright problem is the unauthorized reception (or interception) of blacked-out (see *National Football League of New Haven v. Rondor, Inc.*, 840 F.Supp. 1160 (N.D.Ohio

1993)) or cable (see *Home Box Office v. Champs of New Haven, Inc.*, 837 F.Supp. 480 (D.Conn.1993)) TV sports programming by the way of a satellite dish antenna. In this type of case, the copyright holder will usually prevail and be granted a permanent injunction. Another example is *NBA v. Motorola, Inc.*, 105 F.3d 841 (2d Cir.1997), in which the second circuit ruled that a sports beeper company did not misappropriate the NBA's property by transmitting real-time NBA scores and statistics taken from the broadcasts of games in progress. See also *Score Group, Inc. v. Dad's Kid Corp.*, 1994 WL 794773 (C.D.Cal.1994) (alleged copyright infringement of hologram baseball trading cards); and *Seal–Flex v. Athletic Track & Court Construction*, 870 F.Supp. 753 (E.D.Mich.1994) (copyright infringement over a rubber running track surface).

F. TRADEMARKS

A trademark is a type of symbol used by one to identify a particular set of goods and to distinguish them from another's goods. A trademark owner can prevent others from using the same or similar marks that create a likelihood of confusion or deception. Under trademark law, an individual can establish one's manufactured goods and services from another's (think the Nike SWOOSH).

Trademark law distinguishes between the following: (1) the right to use a mark, (2) the right to exclude others from using a mark, and (3) the right to register the mark.

The Federal Trademark Act of 1946, which is commonly referred to as the Lanham Act, governs the registration and law of trademarks as well as the remedies and enforcement procedure for infringement of trademarks. Under the Lanham Act, a trademark is defined as including "any word, name, symbol, or device or any combination thereof adopted and used by manufacturer or merchant to identify his or her goods and also to distinguish from those manufactured or sold by others." The Lanham Act provides for the registration of service marks, certification marks as well as trademarks. Trademarks actually protect both the consumer and the owner. A consumer can identify the goods and services that have been satisfactory in the past because of a trademark.

In a trademark infringement action, plaintiff must meet five requirements: (1) there must have been either a reproduction or counterfeit of the mark; (2) the reproduction must have occurred without the authority of the registrant; (3) the reproduction has been used in the stream of commerce; (4) the use must have been in the sale, distribution or offering of goods or services; and (5) the use of the reproduction must be likely to cause confusion.

In sports, the most likely conundrum is whether the use of the reproduction is likely to cause confusion. See *National Football League Properties, Inc. v. Wichita Falls Sportswear, Inc.*, 532 F.Supp. 651

(W.D.Wash.1982); and *University of Pittsburgh v. Champion Products*, 686 F.2d 1040 (3d Cir.1982).

There are many trademark and trade dress concerns in the sports cosmos. The battle between golf club manufacturers against knock-off artists is just one example. The problem is, to most consumers, the SWOOSH, or the Shark's Shark, or the Cowboys' logo, IS the product itself. And the trademark holders must enforce their property as vigorously as Coca–Cola® or any other business will, since their identity is so intricately and completely associated with the trademark.

For example, see *Indianapolis Colts v. Metropolitan Baltimore Football Club*, 34 F.3d 410 (7th Cir. 1994), in which Canadian Football League (CFL) team in Baltimore was restrained from using the "Colts" trademark as in the "Baltimore CFL Colts", since "Colts" was already owned by the National Football League "Indianapolis Colts" (formerly of Baltimore). See also *Board of Trustees of the University of Arkansas v. Professional Therapy Services*, 873 F.Supp. 1280 (W.D.Ark.1995) (trademark infringement suit for unauthorized use of the RAZORBACK name and design logo).

Three Blind Mice Designs v. Cyrk, Inc., 892 F.Supp. 303 (D.Mass.1995) (trademark infringement over caricatures of hockey referees in the form of three blind mice); *Fila U.S.A. v. Kim*, 884 F.Supp. 491 (S.D.Fla.1995) (trademark infringement over athletic shoes); *Sports Authority v. Prime Hospitality Corp.*, 877 F.Supp. 124 (S.D.N.Y.1995) (trademark infringement between "The Sports Authority," a warehouse-type sporting good store and "Sports Authority Food, Spirits and Sports"); and *Time Warner Sports Merchandising v. Chicagoland Processing Corp.*, 1995 WL 107145 (N.D.Ill.1995) (dispute over licensing of trademarks and trade names associated with the 1994 World Cup of Soccer).

"March Madness" was upheld as a trademark of the joint venture formed by the National Collegiate Athletic Association (NCAA) and the Illinois High School Association (IHSA). The March Madness Athletic Association, whose only two members are the NCAA and IHSA, filed suit in 2000 against Netfire, Inc., and Sports Marketing International, Inc. (SMI), claiming trademark infringement and cybersquatting for their use of the domain name www.marchmadness.com. The website offered contests and information relating to the annual NCAA basketball championship tournament.

The term "March Madness" was first used by the IHSA in reference to its own male and female high school basketball tournaments. The NCAA and the IHSA had previously battled in court over which party had trademark ownership of the term. The Seventh Circuit court in Chicago ultimately ruled that the IHSA had been the first user, the term had developed a secondary meaning with the NCAA's annual collegiate basketball tournament as well as because of the media's use of the term in that context. See *Illinois High Sch. Ass'n v. GTE Van-*

tage Inc., 99 F.3d 244 (7th Cir.1996). In February of 2000 the two entities created the March Madness Athletic Association, LLC. *March Madness Athletic Ass'n, L.L.C. v. Netfire, Inc.,* 310 F.Supp.2d 786 (N.D.Tex.2003), j/ entered 2003 WL 22173299 (N.D.Tex.2003).

In *Pro Football, Inc. v. Harjo,* 284 F.Supp.2d 96 (D.D.C.2003), the court considered a challenge to the existing marks of the Washington Redskins of the National Football League through a trademark cancellation proceeding. The team challenged the decision of the Trial Trademark and Appeal Board (TTAB) canceling six of its trademark registrations because the TTAB found that the marks disparage Native Americans. The court granted summary judgment for the team, finding that the TTAB did not have substantial evidence to support its conclusion that the marks were disparaging to a substantial composite of Native Americans when used in connection with the team's football entertainment services.

Adidas has used its now infamous "Three-Stripe Mark" on the side of its athletic shoes for over 50 years. The mark is famous because of its use in connection with sports sponsorship. Adidas has multiple federal trademark registrations for the "Three–Stripe Mark" for athletic footwear. In its counterclaim, Adidas alleged that the plaintiff, offered for sale shoes that bear features that are confusingly similar to the "Three–Stripe Mark" (namely, a two-stripe mark). Adidas claimed it was used to intentionally mislead and deceive consumers.

The court held that the two-stripe design was likely to be confused with the Adidas "Three–Stripe Mark." Adidas had shown that there could also be a likelihood of initial-interest, point-of-sale, and post-sale confusion among consumers. Adidas adequately pled its dilution claim by showing that ACI was making commercial use of Adidas' famous mark in commerce. The use of the competing two-stripe mark eroded the distinctiveness of the "Three–Stripe Mark" by its capacity to identify and distinguish goods and services. *ACI Int'l, Inc. v. Adidas–Salomon AG,* 359 F.Supp.2d 918 (C.D.Cal.2005).

G. TRADE DRESS

Trade dress protection is available for non-functional features if they distinguish the goods' origin. The Lanham Act provides protection against the creation of confusion by the simulation of a product or services "trade dress". Trade dress originally meant a products' packaging, but more recent court decisions have extended trade dress to include the configuration and ornamentation of the product.

The signature case is *Pebble Beach Co. v. Tour 18 I, Ltd.*, 942 F.Supp. 1513 (S.D.Tex.1996) which was described as "the celebrated golf course design trade dress suit." Tour 18 is a local golf course outside of Houston that has purposefully attempted to emulate America's most famous golf holes from some of this nation's most prestigious golf courses. Plaintiffs, owners of three of the copied holes, filed a complaint alleging that Tour 18 violated their design proprietary rights, including infringement of their trademarks, trade dress, copyrights, and goodwill. Judge Hittner found trade dress infringement only with respect to the reproduction of the "lighthouse" hole (#18) at Harbour Town; Tour 18 was enjoined from any use of it in its promotions. Tour 18 must disclaim in all promotions, signage, etc., any association with the replicated holes. In short, only the truly distinctive signature holes (like Harbour Town's 18th) deserve trade dress protection; other than that, replica golf courses are legally permissible.

In *Taylor Made Golf Co., Inc. v. Carsten Sports, Ltd.*, 175 F.R.D. 658 (S.D.Cal.1997), plaintiff vigorously asserted its trademark and patented golf clubs against "knock-offs" of these clubs. Among its protected registration is the trade dress of its "BURNER BUBBLE" Metal Wood. Plaintiff's motion for summary judgment was granted, along with a monetary award based on infringer's profits. See also *Taylor Made Golf Co. v. Trend Precision Golf, Inc.*, 903 F.Supp. 1506 (M.D.Fla.1995) (trade dress for Callaway Golf's Big Bertha Irons).

APPENDICES

NOTE

These appendices display documents that represent practical ramifications of athletic participation and representation. These documents are an essential aspect of the practice of sports law and should be read as an adjunct to the chapters on contracts, amateur sports, and drug testing.

UNIFORM PLAYER'S CONTRACT
THE NATIONAL LEAGUE
OF PROFESSIONAL
BASEBALL CLUBS

Parties

Between _____, herein called the Club, and _____ of _____, herein called the Player.

Recital

The Club is a member of the National League of Professional Baseball Clubs, a voluntary association of member Clubs which has subscribed to the Major League Rules with the American League of Professional Baseball Clubs and its constituent Clubs and to The Professional Baseball Rules with that League and the National Association of Baseball Leagues.

Agreement

In consideration of the facts above recited and of the promises of each to the other, the parties agree as follows:

Employment

1.   The Club hereby employs the Player to render, and the Player agrees to render, skilled services as a baseball player during the year(s) 19__ including the Club's training season, the Club's exhibition games, the Club's playing season, the League Championship Series and the World Series (or any other official series in which the Club may participate and in any receipts of which the Player may be entitled to share).

Payment

2.   For performance of the Player's services and promises hereunder the Club will pay the Player the sum of \$_____, in semi-monthly installments after the commencement of the championship season(s) covered by this contract except as the schedule of payments may be modified by a special covenant.   Payment shall be made on the day the amount becomes due, regardless of whether the Club is "home" or "abroad."   If a monthly rate of payment is stipulated above, it shall begin with the commencement of the championship season (or such subsequent date as the Player's services may commence) and end with the termination of the

championship season and shall be payable in semi-monthly installments as above provided.

Nothing herein shall interfere with the right of the Club and the Player by special covenant herein to mutually agree upon a method of payment whereby part of the Player's salary for the above year can be deferred to subsequent years.

If the Player is in the service of the Club for part of the championship season only, he shall receive such proportion of the sum above mentioned, as the number of days of his actual employment in the championship season bears to the number of days in the championship season. Notwithstanding the rate of payment stipulated above, the minimum rate of payment to the Player for each day of service on a Major League Club shall be at the applicable rate set forth in Article VI(B)(1) of the Basic Agreement between the American League of Professional Baseball Clubs and the National League of Professional Baseball Clubs and the Major League Baseball Players Association, effective January 1, 1990 ("Basic Agreement"). The minimum rate of payment for National Association service for all Players (a) signing a second Major League contract (not covering the same season as any such Player's initial Major League contract) or a subsequent Major League contract, or (b) having at least one day of Major League service, shall be at the applicable rate set forth in Article VI(B)(2) of the Basic Agreement.

Payment to the Player at the rate stipulated above shall be continued throughout any period in which a Player is required to attend a regularly scheduled military encampment of the Reserve of the Armed Forces or of the National Guard during the championship season.

Loyalty

3. (a) The Player agrees to perform his services hereunder diligently and faithfully, to keep himself in first-class physical condition and to obey the Club's training rules, and pledges himself to the American public and to the Club to conform to high standards of personal conduct, fair play and good sportsmanship.

Baseball Promotion

3. (b) In addition to his services in connection with the actual playing of baseball, the Player agrees to cooperate with the Club and participate in any and all reasonable promotional activities of the Club and its League, which, in the opinion of the Club, will promote the welfare of the Club or professional baseball, and to observe and comply with all reasonable requirements of the Club respecting conduct and service of its team and its players, at all times whether on or off the field.

Pictures and Public Appearances

3. (c) The Player agrees that his picture may be taken for still photographs, motion pictures or television at such times as the Club may designate and agrees that all rights in such pictures shall belong

to the Club and may be used by the Club for publicity purposes in any manner it desires. The Player further agrees that during the playing season he will not make public appearances, participate in radio or television programs or permit his picture to be taken or write or sponsor newspaper or magazine articles or sponsor commercial products without the written consent of the Club, which shall not be withheld except in the reasonable interests of the Club or professional baseball.

PLAYER REPRESENTATIONS

Ability

4. (a) The Player represents and agrees that he has exceptional and unique skill and ability as a baseball player; that his services to be rendered hereunder are of a special, unusual and extraordinary character which gives them peculiar value which cannot be reasonably or adequately compensated for in damages at law, and that the Player's breach of this contract will cause the Club great and irreparable injury and damage. The Player agrees that, in addition to other remedies, the Club shall be entitled to injunctive and other equitable relief to prevent a breach of this contract by the Player, including, among others, the right to enjoin the Player from playing baseball for any other person or organization during the term of his contract.

Condition

4. (b) The Player represents that he has no physical or mental defects known to him and un-

known to the appropriate representative of the Club which would prevent or impair performance of his services.

Interest in Club

4. (c) The Player represents that he does not, directly or indirectly, own stock or have any financial interest in the ownership or earnings of any Major League Club, except as hereinafter expressly set forth, and covenants that he will not hereafter, while connected with any Major League Club, acquire or hold any such stock or interest except in accordance with Major League Rule 20(e).

Service

5. (a) The Player agrees that, while under contract, and prior to expiration of the Club's right to renew this contract, he will not play baseball otherwise than for the Club, except that the Player may participate in post-season games under the conditions prescribed in the Major League Rules. Major League Rule 18(b) is set forth herein.

Other Sports

5. (b) The Player and the Club recognize and agree that the Player's participation in certain other sports may impair or destroy his ability and skill as a baseball player. Accordingly, the Player agrees that he will not engage in professional boxing or wrestling; and that, except with the written consent of the Club, he will not engage in skiing, auto

racing, motorcycle racing, sky diving, or in any game or exhibition of football, soccer, professional league basketball, ice hockey or other sport involving a substantial risk of personal injury.

Assignment

6. (a) The Player agrees that his contract may be assigned by the Club (and reassigned by any assignee Club) to any other Club in accordance with the Major League Rules and the Professional Baseball Rules. The Club and the Player may, without obtaining special approval, agree by special covenant to limit or eliminate the right of the Club to assign this contract.

Medical Information

6. (b) The Player agrees that, should the Club contemplate an assignment of this contract to another Club or Clubs, the Club's physician may furnish to the physicians and officials of such other Club or Clubs all relevant medical information relating to the Player.

No Salary Reduction

6. (c) The amount stated in paragraph 2 and in special covenants hereof which is payable to the Player for the period stated in paragraph 1 hereof shall not be diminished by any such assignment, except for failure to report as provided in the next subparagraph (d).

Reporting

6. (d) The Player shall report to the assignee Club promptly (as provided in the Regulations) upon receipt of written notice from the Club of the assignment of this contract. If the Player fails to so report, he shall not be entitled to any payment for the period from the date he receives written notice of assignment until he reports to the assignee Club.

Obligations of Assignor and Assignee Clubs

6. (e) Upon and after such assignment, all rights and obligations of the assignor Club hereunder shall become the rights and obligations of the assignee Club; provided, however, that

(1) The assignee Club shall be liable to the Player for payments accruing only from the date of assignment and shall not be liable (but the assignor Club shall remain liable) for payments accrued prior to that date.

(2) If at any time the assignee is a Major League Club, it shall be liable to pay the Player at the full rate stipulated in paragraph 2 hereof for the remainder of the period stated in paragraph 1 hereof and all prior assignors and assignees shall be relieved of liability for any payment for such period.

(3) Unless the assignor and assignee Clubs agree otherwise, if the assignee Club is a National Association Club, the assignee Club shall be liable only to pay the Player at the rate usually paid by said assignee Club to other Players of similar skill

and ability in its classification and the assignor Club shall be liable to pay the difference for the remainder of the period stated in paragraph 1 hereof between an amount computed at the rate stipulated in paragraph 2 hereof and the amount so payable by the assignee Club.

Moving Allowances

6. (f) The Player shall be entitled to moving allowances under the circumstances and in the amounts set forth in Articles VII(F) and VIII of the Basic Agreement.

"Club"

6. (g) All references in other paragraphs of this contract to "the Club" shall be deemed to mean and include any assignee of this contract.

TERMINATION

By Player

7. (a) The Player may terminate this contract, upon written notice to the Club, if the Club shall default in the payments to the Player provided for in paragraph 2 hereof or shall fail to perform any other obligation agreed to be performed by the Club hereunder and if the Club shall fail to remedy such default within ten (10) days after the receipt by the Club of written notice of such default. The Player may also terminate this contract as provided in subparagraph (d)(4) of this paragraph 7. (See Article XV(H) of the Basic Agreement.)

By Club

7. (b) The Club may terminate this contract upon written notice to the Player (but only after requesting and obtaining waivers of this contract from all other Major League Clubs) if the Player shall at any time:

(1) fail, refuse or neglect to conform his personal conduct to the standards of good citizenship and good sportsmanship or to keep himself in first-class physical condition or to obey the Club's training rules; or

(2) fail, in the opinion of the Club's management, to exhibit sufficient skill or competitive ability to qualify or continue as a member of the Club's team; or

(3) fail, refuse or neglect to render his services hereunder or in any other manner materially breach this contract.

7. (c) If this contract is terminated by the Club, the Player shall be entitled to termination pay under the circumstances and in the amounts set forth in Article IX of the Basic Agreement. In addition, the Player shall be entitled to receive an amount equal to the reasonable traveling expenses of the Player, including first-class jet air fare and meals en route, to his home city.

Procedure

7. (d) If the Club proposes to terminate this contract in accordance with subparagraph (b) of this paragraph 7, the procedure shall be as follows:

(1) The Club shall request waivers from all other Major League Clubs. Such waivers shall be good for three (3) business days only. Such waiver request must state that it is for the purpose of terminating this contract and it may not be withdrawn.

(2) Upon receipt of waiver request, any other Major League Club may claim assignment of this contract at a waiver price of $1.00, the priority of claims to be determined in accordance with the Major League Rules.

(3) If this contract is so claimed, the Club shall, promptly and before any assignment, notify the Player that it had requested waivers for the purpose of terminating this contract and that the contract had been claimed.

(4) Within five (5) days after receipt of notice of such claim, the Player shall be entitled, by written notice to the Club, to terminate this contract on the date of his notice of termination. If the Player fails to so notify the Club, this contract shall be assigned to the claiming Club.

(5) If the contract is not claimed, the Club shall promptly deliver written notice of termination to the Player at the expiration of the waiver period.

7. (e) Upon any termination of this contract by the Player, all obligations of both Parties hereunder shall cease on the date of termination, except the obligation of the Club to pay the Player's compensation to said date.

Regulations

8.   The Player accepts as part of this contract the Regulations set forth herein.

Rules

9.   (a) The Club and the Player agree to accept, abide by and comply with all provisions of the Major League Agreement, the Major League Rules, the Rules or Regulations of the League of which the Club is a member, and the Professional Baseball Rules, in effect on the date of this Uniform Player's Contract, which are not inconsistent with the provisions of this contract or the provisions of any agreement between the Major League Clubs and the Major League Baseball Players Association, provided that the Club, together with the other clubs of the American and National Leagues and the National Association, reserves the right to modify, supplement or repeal any provision of said Agreement, Rules and/or Regulations in a manner not inconsistent with this contract or the provisions of any then existing agreement between the Major League Clubs and the Major League Baseball Players Association.

Disputes

9.   (b) All disputes between the Player and the Club which are covered by the Grievance Procedure as set forth in the Basic Agreement shall be resolved in accordance with such Grievance Procedure.

Publication

9. (c) The Club, the League President and the Commissioner, or any of them, may make public the findings, decision and record of any inquiry, investigation or hearing held or conducted, including in such record all evidence or information given, received, or obtained in connection therewith.

Renewal

10. (a) Unless the Player has exercised his right to become a free agent as set forth in the Basic Agreement the Club may, on or before December 20 (or if a Sunday, then the next preceding business day) in the year of the last playing season covered by this contract, tender to the Player a contract for the term of the next year by mailing the same to the Player at his address following his signature hereto, or if none be given, then at his last address of record with the Club. If prior to the March 1 next succeeding said December 20, the Player and the Club have not agreed upon the terms of such contract, then on or before ten (10) days after said March 1, the Club shall have the right by written notice to the Player at said address to renew this contract for the period of one year on the same terms, except that the amount payable to the Player shall be such as the Club shall fix in said notice; provided, however, that said amount, if fixed by a Major League Club, shall be an amount payable at a rate not less than as specified in Article VI, Section D, of the Basic Agreement. Subject to the Player's

rights as set forth in the Basic Agreement, the Club may renew this contract from year to year.

10. (b) The Club's right to renew this contract, as provided in subparagraph (a) of this paragraph 10, and the promise of the Player not to play otherwise than with the Club have been taken into consideration in determining the amount payable under paragraph 2 hereof.

Governmental Regulation—National Emergency

11. This contract is subject to federal or state legislation, regulations, executive or other official orders or other governmental action, now or hereafter in effect respecting military, naval, air or other governmental service, which may directly or indirectly affect the Player, Club or the League and subject also to the right of the Commissioner to suspend the operation of this contract during any national emergency during which Major League Baseball is not played.

Commissioner

12. The term "Commissioner" wherever used in this contract shall be deemed to mean the Commissioner designated under the Major League Agreement, or in the case of a vacancy in the office of Commissioner, the Executive Council or such other body or person or persons as shall be designated in the Major League Agreement to exercise the powers

and duties of the Commissioner during such vacancy.

Supplemental Agreements

The Club and the Player covenant that this contract, the Basic Agreement and the Agreement Re Major League Baseball Players Benefit Plan effective April 1, 1990 and applicable supplements thereto fully set forth all understandings and agreements between them, and agree that no other understandings or agreements, whether heretofore or hereafter made, shall be valid, recognizable, or of any effect whatsoever, unless expressly set forth in a new or supplemental contract executed by the Player and the Club (acting by its President or such other officer as shall have been thereunto duly authorized by the President or Board of Directors as evidenced by a certificate filed of record with the League President and Commissioner) and complying with the Major League Rules and the Professional Baseball Rules.

Special Covenants

_____

_____

_____

Approval

This contract or any supplement hereto shall not be valid or effective unless and until approved by the League President.

Signed in duplicate this ___ day of ___, A.D. 199___

_____   _____
(Player)   (Club)

_____   By _____
(Home address of Player)   (Authorized Signature)

Social Security No. _____

Approved _____, 199___

_____
President, The National
League of Professional
Baseball Clubs

REGULATIONS

1. The Club's playing season for each year covered by this contract and all renewals hereof shall be as fixed by The National League of Professional Baseball Clubs, or if this contract shall be assigned to a Club in another League, then by the League of which such assignee is a member.

2. The Player, when requested by the Club, must submit to a complete physical examination at

the expense of the Club, and if necessary to treatment by a regular physician or dentist in good standing. Upon refusal of the Player to submit to a complete medical or dental examination, the Club may consider such refusal a violation of this regulation and may take such action as it deems advisable under Regulation 5 of this contract. Disability directly resulting from injury sustained in the course and within the scope of his employment under this contract shall not impair the right of the Player to receive his full salary for the period of such disability or for the season in which the injury was sustained (whichever period is shorter), together with the reasonable medical and hospital expenses incurred by reason of the injury and during the term of this contract or for a period of up to two years from the date of initial treatment for such injury, whichever period is longer, but only upon the express prerequisite conditions that (a) written notice of such injury, including the time, place, cause and nature of the injury, is served upon and received by the Club within twenty days of the sustaining of said injury and (b) the Club shall have the right to designate the doctors and hospitals furnishing such medical and hospital services. Failure to give such notice shall not impair the rights of the Player, as herein set forth, if the Club has actual knowledge of such injury. All workmen's compensation payments received by the Player as compensation for loss of income for a specific period during which the Club is paying him in full, shall be paid over by the

Player to the Club. Any other disability may be ground for suspending or terminating this contract.

3. The Club will furnish the Player with two complete uniforms, exclusive of shoes, unless the Club requires the Player to wear non-standard shoes in which case the Club will furnish the shoes. The uniforms will be surrendered by the Player to the Club at the end of the season or upon termination of this contract.

4. The Player shall be entitled to expense allowances under the circumstances and in the amounts set forth in Article VII of the Basic Agreement.

5. For violation by the Player of any regulation or other provision of this contract, the Club may impose a reasonable fine and deduct the amount thereof from the Player's salary or may suspend the Player without salary for a period not exceeding thirty days or both. Written notice of the fine or suspension or both and the reason therefor shall in every case be given to the Player and the Players Association. (See Article XII of the Basic Agreement.)

6. In order to enable the Player to fit himself for his duties under this contract, the Club may require the Player to report for practice at such places as the Club may designate and to participate in such exhibition contests as may be arranged by the Club, without any other compensation than that herein elsewhere provided, for a period beginning not earlier than thirty-three (33) days prior to the start of the championship season, provided, however, that

the Club may invite players to report at an earlier date on a voluntary basis in accordance with Article XIV of the Basic Agreement. The Club will pay the necessary traveling expenses, including the first-class jet air fare and meals en route of the Player from his home city to the training place of the Club, whether he be ordered to go there directly or by way of the home city of the Club. In the event of the failure of the Player to report for practice or to participate in the exhibition games, as required and provided for, he shall be required to get into playing condition to the satisfaction of the Club's team manager, and at the Player's own expense, before his salary shall commence.

7. In case of assignment of this contract the Player shall report promptly to the assignee Club within 72 hours from the date he receives written notice from the Club of such assignment, if the Player is then not more than 1,600 miles by most direct available railroad route from the assignee Club, plus an additional 24 hours for each additional 800 miles.

Post–Season Exhibition Games. Major League Rule 18(b) provides:

(b) EXHIBITION GAMES. No player shall participate in any exhibition game during the period between the close of the Major League championship season and the following training season, except that, with the consent of his club and permission of the Commissioner, a player may participate in exhibition games for a period of not less than thirty (30) days, such period to be designated annually by the Commissioner. Players who participate in barnstorming during this period cannot engage in any Winter League activities. Player conduct, on and off the field, in connection with such post-season exhibition games shall be subject to the discipline of the Commissioner. The Commissioner shall not approve of more than three (3) players of any one club on the same team. The Commissioner shall not approve of more than three (3) players from the joint membership of the World Series participants playing in the same game. No player shall participate in any exhibition game with or against any team which, during the current season or within one year, has had any ineligible player or which is or has been during the current season or within one (1) year, managed and controlled by an ineligible player or by any person who has listed an ineligible player under an assumed name or who otherwise has violated, or attempted to violate, any exhibition game contract; or with or against any team which, during said season or within one (1) year, has played against teams containing such ineligible players, or so managed or controlled. Any player violating this Rule shall be fined not less than Fifty Dollars ($50.00) nor more than Five Hundred Dollars ($500.00), except that in no event shall such fine be less than the consideration received by such player for participating in such game.

PRINTED IN U.S.A. REVISED AS OF MAY 1990

Keeping Faith With The Student-Athlete

A New Model for Intercollegiate Athletics

March 1991

Keeping Faith

LETTER OF TRANSMITTAL

Mr. Lee Hills
Vice Chairman
Board of Trustees
Knight Foundation
2 South Biscayne Boulevard
Miami, Florida 33131

Dear Mr. Hills,

On October 19, 1989, the Trustees of Knight Foundation created this Commission and directed it to propose a reform agenda for intercollegiate athletics. In doing so, they expressed concern that abuses in athletics had reached proportions threatening the very integrity of higher education, which is one of the principal program interests of the Foundation.

It has been our privilege to co-chair this endeavor and on behalf of the members of the Commission we are pleased to transmit this report, *Keeping Faith with the Student-Athlete: A New Model for Intercollegiate Athletics.*

In developing its recommendations, the Commission spent more than a year in study and debate, and benefited from the advice and suggestions of more than 80 experts. During a series of public meetings, we heard from athletics administrators, coaches, student-athletes, scholars, journalists, leaders of professional leagues and others.

The demanding task of monitoring college sports is made all the more difficult today by a confluence of new factors. These include the perception that ethical behavior in the larger society has broken down, the public's insistence on winning local teams, and the growth of television combined with the demand for sports programming, Clearly, universities have not immunized themselves from these developments.

We sense that public concern about abuse is growing. The public appears ready to believe that many institutions achieve goals not through the honest effort but through equivocation, not by hard work and sacrifice but by hook or by crook. If the public's perception is correct, both the educational aims of athletics and the institutions' integrity are called into question.

We have attempted to define the problems as we understand them and to suggest solutions, not search for scapegoats. This report addresses what we consider to be the main issues and does not attempt to treat subordinate matters in any detail. Even in respect to what we see as the major issues, we place less emphasis on specific solutions than on proposing a structure

15

through which these issues -- and others arising in the future -- can be addressed by the responsible administrators.

The first section introduces the core of our interest: the place of athletics on our campuses and the imperative to place the well-being of the student-athlete at the forefront of our concerns. The second section presents our recommendations. It outlines a new structure for intercollegiate athletics in which the well-being of student-athletes, our overarching goal, is attained by what we call the "one-plus-three" model -- presidential control directed toward academic integrity, financial integrity, and independent certification. The third section calls for a nationwide effort, growing from our campuses outward, to put the "one-plus-three" model into effect and suggests appropriate roles for each of the major groups on campus.

The members of the Commission were straightforward in their discussions and are candid in this report regarding both the strengths and the weaknesses of intercollegiate athletics. Although individual members of the Commission may have reservations about the details of some of these recommendations, they are unanimous in their support of the broad themes outlined in this document.

The commission's commitment to the reform of college sport does not end with this report. We will follow through. We plan to monitor the progress in implementing the "one-plus-three" model. In twelve months we will revisit these issues and define what remains to be accomplished.

On a personal note, we want to express our deep sadness on learning, as this document went to press, of the death of a man who played a pivotal role in establishing the Commission, James L. Knight, Chairman of the Knight Foundation. We speak for the entire Commission in expressing our sympathy and our hope that this report keeps faith with Mr. Knight's vision of what intercollegiate sport can be at its best.

Respectfully,

William C. Friday
Co-Chairman
President
William R. Kenan Jr. Fund

Theodore M. Hesburgh, C.S.C.
Co-Chairman
President Emeritus
University of Notre Dame

INTRODUCTION

At their best, which is most of the time, intercollegiate athletics provide millions of people -- athletes, undergraduates, alumni and the general public -- with great pleasure, the spectacle of extraordinary effort and physical grace, the excitement of an outcome in doubt, and a shared unifying experience. Thousands of men and women in the United States are stronger adults because of the challenges they mastered as young athletes.

But at their worst, big-time college athletics appear to have lost their bearings. With increasing frequency they threaten to overwhelm the universities in whose name they were established and to undermine the integrity of one of our fundamental national institutions: higher education.

The Knight Commission believes that intercollegiate athletics, kept in perspective, are an important part of college life. We are encouraged by the energy of the reform movement now under way. But the clamor for reform and the distinguishing signals of government intrusion confirm the need to rethink the management and fundamental premises of intercollegiate athletics.

The Commission's bedrock conviction is that university presidents are the key to successful reform. They must be in charge -- and be understood to be in charge -- on campuses, in conferences and in the decision-making councils of the NCAA.

We propose what we call the "one-plus-three" model, a new structure of reform in which the "one" -- presidential control -- is directed toward the "three" -- academic integrity, financial integrity and independent certification. With such a model in place, higher education can address all of the subordinate difficulties in college sports. Without such a model, athletics reform will continue in fits and starts, its energy squandered on symptoms, the underlying problems ignored.

This is how these recommendations can help change college sports:

PRESIDENTIAL CONTROL

1. Trustees will delegate to the president -- not reserve for the board or individual members of the board -- the administrative authority to govern the athletics program.

2. Presidents will have the same degree of control over athletics that they exercise elsewhere in the university, including the authority to hire, evaluate and terminate athletics directors and coaches, and to oversee all financial matters in their athletics departments.

3. The policy role of presidents will be enhanced throughout the decision-making structures of the NCAA.

4. Trustees, alumni and local boosters will defer to presidential control.

ACADEMIC INTEGRITY

1. Cutting academic corners in order to admit athletes will not be tolerated. Student-athletes will not be admitted unless they are likely, in the judgment of academic officials, to graduate. Junior college transfers will be given no leeway in fulfilling eligibility requirements.

2. "No Pass, No Play" will be the byword of college sports in admissions, academic progress and graduation rates.

3. An athlete's eligibility each year, and each academic term, will be based on continuous progress toward graduation within five years of enrollment.

4. Graduation rates of student-athletes in each sport will be similar to the graduation rates of other students who have spent comparable time as full-time students.

FINANCIAL INTEGRITY

1. Athletics departments will not operate as independent subsidiaries of the university. All funds raised and spent for athletics will go through the university's central financial controls and will be subject to the same oversight and scrutiny as funds in other departments. Athletics foundations and booster clubs will not be permitted to provide support for athletics programs outside the administration's direct control.

2. Contracts for athletics-related outside income of coaches and administrators, including shoe and equipment contracts, will be negotiated through the university.

3. Institutional funds can be spent on athletics programs. This will affirm the legitimate role of athletics on campus and can relieve some of the pressure on revenue-producing teams to support non-revenue sports.

CERTIFICATION

1. Each year, every NCAA institution will undergo a thorough, independent audit of all academic and financial matters related to athletics.

2. Universities will have to withstand the scrutiny of their peers. Each NCAA institution awarding athletics aid will be required to participate in a comprehensive certification program. This program will verify that the athletics department follows institutional goals, that its fiscal controls are sound, and that athletes in each sport resemble the rest of the student body in admissions, academic progress and graduation rates.

The reforms proposed above are designed to strengthen the bonds that connect student, sport and higher learning. Student-athletes should compete successfully in the classroom as well as on the playing field and, insofar as possible, should be indistinguishable from other undergraduates. All athletes -- men or women, majority or minority, in revenue-producing and non-revenue sports -- should be treated equitably.

In order to help presidents put the "one-plus-three" model into effect, the Commission proposes a statement of principles to be used as the basis for intensive discussion at each institution. Our hope is that this discussion will involve everyone on the campus with major responsibilities for college sports. These principles support the "one-plus-three" model and can be employed as a starting point on any campus wishing to take the recommendations of this document seriously. We recommend incorporating these principles into the NCAA's certification process and using that process as the foundation of a nationwide effort to advance athletics reform. Ideally, institutions will agree to schedule only those colleges and universities that have passed all aspects of the certification process. Institutions that refuse to correct deficiencies will find themselves isolated by the vast majority of administrators who support intercollegiate sports as an honorable tradition in college life.

Reform

THE NEED FOR REFORM

As our nation approaches a new century, the demand for reform of intercollegiate athletics has escalated dramatically. Educational and athletics leaders face the challenge of controlling costs, restraining recruiting, limiting time demands, and restoring credibility and dignity to the term "student-athlete." In the midst of these pressures, it is easy to lose sight of the achievements of intercollegiate sports and easier still to lose sight of why these games are played.

The appeal of competitive games is boundless. In ancient times, men at war laid down their weapons to compete in the Olympic games. Today, people around the globe put aside their daily cares to follow the fortunes of their teams in the World Cup. In the United States, the Super Bowl, the World Series, college football and the NCAA basketball tournament command the attention of millions. Sports have helped break down bigotry and prejudice in American life. On the international scene, they have helped integrate East and West, socialist and capitalist. The passion for sport is universal, shared across time and continents.

Games and sports are educational in the best sense of that word because they teach the participant and the observer new truths about testing oneself and others, about the enduring values of challenge and response, about teamwork, discipline and perseverance. Above all, intercollegiate contests — at any level of skill — drive home a fundamental lesson: Goals worth achieving will be attained only through effort, hard work, sacrifice, and sometimes even these will not be enough to overcome the obstacles life places in our path.

The value and success of college sports should not be overlooked. They are the foundation of our optimism for the future. At the 828 colleges and universities which comprise the National Collegiate Athletic Association (NCAA), over 254,000 young men and women participate in 21 different sports each year in about one quarter of a million contests. At the huge majority of these institutions, virtually all of these young athletes participate in these contests without any evidence of scandal or academic abuse. This record is one in which student-athletes and university administrators can take pride and from which the Knight Foundation Commission takes heart.

All of the positive contributions that sports make to higher education, however, are threatened by disturbing patterns of abuse, particularly in some big-time programs. These patterns are grounded in institutional indifference, presidential neglect, and the growing commercialization of sport combined with the urge to win at all costs. The sad truth is that on too many campuses big-time revenue sports are out of control.

The assumption of office by a new executive director of the NCAA coincides with renewed vigor for major reform on the part of athletics administrators and university presidents.

Reform efforts are well underway. One conference has voted to bar from athletics participation all students who do not meet NCAA freshman-eligibility standards. One state has decided to require all students in publicly supported institutions to maintain a "C" average in order to participate in extracurricular activities, including intercollegiate sports. Judging by the tone of recent NCAA conventions, concern for the university's good name and the welfare of the student-athlete — irrespective of gender, race or sport — will be the centerpiece of athletics administration as we approach a new century. We do not want to interfere with that agenda. We hope to advance it.

THE PROBLEM

The problems described to the Commission — in more than a year of meetings and discussions with athletics directors, faculty representatives, coaches, athletes, conference leaders, television officials and accrediting associations - are widespread. They are not entirely confined to big schools ... or to football or basketball ... or to men's sports. But they are most apparent within major athletics programs and are concentrated most strongly in those sports for which collegiate participation serves the talented few as an apprenticeship for professional careers.

Recruiting, the bane of the college coach's life, is one area particularly susceptible to abuse. While most institutions and coaches recruit ethically and within the rules, some clearly do not. Recruiting abuses are the most frequent cause of punitive action by the NCAA. Even the most scrupulous coaching staffs are trapped on a recruiting treadmill, running through an interminable sequence of letters, telephone calls and visits. The cost of recruiting a handful of basketball players each year exceeds, on some campuses, the cost of recruiting the rest of the freshman class.

Athletics programs are given special, often unique, status within the university; the best coaches receive an income many times that of most full professors; some coaches succumb to the pressure to win with recruiting violations and even the abuse of players; boosters respond to athletic performance with gifts and under-the-table payments; faculty members, presidents and other administrators, unable to control the enterprise, stand by as it undermines the institution's goals in the name of values alien to the best the university represents.

These programs appear to promise a quick route to revenue, recognition and renown for the university. But along that road, big-time athletics programs often take on a life of their own. Their intrinsic educational value, easily lost in their use to promote extra-institutional goals, becomes engulfed by the revenue stream they generate and overwhelmed by the accompanying publicity. Now, instead of the institution alone having a stake in a given team or sport, the circle of involvement includes television networks and local stations that sell advertising time, the corporations and local businesses buying the time, the boosters living vicariously through the team's success, the local economies critically dependent on the big game, and the burgeoning population of fans who live and die with the team's fortunes.

In this crucible, the program shifts from providing an exciting avenue of expression and enjoyment for the athletes and their fans to maximizing the revenue and institutional prestige that can be generated by a handful of highly visible teams. The athletics director can become the CEO of a fair-sized corporation with a significant impact on the local economy. The "power coach," often enjoying greater recognition throughout the state than most elected officials, becomes chief operating officer of a multi-million dollar business.

Within the last decade, big-time athletics programs have taken on all of the trappings of a major entertainment enterprise. In the search for television revenues, traditional rivalries have been tossed aside in conference realignments, games have been rescheduled to satisfy broadcast preferences, the number of games has multiplied, student-athletes have been put on the field at all hours of the day and night, and university administrators have fallen to quarreling among themselves over the division of revenues from national broadcasting contracts.

But the promise of easy access to renown and revenue often represents fool's gold. Recognition on the athletic field counts for little in the academic community. Expenses are driven by the search for revenues and the revenue stream is consumed, at most institutions, in building up the program to maintain the revenue. Renown for athletic exploits can be a two-edged sword if the university is forced to endure the public humiliation of sanctions brought on by rules violations. Above all, the fragile institution of the university often finds itself unable to stand up against the commitment, the energy and the passion underlying modern intercollegiate athletics.

In the circumstances we have described, it is small wonder that three out of four Americans believe that television dollars, not administrators, control college sports. But the underlying problems existed long before the advent of television. A 1929 report from the Carnegie Fund for the Advancement of Teaching identified many of the difficulties still with us today. In college athletics, it said, recruiting had become corrupt, professionals had replaced amateurs, education was being neglected, and commercialism reigned. That document still rings true today, reminding us that it is an oversimplification to blame today's problems on television alone. Even so, the lure of the television dollars has unquestionably added a new dimension to the problem and must be addressed.

At the root of the problem is a great reversal of ends and means. Increasingly, the team, the game, the season and "the program" — all intended as expressions of the university's larger purposes — gain ascendancy over the ends that created and nurtured them. Non-revenue sports receive little attention and women's programs take a back seat. As the educational context for collegiate athletics competition is pushed aside, what remains is, too often, a self-justifying enterprise whose connection with learning is tainted by commercialism and incipient cynicism.

In the short term, the human price for this lack of direction is exacted from the athletes whose talents give meaning to the system. But the ultimate cost is paid by the university and by

22

society itself. If the university is not itself a model of ethical behavior, why should we expect such behavior from students or from the larger society?

Pervasive though these problems are, they are not universal. This is true even if the universe is restricted to the roughly 300 institutions playing football or basketball at the highest levels. But they are sufficiently common that it is no longer possible to conclude they represent the workings of a handful of misguided individuals or a few "rotten apples." One recent analysis indicates that fully one-half of Division I-A institutions (the 106 colleges and universities with the most competitive and expensive football programs) were the object of sanctions of varying severity from the NCAA during the 1980s. Other institutions, unsanctioned, graduate very few student-athletes in revenue-producing sports.

The problems are so deep-rooted and long-standing that they must be understood to be systemic. They can no longer be swept under the rug or kept under control by tinkering around the edges. Because these problems are so widespread, nothing short of a new structure holds much promise for restoring intercollegiate athletics to their proper place in the university. This report of the Knight Foundation Commission is designed to suggest such a structure.

We are at a critical juncture with respect to the intercollegiate athletics system. We believe college sports face three possible futures:

- higher education will put its athletics house in order from within;

- athletics order will be imposed from without and college sports will be regulated by government; or

- abuse — unchecked — will spread, destroying not only the intrinsic value of intercollegiate athletics but higher education's claim to the high moral ground it should occupy.

Concern for the health of both intercollegiate athletics and American higher education makes the choice clear.

FOCUS ON STUDENTS

Even clearer, in the Commission's view, is the need to start with the student-athlete. The reforms we deem essential start with respect for the dignity of the young men and women who compete and the conviction that they occupy a legitimate place as students on our campuses. If we can get that right, everything else will fall into place. If we cannot, the rest of it will be all wrong.

Regulations governing the recruitment of student-athletes — including letters-of-intent, and how and under what conditions coaches may contact athletes — take up 30 pages of the NCAA Manual. But there is no requirement that the prospective student-athlete be found academically admissible before accepting a paid campus visit. A prospective player can very easily agree to attend an institution even though the admissions office does not know of the student's existence. Similarly, student-athletes deemed eligible in the fall can compete throughout the year, generally regardless of their academic performance in the first term.

It is hard to avoid the conclusion that there are few academic constraints on the student-athlete. Non-academic prohibitions, on the other hand, are remarkable. Athletics personnel are not permitted to offer rides to student-athletes. University officials are not permitted to invite a student-athlete home for dinner on the spur of the moment. Alumni are not allowed to encourage an athlete to attend their alma mater.

Each of these prohibitions — and the many others in the NCAA Manual — can be understood individually as a response to a specific abuse. But they add up to a series of checks and balances on the student-athlete as an athlete that have nothing to do with the student-athlete as a student. Some rules have been developed to manage potential abuse in particular sports, at particular schools, or in response to the particular circumstances of individual athletes. Whatever the origin of these regulations, the administration of intercollegiate athletics is now so overburdened with legalism and detail that the NCAA Manual more nearly resembles the IRS Code than it does a guide to action.

It is time to get back to first principles. Intercollegiate athletics exist first and foremost for the student-athletes who participate, whether male or female, majority or minority, whether they play football in front of 50,000 or field hockey in front of their friends. It is the university's obligation to educate all of them, an obligation perhaps more serious because the demands we place on them are so much more severe. Real reform must begin here.

A New Model

"ONE-PLUS-THREE"

Individual institutions and the NCAA have consistently dealt with problems in athletics by defining most issues as immediate ones: curbing particular abuses, developing nationally uniform standards, or creating a "level playing field" overseen by athletics administrators.

But the real problem is not one of curbing particular abuses. It is a more central need to have academic administrators define the terms under which athletics will be conducted in the university's name. The basic concern is not nationally uniform standards. It is a more fundamental issue of grounding the regulatory process in the primacy of academic values. The root difficulty is not creating a "level playing field". It is insuring that those on the field are students as well as athletes.

We reject the argument that the only realistic solution to the problem is to drop the student-athlete concept, put athletes on the payroll, and reduce or even eliminate their responsibilities as students.

Such a scheme has nothing to do with education, the purpose for which colleges and universities exist. Scholarship athletes are already paid in the most meaningful way possible: with a free education. The idea of intercollegiate athletics is that the teams represent their institutions as true members of the student body, not as hired hands. Surely American higher education has the ability to devise a better solution to the problems of intercollegiate athletics than making professionals out of the players, which is no solution at all but rather an unacceptable surrender to despair.

It is clear to the Commission that a realistic solution will not be found without a serious and persistent commitment to a fundamental concept: intercollegiate athletics must reflect the values of the university. Where the realities of intercollegiate competition challenge those values, the university must prevail.

The reform we seek takes shape around what the Commission calls the "one-plus-three" model. It consists of the "one" -- presidential control -- directed toward the "three" -- academic integrity, financial integrity and accountability through certification. This model is fully consistent with the university as a context for vigorous and exciting intercollegiate competition. It also serves to bond athletics to the purposes of the university in a way that provides a new framework for their conduct.

The three sides of the reform triangle reinforce each other. Each strengthens the other two. At the same time, the three principles can only be realized through presidential leadership. The coach can only do so much to advance academic values. The athletics director can only go so far to guarantee financial integrity. The athletics department cannot certify itself. But the president, with a transcendent responsibility for every aspect of the university, can give shape and focus to all three.

With such a foundation in place, higher education can renew its authentic claim on public confidence in the integrity of college sports. All of the subordinate issues and problems of intercollegiate athletics -- athletic dorms, freshman eligibility, the length of playing seasons and recruitment policies -- can be resolved responsibly within this model. Without such a base, athletics reform is doomed to continue in fits and starts, its energy rising and falling with each new headline, its focus shifting to respond to each new manifestation of the underlying problems. It is the underlying problems, not their symptoms, that need to be attacked. The "one-plus-three" model is the foundation on which those who care about higher education and student-athletes can build permanent reform.

THE "ONE": PRESIDENTIAL CONTROL

Presidents are accountable for the major elements in the university's life. The burden of leadership falls on them for the conduct of the institution, whether in the classroom or on the playing field. The president cannot be a figurehead whose leadership applies elsewhere in the university but not in the athletics department.

The following recommendations are designed to advance presidential control:

1. Trustees should explicitly endorse and reaffirm presidential authority in all matters of athletics governance. The basis of presidential authority on campus is the governing board. If presidential action is to be effective, it must have the backing of the board of trustees. We recommend that governing boards:

- Delegate to the president administrative authority over financial matters in the athletics program.
- Work with the president to develop common principles for hiring, evaluating and terminating all athletics administrators, and affirm the president's role and ultimate authority in this central aspect of university administration.
- Advise each new president of its expectations about athletics administration and annually review the athletics program.
- Work with the president to define the faculty's role, which should be focused on academic issues in athletics.

2. Presidents should act on their obligation to control conferences. We believe that presidents of institutions affiliated with athletics conferences should exercise effective voting control of these organizations. Even if day-to-day representation at conference proceedings is delegated to other institutional representatives, presidents should formally retain the authority to define agendas, offer motions, cast votes or provide voting instructions, and review and, if necessary, reshape conference decisions.

3. Presidents should control the NCAA. The Knight Commission believes hands-on presidential involvement in NCAA decision-making is imperative. As demonstrated by the overwhelming approval of their reform legislation at the 1991 NCAA convention, presidents have the power to set the course of the NCAA - if they will use it. The Commission recommends that:

- Presidents make informed use of the ultimate NCAA authority - their votes on the NCAA convention floor. They should either attend and vote personally, or familiarize themselves with the issues and give their representatives specific voting instructions. Recent procedural changes requiring that pending legislation be published for review several months before formal consideration simplify this task enormously.

- The Presidents Commission follow up its recent success with additional reform measures, beginning with the legislation on academic requirements it proposes to sponsor in 1992. The Commission can and should consolidate its leadership role by energetic use of its authority to draft legislation, to determine whether balloting will be by roll call or paddle, and to order the convention agenda.

- Presidents must stay the course. Opponents of progress have vowed they will be back to reverse recent reform legislation. Presidents must challenge these defenders of the status quo. They cannot win the battle for reform if they fight in fits and starts — their commitment to restoring perspective to intercollegiate athletics must be complete and continuing.

4. Presidents should commit their institutions to equity in all aspects of intercollegiate athletics. The Commission emphasizes that continued inattention to the requirements of Title IX (mandating equitable treatment of women in educational programs) represents a major stain on institutional integrity. It is essential that presidents take the lead in this area. We recommend that presidents:

- Annually review participation opportunities in intercollegiate programs by gender.

- Develop procedures to insure more opportunities for women's participation and promote equity for women's teams in terms of schedules, facilities, travel arrangements and coaching.

5. Presidents should control their institution's involvement with commercial television. The lure of television dollars has clearly exacerbated the problems of intercollegiate athletics. Just as surely, institutions have not found the will or the inclination to define the terms of their involvement with the entertainment industry. Clearly, something must be done to mitigate the growing public perception that the quest for television dollars is turning college sports into an entertainment enterprise. In the Commission's view it is crucial that presidents, working through appropriate conference and NCAA channels, immediately and critically review contractual relationships with networks. It is time that institutions clearly prescribe the policies,

27

terms and conditions of the televising of intercollegiate athletics events. Greater care must be given to the needs and obligations of the student-athlete and the primacy of the academic calendar over the scheduling requirements of the networks.

THE "THREE": ACADEMIC INTEGRITY

The first consideration on a university campus must be academic integrity. The fundamental premise must be that athletes are students as well. They should not be considered for enrollment at a college or university unless they give reasonable promise of being successful at that institution in a course of study leading to an academic degree. Student-athletes should undertake the same courses of study offered to other students and graduate in the same proportion as those who spend comparable time as full-time students. Their academic performance should be measured by the same criteria applied to other students.

Admissions — At some Division I institutions, according to NCAA data, every football and basketball player admitted in the 1988-89 academic year met the university's regular admissions standards. At others, according to the same data, not a single football or basketball player met the regular requirements. At half of all Division I-A institutions, about 20 percent or more of football and basketball players are "special admits," i.e., admitted with special consideration, That rate is about 10 times as high as the rate for total student body.

The Commission believes that the freshman eligibility rule known as Proposition 48 has improved the academic preparation of student-athletes. Proposition 48 has also had some unanticipated consequences. Virtually unnoticed in the public discussion about Proposition 48 is the requirement that the high school grade point average be computed for only 11 units of academic work. Out of 106 Division I-A institutions, 97 of them (91 percent) require or recommend more than 11 high school academic units for the typical high school applicant. In fact, 73 Division I-A institutions, according to their published admissions criteria, require or recommend 15 or more academic high school units from all other applicants.

Academic Progress — The most recent NCAA data indicate that in one-half of all Division I institutions about 90 percent of all football and basketball players are meeting "satisfactory" progress requirements and are, therefore, eligible for intercollegiate competition. Under current regulations, however, it is possible for a student-athlete to remain eligible each year but still be far from a degree after five years as a full-time student. The 1991 NCAA convention began to address this issue in enacting provisions requiring that at the end of the third year of enrollment, student-athletes should have completed 50 percent of their degree requirements.

The 1991 convention also made significant headway in reducing the excessive time demands athletic participation places on student-athletes. Throughout the 1980s, according to the recent NCAA research, football and basketball players at Division I-A institutions spent approximately 30 hours a week on their sports in season, more time than they spent attending or preparing for class.

Football and basketball are far from the only sinners. Baseball, golf and tennis players report the most time spent on sports. Many other sports for both men and women, including swimming and gymnastics, demand year-round conditioning if athletes are to compete successfully. It remains to be seen whether the recent NCAA legislation will make a genuine dent in the onerous demands on students' time.

Graduation Rates -- At some Division I institutions, 100 percent of the basketball players or the football players graduate within five years of enrolling. At others, none of the basketball or football players graduate within five years. In the typical Division I college or university, only 33 percent of basketball players and 37.5 percent of football players graduate within five years. Overall graduation rates for all student-athletes (men and women) in Division I approach graduation rates for all students in Division I according to the NCAA -- 47 percent of all student-athletes in Division I graduate in five years.

Dreadful anecdotal evidence about academic progress and graduation rates is readily available. But the anecdotes merely illustrate what the NCAA data confirm: About two-thirds of the student-athletes in big-time, revenue-producing sports have not received a college degree within five years of enrolling at their institution.

The Commission's recommendations on academic integrity can be encapsulated in a very simple concept -- "No Pass, No Play." That concept, first developed for high school athletics eligibility in Texas, is even more apt for institutions of higher education. It applies to admissions, to academic progress and to graduation rates.

The following recommendations are designed to advance academic integrity:

1. The NCAA should strengthen initial eligibility requirements. Proposition 48 has served intercollegiate athletics well. It has helped insure that more student-athletes are prepared for the rigors of undergraduate study. It is time to build on and extend its success. We recommend that:

- By 1995 prospective student-athletes should present 15 units of high school academic work in order to be eligible to play in their first year.

- A high school student-athlete should be ineligible for reimbursed campus visits or for signing a letter of intent until the admissions office indicates he or she shows reasonable promise of being able to meet the requirements for a degree.

- student-athletes transferring from junior colleges should meet the admissions requirements applied to other junior college students. Moreover, junior college transfers who did not meet NCAA Proposition 48 requirements when they graduated from high school should be required to sit out a year of competition after transfer.

- Finally, we propose an NCAA study of the conditions under which colleges and universities admit athletes. This study should be designed to see if it is feasible to put in place admissions requirements to insure that the range of academic ability for incoming athletes, by sport, would approximate the range of abilities for the institution's freshman class.

2. The letter of intent should serve the student as well as the athletics department. Incoming freshmen who have signed a letter of intent to attend a particular institution should be released from that obligation if the head coach who recruited them leaves the institution, or if the institution is put on probation by the NCAA, before the enroll. Such incoming student-athletes should be automatically eligible to apply to any other college or university, except the head or assistant coach's new home, and to participate in intercollegiate athletics. Currently student-athletes are locked into the institution no matter how its athletics program changes -- a restriction that applies to no other student.

3. Athletics scholarships should be offered for a five year period. In light of the time demands of athletics competition, we believe that eligibility should continue to be limited to a period of four years, but athletics scholarship assistance routinely should cover the time required to complete a degree, up to a maximum of five years. Moreover, the initial offer to the student-athlete should be for the length of time required to earn a degree up to five years, not the single year now mandated by NCAA rules. The only athletics condition under which the five-year commitment could be broken would be if the student refused to participate in the sport for which the grant-in-aid was offered. Otherwise, aid should continue as long as the student-athlete remains in good standing at the institution.

4. Athletics eligibility should depend on progress toward a degree. In order to retain eligibility, enrolled athletes should be able to graduate within five years and to demonstrate progress toward that goal each semester. At any time during the student-athlete's undergraduate years, the university should be able to demonstrate that the athlete can meet this test without unreasonable course loads. Further, eligibility for participation should be restricted to students who meet the institution's published academic requirements, including a minimum grade point average when applicable.

5. Graduation rates of athletes should be a criterion for NCAA certification. The Commission believes that no university should countenance lower graduation rates for its student-athletes, in any sport, than it is willing to accept in the full-time student body at large. Fundamental to the restoration of public trust is our belief that graduation rates in revenue-producing sports should be a major criterion on which NCAA certification depends.

THE "THREE" : FINANCIAL INTEGRITY

An institution of higher education has an abiding obligation to be a responsible steward of all the recourse that support its activities — whether in the form of taxpayer's dollars, the hard-earned payments of students and their parents, the contributions of alumni, or the revenue stream generated by athletics programs. In this respect, the responsibility of presidents and trustees is singular.

Costs - A 1990 College Football Association study indicated that in the prior four years, the cost of operating an athletics department increased 35 percent while revenues increased only 21 percent. For the first time in its surveys, said the CFA, average expenses exceed average income. Overall, 39 of 53 institutions responding — including some of the largest and presumably the most successful sports programs — are either operating deficits or would be without institutional or state support. More comprehensive data from the NCAA confirm that, on average, the athletics programs of Division I-A institutions barely break even. When athletics expenses are subtracted from revenues, the average Division I-A institutions is left with $39,000.

The Larger Economic Environment - Big-time sports programs are economic magnets. They attract entertainment and business interests of a wide variety. They support entire industries dedicated to their needs and contests. But while college sports provide a demonstrably effective and attractive public showcase for the university, potential pitfalls abound because of the money involved. Particular vigilance is required to assure that central administrators set the terms under which the university engages the larger economic environment surrounding big-time college sports. The lack of such monitoring in the past explains many of the financial scandals that have tarnished college athletics.

The Commission therefore recommends that:

1. Athletics costs must be reduced. The Commission applauds the cost control measures — including reductions in coaching staff sizes, recruiting activities and the number of athletics scholarships — approved at the 1991 NCAA convention. It is essential that presidents monitor these measures to insure that, in the name of "fine tuning," these provisions are not watered down before they become fully effective in 1994. We urge the Presidents Commission, athletics directors and the NCAA leadership to continue the search for cost-reduction measures.

2. Athletics grants-in-aid should cover the full cost of attendance for the very needy. Despite the Commission's commitment to cost reduction, we believe existing grants-in-aid (tuition, fees, books, and room and board) fail to adequately address the needs of some student-athletes. Assuming the ten percent reduction in scholarship numbers approved at the 1991 NCAA convention is put in place, we recommend that grants-in-aid for low-income athletes be expanded to the "full cost of attendance," including personal and miscellaneous expenses, as determined by federal guidelines.

3. The independence of athletics foundations and booster clubs must be curbed.
Some booster clubs have contributed generously to overall athletics revenues. But too
many of these organizations seem to have been created either in response to state laws
prohibiting the expenditure of public funds on athletics or to avoid institutional
oversight of athletics expenditures. Such autonomous authority can severely
compromise the university. Progress has been made in recent years in bringing most of
these organizations under the control of institutions. More needs to be done. The
Commission believes that no extra-institutional organization should be responsible for
any operational aspect of an intercollegiate athletics programs. All funds raised for
athletics should be channeled into the university's financial system and subjected to
the same budgeting procedures applied to similarly structured departments and
programs.

**4. The NCAA formula for sharing television revenue from the national basketball
championship must be reviewed by university presidents.** The new revenue-sharing
plan for distributing television and championship dollars has many promising features
- funds for academic counseling, catastrophic injury insurance for all athletes in all
divisions, a fund for needy student-athletes, and financial support for teams in all
divisions, including increased transportation and per diem expenses. Nonetheless, the
testimony before this Commission made it clear that a perception persists that the plan
still places too high a financial premium on winning and that the rich will continue to
get richer. The Commission recommends that the plan be reviewed annually by the
Presidents Commission during the seven-year life of the current television contract
and adjusted as warranted by experience.

**5. All athletics-related coaches' income should be reviewed and approved by the
university.** The Commission believes that in considering non-coaching income for its
coaches, universities should follow a well-established practice with all faculty
members: If the outside income involves the university's functions, facilities or name,
contracts for particular services should be negotiated with the university. As part of the
effort to bring athletics-related income into the university, we recommend that the
NCAA ban shoe and equipment contracts with individual coaches. If a company is
eager to have an institution's athletes using its product, it should approach the
institution not the coach.

6. Coaches should be offered long-term contracts. Academic tenure is not
appropriate for most coaches, unless they are bona fide members of the faculty. But
greater security in an insecure field is clearly reasonable. The Commission suggests
that within five years of contractual employment, head and assistant coaches who meet
the university's expectations, including its academic expectations, should be offered
renewable, long-term contracts. These contracts should specifically address the
university's obligations in the event of termination, as well as the coach's obligations
in the event he or she breaks the contract by leaving the institution.

32

7. Institutional support should be available for intercollegiate athletics. The Commission starts from the premise that properly administered intercollegiate athletics programs have legitimate standing in the university community. In that light, general funds can appropriately be used when needed to reduce the pressure on revenue sports to support the entire athletics program. There is an inherent contradiction in insisting on the one hand that athletics are an important part of the university while arguing, on the other hand, that spending institutional funds for them is somehow improper.

THE "THREE": CERTIFICATION

The third leg of our triangle calls for independent authentication by an outside body of integrity of each institution's athletics program. It seems clear that the health of most college athletics programs, like the health of most individuals, depends on periodic checkups. Regular examinations are required to ensure the major systems are functioning properly and that problems are treated before they threaten the health of the entire program. Such checkups should cover the entire range of academic and financial issues in intercollegiate athletics.

The academic and financial integrity of college athletics is in such low repute that authentication by an outside agency is essential. Periodic independent assessments of a program can go a long way toward guaranteeing that the athletics culture on campus responds to academic direction, that expenditures are routinely reviewed, that the president's authority is respected by the board of trustees, and that the trustees stand for academic values when push comes to shove in the athletics department.

Regarding independent certification, the Commission therefore recommends:

1. The NCAA should extend the certification process to all institutions granting athletics aid. The NCAA is now in the midst of a pilot effort to develop a certification program which will, when in place, certify the integrity of athletics programs. We recommend that this pilot certification process be extended on a mandatory basis to all institutions granting athletics aid. Of critical importance to the Commission in its support of this new activity is the assurance of NCAA officials that certification will depend, in large measure, on the comparison of student-athletes, by sport, with the rest of the student body in terms of admissions, academic progress and graduation rates. Equally important are plans to publicly identify institutions failing the certification process.

2. Universities should undertake comprehensive, annual policy audits of their athletics program. We urge extending the annual financial audit now required by the NCAA to incorporate academic issues and athletics governance. The new annual review should examine student-athletes' admissions records, academic progress and graduation rates, as well as the athletics department's management and budget. This activity should serve as preventive maintenance to insure institutional integrity and can provide the annual raw data to make the certification process effective.

3. The certification program should include the major themes put forth in this document. If the new certification program is to be effective and institutions are to meet its challenge, we believe colleges and universities will be forced to undergo the most rigorous self-examination of the policies and procedures by which they control their sports programs. This document concludes with ten principles that, in the form of a restatement of the Commission's implementing recommendations, can serve as a vehicle for such self-examination. We urge the NCAA to incorporate these principles into the certification process.

Putting Principles Into Action

PRINCIPLES INTO ACTION

Reform will not be realized with calls for improvement or with recommendations that sit on a shelf. What is required is a great nationwide effort to move reform from rhetoric to reality. This campaign should be directed at putting the "one-plus-three" model into place and ridding intercollegiate athletics of abuse.

This effort must take root on individual campuses; it cannot be imposed from without. It should draw on the energy of university presidents and trustees. It should seek the counsel of athletics directors, coaches, faculty and alumni, and call forth the best that is in our student-athletes. This campaign needs the assistance of secondary school administrators and the staunch support of the NCAA. With these elements in place, college sports can be transformed.

If that is to happen, the major actors involved in intercollegiate athletics must clearly understand their roles. The Commission wishes to speak directly to each of them.

TO COLLEGE AND UNIVERSITY PRESIDENTS:

Your success at the 1991 NCAA convention confirms what we believe: You are the linchpin of the reform movement. At your own institution, your efforts are critical to a sound athletics program, one that honors the integrity of both your institution and the students wearing your colors. Together with your colleagues across the nation you can assure that college athletics serve the best ideals of higher education.

This report suggests how you can make a difference on your campus. It recommends your involvement in directing your athletics conference and in strengthening the policy-making role of presidents within the NCAA. It insists that you pay greater attention to the academic and financial functioning of your athletics department. We ask that you maintain open lines of communication with your athletics director; there should be no misunderstanding about your institution's academic and athletics goals. The burden is on you to insist that athletics reform is a matter of utmost concern in your institution's academic principles.

TO CHAIRS OF GOVERNING BOARDS:

When you support your president in these reforms, success will be assured. If you do not, we do not know how reform can be accomplished.

The proper role of a board is policy and oversight, not management and personnel actions. The board you lead can be the conscience of the university and the strong right arm of the president. But, without your firm hand, your board can easily lose its way amidst the doubts and misgivings that attend any great undertaking. Your task is to assure unity of purpose and firmness of resolve. Your reward will be an institution secure in the knowledge that no crisis of public confidence can arise from scandal in the athletics program.

TO THE FACULTY:

You are the inheritors of a tradition stretching back through the centuries. It holds that the faculty is responsible for academic standards and protecting the curriculum.

Your first responsibility is to that inheritance. If your institution offers classes or courses of study designed largely for student-athletes, you have fallen short. You cannot remain true to the tradition you bear by permitting athletes to masquerade as students.

Your second task is to help insure that your institutional representatives to the NCAA are not confused about their purpose. The evidence presented to the Commission indicates that some faculty athletics representatives have not fulfilled their potential as guardians of the academic interest. Working with the president, you must make it clear that these faculty members attend athletics meetings to represent the academic values of the institution.

TO ATHLETICS DIRECTORS:

It is up to you to put muscle and sinew on the framework we have suggested here and to oversee its day-to-day implementation. Most of you understand the importance of what we are proposing and have already supported essential elements of our plan within the councils of the NCAA.

Your most difficult task will be to counterbalance the traditional demand for winning teams with the renewed call for integrity and the equitable treatment of all athletes. Your best guide will come not from boosters with short memories, but from your president and your institution's trustees. Their larger vision of the university's responsibilities and their longer memory of its achievements represent your surest standards.

Your success as a leader in athletics reform will undoubtedly be judged by your ability to transform the athletics culture on your campus. That culture must be reshaped from one in which winning is everything to one in which competition is grounded in the "one-plus-three" model.

TO COACHES:

We know that at their best coaches are educators, mentors, and loyal advocates for the institutions and for higher education. We understand that you are on the front line - forced to make career-shaping decisions under great pressure, constantly on the alert to insure that rivals do not gain an advantage over you, your program or your institution.

You and your colleagues are the adults with the greatest day-to-day contact with our student-athletes. You must make them understand that fewer than one in a hundred will ever make a living from their athletic ability. Emphasize to them the value of a college degree. Insist that the privilege of being a member of your squad carries with it the obligation of being a student in good standing. Search out every opportunity to drive home the point that your athletes' behavior, on and off the field, is important not merely because of what it says about them. Your satisfaction will be a lifetime associated with adults who have, with your assistance, achieved their full potential.

Your most difficult challenge may be to take to heart the warning in this document that if intercollegiate sport will not police itself, others will. That is no empty threat. It is essential that you forego the temptation to cynicism and, with your colleagues throughout the coaching profession, forge a coalition for reform built around the "one-plus-three" model.

TO THE ALUMNI:

As a product of your institution, you have a critical role to play in safeguarding its reputation. University presidents, faculty members and members of governing boards come and go, but you remain.

In the marketplace, the value of your degree is based on your institution's reputation today, not the reputation it enjoyed when you were students. You can help protect the stake you hold in that degree by insisting that the athletics program is directed along ethical lines. Through your formal participation in structures such as governing boards, alumni boards, athletics councils and local alumni clubs, you can insist that your institution holds fast to the reform model we present here.

TO STUDENT-ATHLETES:

No one has a greater stake in the outcome of the issues described here than you. With this document the Commission has placed your concerns at the heart of athletics administration. If these reforms are adopted, letters of intent will no longer bind so tightly, the initial grant-in-aid offer will no longer be for only one year, and our institutions will renew their commitment to deliver educationally even if you are injured and unable to play.

You must deliver, too. University presidents, trustees, athletics directors and coaches have the power only to create the conditions under which you can reap the rewards of a university education. You must gather that harvest. We plead with you to understand that — unless you are one of the remarkably talented and very lucky — when your athletics eligibility has expired *your playing days are over*. Your task, even if you are one of the fortunate few, is to prepare yourself for the years and decades that stretch ahead of you beyond college. Boosters and alumni cannot do that for you. Presidents and coaches cannot create your future. You must create it yourself. The best place to do that is in the classroom, the library and the laboratory.

TO SECONDARY SCHOOL OFFICIALS:

Many of you have objected over the years to the overemphasis on athletics at the collegiate level. But the nature of the problem has, in recent years, changed. We sense that some secondary school programs now emulate the worst features of too many collegiate programs: recruiting abuses, permitting athletics to interfere with college preparation, standing by as coaches enter into shoe contracts, permitting the time demands for team travel to grow beyond reason, and pursuing television exposure and national rankings with the same passion as colleges and universities.

With this report, we are doing our very best to re-establish important values at the center of intercollegiate sport — and to restore the student-athlete to the center of our concern. We ask you to join us in this effort.

In particular, we ask you to cooperate with us in putting an end to all-star games during the academic year, and to summer camps and leagues dominated by commercial interests. These activities promote a false sense of the importance of athletics in the student's long-term future. We urge you to encourage high school athletes to spend as much time preparing themselves academically as they do preparing themselves athletically. We suggest that you guide them toward institutions that will put their welfare as students and their maturation as young adults ahead of their performance as athletes. We encourage you to make them aware of the importance of attending institutions that have adopted the "one-plus-three" model set forth in this report.

TO THE NATIONAL COLLEGIATE ATHLETIC ASSOCIATION:

Finally, we address the National Collegiate Athletic Association — both our colleagues in the institutions which constitute the Association and the staff which directs the organization in their name. Throughout this document we have alluded to the NCAA. We have applauded it when justified and taken it to task when appropriate.

The NCAA has many critics. Aggrieved institutions and coaches complain about it. Disappointed boosters and politicians disagree with it. Enraged editors attack it. Presidents and academics complain that its investigative techniques are unfair. Some of the members of this Commission are among the organization's more severe critics; most of us are not.

We want to make a few major points with respect to the NCAA. First, if it did not exist, higher education would have to create it, or something very much like it. It is clear that a governing, rulemaking and disciplinary body of some sort is required. This Commission cannot impose progress; major change has to grow from within and mature through governing bodies. Handcuffing the NCAA is no way to advance athletics reform.

Second, critics of the NCAA -- particularly those in higher education - should be reminded that it is not some mysterious, omnipotent, external force. It is simply the creature of its own members. Colleges and universities have only themselves to blame for its shortcomings, real or imagined; the power to change the Association rests entirely within their hands.

Third, our recommendation for advancing reform through the NCAA is built on our bedrock principle of presidential control. In fact, the organization itself preaches presidential authority on campus. The activities of the Association should reflect that conviction.

Finally, with that change in place we ask that the NCAA apply itself to the task of simplifying and codifying complex NCAA rules and procedures. Any man or woman on the street should be able to understand what the NCAA does, how it works, how it makes its decisions, and, in particular, how it determines its sanctions. As it stands, not only can the average citizen not answer those questions, but very few presidents, athletics directors, coaches or student-athletes can predict what it is likely to do in any given circumstance. This situation must be addressed.

PRINCIPLES FOR ACTION

It is clear that this nationwide effort must grow from our campuses. We have reduced the essence of our concerns to the "one-plus-three" model. We have expanded this model through the implementing recommendations that form the core of Chapter II. But the question remains, where to begin?

We believe that any institution wishing to take seriously the "one-plus-three" model would do well to start with the following statement of principles which recasts this report's main themes. We urge presidents to make this statement the vehicle for serious discussions within their institutions and, in particular, with the members of the governing board. Each principle is significant. Each deserves a separate conversation. Together they can define what the university expects, and how it hopes to realize its expectations.

A STATEMENT OF PRINCIPLES

Preamble: This institution is committed to a philosophy of firm institutional control of athletics, to the unquestioned academic and financial integrity of our athletics program, and to the accountability of the athletics department to the values and goals befitting higher education, in support of that commitment, the board, officers, faculty and staff of this institution have examined and agreed to the following general principles as a guide to our participation in intercollegiate athletics:

I. The educational values, practices and mission of this institution determine the standards by which we conduct our intercollegiate athletics program.

II. The responsibility and authority for the administration of the athletics department, including all basic policies, personnel and finances, are vested in the president.

III. The welfare, health and safety of student-athletes are primary concerns of athletics administration on this campus. This institution will provide student-athletes with the opportunity for academic experiences as close as possible to the experiences of their classmates.

IV. Every student-athlete -- male and female, majority and minority, in all sports -- will receive equitable and fair treatment.

V. The admission of student-athletes -- including junior college transfers -- will be based on their showing reasonable promise of being successful in a course of study leading to an academic degree. That judgment will be made by admissions officials.

VI. Continuing eligibility to participate in intercollegiate athletics will be based on students being able to demonstrate each academic term that they will graduate within five years of their enrolling. Students who do not pass this test will not play.

VII. Student-athletes, in each sport, will be graduated in at least the same proportion as non-athletes who have spent comparable time as full-time students.

VIII. All funds raised and spent in connection with intercollegiate athletics programs will be channeled through the institutions general treasury, not through independent groups, whether internal or external. The athletics department budget will be developed and monitored in accordance with general budgeting procedures on campus.

IX. All athletics-related income from non-university sources for coaches and athletics administrators will be reviewed and approved by the university. In cases where the income involved the university's functions, facilities or name, contracts will be negotiated with the institution.

X. We will conduct annual academic and fiscal audits of the athletics program. Moreover, we intend to seek NCAA certification that our athletics program complies with the principles herein. We will promptly correct any deficiencies and will conduct our athletics program in a manner worthy of this distinction.

We believe these 10 principles represent a statement around which our institutions and the NCAA can rally. It is our hope that this statement of principles will be incorporated into the Association's developing certification program. The Commission believes that the success of the NCAA certification program must be judged on the degree to which it advances these principles as the fundamental ends of intercollegiate programs. Ideally, institutions will agree to schedule only those colleges and universities that have passed all aspects of the certification process: Institutions that refuse to correct deficiencies will find themselves isolated by the vast majority of athletics administrators who support intercollegiate athletics as an honorable tradition in college life.

The members of the Knight Foundation Commission are convinced, as we know most members of the public and of the athletic and academic worlds are convinced, that changes are clearly required in intercollegiate athletics. Making these changes will require courage, determination and perseverance on the part of us all. That courage, determination and perseverance must be summoned. Without them, we cannot move forward. But with them and the "one-plus-three" model we cannot be held back. The combination makes it possible to keep faith with our student-athletes, with our institutions, and with the public that wants the best for them both.

Appendix: Action On Knight Commission Recommendations

I. PRESIDENTIAL CONTROL

Trustees should explicitly endorse and reaffirm presidential authority in athletics governance, delegate authority over finances, affirm the president's authority for personnel and annually review athletics program.

Implementation of this recommendation requires action on individual campuses. Although no detailed records are available, more than 100 institutions and organizations have reported adoption of this principle.

Presidents should act on their obligation to control conferences.

The 1992 NCAA convention addressed the issue of presidential control, amending Article 5 of the NCAA Constitution so to require presidential approval of conference-sponsored legislative initiatives.

Presidents should control the NCAA.

Legislation passed at the 1993 NCAA convention formalized the governance role of presidents within the organization by the creation of a Joint Policy Board comprised of officers of the NCAA and the Presidents Commission.

Presidents should commit their institutions to equity in all aspects of intercollegiate athletics.

The 1992 NCAA convention delayed reductions in financial aid for Division I women's sports. Also, the NCAA appointed a Gender-Equity Task Force which issued its findings and recommendations in the Summer of 1993. Additional gender equality legislation is anticipated for the 1994 NCAA convention.

Presidents should control their institution's involvement with commercial television.

The 1992 NCAA convention directed that the Special Committee on Financial Conditions in Intercollegiate Athletics examine the issue of media revenues, among other financial considerations.

10

II. ACADEMIC INTEGRITY: "NO PASS, NO PLAY"

• **The NCAA should strengthen initial eligibility requirements: By 1995, initial eligibility should be based on a 2.00 average in 15 units of high school academic work and a combined score of 700 on the SAT or 17 on the ACT.**

The 1992 NCAA convention established core curriculum requirements of 13 units, and an initial eligibility index of 2.5 GPA in the core combined with an SAT score of 700 (ACT score of 17).

• **High school student-athletes should be ineligible for reimbursed campus visits (or signing a letter of intent) until they show reasonable promise of being able to meet degree requirements.**

The 1992 NCAA convention prohibited official visits prior to the early signing period in Division I sports if student-athletes do not present as SAT score of 700 (ACT score of 17) and a minimum 2.00 GPA in seven core courses. Under current bylaws, prospects may visit campus after the early signing period even if they do not meet SAT or ACT minimum requirements.

• **Junior college transfers who did not, on graduating from high school, meet proposition 48 requirements, should "sit out" a year of competition after transfer.**

This recommendation is substantially incorporated in a new progress toward degree requirement adopted at the 1992 NCAA convention (see below).

• **The NCAA should study the feasibility of requiring the range of academic abilities of incoming athletes to approximate the range of abilities of the entire freshman class.**

The NCAA's new certification program (see section IV below) requires institutions to compare academic performance of incoming athletes with the rest of the freshman class.

The letter of intent should serve the student as well as the athletics department.
No action to date.

Athletics scholarships should be offered for a five-year period.
No action to date.

Athletics eligibility should depend on progress toward a degree.

The 1992 NCAA convention created new Division I requirements governing: mid-year transfer students, credits to be earned during the regular academic year, proportion of credits toward a specific degree, and minimum GPA toward that degree. The credit and GPA requirements govern athletics eligibility in years 3 and 4.

Graduation rates of athletes should be a criterion for NCAA certification.

The certification process (below) incorporates graduation rates as a major criterion.

III. FINANCIAL INTEGRITY

Athletics cost must be reduced, and cost control measures adopted in 1991 must not be "fine tuned" out of existence.

The 1992 NCAA convention reduced the allowable number of grants-in-aid. Also, the NCAA appointed a special Committee to Review Financial Conditions in Intercollegiate Athletics which issued a report in June 1993. Based upon the recommendations of the Special Committee, additional "cost-cutting" legislation will be introduced at the 1994 NCAA convention.

Athletics grants-in-aid should cover the full cost of attendance for the very needy.

No action to date.

The independence of athletics foundations and booster clubs must be curbed.

The 1992 NCAA convention directed the Special Committee to Review Financial Conditions in Intercollegiate Athletics to examine the role of booster clubs, among other financial considerations;

The NCAA formula for sharing television revenue from the national basketball championship must be viewed by university presidents.

The Presidents Commission reviewed the revenue-sharing formula, approved it, and recommended reserving additional moneys for the membership fund.

All athletics-related coaches' income should be reviewed and approved by the university.

The 1992 NCAA convention required annual written approval from the institution's CEO for all athletically related income.

Coaches should be offered long-term contracts.

Implementation of this recommendation requires action on individual campuses.

Institutional support should be available for intercollegiate athletics.

Implementation of this recommendation requires action on individual campuses.

IV. CERTIFICATION

The NCAA should extend the certification process to all institutions granting athletics aid.

The 1993 NCAA convention adopted a new athletics certification program for Division I institutions.

Universities should undertake comprehensive, annual policy audits for their athletics program.

The NCAA certification program entails an annual compilation of this and other data.

The certification program should include the major themes advanced by the Knight Commission, i.e., the "One-Plus-Three" model.

The NCAA certification program substantially incorporates the fundamental principles of the "One-Plus-Three" model.

REPORT TO THE COMMISSIONER OF BASEBALL OF AN INDEPENDENT INVESTIGATION INTO THE ILLEGAL USE OF STEROIDS AND OTHER PERFORMANCE ENHANCING SUBSTANCES BY PLAYERS IN MAJOR LEAGUE BASEBALL

GEORGE J. MITCHELL

DLA PIPER US LLP

December 13, 2007

TABLE OF CONTENTS

TABLE OF CONTENTS
(continued)

TABLE OF CONTENTS
(continued)

TABLE OF CONTENTS
(continued)

**REPORT TO THE COMMISSIONER OF BASEBALL
OF AN INDEPENDENT INVESTIGATION INTO
THE ILLEGAL USE OF STEROIDS AND OTHER
PERFORMANCE ENHANCING SUBSTANCES
BY PLAYERS IN MAJOR LEAGUE BASEBALL**

SUMMARY AND RECOMMENDATIONS

Summary and Recommendations

    For more than a decade there has been widespread illegal use of anabolic steroids and other performance enhancing substances by players in Major League Baseball, in violation of federal law and baseball policy. Club officials routinely have discussed the possibility of such substance use when evaluating players. Those who have illegally used these substances range from players whose major league careers were brief to potential members of the Baseball Hall of Fame. They include both pitchers and position players, and their backgrounds are as diverse as those of all major league players.

    The response by baseball was slow to develop and was initially ineffective, but it gained momentum after the adoption of a mandatory random drug testing program in 2002. That program has been effective in that detectable steroid use appears to have declined. But the use of human growth hormone has risen because, unlike steroids, it is not detectable through urine testing.

    This report, the product of an intensive investigation, describes how and why this problem emerged. We identify some of the players who were caught up in the drive to gain a competitive advantage through the illegal use of these substances. Other investigations will no doubt turn up more names and fill in more details, but that is unlikely to significantly alter the description of baseball's "steroids era," as set forth in this report.

    From hundreds of interviews and thousands of documents we learned enough to accurately describe that era. While this investigation was prompted by revelations about the involvement of players with the Bay Area Laboratory Co-Operative, the evidence we uncovered indicates that this has not been an isolated problem involving just a few players or a few clubs. It has involved many players on many clubs. In fact, each of the thirty clubs has had players who have been involved with performance enhancing substances at some time in their careers.

The illegal use of these substances was not limited to the players who are identified in this report. There have been many estimates of use. In 2002, former National League Most Valuable Player Ken Caminiti estimated that "at least half" of major league players were using anabolic steroids. Dave McKay, a longtime coach for the St. Louis Cardinals and the Oakland Athletics, estimated that at one time 30% of players were using them. Within the past week, the former Cincinnati Reds pitcher Jack Armstrong estimated that between 20% and 30% of players in his era, 1988 to 1994, were using large doses of steroids while an even higher percentage of players were using lower, maintenance doses of steroids. There have been other estimates, a few higher, many lower, all impossible to verify.

However, it is a fact that between 5 and 7 percent of the major league players who participated in anonymous survey testing in 2003 tested positive for performance enhancing substances. Those figures almost certainly understated the actual level of use since players knew they would be tested at some time during the year, the use of human growth hormone was not detectable in the tests that were conducted, and, as many have observed, a negative test does not necessarily mean that a player has not been using performance enhancing substances.

Mandatory random testing, formally started in 2004 after the survey testing results, appears to have reduced the use of detectable steroids, but players switched to human growth hormone precisely because it is not detectable. Players who use human growth hormone apparently believe that it assists their ability to recover from injuries and fatigue during the long baseball season; this also is a major reason why players used steroids. Human growth hormone was the substance most frequently sold to players by Kirk Radomski, a former New York Mets clubhouse employee who was a significant source of illegal performance enhancing substances until late 2005. Separately, a number of players reportedly purchased human growth hormone

SR-2

through "anti-aging" centers using dubious prescriptions written by physicians who never examined, or even met, the customers for whom they were writing prescriptions.

At the beginning of this investigation, I said that I would conduct a "deliberate and unbiased examination of the facts that will comport with basic American values of fairness." To honor that commitment, I invited each current or former player about whom allegations were received of the illegal possession or use of performance enhancing substances to meet with me so that I could inform him of the evidence supporting the allegations and give him a chance to respond. The explanations provided by those players who we did interview were taken into account and are reflected in this report.

Among current players I asked to interview were five who have spoken publicly about the issue. When I did so, I made clear that there was no suggestion that any of the five had used performance enhancing substances, and I repeat here that clarifying statement. Four of the five declined. One of them, Frank Thomas of the Toronto Blue Jays, agreed. His comments were informative and helpful.

Since 1986, drug testing has been subject to collective bargaining in Major League Baseball. For many years, citing concerns for the privacy rights of players, the Players Association opposed mandatory random drug testing of its members for steroids or other substances. On the other side of the bargaining table, the owners and several Commissioners proposed drug testing programs but gave the issue a much lower priority in bargaining than economic issues. But when the opportunity was presented in 2002 to achieve agreement on a system of mandatory random drug testing, the Commissioner pressed hard on the issue and the Players Association agreed to the basic elements of the program that is in place today.

SR-3

No drug testing program is perfect. The current drug testing program in Major League Baseball is the product of the give and take inherent in collective bargaining. It appears to have reduced the use of detectable steroids but by itself has not removed the cloud of suspicion over the game. Even as this investigation was underway, developments in several government investigations exposed the depth and breadth of the continuing illegal use of these substances in baseball (and in other sports) and made clear that this problem continues, years after mandatory random testing began and stringent penalties for failing those tests were adopted.

Plainly, baseball needs to do more to effectively address this problem. I have never met or talked with Jeff Kent of the Los Angeles Dodgers, but he appears to have understood this when he said in September, as reported in several newspapers: "Major League Baseball is trying to investigate the past so they can fix the future."

That is the purpose of the recommendations that are set forth in detail in this report. In summary, they fall into three categories: (1) Major League Baseball must significantly increase its ability to investigate allegations of use outside of the testing program and improve its procedures for keeping performance enhancing substances out of the clubhouse; (2) there must be a more comprehensive and effective program of education for players and others about the serious health risks incurred by users of performance enhancing substances; and (3) when the club owners and the Players Association next engage in collective bargaining on the joint drug program, I urge them to incorporate into the program the principles that characterize a state-of-the-art program, as described in this report.

Although I sought and received a wide range of views, including the opinions of many experts in the field, the conclusions and recommendations in this report are mine alone, following close consultation and extensive discussions with the very talented members of the

staff I assembled to assist me in this effort.[1]

A.   The Investigation and this Report

On March 30, 2006, the Commissioner of Baseball, Allan H. ("Bud") Selig, asked

me to investigate allegations that a number of players in Major League Baseball had illegally

used steroids and other performance enhancing substances. I accepted on the conditions that

(1) I have total independence in conducting the investigation and in preparing this report; and

(2) I have full freedom and authority to follow the evidence wherever it might lead, so that the

investigation would not be limited to any one player or team. The Commissioner readily agreed.

He pledged that this report, when completed, would be made public, a decision I agreed with.

He promised his full support and he kept his promise.

The Commissioner retained the authority to determine whether any activities in

the conduct of this investigation might violate his obligations under the Basic Agreement,

including the joint drug program. I agreed to be bound by his decisions in that regard.

The Commissioner also retained the right to prohibit publication in this report of

any information that he is under a legal duty to keep confidential. To enable him to make that

determination, I agreed to provide his office the opportunity to review this report three business

days before it was released publicly. No material changes were made as a result of that review.

I was assisted in this investigation by lawyers from the firm of DLA Piper US

LLP and by several experts. They include Richard V. Clark, M.D., Ph.D., a leader in the fields

---

[1] I personally conducted many of the interviews that form the basis for this report, but because more than 700 interviews were taken during this investigation it was not possible for me to conduct all of them. Lawyers on my staff from the law firm of DLA Piper conducted the interviews that I did not attend. In this report, I use the pronouns "I" and "we" interchangeably because its findings are based on our work collectively, under my direction.

of andrology and endocrinology and Richard H. McLaren, HBA, LL.B., LL.M., C. Arb., a professor of law at the University of Western Ontario and a distinguished arbitrator for the Court of Arbitration for Sport.[2]

I requested the production of relevant documents from the Commissioner's Office, each of the thirty major league clubs, and the Players Association. We received and reviewed more than 115,000 pages of documents from the Commissioner's Office and the thirty clubs and over 20,000 electronic documents that were retrieved from the computer systems of the Commissioner's Office and some of the clubs. We also gathered and reviewed many documents from other sources, some of them public.

In the course of the investigation, we interviewed more than 700 witnesses in the United States, Canada, and the Dominican Republic. Over 550 of these witnesses were current or former club officials, managers, coaches, team physicians, athletic trainers, or resident security agents. We also interviewed 16 persons from the Commissioner's Office, including Commissioner Selig, president and chief operating officer Robert DuPuy, executive vice president for labor relations Robert D. Manfred, Jr., and former senior vice president for security and facility management Kevin Hallinan.

We sought to interview as many current and former players as possible. We attempted to reach almost 500 former players. Many of them declined to be interviewed, but 68 did agree to interviews. In addition, interviews of 3 former players were arranged through the assistance of federal prosecutors and law enforcement agents.

---

[2] Lawyers from Foley & Lardner LLP played a separate but important role as counsel for the Commissioner and Major League Baseball. Lawyers from Foley & Lardner did not participate in many of the interviews that we conducted and had no role in preparing this report other than reviewing it, as representatives of the Commissioner, three days before its release.

The Players Association was largely uncooperative. (1) It rejected totally my requests for relevant documents. (2) It permitted one interview with its executive director, Donald Fehr; my request for an interview with its chief operating officer, Gene Orza, was refused. (3) It refused my request to interview the director of the Montreal laboratory that analyzes drug tests under baseball's drug program but permitted her to provide me with a letter addressing a limited number of issues. (4) I sent a memorandum to every active player in Major League Baseball encouraging each player to contact me or my staff if he had any relevant information. The Players Association sent out a companion memorandum that effectively discouraged players from cooperating. Not one player contacted me in response to my memorandum. (5) I received allegations of the illegal possession or use of performance enhancing substances by a number of current players. Through their representative, the Players Association, I asked each of them to meet with me so that I could provide them with information about the allegations and give them a chance to respond. Almost without exception they declined to meet or talk with me.

My goal in preparing this report was to provide a thorough, accurate, and fair accounting of what I learned in this investigation about the illegal use of performance enhancing substances by players in Major League Baseball. To provide context for my conclusions and recommendations, I also include in the report the medical, legal, and historical issues that are part of this complex problem.

I have not included every allegation that we received or the results of every interview we conducted or every document we reviewed. Inevitably, much of that information was cumulative, not relevant, or of only marginal relevance. None of it would have materially altered the account that is provided.

B.   The Problem Is Serious

The illegal use of performance enhancing substances poses a serious threat to the integrity of the game. Widespread use by players of such substances unfairly disadvantages the honest athletes who refuse to use them and raises questions about the validity of baseball records. In addition, because they are breaking the law, users of these substances are vulnerable to drug dealers who might seek to exploit their knowledge through threats intended to affect the outcome of baseball games or otherwise.

The illegal use of these substances to improve athletic performance also carries with it potentially serious negative side effects on the human body. Steroid users place themselves at risk for psychiatric problems, cardiovascular and liver damage, drastic changes to their reproductive systems, musculoskeletal injury, and other problems. Users of human growth hormone risk cancer, harm to their reproductive health, cardiac and thyroid problems, and overgrowth of bone and connective tissue.

Apart from the dangers posed to the major league player himself, however, his use of performance enhancing substances encourages young athletes to use those substances. Young Americans are placing themselves at risk of serious harm. Because adolescents are already subject to significant hormonal changes, the abuse of steroids and other performance enhancing substances can have more serious effects on them than they have on adults.[3]

Some estimates appear to show a recent decline in steroid use by high school students; they range from 3 to 6 percent.[4] But even the lower figure means that hundreds of

---

[3] *See Restoring Faith in America's Pastime: Evaluating Major League Baseball's Efforts to Eradicate Steroid Use: Hearing Before the H. Comm. on Gov't Reform,* 109th Cong. 307 (2005) (statement of Dr. Kirk Brower).

[4] National Institute on Drug Abuse, Monitoring the Future: Nat'l Survey Results on Drug Use, 1975-2006, Vol. 1, at 44 (2006); Centers for Disease Control and Prevention, *National*

thousands of high school-aged young people are still illegally using steroids. It's important to devote attention to the Major League Baseball players who illegally used performance enhancing substances. It's at least as important, perhaps even more so, to be concerned about the reality that hundreds of thousands of our children are using them. Every American, not just baseball fans, ought to be shocked into action by that disturbing truth. The recent decline is welcome, but we cannot be complacent.

Don Hooton, whose son committed suicide after abusing anabolic steroids, created the Taylor Hooton Foundation for Fighting Steroid Abuse. In 2005 congressional testimony, Mr. Hooton said:

> I believe the poor example being set by professional athletes is a major catalyst fueling the high usage of steroids amongst our kids. Our kids look up to these guys. They want to do the things the pros do to be successful.
>
> *   *   *
>
> Our youngsters hear the message loud and clear, and it's wrong. "If you would want to achieve your goal, it's OK to use steroids to get you there, because the pros are doing it." It's a real challenge for parents to overpower the strong message that's being sent to our children by your behavior.[5]

Finally, the illegal use in baseball of steroids and other performance enhancing substances victimizes the majority of players who do not use those substances. A September 2000 study by the National Center on Addiction and Substance Abuse observed that:

> 'Clean' athletes face three choices: (1) compete without performance-enhancing substances, knowing that they may lose to competitors with fewer scruples; (2) abandon their quest because they are unwilling to use performance-enhancing substances to achieve a decisive competitive

---

Youth Risk Behavior Survey: 1991-2003: Trends in the Prevalence of Marijuana, Cocaine and Other Illegal Drug Use (2004).

[5] *Restoring Faith in America's Pastime: Evaluating Major League Baseball's Efforts to Eradicate Steroid Use: Hearing Before the H. Comm. on Gov't Reform*, 109th Cong. 307 (2005) (statement of Donald M. Hooton, president & director, Taylor Hooton Foundation).

advantage; or (3) use performance-enhancing substances to level the
playing field.[6]

We heard from many former players who believed it was grossly unfair that some players were

using performance enhancing substances to gain an advantage. One former player told us that

one of the "biggest complaints" among players was that a "guy is using steroids and he is taking

my spot."

C.   Governing Laws and Major League Baseball Policies

Anabolic steroids are listed as controlled substances under the federal Controlled

Substances Act. Since 2004, the dietary supplement androstenedione and other steroid

precursors have been as well. That means that it is illegal to use or possess steroids or steroid

precursors without a valid physician's prescription. Violations of this law carry penalties similar

to those applicable to the illegal use or possession of narcotics. Human growth hormone is a

prescription medication. It is illegal to issue a prescription for human growth hormone except

for very limited purposes. Human growth hormone never has been approved for cosmetic or

anti-aging uses, or to improve athletic performance. Issuing a prescription for human growth

hormone for any of these unauthorized purposes is a violation of federal law.

Many have asserted that steroids and other performance enhancing substances

were not banned in Major League Baseball before the 2002 Basic Agreement. This is not

accurate. Beginning in 1971 and continuing today, Major League Baseball's drug policy has

prohibited the use of any prescription medication without a valid prescription.[7] By implication,

---

[6] National Center on Addiction and Substance Abuse at Columbia University, *Winning at Any Cost*, at 3 (Sept. 2000).

[7] *See* Notice No. 12, Memorandum from Major League Baseball Office of the Commissioner to Administrative Officials of Major and Minor League Ball Clubs Re: Drug Education and Prevention Program, dated Apr. 5, 1971, ¶ 9 ("Baseball must insist its personnel

this prohibition applied to steroids even before 1991, when Commissioner Fay Vincent first expressly included steroids in baseball's drug policy. Steroids have been listed as a prohibited substance under the Major League Baseball drug policy since then, although no player was disciplined for steroid use before the prohibition was added to the collective bargaining agreement in 2002.

It is also inaccurate to assert, as some have, that baseball's drug policy was not binding on players before it was added to the collective bargaining agreement. Many players were suspended for drug offenses before 2002, even though none of those suspensions related to the use of steroids or other performance enhancing substances. Some suspensions were reduced in grievance arbitrations brought by the Players Association, but no arbitrator ever has questioned the authority of the Commissioner to discipline players for "just cause" based on their possession, use, or distribution of prohibited drugs.

For many years before 2002, the Players Association opposed any drug program that included mandatory random testing, despite several proposals for such a program from different Commissioners. The early disagreements on this issue centered around testing for cocaine and other "recreational" drugs, not steroids, but the effect of the Players Association's opposition was to delay the adoption of mandatory random drug testing in Major League Baseball for nearly 20 years.

However, opposition by the Players Association was not the only reason that mandatory random drug testing was not adopted. In 1994, Commissioner Selig and the club owners proposed a drug program that would have included some forms of testing and would have listed steroids among baseball's prohibited substances. Robert D. Manfred, Jr., who is now

comply with the federal and state drug laws. It is your obligation to be familiar with these drug laws.").

executive vice president for labor relations in the Commissioner's Office, recalled that anabolic steroids were included in the 1994 proposal to be proactive, and the decision to include steroids in the proposal was not based on any particular concern about the use of those substances in baseball at that time. He acknowledged that at the time the drug program was not as high a priority as economic issues.

The Players Association did not agree to the proposal. Officials of the Players Association said that the clubs did not appear to regard the 1994 proposal as a high priority and did not pursue its adoption vigorously. Indeed, Players Association executive director Donald M. Fehr recalled that the proposal never even reached the main bargaining table during negotiations.

Later that year, a work stoppage ended the season and resulted in the cancellation of the World Series. Play resumed in 1995 without a collective bargaining agreement, and the owners made no attempt to renew the drug program proposal when collective bargaining resumed. That bargaining resulted in an agreement that remained in effect until 2002, so the next proposal for a mandatory random drug testing program was made in those negotiations with the Players Association in early 2002.

In 2001, the Commissioner had unilaterally implemented drug testing throughout baseball's affiliated minor leagues. He used that program as the basis for his 2002 proposal to the Players Association for a major league program. The proposal included many of the elements of the current Major League Baseball joint program. Building from that proposal, the Players Association and the clubs negotiated the terms of a joint drug program as part of the 2002 Basic Agreement. For the first time, there was a program; it provided for the possibility of mandatory random drug testing of all major league players if more than 5% of players tested

SR-12

positive for steroids during anonymous survey testing in 2003. After that did in fact occur, mandatory random drug testing began in Major League Baseball in 2004. That year, there were 12 undisputed positive tests for steroids. No player was suspended because the program did not provide for suspensions of first-time offenders at that time.

The Major League Baseball Joint Drug Prevention and Treatment Program has been modified twice since it originally was agreed to in 2002. In January 2005, human growth hormone (along with seventeen other compounds) was added to the list of prohibited substances. In addition, the Players Association agreed to more stringent penalties for a positive test for steroids (or similar substances) including, for the first time, a suspension of ten days for a player's first positive test. In 2005, 12 players tested positive for steroids and were suspended for ten days.

Later that year, further revisions were agreed to, including significant increases in penalties: a 50-game suspension for a first positive test; a 100-game suspension for a second positive test; and a permanent suspension for a third positive test. The penalties are unchanged since those revisions. The penalties for positive drug tests under the major league program are the strongest in major U.S. professional sports leagues.[8] In 2006, two players tested positive for steroids and were suspended for 50 games. In 2007, three players were suspended for 50 games each for positive steroids tests.

In addition, in June 2006 Arizona Diamondbacks pitcher Jason Grimsley was suspended for 50 games based on "non-analytic" evidence that he had violated the policy,

---

[8] In major professional sports leagues in the United States, athletes are represented in collective bargaining by players associations. Under federal law, drug testing is a subject of collective bargaining and, in this context, requires the agreement of the players associations. That is not the case with the Olympics or other traditionally amateur sports; there the governing bodies may unilaterally impose any program of their choice.

specifically, his reported admissions to federal agents that he had used steroids and human growth hormone. In September 2007, Cincinnati Reds catcher Ryan Jorgenson also was suspended for 50 games based on non-analytic evidence that he had violated the joint program. In December 2007, two players, Jay Gibbons and Jose Guillen, were each suspended for 15 days based on non-analytic evidence of past violations of the joint program.

    D.   The Rise of the "Steroids Era"

Reports of steroid use in Major League Baseball began soon after the widely publicized discipline of Canadian sprinter Ben Johnson at the Summer Olympic Games in September 1988. Jose Canseco of the Oakland Athletics was the subject of the first media speculation about his use of steroids, and Boston Red Sox fans taunted him for his alleged steroids use during the 1988 American League Championship Series.

News reports about alleged steroid use in baseball grew more frequent throughout the 1990s. In 1996, after a dramatic increase in offense throughout Major League Baseball, Ken Caminiti of the San Diego Padres was voted the National League's Most Valuable Player. In a 2002 Sports Illustrated article, he admitted that he had been using steroids that season and credited them for his increased power. In August 1998, coverage of the issue reached what seemed at the time to be a peak, when an article reported that Mark McGwire was using the then-legal steroid precursor androstenedione while chasing the single-season home run record.

With the benefit of hindsight, it is clear that baseball missed the early warning signs of a growing crisis. Then, beginning in the summer of 2000, a number of incidents involving steroids or drug paraphernalia came to the attention of club and Commissioner's Office officials, and the Players Association. They included:

- In June 2000, state police in Boston discovered steroids and hypodermic needles in the glove compartment of a vehicle belonging to a Boston Red Sox infielder;

- Also in June 2000, a clubhouse attendant found a paper bag containing six vials of steroids and over two dozen syringes in the locker of a pitcher with the Florida Marlins;

- In mid-September 2000, a clubhouse employee discovered a bottle of steroids and several hundred diet pills in a package that had been mailed to the ballpark for an Arizona Diamondbacks infielder;

- In October 2001, officers with the Canadian Border Service discovered steroids, syringes, and other drugs in an unmarked bag that came from the entourage of a Cleveland Indians outfielder;

- In September 2002, a bullpen catcher with the Montreal Expos was arrested for trying to send marijuana back to Florida with the Florida Marlins' luggage. He later told Major League Baseball security officials that he had supplied drugs to nearly two dozen major league players, including eight players for whom he said he had procured steroids.

Further inquiries were made in the Arizona and Montreal incidents, but in some of these cases, little investigation was conducted. Almost without exception, before this investigation began active major league players were not interviewed in investigations into their alleged use of performance enhancing substances.

Instead, players under suspicion frequently were subjected to "reasonable cause" testing for steroid use. Prior to the 2002 Basic Agreement those tests were the subject of an informal arrangement between the Commissioner's Office and the Players Association that involved negotiations in each case as to whether testing of a player would be conducted and, if so, when. As a result, when they did occur, the tests were administered long after the allegations were received, and no suspected player ever tested positive for steroids in these tests.

Commissioner Selig and Rob Manfred both recognized the flaws in "reasonable cause" testing as it was conducted during those years. In 2002, Manfred told a Senate subcommittee that the process was "ad hoc at best, and dysfunctional at worst."[9] To remedy the problems, they focused their efforts on negotiating a comprehensive drug program with the Players Association which, when it was agreed to, included both mandatory random drug testing and its own formal procedure for reasonable cause testing.

More recently, the Commissioner's Office has been more aggressive in responding to allegations of the use of steroids or other performance enhancing substances. Examples include:

- In June 2004, a minor league athletic trainer discovered a vial of steroids in a package that had been mailed by a player on a major league 40-man roster. Manfred and his deputy investigated the incident and negotiated a resolution with the Players Association under which the player was immediately separated from his team and was required to submit to a drug test if he ever attempted to return to Major League Baseball;

- In June 2006, the Commissioner suspended Arizona Diamondbacks pitcher Jason Grimsley for 50 games based on admissions he reportedly made to federal law enforcement officers about his illegal use of performance enhancing substances. The joint drug program did not expressly provide for a suspension under those

---

[9] *Steroid Use in Professional Baseball and Anti-Doping Issues in Amateur Sports: Hearing Before the Subcomm. on Consumer Affairs, Foreign Commerce and Tourism of the S. Comm. on Commerce, Science and Transp.*, 107th Cong. 7 (2002).

circumstances, but as part of a later settlement the Players Association agreed that the suspension was appropriate and could be a precedent in the future;

- During 2007, the Commissioner's Office interviewed several players, and to date has suspended two of them, after news articles appeared alleging their past illegal use of performance enhancing substances.

E.   The BALCO Investigation

Commissioner Selig asked me to conduct this investigation after the publication of *Game of Shadows*, a book that contained allegations about the illegal use of performance enhancing substances by major league players that were supplied by BALCO and the personal trainer Greg Anderson.

Throughout this investigation, a federal criminal investigation related to BALCO was ongoing. On November 15, 2007, former San Francisco Giants outfielder Barry Bonds was indicted for perjury and obstruction of justice based on his grand jury testimony in that investigation. The ongoing criminal investigation, and the resulting unwillingness of many participants to cooperate with me, limited my ability to gather information that was not already in the public record about the involvement of major league players with BALCO. The information that we did obtain is set forth in Chapter VII.

F.   Evidence Obtained of Other Players' Possession or Use

Through the efforts of the United States Attorney's Office for the Northern District of California and federal law enforcement agencies, we obtained the cooperation of former New York Mets clubhouse employee Kirk Radomski. Radomski was interviewed by me and members of my investigative staff on four occasions, with federal law enforcement representatives participating in all interviews and his lawyer participating in three of them.

Radomski identified a large number of current or former major league players to whom he said
he illegally sold steroids, human growth hormone, or other substances.

Radomski also provided me with a number of documents relating to his
transactions with players in Major League Baseball, including copies of deposited checks that he
retrieved from his banks, copies of some shipping labels or receipts, his telephone records for
two years, and a copy of his address book in the form in which it was seized by federal agents
when they executed a search warrant at his home.

We also obtained information from sources other than Radomski about players'
possession or use of performance enhancing substances. These included several former major
league players and two former strength and conditioning coaches, some of whom met with us
voluntarily; others did so at the request of federal law enforcement officials.

As a result, we gathered sufficient evidence about their alleged illegal possession
or use of performance enhancing substances to identify in this report dozens of current or former
players in Major League Baseball. Each of the players was invited to meet with me to provide
him with information about the allegations against him and give him an opportunity to respond.

Both pitchers and position players are named in this report. Some of those named
are prominent, including winners of significant post-season awards. Many played in the World
Series or in All-Star games. Others are less well known, and some had only brief careers at the
major league level. The players were with clubs spread throughout Major League Baseball, as
Radomski's customers referred their friends and teammates to him as they moved from club to
club.

I carefully reviewed and considered all of the information we received about the purchase, possession, or use of performance enhancing substances by Major League Baseball players.

1.   Kirk Radomski provided substantial information about the distribution of performance enhancing substances, and in many cases his statements were corroborated by other evidence. He did not, however, observe or participate in the use of performance enhancing substances by any player named in this report, with one exception that is described below.

The corroboration took many forms, including: (a) the admission by eleven players that Radomski had supplied them with performance enhancing substances, as he had said in our interviews of him;[10] (b) checks or money orders written to Radomski by some players in appropriate amounts; (c) mailing receipts for shipments of performance enhancing substances by Radomski to some players; (d) statements by other witnesses supporting the allegations of use by some players; (e) the names, addresses, and/or telephone numbers of many players were found in Radomski's seized address book; (f) telephone records showing calls between Radomski and some players; and (g) a positive drug test.

I did not include in this report the names of three players to whom Radomski said he sold performance enhancing substances: two of them because the players had retired from Major League Baseball by the time of the alleged sales; and one of them because the player admitted that he had purchased and possessed the substances but denied that he had used them and his version of events was corroborated by other credible evidence.

I interviewed Radomski four times (in June, July, October, and November 2007), three times in person, once by telephone. His personal lawyer participated in three of the

---

[10] Two players admitted receipt and possession of illegal performance enhancing substances sold by Radomski but denied they ever used them.

interviews. Federal law enforcement officials and members of my staff participated with me in all of the interviews. No one from the Commissioner's Office, any club, or the Players Association participated in these interviews.

During each of the interviews, the law enforcement officials warned Radomski that if he made any false statements he would forfeit their commitment to recommend a more lenient sentence and he would face further criminal jeopardy. Before the interviews, Radomski had been debriefed extensively by federal prosecutors and agents. They subsequently confirmed that the information he provided to us in his interviews was consistent with the information he had previously provided to them.

2.   Six players are named based on information obtained from persons other than Radomski or former major league strength and conditioning coach Brian McNamee. In each case, these allegations are supported by one or more of the following: (a) checks; (b) prior consistent statements; (c) a statement made about a player's use where the witness was a friend of the player identified and under circumstances in which the witness faced criminal exposure for making a false statement; (d) statements reporting a witness's direct observation of the player using a performance enhancing substance; (e) the player's own admission of his use.

3.   Brian McNamee said that he was a direct eyewitness and participant in alleged illegal use by three players who he served as a personal trainer. I interviewed him three times (in July, October, and December 2007), once in person and twice by telephone.[11] His personal lawyer participated in each interview. Federal law enforcement officials and members of my staff participated with me in all of the interviews. No one from the Commissioner's Office, any club, or the Players Association participated in these interviews.

---

[11] In addition, a member of my investigative staff interviewed him by telephone on a fourth occasion in December 2007; his personal lawyer also participated.

During each of the interviews, the law enforcement officials warned him that he faced criminal jeopardy if he made any false statements. With respect to two of the players, McNamee was acting against his financial interest in disclosing this information. Before the interviews, McNamee had been debriefed extensively by federal prosecutors and agents. They subsequently confirmed that the information he provided to us in his interviews was consistent with the information he had previously provided to them.

In some cases, I include statements by club personnel in emails or other documents commenting on a player's alleged drug use. Those statements are cited as corroboration of other evidence that a player possessed or used performance enhancing substances; they did not serve as the primary basis for any of the decisions I made. No player is identified in this report on the basis of mere suspicion or speculation.

Radomski met with many players while they were in New York, where he lives. Most of his business, however, was conducted by telephone and mail or overnight delivery. He sent drugs to their homes, to hotels, and in some cases to major league clubhouses. He was paid by check, by money order, or in cash.

Even before mandatory random drug testing began in Major League Baseball, Radomski observed players moving away from oil-based steroids that stay in the body for a long time, to water-based steroids that clear the body faster. Because human growth hormone cannot be detected in a urine test, as mandatory random drug testing was implemented many players switched to it even when they concluded that it was less effective than steroids.

A detailed discussion of Radomski's network of customers, and other players for whom evidence has been obtained of their alleged possession or use of performance enhancing substances, is provided in Chapter VIII of the report.

G.   <u>Players' Use of Substances Purchased from Anti-Aging Centers</u>

In February 2007, a government task force executed search warrants on Signature Compounding Pharmacy in Orlando, Florida and other businesses, including several so-called "rejuvenation centers," exposing another source of illegal performance enhancing substances. Some businesses that describe themselves as anti-aging or rejuvenation centers sell steroids or human growth hormone and arrange for buyers to obtain prescriptions for those substances from corrupt or suspended physicians or even, in some cases, a dentist. The prescriptions are then filled by a compounding pharmacy affiliated with the center and delivered to the buyer either through the mail or at the "clinic."

In a series of news reports during 2007, eight active major league players and eight former players were identified as appearing in the customer records of either anti-aging clinics or compounding pharmacies that are involved in this illegal trade. Those players reportedly purchased steroids, human growth hormone, and other drugs used to counteract the effects of steroid use.

Several players mentioned in these news reports admitted that they purchased human growth hormone from an anti-aging clinic or rejuvenation center and claimed that the purchases were to treat an injury or other medical condition. The Food and Drug Administration has never approved the use of human growth hormone to treat an athletic injury, to become more lean, or to improve athletic performance. The use of human growth hormone is a violation of federal law if not for an authorized purpose, even if with a prescription. In any event, based on the news reports it is doubtful that the prescriptions were valid.

In the section of this report entitled "Alleged Internet Purchases of Performance Enhancing Substances By Players in Major League Baseball," I briefly describe alleged purchases by sixteen players. The information in that section was obtained from public sources, primarily news articles. All of these disclosures arose out of investigations by federal and state law enforcement agencies.

H.   Major League Baseball's Joint Drug Prevention and Treatment Program

The joint drug prevention and treatment program was added to the Basic Agreement in 2002. Under that program, testing has been conducted of players in Major League Baseball since 2003, first in the form of anonymous survey testing in 2003, and thereafter in mandatory random testing that now carries with it severe penalties for violations. The program has been amended formally twice since 2002 as the result of negotiations between the Commissioner and the Players Association, and other minor modifications also have been made. As a result, penalties have been increased, the list of prohibited substances has been lengthened, and some improvements in procedures have been made.

Adoption of the current program was a positive first step. The information obtained in this investigation suggests that the use of detectable steroids by players in Major League Baseball has declined but the use of human growth hormone has increased. In some respects, however, the program still falls short of current best practices in drug testing for the use of performance enhancing substances.

The drug testing programs in all sports, including the Olympics, have evolved over time through a process of trial and error, as the programs were modified to address problems and concerns. In that respect, baseball's program has been like all the others. The challenge now is to take the program to a new and higher level and to then continue the process of improvement to deal with the problems and concerns which cannot be foreseen but which inevitably will arise. Certain characteristics are now widely recognized as essential to an effective testing program. These are: independence of the program administrator; transparency and accountability; effective, year-round, unannounced testing; adherence to best practices as they develop; due process for athletes; adequate funding; and a robust education program.

Programs based on these principles can more readily adapt to changing circumstances in the ongoing contest between athletes who compete clean and those who do not, although even the strongest program by itself cannot entirely eradicate the use of banned substances. The Major League Baseball joint drug program can be strengthened in several of these areas. Most notably, the program is not administered by a truly independent authority. Although in their latest revisions to the program the parties established an "independent program administrator," the Commissioner's Office and the Players Association continue to retain authority over the program administrator and other important issues.

The current program also lacks transparency, an essential attribute to demonstrate the integrity and effectiveness of the program to outside observers. Transparency is most often obtained by issuing periodic reports on a program's operations, including reporting aggregate data on testing, and by regular audits, neither of which is now done under the joint program.

Concerns have been raised about the collection procedures used, including allegations that some players received advance notice of testing. In *Game of Shadows*, and in an earlier San Francisco Chronicle article, the authors described a surreptitious recording of a conversation that reportedly occurred in spring 2003 between Greg Anderson and an unidentified person. In that conversation, Anderson reportedly claimed that he would receive notice of upcoming tests between one and two weeks in advance. He also reportedly claimed that testing was "going to be either at the end of May or beginning of June . . ."

I could not obtain a copy of the recording or otherwise confirm that Anderson made these statements, or that he made them before late May 2003 as reported by the authors.

SR-24

However, records that we obtained from the contractor who administered his tests show that Bonds was tested on May 28 and June 4, 2003. Therefore, if the report of this conversation is accurate Anderson correctly predicted the dates of testing, at least for his client Barry Bonds.

We interviewed the relevant personnel from Comprehensive Drug Testing, Inc., the company responsible for sample collection under the Major League Baseball joint drug program. Those witnesses denied that they provided advance notice of test dates to Bonds or anyone else. CDT witnesses also told us that advance notice of testing dates was never provided to Quest Diagnostics, Inc., the laboratory that processed test samples, so Quest personnel could not have been the source of advance notice to anyone else. A Quest spokesman was reported to have said the same thing in the original news article about the recording.

I also investigated other allegations that some players received advance notice of tests in 2004. In April 2004 federal agents executed search warrants on the two private firms involved in the 2003 survey testing, Comprehensive Drug Testing, Inc. and Quest Diagnostics, Inc.; the warrants sought drug testing records and samples for ten major league players connected with the BALCO investigation. In the course of those searches, the agents seized data from which they believed they could determine the identities of the major league players who had tested positive during the anonymous survey testing.

Shortly after these events, the Players Association initiated discussions with the Commissioner's Office regarding a possible suspension of drug testing while the federal investigation proceeded. Manfred said the parties were concerned at the time that test results that they believed until then raised only employment issues had now become an issue in a pending criminal investigation. Ultimately, the Commissioner's Office and the Players Association agreed to a moratorium on 2004 drug testing. While the exact date and length of this moratorium is uncertain, and the relevant 2004 testing records have been destroyed, Manfred stated that the moratorium commenced very early in the season, prior to the testing of any significant number of players. Manfred stated that the Players Association was not authorized to advise its members of the existence of the moratorium.

According to Manfred, the moratorium lasted for a short period. For most players, drug tests then resumed. With respect to the players who the federal agents believed had tested positive during 2003 survey testing, however, the Commissioner's Office and the Players Association agreed that: (1) the Players Association would be permitted to advise those players of this fact, since that information was now in the hands of the government; (2) the testing moratorium would continue with respect to those players until the Players Association had an opportunity to notify them; and (3) the Players Association would not advise any of the players of the limited moratorium.

Sometime between mid-August and early September 2004, Manfred contacted Orza because the Players Association had not yet notified the players involved. The 2004 season was drawing to a close without those players having been tested because they remained under the moratorium. Manfred said that he pressed Orza to notify the players as soon as possible so that they could be tested. All of the players were notified by early September 2004.

A former major league player stated that in 2003 he was tested as part of the survey testing program. He said that in September 2004, Gene Orza of the Players Association told him that he had tested positive in 2003 and that he would be tested in the next two weeks. Independently, Kirk Radomski told us that this former player had earlier told him the same thing about Orza's statements shortly after the conversation between Orza and the former player occurred. In addition, the former player Larry Bigbie told us that the same former player had told him the same thing about his conversation with Orza.

Furthermore, according to Bigbie, in 2004 a current player admitted to Bigbie that he also had been told by a representative of the Players Association that he had tested positive for steroids in 2003.

I am not permitted to identify either the former player with whom we spoke or the current player who made the admission to Bigbie because the Commissioner's Office and the Players Association have concluded that for me to do so would violate the confidentiality provisions of the joint program.

According to the redacted affidavit filed in support of a search warrant sought for Jason Grimsley's residence, Grimsley told federal agents that he, too, was informed that he had tested positive for anabolic steroids in 2003. The identity of the person who so advised Grimsley is redacted in the public version of the affidavit, and I did not have access to the unredacted version.[12]

Other players may have received similar notice, since (1) the program required that each player be tested once during the 2004 season, (2) the Commissioner's Office and the Players Association agreed that, since the government had the names of the players who they believed had tested positive in 2003, those players should be notified and should not be tested in 2004 until that notification had taken place, and (3) that notification did not take place until late August or early September 2004, just weeks before the season ended.

Orza declined my request for an interview.

---

[12] Affidavit of IRS Special Agent Jeff Novitzky in Support of Search Warrant, sworn to on May 31, 2006, ¶ 16.

Officials of the Commissioner's Office emphasized that the circumstances

described above represented an emergency response to an unforeseen event: a government

investigation that obtained the names of players who had tested positive in the 2003 survey

testing, information that the parties had agreed in advance would be anonymous. Consequently,

they assert that it does not describe the normal operation of the program.

The Players Association objected to my making any reference to this matter in

this report. I offered to include a statement by the Association and they provided me with the

following:

> Because of certain actions by the Government in 2004 (which led to
> litigation, much of which has been under seal), the parties were forced to
> confront a serious threat to the confidentiality and integrity of our
> program. To combat that threat, and indeed to save the credibility of our
> program, the parties undertook certain measures in that year only. These
> were not unilateral actions undertaken by the MLBPA, but actions
> discussed and agreed upon between the MLBPA and the Commissioner's
> Office. Each party was fully aware and in agreement with the steps the
> other was taking.
>
> The MLBPA believes that, by publishing in this Report anything related to
> these subjects, Senator Mitchell and the Commissioner's Office are
> breaching promises of confidentiality made to the MLBPA and to its
> members.

1.   Recommendations

To prevent the illegal use of performance enhancing substances in Major League

Baseball, I make a series of recommendations. Some can be implemented by the Commissioner

unilaterally; some are subject to collective bargaining and therefore will require the agreement of

the Players Association.

The recommendations below focus on three principal areas: investigations based

upon non-testing evidence; player education; and further improvements in the testing program.

These recommendations are designed to work in combination with one another to more effectively combat performance enhancing substance violations. It bears emphasis that no testing program, standing alone, is enough. Certain illegal substances are difficult or virtually impossible to detect, and law enforcement investigations of Kirk Radomski and compounding pharmacies and anti-aging clinics show that, even in this era of testing, players can continue to use performance enhancing substances while avoiding detection. Indeed, one leading expert has argued that "testing only scratches the surface." The ability to investigate vigorously allegations of performance enhancing substance violations is an essential part of any meaningful drug prevention program.

First, the Commissioner should create a Department of Investigations, led by a senior executive who reports directly to the president of Major League Baseball, to respond promptly and aggressively to allegations of the illegal use or possession of performance enhancing substances. The success of that official will depend in part upon his interaction with law enforcement officials, who in the course of their own investigations obtain evidence of athletes' possession or use of illegal substances that, under appropriate circumstances, can be shared with sports leagues, as recent events in both Major League Baseball and other sports have demonstrated.

The Commissioner also should strengthen existing efforts to keep illegal substances out of major league clubhouses. Given the evidence that many players have had steroids and human growth hormone shipped to them at major league ballparks, packages delivered to players through their clubs should be logged and tracked. Clubs also should be required to adopt policies to ensure that allegations of a player's possession or use of performance enhancing substances are reported promptly to the Department of Investigations.

Second, improved educational programs about the dangers of substance use are critical to any effort to deter performance enhancing substance use. Over the last several years, the Commissioner's Office and the Players Association have made an increased effort to provide players and some club personnel with educational materials on performance enhancing substances. Some of these efforts have been effective, but we heard criticism from both former players and club personnel about the anti-steroids education programs.

Most of the educational programs we reviewed address the side effects of performance enhancing substance use and the deleterious health effects of long-term use. According to Dr. Jay Hoffman, a former professional athlete and expert in the field, discussions of health risks alone, although important, generally will not deter a player from using these substances because players who consider using performance enhancing substances do not view them as dangerous if used properly. To counter this skepticism, Dr. Hoffman proposes that education about the dangers of performance enhancing substances be combined with education on how to achieve the same results through proper training, nutrition, and supplements that are legal and safe.

Another health risk associated with performance enhancing substances is the unknown nature and origin of the substances. Players need to be aware of the risks associated with buying black market drugs.

The public outcry over the use of performance enhancing substances in professional sports has provided the substance dealer with an opportunity to exploit his relationship with a player. Those players who buy and use illegal performance enhancing substances place their livelihoods and reputations in the hands of drug dealers. Players also should be reminded of their responsibilities as role models to young athletes, who in emulating major league players' illegal substance use will place themselves at risk.

Third, although it is clear that even the best drug testing program is, by itself, not sufficient, drug testing remains an important element of a comprehensive approach to combatting the illegal use of performance enhancing substances. In Major League Baseball, however, the Commissioner does not have the authority to act unilaterally on drug testing; the agreement of the Players Association is required. The current joint drug program is part of the Basic Agreement that was agreed to in 2006 and will remain in effect until 2011. Any changes to the program therefore must be negotiated with and agreed to by the Players Association. Neither party is obligated to agree to reopen the Basic Agreement to address the program, even though that is what happened in 2005. There is no way for me to know whether that will happen again.

In recognition of the uncertainties associated with both the timing of further action on drug testing and the position of the parties when that action does take place, I set forth in this report the principles that presently characterize a state-of-the-art drug testing program. Every program should be updated regularly to keep pace with constantly changing challenges and best practices. It will be for the clubs and the Players Association to decide when to undertake a fresh review of these issues. When they do, I urge them to incorporate into the Major League Baseball joint drug program the principles described in this report.

The program should be administered by a truly independent authority that holds exclusive authority over its structure and administration. This could be in the form of an independent expert who cannot be removed except for good cause, an independent non-profit corporation, or another structure devised and agreed to by the Players Association and the major league clubs.

The program should be transparent to the public, by allowing for periodic audits of its operations and providing regular reports of aggregate data on testing and test results. The program should include adequate year-round, unannounced testing and employ best practices as they develop. How the program achieves those objectives is best left to a truly independent administrator to decide. To ensure that he can accomplish these objectives, the program should receive sufficient funding. The program should continue to respect the legitimate privacy and due process rights of the players.

*   *   *

All of these recommendations are prospective. The onset of mandatory random drug testing, the single most important step taken so far to combat the problem, was delayed for years by the opposition of the Players Association. However, there is validity to the assertion by the Players Association that, prior to 2002, the owners did not push hard for mandatory random drug testing because they were much more concerned about the serious economic issues facing baseball.

To prolong this debate will not resolve it; each side will dig in its heels even further. But it could seriously and perhaps fatally detract from what I believe to be a critical necessity: the need for everyone in baseball to work together to devise and implement the strongest possible strategy to combat the illegal use of performance enhancing substances, including the recommendations set forth in this report.

I was asked to investigate the use of performance enhancing substances by major league players and to report what I found as fairly, as accurately, and as thoroughly as I could. I have done so.

Only the Commissioner is vested with authority to take disciplinary action. Any such determination is properly for the Commissioner to make, subject to the players' right to a hearing.

I urge the Commissioner to forego imposing discipline on players for past violations of baseball's rules on performance enhancing substances, including the players named in this report, except in those cases where he determines that the conduct is so serious that discipline is necessary to maintain the integrity of the game. I make this recommendation fully aware that there are valid arguments both for and against it; but I believe that those in favor are compelling.

First, a principal goal of this investigation is to bring to a close this troubling chapter in baseball's history and to use the lessons learned from the past to prevent the future use of performance enhancing substances. While that requires us to look back, as this report necessarily does, all efforts should now be directed to the future. That is why the recommendations I make are prospective. Spending more months, or even years, in contentious disciplinary proceedings will keep everyone mired in the past.

Second, most of the alleged violations in this report are distant in time. For current players, the allegations of possession or use are at least two, and as many as nine years old. This covers a period when Major League Baseball made numerous changes in its drug policies and program: it went from limited probable cause testing to mandatory random testing; since 2002, the penalties under the program have been increased several times; human growth hormone was not included as a prohibited substance under the joint drug program until 2005. Under basic principles of labor and employment law, an employer must apply the policies in place at the time of the conduct in question in determining what, if any, discipline is appropriate.

SR-33

Until 2005, there was no penalty for a first positive drug test under the joint drug program, although the Commissioner has always had the authority to impose discipline for "just cause" for evidence obtained outside of the program.[13]

Third, and related, more than half of the players mentioned in this report are no longer playing in Major League Baseball or its affiliated minor leagues and thus are beyond the authority of the Commissioner to impose discipline.

Fourth, I have reported what I learned. But I acknowledge and even emphasize the obvious: there is much about the illegal use of performance enhancing substances in baseball that I did not learn. There were other suppliers and there have been other users, past and present. Many of those named in this report were supplied by Kirk Radomski. Yet plainly he was not the only supplier of illegal substances to major league players. Radomski himself said that some players told him they had other sources. And the evidence demonstrates that a number of players have obtained performance enhancing substances through so-called "rejuvenation centers" using prescriptions of doubtful validity.

Fifth, the Commissioner promised, and I agreed, that the public should know what I learned from this investigation. Perhaps the most important lesson I learned is that this is a serious problem that cannot be solved by anything less than a well-conceived, well-executed, and cooperative effort by everyone involved in baseball. From my experience in Northern Ireland I learned that letting go of the past and looking to the future is a very hard but necessary step toward dealing with an ongoing problem. That is what baseball now needs.

---

[13] It should be noted, however, that the rule that there would be no discipline for the first positive test was part of the quid pro quo for the Players Association's agreement to mandatory random drug testing. Indeed, the Basic Agreement protects a "First Positive Test Result" from discipline but does not similarly protect the first use of steroids from discipline. The primary evidence of wrongdoing in this report was not obtained from baseball's testing program but rather from an independent investigation.

The Commissioner should give the players the chance to make a fresh start, except where the conduct is so serious that he must act to protect the integrity of the game. This would be a tangible and positive way for him to demonstrate to the players, to the clubs, to the fans, and to the general public his desire for the cooperative effort that baseball needs to deal effectively with this problem. It also would give him a clear and convincing basis for imposing meaningful discipline for future violations.

J.   Conclusions

There has been a great deal of speculation about this report. Much of it has focused on players' names: how many and which ones. After considering that issue very carefully I concluded that it is appropriate and necessary to include them in this report. Otherwise I would not have done what I was asked to do: to try to find out what happened and to report what I learned accurately, fairly, and thoroughly.

While the interest in names is understandable, I hope the media and the public will keep that part of the report in context and will look beyond the individuals to the central conclusions and recommendations of this report. In closing, I want to emphasize them:

1.   The use of steroids in Major League Baseball was widespread. The response by baseball was slow to develop and was initially ineffective. For many years, citing concerns for the privacy rights of the players, the Players Association opposed mandatory random drug testing of its members for steroids and other substances. But in 2002, the effort gained momentum after the clubs and the Players Association agreed to and adopted a mandatory random drug testing program. The current program has been effective in that detectable steroid use appears to have declined. However, that does not mean that players have stopped using performance enhancing substances. Many players have shifted to human growth hormone, which is not detectable in any currently available urine test.

SR-35

2.   The minority of players who used such substances were wrong. They violated federal law and baseball policy, and they distorted the fairness of competition by trying to gain an unfair advantage over the majority of players who followed the law and the rules. They – the players who follow the law and the rules – are faced with the painful choice of either being placed at a competitive disadvantage or becoming illegal users themselves. No one should have to make that choice.

3.   Obviously, the players who illegally used performance enhancing substances are responsible for their actions. But they did not act in a vacuum. Everyone involved in baseball over the past two decades – Commissioners, club officials, the Players Association, and players · shares to some extent in the responsibility for the steroids era. There was a collective failure to recognize the problem as it emerged and to deal with it early on. As a result, an environment developed in which illegal use became widespread.

4.   Knowledge and understanding of the past are essential if the problem is to be dealt with effectively in the future. But being chained to the past is not helpful. Baseball does not need and cannot afford to engage in a never-ending search for the name of every player who ever used performance enhancing substances. The Commissioner was right to ask for this investigation and report. It would have been impossible to get closure on this issue without it, or something like it.

5.   But it is now time to look to the future, to get on with the important and difficult task that lies ahead. Everyone involved in Major League Baseball should join in a well-planned, well-executed, and sustained effort to bring the era of steroids and human growth hormone to an end and to prevent its recurrence in some other form in the future. That is the

only way this cloud will be removed from the game. The adoption of the recommendations set forth in this report will be a first step in that direction.

XI.   Recommendations

To prevent the illegal use of performance enhancing substances in Major League Baseball, I make a series of recommendations. Some can be implemented by the Commissioner unilaterally; some are subject to collective bargaining and therefore will require the agreement of the Players Association.

First, the Commissioner's Office should place a higher priority on the aggressive investigation of non-testing (so-called "non-analytic") evidence of possession or use, enhance its cooperation with law enforcement authorities, and make other improvements designed to keep performance enhancing substances out of major league clubhouses.

Second, Major League Baseball needs a compelling and greatly enhanced educational program that focuses on real-life stories as well as on all the risks involved in the use of performance enhancing substances. These include health risks, career risks, and the many dangers that can result from associating with drug dealers. This program should also give significant attention to the status that major league players enjoy as role models and how their use affects the decisions of young people throughout the country.

I have been warned by a number of former players that some players will use performance enhancing substances no matter what they are told. They may be right. But I also heard from other former players who wrestled long and hard with the decision to use performance enhancing substances. An education program that effectively communicates the messages described above might not deter all players from use, but it surely will deter some.

Third, although it is clear that even the best drug testing program is, by itself, not sufficient, drug testing remains an important part of a comprehensive approach to combatting the illegal use of performance enhancing substances. The Commissioner does not have the authority to act unilaterally on drug testing, however; the agreement of the Players Association is required. The current joint drug program is part of the Basic Agreement that was agreed to in 2006 and will remain in effect until 2011. Any changes to the program therefore must be negotiated with and agreed to by the Players Association. Neither party is obligated to agree to reopen the Basic Agreement to address the program, even though that is what happened in 2005. There is no way for me to know whether that will happen again.

In recognition of the uncertainties in both the timing of further action on drug testing and in the positions of the parties when that action does take place, I set forth here a set of principles and best practices that presently characterize a state-of-the-art drug testing program. Every program should be updated regularly to keep pace with constantly changing challenges and best practices. It will be for the clubs and the Players Association to decide when to undertake a fresh review of these issues. When they do, I urge them to incorporate the principles described in this report into Major League Baseball's joint drug program.

A.   Recommendations for Investigation of Non-Testing Based
      Allegations of Performance Enhancing Substance Possession or Use

As described elsewhere in this report, the Commissioner's Office has conducted several investigations into allegations of the use of performance enhancing substances by Major League Baseball players.[566] These investigations were limited by a number of restrictions, some self-imposed, some based upon collective bargaining obligations or interpretations of those obligations. As a result, they were in many cases ineffective.

It is imperative that the Commissioner's Office have a more robust investigative ability to respond promptly and effectively to allegations of the illegal use or possession of performance enhancing substances. This report and recent law enforcement efforts show that

---

[566] *See supra* at 91-108.

non-analytic evidence of use can be obtained. The Commissioner's Office must vigorously respond when such allegations are made, particularly as violators continue to shift their use to substances such as human growth hormone that are difficult or impossible to detect through currently available testing procedures.

Set forth below are recommendations that, if adopted, should materially enhance that investigative capability. This is critical to effectively identifying and disciplining those players who continue to violate Major League Baseball's rules and policies. These recommendations also are consistent with new approaches to enforcement efforts adopted by anti-doping agencies.[567] One agency head has concluded that drug testing "barely scratches the surface." Accordingly, in addition to a vigilant drug testing program, the Commissioner's Office must also "focus . . . on building detection capability for serious non-analytical anti-doping violations."[568]

1.   The Commissioner Should Establish
a Department of Investigations

The principal responsibility of the labor relations department of the Commissioner's Office is to oversee the collective bargaining relationship with the Players Association, particularly the periodic negotiation of the Basic Agreement. This responsibility carries with it enormous implications for the financial health of all of baseball. In recent years the labor relations department has performed that role well. Since 1994-95, there have been no work stoppages in Major League Baseball. This fact, perhaps more than any other, explains why Major League Baseball today is on much firmer economic ground than it was just a decade ago.

---

[567] Richard Ings, *Australia: Revolutionary Model Battles Doping on all Eight Fronts of the Code*, 1 Play True (World Anti-Doping Agency 2007), at 10.

[568] *Id.*

That primary responsibility, however, also complicates the ability of the labor relations department to meet another of its responsibilities, to investigate allegations of player wrongdoing. The department must maintain good relations with the Players Association; but aggressive, thorough investigations of the alleged possession or use by players of performance enhancing substances may be inconsistent with that objective. Many of the investigations involving performance enhancing substances have not been aggressive or thorough. Before this investigation, with few exceptions, the Commissioner's Office had not conducted investigative interviews of current major league players regarding alleged possession or use of performance enhancing substances, by that player or by others.

The Commissioner's Office security department has been responsible for parts of some investigations into the use or distribution of performance enhancing substances. That department's primary function, however, is to provide security for the players and the playing environment. That also places security officials in a difficult situation when they are asked to investigate the very persons they are responsible for protecting.

The Commissioner should create a Department of Investigations, led by a senior executive who reports directly to the president of Major League Baseball. Ideally, this senior executive should have experience as a senior leader in law enforcement, with the highest credibility among state and federal law enforcement officials; the success of this department will depend in part upon how well it interacts with law enforcement authorities. The senior executive should have sole authority over all investigations of alleged performance enhancing substance violations and other threats to the integrity of the game, and should receive the resources and other support needed to make the office effective.

The Commissioner's Office should establish policies to ensure the integrity and independence of the department's investigations, including the adoption of procedures analogous to those employed by internal affairs departments of law enforcement agencies. The adoption of and adherence to these policies can serve to ensure public confidence that the Commissioner's Office is responding vigorously to all serious allegations of performance enhancing substance violations.

The Commissioner's Office has never published a written policy describing who should receive and act on evidence of possible performance enhancing substance use violations. The Commissioner's Office should adopt a written policy requiring that all information received by club or Commissioner's Office personnel about possible performance enhancing substance use (other than through the drug testing program) must be reported immediately and directly to the senior executive in charge of the Department of Investigations.

In turn, that senior executive should be required to report immediately all significant allegations of player substance use directly to both the Commissioner and the president of Major League Baseball; this has not always happened in the past. Additionally, the Department of Investigations should make quarterly reports to the Commissioner and president describing the Department's investigatory efforts.

The administrator of the drug testing program should also receive any information that, in the view of the senior executive in charge of investigations, might be helpful in tailoring the procedures of the testing program and would not compromise ongoing investigations or, where it is required, confidentiality. For an obvious example, should the Department of Investigations obtain information about possible countermeasures players are taking to avoid

289

detection on drug tests, such information should be reported immediately to the program administrator.

    2.   The Commissioner's Office Should More Effectively
             Cooperate with Law Enforcement Agencies

No matter how skilled, the Commissioner's Office's investigators face significant disadvantages in investigating illegal performance enhancing substance use compared to law enforcement officials. Law enforcement officials, of course, have a broad array of investigatory powers, including search warrants and subpoena power.

Recently, law enforcement agencies have become increasingly flexible and creative in sharing with professional sports organizations information gathered during investigations. This practice makes sense because law enforcement agencies typically focus their efforts in illegal drug investigations on prosecution of the manufacturers, importers, and distributors, not on the athletes who are the end users. During these investigations, however, law enforcement agencies often accumulate evidence of use by individuals.

This is what happened in the prosecution of Kirk Radomski by the United States Attorney's Office for the Northern District of California. As described in this report, the Radomski investigation yielded information regarding performance enhancing substance use by major league players, much of it corroborated by documentary or other evidence.

The appointment of an senior executive in charge of investigations, with an impeccable law enforcement reputation and the resources and authority needed to perform effectively the duties of that office, will be an important first step to improving relations with law enforcement agencies. One law enforcement official advised us in frustration that there is no clearly designated person in the Commissioner's Office to call when law enforcement does have information. The senior executive in charge of investigations would be that person.

Improved relations with law enforcement agencies and customs officials may also serve as a deterrent to substance use by players. The Radomski case, the Signature Pharmacy investigation, and other performance enhancing substance investigations, for example, may have implications beyond the individual players identified in those cases. If nothing else, they serve as a warning to all players that no one is protected from being identified by his supplier. And suppliers may be more wary of supplying professional athletes if they know that sports organizations are aggressively seeking to identify and facilitate the prosecution of those who supply illegal substances to athletes.

      3.   The Commissioner's Office Should Actively Use the Clubs'
              Powers, as Employer, to Investigate Violations of the Joint Program

One of the critical tools available to all employers is the investigatory interview. Generally, an employer may compel union-represented employees to attend and truthfully respond during any interview conducted by or on behalf of the employer.[569]

The Ferguson Jenkins arbitration decision has played a role in the interpretation of a player's rights during an investigatory interview.[570] In Jenkins, an arbitrator ruled that the Commissioner could not impose discipline upon Jenkins for refusing to answer questions about alleged possession of drugs of abuse while Jenkins was facing criminal charges for the same conduct.

According to the Commissioner's Office and the Players Association, however, no major league player ever has been convicted of a criminal offense for the use or possession of

---

[569] Where the employee reasonably believes the investigatory interview might result in disciplinary action, he has the right to representation at that interview. *See NLRB v. J. Weingarten, Inc.*, 420 U.S. 251, 257 (1975) ("[T]he employee's right to request representation as a condition of participation in an interview is limited to situations where the employee reasonably believe[s] the investigation will result in disciplinary action."). The Basic Agreement also requires advance notice of such an interview. Basic Agreement, Art. XII(E).

[570] *See supra* at 29-31.

performance enhancing substances. And, as noted elsewhere in this report, the policy of the Department of Justice, and of other prosecutors, is to prosecute the manufacturers, importers, and distributors of performance enhancing substances, not the athletes who use them. Thus, the basis on which the Jenkins arbitrator relied – pending criminal charges against the athlete based on the same conduct – will rarely be an issue.

The Commissioner's Office has these interview rights to ensure that its rules are followed, but before this investigation began active major league players were rarely required to participate in investigatory interviews regarding alleged performance enhancing substance violations. Since this investigation began, however, the Commissioner's Office has conducted a number of interviews of major league players accused of performance enhancing substance violations, and the Commissioner has disciplined some of those players.

Unless there are compelling individual circumstances to the contrary, the Department of Investigations, once established, should promptly seek to interview any player about whom allegations are received of performance enhancing substance violations and insist upon full cooperation. Where law enforcement efforts have been the source of the information, the Department should seek corroboration where possible (for example, records indicating the ordering or receipt of such substances) so that it has evidence to present to the player. This practice would bring Major League Baseball into conformity with other employers.

4.   All Clubs Should Have Clear, Written, and Well-Publicized
      Policies for Reporting Information Relating to Possible
      Performance Enhancing Substance Violations

Since 1991, Major League Baseball's Drug Policy has covered performance enhancing substances expressly. That policy states in part:

If any club covers up or fails to disclose to [the Commissioner's] office any information concerning drug use by a player, the Club will be fined in an amount up to $2 million, the highest allowable amount under the Major League Constitution.[571]

Many club personnel told us that they were not aware of the policy. The Commissioner's Office should actively publicize its policy regarding performance enhancing substances to club personnel and require each club to adopt a uniform, written policy for reporting information about possible substance violations. The club policy should state that any information concerning a player's possible use, possession, or distribution of performance enhancing substances must be reported to a designated club contact immediately. The club contact, in turn, should be required to promptly report all such information to the Department of Investigations.

At least one exception to this reporting requirement should be included in the club policy. Physicians and club athletic trainers should not be required to report such information if to do so would cause them to violate federal or state law relating to the confidentiality of patient communications or information.[572]

To ensure that the clubs are meeting their long-standing obligations to report all information concerning possible possession or use, the Commissioner's Office should require all club personnel with responsibility affecting baseball operations to sign annual certifications. These certifications should affirm that the club employee has no undisclosed, actual knowledge of any possible possession or use of performance enhancing substances by any current major league player. This certification should provide an exception for athletic trainers, to the extent

---

[571] *See* Memorandum from Commissioner Selig to All Clubs Re: Baseball's Drug Policy and Prevention Program, dated Mar. 2, 2005, at 2. The amount of the fine has varied over time.

[572] At the same time, the Commissioner's Office should revise its substance policy to exempt clubs from sanctions for failure to provide other reportable information where the disclosure of such information by a physician or athletic trainer would violate the law.

that they are in receipt of responsive information the disclosure of which would violate the law or the rules of applicable licensing organizations.[573]

In the event of a failure to certify, or should the Commissioner's Office determine that a certification was false, the Commissioner should exercise his discretion under the "best interests of the game" clause to impose discipline appropriate to the circumstances.

5.   Logging Packages Sent to Players at Major League Ballparks

In a number of incidents of players' possession or use that have been described in this report, a major league player reportedly received deliveries of performance enhancing substances through clubhouse attendants at Major League Baseball facilities. Kirk Radomski shipped illegal substances to some of his customers at major league clubhouses. Some players who purchased performance enhancing substances through rejuvenation centers also reportedly had the purchases shipped to them at their clubhouses.

We interviewed clubhouse personnel throughout Major League Baseball. It is apparent from those interviews that players receive a significant volume of mail, most of it entirely legitimate, in care of their clubhouse managers. In response to recent news reports that players have received shipments of human growth hormone and other substances from compounding pharmacies at major league ballparks, George Hanna, who is the current director of investigations for the security department in the Commissioner's Office, has suggested that all packages received for players at major league clubhouses be logged.

The Commissioner's Office should require each major and minor league club to establish a system to log every package received for a player at its facilities. These logs should record the sender, the sender's address and phone number, the recipient, the date of delivery, and

---

[573] Physicians are typically not club employees, and thus would be exempt from this certification requirement.

the type of package. Copies of these logs should be maintained for a period of time sufficient to aid in any subsequent investigations.

B.   <u>Additional Actions to Address Performance Enhancing Substance Violations</u>

There are several other actions that the Commissioner can take to address the issue that do not require collective bargaining.

1.   <u>Background Investigations of Prospective Clubhouse Personnel</u>

Kirk Radomski and Luis Perez vividly demonstrate that sources of supply can come from within the clubhouse. The Commissioner's Office must require all clubs to submit to it the names of proposed clubhouse personnel hires for appropriate background checks.

2.   <u>Random Drug Testing of Clubhouse Personnel</u>

In 2003, the security department of the Commissioner's Office recommended possible random drug testing of clubhouse personnel in conjunction with its investigation of the Luis Perez incident that is described earlier in this report. Baseball's drug policy has provided for the possibility of random testing of non-playing personnel for decades. Kirk Radomski admitted that he was using steroids while he was a clubhouse attendant with the Mets, a time when he began building the relationships that would ultimately facilitate his distribution of performance enhancing substances to players after he left the Mets.

The 2003 proposal to implement mandatory, random, unannounced drug testing for clubhouse personnel was never adopted, but officials in the security department continue to recommend it. The testing could be conducted in conjunction with testing of major league players under the joint drug program.

3.   <u>Hot Line for Reporting Anonymous Tips</u>

Sources both currently and formerly associated with Major League Baseball have suggested that an anonymous hotline or ethics committee for reporting tips may prove useful.

USADA and its counterparts have employed such hotlines for some time and report that they
have yielded information that resulted in the detection of drug violations.

4.   The Top Draft Prospects Should Be Tested
      Prior to the Major League Draft

The Major League Baseball Scouting Bureau identifies the top 100 draft eligible
prospects annually. The scouting bureau has proposed that those prospects be subjected to drug
tests before the draft each year. It has had preliminary contacts with the National Collegiate
Athlete Association to discuss the feasibility of this proposal.

As with the minor league testing program, unannounced tests will discourage the
use of performance enhancing substances from the very beginning of a player's professional
career. The testing of draft prospects could be administered as an adjunct of the minor league
testing program.

C.   Educational and Related Recommendations to Decrease
      Use of Performance Enhancing Substances

Critical to any effort to deter performance enhancing substance use in Major
League Baseball is an effective educational program designed to inform players about the
dangers of substance use in a way that will resonate with them. Over the last several years, the
Commissioner's Office and the Players Association have made an increased effort to provide
players and some club personnel with educational materials on performance enhancing
substances.

Some of these efforts have been effective. For example, in 2003 the
Commissioner's Office hired Dr. Gary Green as a consultant responsible for, among other things,
"[d]eveloping and implementing educational programs and materials for Major League and
minor league players" regarding "anabolic steroids and [other] performance enhancing

agents."[574] Dr. Green has done an effective job of educating doctors and other medical personnel on the dangers of performance enhancing substances. The Texas Rangers have retained Dr. Jay Hoffman, Professor in Health and Education Science and a former National Football League player, as a confidential resource for its players regarding performance enhancing substance use.

Additional efforts have included the production of an educational video, in both English and Spanish, that is shown to all players in spring training and the distribution of posters and educational pamphlets. Spring training educational meetings for players have been arranged. Dr. Green also has conducted annual educational sessions for team physicians, athletic trainers, and club employee assistance professionals.

Nevertheless, we heard criticism from both former players and club personnel about the current anti-steroids education programs. Some criticized the perceived shallowness of the efforts, while others could not remember the programs at all, even though they were with clubs when the programs were supposed to have been presented. Plainly, there is much room for improvement.

In contrast, the issues of gambling, other threats to the integrity of the game, and players' safety receive prominent educational attention. Nearly everyone we interviewed could vividly recall an educational program addressing gambling.[575] Major League Baseball's

---

[574] Dr. Green has a long background in testing for, and education related to, performance enhancing substances, including serving as director of UCLA's intercollegiate drug testing program, as the chairman of the NCAA's Subcommittee on Drug Testing and Drug Education, and as a USADA panel member.

[575] The problem of gambling predates the Players Association and collective bargaining by many decades. Gambling by players on the Chicago White Sox was the impetus for the creation of the position of Commissioner of Baseball in 1920. For that reason, the Commissioner can act unilaterally with respect to gambling (although even for gambling his disciplinary powers are subject to the "just cause" limitation of the Basic Agreement).

educational programs regarding player safety include dramatic role playing and memorable personal testimonials that are particularly effective in conveying their messages.

In this section I propose a series of recommendations intended to improve Major League Baseball's performance enhancing substance education program. These recommendations are derived from many of the interviews conducted in this investigation, including interviews of a number of experts who have first-hand experience with educating elite athletes on the dangers of performance enhancing substances.

1.   The Design and Implementation of the Educational Program
      Should Be Centralized with the Independent Program Administrator

As with an effective testing program, an effective educational program must be focused, independent, and transparent. The best and most efficient way to achieve this is to delegate to the independent program administrator the responsibility for designing and implementing the educational program. This will ensure that the program is unbiased and operates consistently with the goals of the testing program. Further, centralizing the educational program will ensure the consistency and effectiveness of its message.

2.   Spring Training Programs Should Include Testimonials
      and Other Speakers and Presentations

As explained above, Major League Baseball does an effective job of communicating its "no gambling" message through testimonials and dramatic role playing. The same methods should be used for performance enhancing substance education as well. The following are examples of such methods that have been used effectively in this area.

Dr. Jay Hoffman is a professor who has written extensively about the effects of performance enhancing substances on the body. Dr. Hoffman also admits that he used anabolic steroids when he played college and professional football during the mid-1980s.

Jamie Reed, head athletic trainer for the Texas Rangers and President of the Professional Baseball Athletic Trainer Society, told us that because Dr. Hoffman is a former athlete, players respond very well to his anti-steroid message and are more open to accept his attestations concerning its use. Other athletic trainers and strength coaches echoed the opinion that Dr. Hoffman is an effective speaker on these issues. For example, Rick Slate, the New York Mets' strength and conditioning coach, identified Dr. Hoffman as a "tremendous help" to the Professional Baseball Strength and Conditioning Coaches Society in formulating its policies.

The Taylor Hooton Foundation was founded in memory of Taylor Hooton, a high school baseball player who committed suicide after taking anabolic steroids. Taylor's father, Don Hooton, created the Foundation and has educated high school and world class athletes around the country about the dangers of performance enhancing substances. Mr. Hooton's message painfully demonstrates that, when major league players use performance enhancing substances, the ramifications go far beyond the players themselves. Whether they like it or not, Major League Baseball players are role models for young athletes, and what they do – right or wrong – affects those young people. Telling the story of Taylor Hooton, and those like him, to players – many of whom are fathers or are considering becoming fathers – will serve to underscore the profound social dangers associated with performance enhancing substance use by high profile athletes.

Law enforcement agency personnel have offered presentations to players during spring training concerning the use of drugs of abuse and gambling, and some individuals we interviewed reported that these talks were memorable. Law enforcement speakers also should be employed to discuss the dangers of performance enhancing substances from their institutional perspective. Law enforcement personnel are uniquely suited to emphasize the criminal

299

implications of buying, selling, and using these types of substances, and of consorting with those who engage in illegal trafficking.

> 3.   Explain the Health Risks in Context and Provide Education
> on Alternative Methods to Achieve the Same Results

Most of the performance enhancing substance educational programs we reviewed address the side effects of performance enhancing substance use and the deleterious health effects of long-term use. According to Dr. Hoffman, however, these health risks, although important, generally will not deter a player from using these substances. This is because players who use or are considering using performance enhancing substances do not consider them dangerous if used properly. This view is reinforced when players see that other players who they know are using performance enhancing substances are not experiencing the adverse health effects described in the educational materials.

To counter this skepticism, Dr. Hoffman proposes that, while it is important to educate players about the dangers of performance enhancing substances, it is just as important to educate them on how to achieve the same results through proper training, nutrition, and supplements that are legal and safe. While the clubs have done a better job in recent years of informing players of the importance of fitness and proper nutrition through their strength and conditioning coaches, this message should be delivered in the context of substance use prevention, so that the players understand they can achieve some of the same benefits through training and fitness and, if necessary, legal supplements.

Another health risk associated with performance enhancing substances is the unknown nature and origin of the substances. Players need to be aware of the risks associated with buying black market drugs. Veterinary steroids are sometimes sold illegally to steroid abusers.[576] Similarly, many of the home laboratories that were raided by the Drug Enforcement Administration as part of its "Operation Raw Deal" in 2007 were unsanitary, with steroids being mixed in bathtubs or bathroom sinks in some instances.[577] An effective education program must highlight the potential health risks associated with taking drugs of unknown origin without a prescription.

4. Players Need to Understand the Non-Health Effects of Buying Performance Enhancing Substances from Street Dealers and "Internet Pharmacies"

In addition to the obvious health risks of using performance enhancing substances of unknown origin, players place their livelihoods and reputations in the hands of drug dealers. The public outcry over the use of performance enhancing substances in professional sports has provided the substance dealer with an opportunity to exploit his relationship with a player. The Commissioner's Office has been concerned for decades that drug dealers could blackmail a player to alter the outcome of a game in exchange for maintaining the secrecy of the player's substance use.[578] Such threats to the integrity of the game are as serious as gambling. Major League Baseball's performance enhancing substance educational program must convey the gravity of these dangers to the reputation and integrity of the players and of the game.

[576] Many Mexican manufacturers of veterinary steroids altered their production to account for increased demand for human use of steroids in the United States. *See* George Dohrmann & Luis Fernando Llosa, *Special Report: Steroid Trafficking – the Mexican Connection*, Sports Illustrated, Apr. 24, 2006, at 68. In December 2005, the DEA announced a law enforcement operation, called "Operation Gear Grinder," in which eight veterinary steroid manufacturers were raided by federal law enforcement authorities. *See* Press Release, DEA Leads Largest Steroids Bust in History (Dec. 15, 2005); *see also* Michael O'Keeffe, *Drug Enforcement Administration Steroid Crackdown Hits Home*, N.Y. Daily News, Dec. 18, 2005.

[577] *See* Press Release, Drug Enforcement Administration, DEA Announces Largest Steroid Enforcement Action in U.S. History (Sept. 24, 2007).

[578] *See* Memorandum from Commissioner Peter Ueberroth to All Clubs Re: Baseball's Drug Education and Prevention Program, dated May 14, 1985, at 1.

5.   Prominently Display Posters About
         Performance Enhancing Substance Use Prevention

Performance enhancing substance prevention should receive the same educational

priority as gambling. Each club should distribute educational materials to players, and each

clubhouse, weight room, and training room should prominently display posters about

performance enhancing substance use prevention that (1) forcefully articulate Major League

Baseball's rule against performance enhancing substance use, (2) inform players of the dangers

of performance enhancing substance use, and (3) explain the penalties associated with

performance enhancing substance use.

D.   Recommendations for Further Improvement of the
         Joint Drug Prevention and Treatment Program

There have been a number of improvements in Major League Baseball's drug

testing program since the Joint Drug Prevention and Treatment Program became effective in

2003. Because of the constantly evolving nature of this problem, however, further improvements

are necessary.

As noted earlier, the clubs and the Players Association are under no obligation to

bargain, or even to discuss the joint program, until the current Basic Agreement expires in 2011.

Neither has the authority to change the current program unilaterally.

When the parties do address the drug testing program and related enforcement

issues, I urge them to make certain that their program is consistent with the following

principles.[579] In the previous chapter, I described a number of concerns that have arisen with

---

[579] The principles described below apply only to those aspects of the joint program that
are applicable to performance enhancing substances. I am not suggesting modifications to the
provisions of the program to the extent that it governs use of other drugs unrelated to athletic
performance.

respect to Major League Baseball's joint program. Where applicable, I also described the initiatives adopted by the Commissioner and the Players Association to address these concerns.

It is not necessary for me to recommend even more detailed refinements to the joint program. First, the details of specific operating procedures are best left to the discretion of an independent program administrator who will have the benefit of all the relevant facts as of the time the decision is to be made. Second, any changes in such procedures are likely to have a limited period of utility given the dynamic nature of illegal drug use and of testing programs.

All drug program administrators face a never ending series of challenges, the details of which are often not foreseeable. Accordingly, my recommendations address the principles that parties should adopt in their drug program.

1. The Program Should Be Independent

Independence is the most important principle of an effective drug testing program. The parties previously have recognized the importance of this principle by delegating some of the administrative authority for the program to an independent program administrator. However, under the current program, both the independence of the program administrator and the level of authority that has been delegated to him are limited.

There are a number of methods by which true independence may be achieved. The precise form is for the parties to decide through collective bargaining. The independent program administrator could serve for a substantial fixed term, not subject to removal except for good cause. Alternatively, the parties could establish a self-perpetuating, non-profit corporation that is completely independent of the parties. There may be other alternatives. Whatever form they choose, the independent program administrator should hold exclusive authority over all aspects of the formulation and administration of the program.

It is likely, and understandable, that the Players Association will not agree to relinquish authority over the length·of penalties to an independent program administrator. Delegation of that aspect of the program might not be necessary, however, given that the penalties now in effect under the joint program are the strongest of any major professional sports league in the United States.[580]

2.   The Program Should Be Transparent

Drug testing programs must respect the privacy rights of the athletes who are tested. Yet to instill public trust and ensure accountability, they must be as transparent as possible consistent with protecting those rights. Transparency can be achieved by such actions as submitting to outside audits, and publishing periodic reports of de-identified aggregate testing results, retaining records of negative test results so that confirmation is available to correctly interpret subsequent tests, which may inure to the benefit of a player charged with a positive result in a later test. A transparent program should provide the public with aggregate data that demonstrates the work of the program and the results achieved by it (but that does not reveal or permit the determination of individual identities).

The importance of transparency is illustrated by an article about the Major League Baseball joint drug program that appeared in the San Diego Union-Tribune in May 2007.[581] The article reported that the number of positive tests reported by the Montreal testing laboratory that is used by Major League Baseball and other organizations increased from around 20 in 2005 to 104 in 2006. Under WADA standards, the laboratory was required to segregate its reported data

---

[580] *See supra* at 276-77.

[581] Mark Zeigler, *Report: Stimulant Positive Tests Up; Strong Indication of Use in Baseball*, San Diego Union-Tribune, May 11, 2007.

by sport but not by client, and that laboratory has other clients whose data are included in the laboratory's aggregate baseball/softball data.

Nevertheless, the article drew speculative conclusions from the aggregate data about the effects of including stimulants among the prohibited substances under the joint program, observing that "in the absence of a fully transparent testing program by baseball, the WADA report may be the closest thing to real numbers of positive tests."[582]

3. There Should Be Adequate Year-Round, Unannounced Drug Testing

Adequate year-round, unannounced testing is essential to any effective drug testing program. While strong sanctions for violators are necessary, those sanctions are meaningless unless testing maximizes the chance that violators will be detected. If tests are limited, predictable, or announced in advance, players can avoid detection and evade discipline.

The formulation of what is adequate is best left for determination by a truly independent program administrator. It is likely that the appropriate amount of testing, allocations between in-season and out-of-season testing, and allocation of resources between targeted and random testing will not be static.

4. The Program Should Be Flexible Enough to Employ Best Practices as They Develop

A state of the art drug testing program must employ best practices as they develop. Just as the methods that violators employ to avoid detection are not static, neither are these best practices. This may involve modification of the program as enhanced techniques, new tests, and best practices evolve.

---

[582] *Id.*

305

5.   The Program Should Continue to Respect the Legitimate Rights of Players

While I believe that changes are necessary to make the drug testing program more effective, there is nothing inconsistent between my recommendations and continued respect for the legitimate privacy and due process rights of players. The principles upon which I have based my analysis of the current program and my recommendations require that an effective drug testing program recognize the legitimate privacy and due process rights of all players. Although there obviously have been some differences and disagreements in recent years, the parties generally appear to have respected players' rights, and I recommend that any changes to the program in the future continue to recognize and respect the legitimate rights of players.

6.   The Program Should Have Adequate Funding

A meaningful program requires the funding necessary to be effective. It would be contrary to Major League Baseball's and the Players Association's self-interests to deny needed resources to a truly independent program.

*   *   *

These recommendations are designed to work in combination with one another to create a new environment, one that is more aggressive in deterring the use of performance enhancing substances, while still protecting the rights of the players. I believe that the principal beneficiaries of these reforms will be the majority of major league players who play clean and follow the rules. These players have been harmed by having to play against violators who gained an unfair advantage, and further harmed by having the legitimacy of their fairly-earned accomplishments frequently questioned. The clean major league players deserve far better than they have had to endure.

E.   We Need to Look to the Future

All of these recommendations are prospective. The onset of mandatory random drug testing, the single most important step taken so far to combat the problem, was delayed for years by the opposition of the Players Association. However, there is validity to the assertion by the Players Association that, prior to 2002, the owners did not push hard for mandatory random drug testing because they were much more concerned about the serious economic issues facing baseball.

To prolong this debate will not resolve it; each side will dig in its heels even further. But it could seriously and perhaps fatally detract from what I believe to be a critical necessity: the need for everyone in baseball to work together to devise and implement the strongest possible strategy to combat the illegal use of performance enhancing substances, including the recommendations set forth in this report.

I was asked to investigate the use of performance enhancing substances by major league players and to report what I found as fairly, as accurately, and as thoroughly as I could. I have done so.

Only the Commissioner is vested with authority to take disciplinary action. Any such determination is properly for the Commissioner to make, subject to the players' right to a hearing.

I urge the Commissioner to forego imposing discipline on players for past violations of baseball's rules on performance enhancing substances, including the players named in this report, except in those cases where he determines that the conduct is so serious that discipline is necessary to maintain the integrity of the game. I make this recommendation fully aware that there are valid arguments both for and against it; but I believe that those in favor are compelling.

First, a principal goal of this investigation is to bring to a close this troubling chapter in baseball's history and to use the lessons learned from the past to prevent the future use of performance enhancing substances. While that requires us to look back, as this report necessarily does, all efforts should now be directed to the future. That is why the recommendations I make are prospective. Spending more months, or even years, in contentious disciplinary proceedings will keep everyone mired in the past.

Second, most of the alleged violations in this report are distant in time. For current players, the allegations of possession or use are at least two, and as many as nine years old. This covers a period when Major League Baseball made numerous changes in its drug policies and program: it went from limited probable cause testing to mandatory random testing; since 2002, the penalties under the program have been increased several times; human growth hormone was not included as a prohibited substance under the joint drug program until 2005. Under basic principles of labor and employment law, an employer must apply the policies in place at the time of the conduct in question in determining what, if any, discipline is appropriate. Until 2005, there was no penalty for a first positive drug test under the joint drug program, although the Commissioner has always had the authority to impose discipline for "just cause" for evidence obtained outside of the program.[583]

Third, and related, more than half of the players mentioned in this report are no longer playing in Major League Baseball or its affiliated minor leagues and thus are beyond the authority of the Commissioner to impose discipline.

---

[583] It should be noted, however, that the rule that there would be no discipline for the first positive test was part of the quid pro quo for the Players Association's agreement to mandatory random drug testing. Indeed, the Basic Agreement protects a "First Positive Test Result" from discipline but does not similarly protect the first use of steroids from discipline. The primary evidence of wrongdoing in this report was not obtained from baseball's testing program but rather from an independent investigation.

Fourth, I have reported what I learned. But I acknowledge and even emphasize the obvious: there is much about the illegal use of performance enhancing substances in baseball that I did not learn. There were other suppliers and there have been other users, past and present. Many of those named in this report were supplied by Kirk Radomski. Yet plainly he was not the only supplier of illegal substances to major league players. Radomski himself said that some players told him they had other sources. And the evidence demonstrates that a number of players have obtained performance enhancing substances through so-called "rejuvenation centers" using prescriptions of doubtful validity.

Fifth, the Commissioner promised, and I agreed, that the public should know what I learned from this investigation. Perhaps the most important lesson I learned is that this is a serious problem that cannot be solved by anything less than a well-conceived, well-executed, and cooperative effort by everyone involved in baseball. From my experience in Northern Ireland I learned that letting go of the past and looking to the future is a very hard but necessary step toward dealing with an ongoing problem. That is what baseball now needs.

The Commissioner should give the players the chance to make a fresh start, except where the conduct is so serious that he must act to protect the integrity of the game. This would be a tangible and positive way for him to demonstrate to the players, to the clubs, to the fans, and to the general public his desire for the cooperative effort that baseball needs to deal effectively with this problem. It also would give him a clear and convincing basis for imposing meaningful discipline for future violations.

XII. Conclusions

There has been a great deal of speculation about this report. Much of it has focused on players' names: how many and which ones. After considering that issue very carefully I concluded that it is appropriate and necessary to include them in this report. Otherwise I would not have done what I was asked to do: to try to find out what happened and to report what I learned accurately, fairly, and thoroughly.

While the interest in names is understandable, I hope the media and the public will keep that part of the report in context and will look beyond the individuals to the central conclusions and recommendations of this report. In closing, I want to emphasize them:

1.   The use of steroids in Major League Baseball was widespread. The response by baseball was slow to develop and was initially ineffective. For many years, citing concerns for the privacy rights of the players, the Players Association opposed mandatory random drug testing of its members for steroids and other substances. But in 2002, the effort gained momentum after the clubs and the Players Association agreed to and adopted a mandatory random drug testing program. The current program has been effective in that detectable steroid use appears to have declined. However, that does not mean that players have stopped using performance enhancing substances. Many players have shifted to human growth hormone, which is not detectable in any currently available urine test.

2.   The minority of players who used such substances were wrong. They violated federal law and baseball policy, and they distorted the fairness of competition by trying to gain an unfair advantage over the majority of players who followed the law and the rules. They – the players who follow the law and the rules – are faced with the painful choice of either being placed at a competitive disadvantage or becoming illegal users themselves. No one should have to make that choice.

3.   Obviously, the players who illegally used performance enhancing substances are responsible for their actions. But they did not act in a vacuum. Everyone involved in baseball over the past two decades – Commissioners, club officials, the Players Association, and players – shares to some extent in the responsibility for the steroids era. There was a collective failure to recognize the problem as it emerged and to deal with it early on. As a result, an environment developed in which illegal use became widespread.

4.   Knowledge and understanding of the past are essential if the problem is to be dealt with effectively in the future. But being chained to the past is not helpful. Baseball does not need and cannot afford to engage in a never-ending search for the name of every player who ever used performance enhancing substances. The Commissioner was right to ask for this investigation and report. It would have been impossible to get closure on this issue without it, or something like it.

5.   But it is now time to look to the future, to get on with the important and difficult task that lies ahead. Everyone involved in Major League Baseball should join in a well-planned, well-executed, and sustained effort to bring the era of steroids and human growth hormone to an end and to prevent its recurrence in some other form in the future. That is the only way this cloud will be removed from the game. The adoption of the recommendations set forth in this report will be a first step in that direction.

*

INDEX

References are to Pages

✝